LAND AND SOCIETY
IN EARLY SCOTLAND

LAND AND SOCIETY
IN EARLY SCOTLAND

by

ROBERT A. DODGSHON

CLARENDON PRESS · OXFORD
1981

Oxford University Press, Walton Street, Oxford OX2 6DP
London Glasgow New York Toronto
Delhi Bombay Calcutta Madras Karachi
Kuala Lumpur Singapore Hong Kong Tokyo
Nairobi Dar es Salaam Cape Town
Melbourne Auckland
and associate companies in
Beirut Berlin Ibadan Mexico City

Published in the United States by
Oxford University Press, New York

© Robert A. Dodgshon 1981

British Library Cataloguing in Publication Data

Dodgshon, Robert A.
  Land and society in early Scotland.
  1. Scotland—Rural conditions—History
  I. Title
  941.1   HN385
  ISBN 0-19-822660-8

Filmset by DBM Typesetting (Oxford)
Printed in Great Britain
at the University Press, Oxford
by Eric Buckley
Printer to the University

For my mother and father

Preface

Books can be written for a variety of reasons. In writing this book, I confess to being prompted more by reasons to do with myself than the needs of any potential readership. Having carried out a series of detailed thematic studies on the relationship between land and society in early Scotland, I felt it would greatly help my thinking if I attempted a more general synthesis of the problem. Producing such a text has made me even more conscious of the many gaps and lacunae in our understanding. However, I have been equally conscious of the fact that only through a synthesis can we begin to set the broader trends of Scottish rural history in focus. I have chosen to start my discussion back in the prehistoric period, largely because of a growing belief that the relationship between land and society probably experienced more continuity than discontinuity in its progress from prehistory to history. At the other end of my text, I have chosen to terminate the discussion in the mid-eighteenth century, on the eve of the Improvers' Movement. I have done so for the simple reason that the history of land and society during the centuries that stretch back before the Improvers' Movement has generally been neglected. Having myself been more concerned with these earlier phases of Scottish rural history, it seemed appropriate to structure my text around this bias.

Since starting research work on Scotland back in 1963, I have received help from a number of individuals and institutions. My postgraduate or doctoral work under Professor Richard Lawton of Liverpool University provided an excellent foundation. Subsequent posts at Reading University and, from 1970 at the University College of Wales, Aberystwyth, have enabled me to broaden my interests from the Borders to the Scottish countryside at large. Researching on Scotland from a base at Aberystwyth has never struck my colleagues as a particularly sensible arrangement, given the distances to be travelled in order to reach the prime archives or libraries. However, having the resources of the National Library of Wales closer to hand has eased the task considerably. Furthermore, my College has always been generous in its funding of my trips to Edinburgh. Whilst in

Edinburgh, the Scottish Record Office has given me valuable assistance over the years with the locating of manuscripts and with photocopying. I have also benefited from the help given by the National Library of Scotland. During my stays in Edinburgh, it has become my custom to spend the early part of the evening working through the shelves of the Scottish Room of the Edinburgh Public Library. At a time when many libraries are restricting access to their more specialized collections, I have appreciated having such a good range of Scottish material on open shelf.

The labour of actually writing the text began in 1975. Demands from other books and writing commitments have spread its preparation and revision over four years. A number of people have helped with its production, either directly or indirectly. I am especially indebted to Professor A. A. M. Duncan of Glasgow University who kindly worked through two drafts of the book and not only offered many corrections but advised me on numerous matters of interpretation. Other scholars, but notably Professors G. W. S. Barrow (Edinburgh), G. Donaldson (Edinburgh), E. L. Jones (La Trobe), and T. C. Smout (St Andrews), have also played a part through their comments on previous published work. My colleagues in the Annexe at Aberystwyth—as well as those who inhabit the remoter heights of the Llandinam Tower—have been a regular source of support and discussion, but particularly Bill Edwards, Tony Moyes, and John Walton, Between them, my Department's various secretaries kindly typed the first full draft. Donald Williams and Michael Gelli Jones drew the maps and David Griffiths carried out all the photographic work. My wife, Katherine, and daughters, Clare and Lucy, made their contribution too, not least by their willingness to endure wet and windy holidays from Ardnamurchan to Inverkirkaig. Finally, my parents—to whom the book is dedicated—helped not only in the sense of being *prima causa*, but also, by their unquestioning faith in the value of university education and research. Sadly, whilst my father (Robert C. Dodgshon 1911 to 1964) saw the start of my work on Scotland, he was not able to see any of its results.

Robert A. Dodgshon
University College of Wales, Aberystwyth

Contents

Plates

(between pages 178 and 179)

Figures

Tables

Abbreviations

AHR	*Agricultural History Review*
APS	*Acts of Parliament of Scotland*
EcHR	*Economic History Review*
HMC	Historical Manuscripts Commission
NSA	*New Statistical Account*
OSA	*Old Statistical Account*
PSAS	*Proceedings of the Society of Antiquaries of Scotland*
RCAM	Royal Commission on Ancient Monuments
SAF	*Scottish Archaeological Forum*
SGM	*Scottish Geographical Magazine*
SHR	*Scottish Historical Review*
SRO	Scottish Record Office
SRS	Scottish Record Society
SS	*Scottish Studies*
STS	Scottish Text Society
TDGNHAS	*Transactions of the Dumfriesshire and Galloway Natural History and Antiquities Society*
TIBG	*Transactions of the Institute of British Geographers*

Chapter 1

Prehistoric Man
and the Scottish Landscape

Paleolithic man first appeared in Britain just over 200,000 years ago during a phase of warmer climate that occurred towards the close of the second of Britain's four main glaciations, or the Clactonian. However, it was not until after the last glaciation that he ventured north into Scotland. Even then, his arrival was hardly on the heels of the retreating ice sheets. Radio-carbon assay (carbon-14) has dated the start of the final retreat after the Lomond advance to about 12000 BC, with the last major ice sheets disappearing completely by 8000 BC. The first human communities make their tardy appearance in the Scottish archaeological record around 7000 BC, at a time when the earliest phase of human culture, or the Paleolithic, had started to give way in other parts of Britain to the Mesolithic.

The Paleolithic/Mesolithic

Our appreciation of early man in Scotland has long been hampered by a lack of adequately excavated sites. Fortunately, this situation has begun to alter. Not only are more sites being excavated by scientific methods, but the application of carbon–14 dating has given our understanding a more precise chronology. In fact, within the last decade, the dating of the earliest sites has been pushed back from around 3000 to 4000 BC to 6000 to 7000 BC. Ultimately, this more exact dating may produce a new classification for Scotland's hunter–gatherer communities. But until a new model is constructed using the data now emerging, we must be content with the classification put forward by A. D. Lacaille on the basis of their material culture.[1]

An important group of sites lie scattered along the coast and estuaries of the south-west, from Argyll southwards through Renfrew and Ayrshire, to Galloway. These sites form the Scottish counterpart to a culture called the Larnian whose province lay

[1] A. D. Lacaille, *The Stone Age of Scotland* (Oxford, 1954), pp. 92–245.

astride the North Channel. In terms of material equipment, it is characterized by a stone-working industry in which flint assemblages predominate and from which the microliths typical of other Mesolithic sites are absent. These assemblages, comprising struck flakes and blades, usually occur as deposits incorporated into the 25-feet postglacial raised beach. It was a culture developed around a fishing and strand-looping economy, at least for part of the year. A typical site is that at Ballanstrae in Ayrshire, where Larnian artefacts have been found embedded in the 25-feet raised beach on the south side of the Stinchar estuary. The community who occupied this area must have had access to a wide variety of marine- and riverine-based resources: salt and fresh-water fish, molluscs, wildfowl, and small game as well as the larger land mammals, like the aurochs, which must have roamed the estuary area. Such coastal sites are characteristic of the late Mesolithic in Britain.[2] They have been interpreted as manifesting a rather impoverished and degraded 'limpet-bashing' economy when compared with the well-developed hunting and gathering economies of the early Mesolithic.[3] Alternatively, they may have formed part of a territorial strategy in which hunting groups adopted a quite different economy, like strand-looping, during the lean months of the year.[4]

Within the last few years, sites have been discovered at Lussa Bay on Jura which yield flint assemblages of a strongly Paleolithic character and which date from around 7000 BC.[5] Not only does this make them the oldest sites known for Scotland but it throws some light on the possible ancestry of groups like the Larnian. In particular, it adds plausibility to F. Mitchell's argument that about 7700 BC, groups with a strong Paleolithic element in their cultural make-up reached the North Channel

[2] See, e.g., the discussion in P. Evans, 'The Intimate Relationship: An Hypothesis Concerning Pre-Neolithic Land Use', pp. 44–8 in J. G. Evans, S. Limbrey, and H. Cleere (eds.), *The Effect of Man on the Landscape: The Highland Zone*, Council for British Archaeology research report no. 11 (London, 1975), pp. 44–8.

[3] Echoes of this view can be found in R. J. C. Atkinson, 'Farmers and Fishermen', pp. 1–38 in S. Piggott (ed.), *The Prehistoric Peoples of Scotland* (London, 1952), pp. 1–6.

[4] W. F. Cormack and J. M. Coles, 'A Mesolithic Site at Low Clone, Wigtonshire', *TDGNHAS* xlv (1968), pp. 44–72.

[5] J. Mercer, 'New C14 Dates from the Isle of Jura, Argyll', *Antiquity,*, xlviii (1974), pp. 65–6; J. Mercer, 'Flint Tools from the Present Tidal Zone, Lussa Bay, Isle of Jura, Argyll', *PSAS* cii (1969–70), pp. 25 and 28.

area and developed in some degree of isolation for the next three or four millennia. The outcome of this isolation was the Larnian.[6] The isolation of the area ended with the arrival of Neolithic communities towards the end of the fourth millennium BC, an event which appears to have re-invigorated the Larnian. Not only did they undergo an expansion of numbers but there may also have been some kind of symbiosis between the two, with the Larnian possibly surviving for a time as 'fish merchants' to early farming settlements.[7]

Overlapping with the Larnian in both time and space was a culture known as the Obanian. Judging from the finds made so far, the territory of the Obanian was again predominantly coastal, stretching from Kintyre northwards through the islands and littoral of Argyll as far north as Moidart and Morvern. Typical of its sites are the caves around Oban, such as Mackay, MacArthurs, and Distillery Caves and the Drumvargie rock shelter, together with open-air cooking hearths and shell mounds, such as those at Cnoc Sligeach (Oronsay) or on Risga Island in Loch Sunart. In character, their sites all have the appearance of an economy based partly on hunting and partly on the collecting of sea-food and fishing. Their material culture includes not only scrapers and picks for the treatment of animal bones and skins, but also, limpet scoops and harpoon spears. An important feature of their material equipment is the use of bone and antler for the manufacture of barbed spear-heads and harpoons, as well as for tools like adzes, chisels, awls, and pins.[8] According to J. Mercer, the Obanian culture—like the Larnian—evolved from Paleolithic groups who moved into the region around 8000 to 7000 BC.[9] As a separate culture, the Obanian had taken shape soon after the start of the fourth millennium BC. The shell-middens at Caisteal nan Gillean (Oronsay) have been dated to around 3900 BC, whilst those at

---

[6] G. F. Mitchell, 'The Larnian Culture. A Minimal View', *Proc. Prehistoric Soc.*, xxxvii (1971), p. 282.

[7] Ibid., pp. 282–3. See also, Mercer, 'New C14 Dates', p. 66.

[8] Lacaille, op. cit., pp. 196–245.

[9] Mercer, 'New C14 Dates', p. 66. The idea that the Obanian and Larnian were connected was originally put forward by J. G. D. Clark, 'Notes on the Obanian with Special Reference to Antler- and Bone-Work', *PSAS* lxxxix (1955–6), p. 103. They were, he wrote, 'part of a unitary, intrusive culture'.

nearby Cnoc Sligeach in Loch Sunart have yielded a date of
3755 BC, though activity at the site continued down to 2500 to
2300 BC.[10]

As the ice sheets in Europe retreated after the last glaciation,
and the tundra-like conditions of de-glaciated areas gave way to
forest cover, many parts of northern Europe bordering the North
Sea, saw the emergence of a culture called the Maglemosian or
Forest culture. The marsh and fen-like conditions that prevailed
along the valleys of the Forth and Tay during the Mesolithic
period replicated the habitat in which Forest cultures thrived
elsewhere in Europe. It is not surprising, therefore, that such
communities were to be found in these valleys. Apart from fishing
and wildfowling, they relied a great deal on the hunting of both
sea and land mammals. A revealing glimpse of their dietary and
material needs is provided by the stripped whale carcases which
have been found buried in the coarse clays of the Forth, on either
side of Stirling. Such whales were probably stranded by the tide
rather than hunted off shore. Apart from the harvest of the inter-
tidal zone, it is likely that these Mesolithic communities also
hunted deer. Recent thinking about such Forest cultures has
tended to stress the extent to which they were associated with
deer herds, arguing that they may have manipulated the grazing
movements of deer by burning small patches of woodland cover
in order to create pockets of younger and more herbaceous
growth.[11]

Although possessing a different kind of material equipment
from other Mesolithic sites in the Forth and Tay valleys, mention
might also be made here of the site at Morton, six miles north-
north-west of St Andrews, which has produced dates of around
6000 BC for its earliest occupation layers. Even its more recent
layers date from around 4200 BC. It comprises a small collection
of domestic sites on what must have been, at the time of their
occupation, an island just off the north-east tip of Fife. They are
evidenced on the ground by a series of post marks and cooking
hearths. The post marks represent the supports of semicircular or

[10] P. A. Mellars, 'The Paleolithic and Mesolithic', pp. 41–99 in C. Renfrew (ed.),
British Prehistory (London, 1974), pp. 98–9.

[11] See, e.g., P. Mellars, 'Ungulate Populations, Economic Patterns, and the Mesolithic
Landscape', pp. 49–56 in Evans, Limbrey, and Cleere (eds.), op. cit., pp. 52–4; M. R.
Jarman, 'European Deer Economies and the Advent of the Neolithic', pp. 125–45 in E. S.
Higgs (ed.), *Papers in Economic Prehistory* (Cambridge, 1973), pp. 125–45.

arc-shaped shelters. An analysis of the refuse of the site suggests a dietary regime of typical coastal dwellers, with an emphasis on small game, birds, fish, and vegetables gathered from the wild. The excavators of the site were at pains to point out that this may only have been a seasonally occupied camp, its occupants moving on to different environments (i.e. the Ochil Hills) at other times of the year, where they presumably had command over a different set of resources.[12]

The most typical artefact of the Mesolithic period consists of small microlithic points, arrow-heads, burin scrapers, and the like. At first, these had an irregular, non-geometric shape, but towards the latter part of the Mesolithic, they take on a more regular, geometric form. In Scotland, such microliths are to be found largely in the south-east, especially along the Tweed valley.[13] Their occurrence elsewhere tends to be thin and scattered. In all probability, the hunting groups who manufactured these microliths were linked to similar communities who roamed the valleys and hill ground of northern England. Most of the Scottish finds have been turned up by the plough. The kind of understanding that can be gained from the excavation of a well-stratified site, therefore, is lacking.

The Neolithic Period

As a separate phase of prehistory, the Neolithic period is distinguished above all by the arrival of communities which practised farming. Their spread into northern Britain was by sea not land. Some arrived via the western or Atlantic seas. Others arrived via the eastern or continental seas. Emphasizing the importance of the sea as the means of transport and contact is the fact that these two routes spawned cultures which show relatively little sign of cross-fertilization. As one writer has said, it was a case of the 'sea unites and watersheds divide'.[14]

In Skara Brae and Rinyo, Scotland has the finest examples of

[12] J. M. Coles, 'The Early Settlement of Scotland: Excavations at Morton, Fife', *Proc. Prehistoric Soc.*, xxxvii (1971), p. 362.
[13] A review of these communities can be found in H. Mulholland, 'Microlithic Industries in the Tweed Valley', *TDGHNAS* xlvii (1970), p. 86.
[14] W. Kirk, 'The Primary Agricultural Colonisation of Scotland', *SGM* lxxiii (1957), p. 86.

Neolithic settlement in the whole of Britain. Unfortunately, such well-preserved sites are rare as well as atypical in their character. More abundant evidence survives in the form of chambered tombs and long mounds. Indeed, if we wish to understand the spread of Neolithic cultures into Scotland, and to grasp something of its regional differences, then we must do so through the evidence of the dead rather than the living. As a field monument, chambered tombs are to be found throughout western and northern Britain. Traditionally, they have been seen as the more manifest and durable signs of a religious cult which spread into Britain from a source-area in the Mediterranean. The application of carbon-14 dating has exploded this fallacy, for it has shown that chambered tombs in western and northern Britain were older than those from which they were supposedly derived in the Mediterranean. The view which has replaced it is that the chambered tombs of Highland Britain, together with the long mounds of the extreme north of Scotland, were developed *in situ* without external influence.[15]

Viewed overall, Scottish chambered tombs have a distribution that is overwhelmingly coastal or riverine. Within this over-all pattern, certain regional differences based on design can be perceived. Three types in particular can be recognized.[16] These comprise two types of chambered tomb plus the long mounds or cairns. The long mounds are concentrated in eastern Scotland, with important offshoots westwards into Galloway, Wigtonshire, and Dumfriesshire. The subdivision of chambered tombs into two classes is based on whether their entrance opens directly into a burial chamber, a type which used to be known as a gallery grave but which has been re-named Clyde cairns by A. Henshall, or whether one approaches the burial chamber through a stone-pillared passage, a type called passage graves. The former are located primarily in the south-west and in Argyll, whilst the latter are found mainly in the far north, stretching from Sutherland and Caithness across into Orkney and Shetland, and

[15] This view has been developed by C. Renfrew, *Before Civilisation: The Radiocarbon Revolution and Prehistoric Europe* (Harmondsworth, 1976), esp. chs. 6 and 7. A Scottish view is provided by A. Henshall, *Chambered Tombs in Scotland*, 2 vols. (Edinburgh, 1963 and 1972).
[16] Based on the scheme put forward by A. Henshall, 'Scottish Chambered Tombs and Long Mounds', pp. 137–64 in Renfrew (ed.), *British Prehistory*, pp. 137–64.

in the Outer Hebrides, particularly on the Uists. Although defined here as simple and easily recognized categories of monument, it must be stressed that both Clyde cairns and passage graves are complex types. Many examples are thought to be composite structures, built over a long period by different social groups rather than monuments designed and built at one point in time.

The idea that chambered tombs and long mounds can be used to indicate the areas in which Neolithic communities settled obviously involves assumptions regarding the link between the actual site of domestic settlement and their funerary monuments. As long ago as 1946, Gordon Childe noted how, on Rousay, 'each tomb corresponds to a natural agricultural unit, generally still or till recently farmed by a community and comprising in each case a stream, a strip of good arable below, and a tract of pasture above the tomb.'[17] Similar locations have been claimed for tombs on Bute, Arran, and in Kintyre. The implication is clear: tombs were related to specific areas or units of settlement. One writer has gone further and speculated that each patch of arable was the territory of a particular family or descent group, the tomb being a sort of family vault.[18] The monolithic scale of many of these tombs would certainly necessitate some kind of communal effort such as would be available within an extended family or kinship system. A detailed study of the cairn at Quanterness (Orkney) has refined these arguments further. It concluded that the cairn 'served a local residential group of some twenty persons, all of whom, other than infants, would be buried in the tomb as death came'.[19] Equally relevant, the study stressed that such tombs were not a resting place for prominent chiefs or their families, 'but the ritual and mortuary forms for small egalitarian communities'.[20] Altogether, the pattern envisaged in Orkney, *c*.3000 BC, is of 'a mosaic of small communities, each autonomous and independent of its neighbours—although enjoying close relations with them, as the evidence for the exchange of pottery indicates'.[21]

[17] V. G. Childe, *Scotland Before the Scots* (London, 1946), p. 34.
[18] Renfrew, *Before Civilisation*, pp. 146–52.
[19] C. Renfrew, D. Harkness, and R. Switsur, 'Quanterness, Radiocarbon and the Orkney Cairns', *Antiquity*, I (1976), p. 200.
[20] Ibid., p. 201.
[21] Ibid., p. 201.

However, such a tidy accordance between arable land and chambered tombs does not hold true everywhere. Indeed, a recent analysis even of Rousay, whilst emphasizing the concentration of chambered cairns on the island, went on to say that it was not a particularly fertile island and, therefore, it was not one on which a dense settlement by farmers would be expected so early in the process of pioneer colonization. More pointedly, on the matter of where chambered cairns were actually sited, the authors of this study argue that the results of their analysis 'play down the relevance of agricultural land and stress instead the commanding nature of the sites, as well as drawing attention to the importance of the sea which was presumably used for transport as well as for a source of food'.[22] In short, the governing factor behind the location of these tombs may have been the desire amongst Neolithic colonizers that their sepulchral monuments should be visible over a wide area as well as accessible when need arose.

A similar challenge to the notion that chambered tombs may identify the patches of land cultivated by Neolithic settlers comes from a closer study of tomb sites on Arran. Despite generalizations to the contrary, tombs do occur inland on ground unsuited to arable farming. Furthermore, these inland tombs tend to be façaded types, whilst those sited along the coast, usually on raised-beach platforms, are non-façaded. Given that the more elaborate façaded tombs are now seen as later in construction than the simpler, non-façaded ones, this suggests that settlement began along the coast and not inland as once believed.[23] Anticipating this revision of ideas back in 1962, W. Kirk also anticipated its likely significance, and that is, 'the higher, inland and more elaborate' examples could 'represent the growing power and cultural evolution of coastal farming communities'.[24]

Although the debate on Neolithic settlement must of necessity be sustained largely through the indirect evidence of funerary monuments, a few domestic sites have survived from the period. Mention has already been made of those at Skara Brae, Rinyo,

[22] D. A. Davidson, R. L. Jones, and C. Renfrew, 'Paleoenvironmental Reconstruction and Evaluation. A Case Study from Orkney', *TIBG*, n.s. i (1976), p. 360.
[23] Henshall, 'Scottish Chambered Tombs', pp. 144–8.
[24] Kirk, op. cit., p. 81.

and Jarlshof, which rank among the best preserved of Neolithic settlement sites in Britain. In each case, the nucleus of the settlement comprises small circular huts built of drystone coursing. At Jarlshof, only one hut survives. At Skara Brae and Rinyo, there exists a small group of huts huddled together as a single, structural unit, and linked by common access passages. Each hut has a central hearth with cubicles and recesses along its outer wall. In the case of Skara Brae, stone dressers and sleeping quarters can be identified. The comfort of its inhabitants was increased by infilling the non-service gaps between each hut with domestic waste thereby making the habitable part of the site windproof, whilst sanitation was effected by means of underfloor drains which fed into a common sewer outside.[25]

Though by far the most publicized, Skara Brae, Jarlshof, and Rinyo are not the only Neolithic habitation sites in the Northern Isles. A recent re-excavation of two small, rectangular huts at Knap of Howar on Papa Westray, the most northerly of Orkney's islands, has shown them to have been occupied around 3500 to 3100 BC, a date which establishes them as the oldest stone huts known for Scotland.[26] By their date and form, they are possibly the prototypes for those later built at sites like Skara Brae and Jarlshof. Also attributed to the Neolithic period are various drystone huts to be found in Shetland. In all, just over seventy of these hut sites have been discovered,[27] with notable concentrations occurring in the Gruting, Nesting, and Mavisgrind districts. Each of these sites comprises either a single hut or a small cluster of up to four. In design, the huts are oval or circular, with walls that might be as much as three metres thick. Some, such as those at Standydale and The Gairdie, show signs of having an internal cellular structure. In a number of cases, such as those at Scord of Brouster, Ness of Gruting, Dalsetter, and Boddam, the huts are set in the midst of small fields that are bounded by boulder trails and surrounded by cairns of cleared stones known locally as 'roonies'. With such a long and

[25] V. G. Childe, *Ancient Dwellings at Skara Brae* (Edinburgh, 1950); J. R. C. Hamilton, *Jarlshof* (Edinburgh, 1953); V. G. Childe, 'A Stone-Age Settlement at Rinyo', *PSAS* lxxxi (1948), pp. 16–42.

[26] Cited in E. W. MacKie, *Scotland: An Archaeological Guide* (London, 1975), pp. 258–9.

[27] This estimate is given by L. Laing, *Orkney and Shetland: An Archaeological Guide* (Newton Abbot, 1974), p. 71.

continuous tradition of stone-hut building in Shetland, the exact dating of these huts poses difficulties, but on the strength of those excavated at Stanydale and Ness of Gruting, a late Neolithic (2000 to 1500 BC) occupation seems likely.[28]

What evidence can be adduced for the kind of farming which these Neolithic settlers brought with them into Scotland? It has already been mentioned that some writers believed chambered tombs picked out the locally available plots of cultivable land, thus implying that the builders of these monuments were arable farmers. Given the reservations entered earlier over precisely what factors did determine the location of tombs, this can hardly be used to frame a view of the Neolithic economy. However, less disputable evidence is available. The stone field-walls and clearance cairns associated with Neolithic huts in Shetland indicate as graphically as possible that these early farming communities practised arable farming. A similar conclusion might be drawn from a site recently discovered at Black Crofts near North Connell in Argyll, where field dykes, clearance cairns, and chambered tombs occur in close association.[29] Material evidence for early cultivation is also afforded by finds of cereal grains or pollen at sites like Skara Brae, Maeshowe, or Ness of Gruting, and of querns at sites like the Knap of Howar.[30] However, although this evidence for arable farming is unequivocal, it seems likely that Neolithic settlers were, at the outset, mainly pastoralists, and only during the later stages of their settlement did arable cropping become important. That they were at some point engaged in livestock farming has long been known from finds of sheep and cattle bones at sites like Skara Brae. An idea of the over-all relationship between stock and arable farming can be gained from pollen analysis. At present, the earliest indication of man's interference with surface vegetation dates from around 3000 BC when a marked decline occurs in the frequency of elm pollen in pollen profiles for central

[28] Much of this discussion is based on C. S. T. Calder, 'Report on the Discovery of Numerous Stone Age House-Sites in Shetland', *PSAS* lxxxix (1956–6), pp. 340–97.

[29] A. Ritchie, G. Ritchie, G. Whittington, and J. Soulsby, 'A Prehistoric Field Boundary From Black Crofts North Connell, Argyll', *Glasgow Arch. Jnl.*, iii (1974), pp. 66–70.

[30] Calder, op. cit., p. 353. The site at Ness of Gruting yielded 28 lb. of carbonized grain, mostly naked and hulled barley.

and southern Scotland.[31] One interpretation of this selective decline in elm pollen is that it reflects the spread into Scotland of a leaf-foddering culture, that is, of pastoralists who used the leaves and shoots of elm to feed stock. Strong reservations over such a view still remain, partly because it would compress the diffusion of Neolithic settlers into too brief a time period to be convincing. A firmer basis for interpretation is provided by the general but temporary decline in all tree pollen that tends to occur soon after the elm decline.[32] As in other parts of Britain, these early signs of man's impact on vegetation suggest a sporadic and impermanent occupation of arable, with forest land being cropped temporarily, before being allowed to regenerate, the entire sequence forming what is known as a landnam episode. In some areas, clearances appear to have been more permanent, even at this early date. The recent excavation of the Dalladies long barrow in north-east Scotland reached the conclusion that large areas must have been converted from forest to pasture to enable so much turf to be spared for the construction of the barrow. The fact that pollen analysis of the site revealed no cereal pollen, only grass pollen, suggests that this reservoir of turf was linked to a pastoral system.[33] Altogether, though, it is difficult to typecast the efforts of early farmers. Rather should we envisage the use of a range of cropping systems according to the local situation. The point is well made by the study of the chambered cairn site at Maeshowe. There, pollen analysis of a ditch presumed to be connected with the cairn implied 'varied and intensive agrarian practices close at hand' during the late Neolithic. It was concluded that in Orkney the late Neolithic period saw the continuance of a predominantly pastoral system but with the adoption of more intense and diverse farming systems around sites of importance like Maeshowe.[34]

---

[31] H. H. Birks, 'Studies in the Vegetational History of Scotland II. Two Pollen Diagrams from the Galloway Hills, Kirkcudbrightshire', *Jnl. of Ecology*, lx (1972), p. 208; J. Turner, 'Post-Neolithic Disturbances of British Vegetation', pp. 97–116 in D. Walker and R. G. West (eds.), *Studies in the Vegetational History of the British Isles* (Cambridge, 1970), p. 97.

[32] S. Piggott, 'The Dalladies Long Barrow: NE Scotland', *Antiquity*, xlvii (1973), pp. 32–6.

[33] See, for instance, Birks, op. cit., pp. 209–10.

[34] Davidson, Jones, and Renfrew, op. cit., p. 354.

The Bronze Age

The opening of the Bronze age marks the arrival of the first metal-bearing cultures. The long-held view was that its earliest phases were marked by the sequential intrusions of new cultures from abroad. The first of these were the Beaker folk, a group distinguished by the presence of small drinking beakers amongst their grave goods. The character of their burials is also distinct for, in contrast to the collective inhumation techniques of the earlier Neolithic, Beaker burials took the form of single-body cist burials. The physical appearance of the Beaker folk also set them apart, since they were much taller and had broader foreheads than Neolithic peoples. These differences from established communities clearly implied that the Beaker folk were a new, immigrant group. The Beaker folk were thought by prehistorians to have been replaced by the Food-Vessel culture. The communities who made up the Food-Vessel culture were indigenous rather than of immigrant background, but our view of them has now been revised to the extent that they are seen as contemporaneous with rather than a replacement for the Beaker folk. With this revised chronology have come new possibilities on how they originated. S. Piggott once commented that it 'is tempting, but unproven, to think of the Food Vessel in north Britain as originating as a "native" counterpart of the exotic Beaker'.[35] In fact, this is the view now favoured. As one writer has put it, 'food vessel communities were probably the most strongly beaker-influenced element in the native population, and their distribution coincides with the major beaker concentrations in the east.'[36] This overlap in time and space is clearly demonstrated by Scottish evidence. Maps of the different types of Beakers (long-necked and bell) and Food Vessels display a virtually identical pattern, with heavy concentrations in the eastern Lowlands, from south-east Sutherland in the north, through the north-east Lowlands, Angus, and Fife, to the Lothians. Only in the central valley is there a significant offshoot towards the west coast, an offshoot which curves both north- and southwards as it nears the coast, reaching into Argyll and the extreme south-

---

[35] S. Piggott, 'Traders and Metalworkers', pp. 73–103 in Piggott (ed.), *Prehistoric Peoples of Scotland*, p. 85.

[36] C. Burgess, 'The Bronze Age', pp. 165–232 in Renfrew (ed.), *British Prehistory*, p. 175.

west.[37] Since both the latter areas possessed resources of tin and copper, the basis of bronze, it is hardly surprising that the Beaker-folk and Food-Vessel communities should show an interest in these latter two areas.

Adding still more complexity to this interweave of cultures is a third group of communities known as the Urn people. Although they were thought to have succeeded the Food-Vessel culture, carbon-14 dates now available make it clear that they too overlapped in time with the Food-Vessel and Beaker cultures. Furthermore, their burials share a broadly similar distribution. In Scotland, the only real difference is that the Urn burials are better represented in southern Scotland. However, the main component of their distribution, or a heavy emphasis in the eastern lowland areas, is the same. Unlike the other two cultures of the early Bronze age, the Urn folk practised cremation. Otherwise, their most notable contribution to the landscape was in continuing the henge tradition which had emergd during the Neolithic period, a tradition best illustrated by sites like Callanish (Lewis) and the Ring of Brodgar (Orkney).

The latter part of the Bronze age was a time of considerable activity in Scotland. The application of carbon-14 dating to sites in eastern and northern Scotland has shown that some which were considered to be Iron age in date were, in fact, developed during the close of the Bronze age. Notable amongst those which have been re-dated are the vitrified and associated drystone forts of east-central Scotland. Examples like that at Finavon in Angus or that of Dun Lagaiadh in Loch Broom are known to have been built by the seventh century BC, or the late Bronze age. As a class of monuments, these forts extend over a wide range of design and layout. In the case of the example at Abernethy, a fort which Childe used to typify the entire complex of vitrified and drystone forts, we are dealing with a small, circular, walled fort. That at Finavon is much larger and oval in shape. Those of Craig Phadraig in Inverness-shire and Forgandenny in Angus are defended not just by one but by two concentric stone walls. In other cases, we are dealing with drystone forts which have never been vitrified or even timber-laced. In this category fall the very large and defensively complex forts like the Barmekin of Echt

[37] See, e.g., those provided by Piggott, 'Traders and Metalworkers', pp. 78, 83, and 87.

(Aberdeenshire) or the Brown Caterthun (Angus). We cannot say for certain whether all these different types were built by the late Bronze age, or whether some were not built until much later, but the tradition of stone-fort building had certainly begun by then. Owing to their occurrence in the area later occupied by the Picts, the identity of those who actually built them has received more than an average amount of attention. Excavation has not answered the question. However, there are some signs that new immigrants were arriving in Scotland during the late Bronze age.[38]

A comparable re-dating has taken place with regard to the so-called palisaded enclosures of the south-east. These comprise defensive enclosures whose outer boundary was formed by a palisade set in a narrow bedding trench. The largest, or those on White Hill (Peeblesshire) or Hayhope Knowe (Roxburghshire), are up to 5 acres (2 ha) in extent. Within their bounds, these larger palisaded enclosures can possess up to fifteen hut sites. Whilst not all these sites were occupied at the same point in time, these were group settlements inhabited by social units whose scale, at the very least, was equivalent to that of the extended family. Contrasted with these larger palisaded enclosures are smaller examples, under an acre or so ($\frac{1}{2}$ ha) in extent, that contained no more than two or three hut sites. These smaller versions are best classed as homesteads rather than group settlements. Traditionally, the origin of these enclosures has been regarded as a problem of the Iron age. Now, there is good reason for believing that the larger sites date back to the seventh or sixth centuries BC. E. MacKie sees them as built by new migrants moving into the area from the south.[39] But A. Ritchie prefers to see them as representing nothing more than 'the development of widespread, permanent settlement in place of the impermanent and insubstantial settlement that must be assumed, in the absence of evidence to the contrary, for earlier periods'.[40]

The late Bronze age may also have been a time of change in the

[38] E. W. MacKie, 'The Vitrified Forts of Scotland', pp. 205–36 in D. W. Harding (ed.), *Hillforts* (London, 1977), pp. 244–5; E. W. MacKie, 'Radio-Carbon Dates and the Scottish Iron Age', *Antiquity*, xliii (1969), pp. 15–26.

[39] E. W. MacKie, 'The Scottish "Iron Age"', *SHR* xlix (1970), pp. 14–17.

[40] A. Ritchie, 'Palisaded Sites in North Britain: Their Context and Affinities', *SAF* (1970), p. 56. But see also the reply by E. W. MacKie, 'The Hownam Culture: A Rejoinder to Ritchie', *SAF* (1970), pp. 68–72.

Prehistoric Man and the Scottish Landscape 15

far north. It has been argued that the stone huts and field systems that lie scattered across Shetland and which were provisionally classified earlier as late Neolithic (p. 9) may well be late Bronze age in origin.[41] More certainly, we know that at Jarlshof, the late Bronze age saw the construction of a cluster of courtyard houses, similar to their Neolithic antecedents but more regular in plan and having more pronounced internal cells that open out to a central courtyard. Of equal interest are the drystone huts to be found in eastern Sutherland, or the 'wags'. Over 2,000 are estimated to exist. Most are situated on ground lying between 60 and 120 metres above sea level. The better-preserved examples, such as those at Kildonan, Ord of Lairg, Kilphedir, or in upper Strathnaver, are linked to clearance cairns or field systems, part of which are now partially covered by peat deposits. Detailed ground study has distinguished between two types of site, the one a simple circular enclosure on a prepared platform and the other, a more massively built structure reinforced along its inner edge with slabs and sometimes elaborated with an entrance passage. Other features sharpen this distinction. Thus, the former are linked with clearance cairns, whilst the latter are associated with trailing banks and boulder trails. The former are found generally throughout eastern Sutherland, whereas the latter are more confined to the south-east. Lastly, there is a difference of chronology. The former is older. Carbon-14 dating on the site at Kilphedir has yielded a date of around 500 to 400 BC. Whether this is seen as late Bronze age or early Iron age is open to debate. Possibly the most revealing conclusion reached by the excavation of Kilphedir is that 'its occupants may have been still largely stone using.'[42] In other words, some of these northern sites are not easily accommodated into a classification scheme based on whether their occupants were bronze- or iron-using.

Pollen diagrams inform us that the Bronze age saw a significant increase in arable farming, with signs of forest clearance for cultivation becoming more widespread by 1800 BC. These signs still take the form of landnam episodes. Excellent studies of such episodes in a Scottish context are provided by J. Turner's work on Lennox and Bloak mosses (Ayrshire). Her work

[41] Laing, op. cit., pp. 71–2.
[42] H. Fairhurst and D. B. Taylor, 'A Hut-Circle Settlement at Kilphedir, Sutherland', *PSAS* ciii (1970–1), pp. 65–99.

is especially informative in that it shows sequences of landnam episodes such as might result from a system of shifting cultivation.[43] But whilst shifting and temporary cropping may have been the rule, traces of permanently occupied field systems dating from the late Bronze age do occur in parts of southern Scotland.[44] Pollen work by R. E. Durno on sites in the north-east, such as at Dalnagar, evidence a comparatively limited amount of forest clearance and cultivation during the Bronze age, but with a marked increase in human activity towards the close, or around 700 to 500 BC.[45]

The Iron Age

In a fresh appraisal of the evidence,[46] MacKie has argued that the Iron age saw the consolidation of those groups who had emerged in eastern and south-eastern Scotland during the late Bronze age, together with the arrival in the north and north-west of new influences, and possibly new migrants, from southern England. If we add to these three regions that of the south-west, then it gives us four main cultural regions around which any discussion of the Scottish Iron age must be based.

It was said earlier that the south-east was characterized by palisaded enclosures which first appeared during the late Bronze age. These sites continued to be occupied, without any major break or discontinuity, throughout the Iron age. As MacKie put it, once established, we must think 'in terms of a population (whose language and cultural origin are still unknown) which remained relatively static and unchanged from the late Bronze age in the seventh century BC, and perhaps earlier, for several centuries until the Votadini were overrun by the Romans in about AD 80. In this case the population would simply have assimilated new ideas and techniques from the south of the Border.'[47] These new techniques and ideas to which he refers are expressed in the changes of design and layout which palisaded settlements underwent. The well-documented example of

---

[43] Turner, op. cit., pp. 86–95.

[44] R. Feachem, 'Ancient Agriculture in the Highland of Britain', *Proc. Prehistoric Soc.*, xxxviii (1972), pp. 339–47.

[45] S. E. Durno, 'Pollen Analysis of Peat Deposits in Scotland', *SGM* lxxii (1956), pp. 176–84.

[46] MacKie, 'The Scottish "Iron Age" ', pp. 1–32.

[47] Ibid., p. 16.

Hownam Rings (Roxburghshire), for instance, began as an open or unenclosed settlement before being palisaded. After being palisaded, it subsequently had its palisade replaced by a drystone wall, and eventually finished up as a multi-vallum fort, or one defended by a series of bank and ditch systems. In other places, the elaboration of the defences took the form of extra palisades. By far the most important change occurred during the fourth, third, and second centuries BC, with the widespread emergence of small enclosures, or the palisaded homesteads. The sheer number of these homesteads has suggested to some that their development was a direct and simple response to population growth.[48] Alternatively, it may signify 'a development in social conditions and an elaboration of social organization', with the larger palisaded settlements or large social groupings being replaced by smaller, possibly more family-based units of settlement.[49]

Continuity of settlement from the late Bronze age down through the Iron age is also arguable for east-central Scotland. Some new influences were absorbed by trade and through the settlement of fresh communities along the southern fringes of the Highlands, but these were not sufficient to overwhelm the existing Bronze-age characteristics of the local population. This continuity is demonstrated by the continued occupation of vitrified forts, though the technique of timber-facing was abandoned in new constructional work around the fourth century BC. This admixture of surviving Bronze-age with later, intrusive Iron-age cultural strands is of interest because it provides a cultural context for the later Picts.

The brochs and wheelhouses of the north-west and north, or Atlantic Province, provide us with Scotland's most impressive Iron-age settlements. The former consist of stone-built circular towers, rising in some cases to over 15 metres, though only the example at Mousa survives to anything like this height today. Their construction was no mean technical feat. It was achieved by using a hollow-wall technique and tapering the tower as it

---

[48] G. Jobey, 'Excavations at Boonies, Westerkirk, and the Nature of Romano–British Settlement in Eastern Dumfries-shire', *PSAS* cv (1972), p. 13. See also, G. Jobey, 'Homesteads and Settlements of the Frontier Area', pp. 1–14 in C. Thomas (ed.), *Rural Settlement in Roman Britain*, Council for British Archaeology research report no. vii (London, 1966), pp. 9–10.

[49] Ritchie, op. cit., p. 55.

gained height, the hollow wall being formed out of two concentric walls tied together at certain levels by cross-stones or lintels. At the base of the tower, these two concentric walls were sufficiently far apart to enable passages and guard chambers to be installed within them, but towards the top of the broch, the gap between them decreased as its profile tapered.

For a long time, the view was held that because the largest and technically most sophisticated examples were in Orkney and Shetland, their origin must be sought there. This view has recently been subjected to detailed and careful investigation, out of which have come two interpretations, one favouring it and one rejecting it. The argument in favour has been developed by J. R. C. Hamilton, using evidence provided by the excavation of a broch at Clickhimmin in Shetland.[50] The alternative interpretation advanced by MacKie is rooted in a detailed analysis of the broad areal variations in broch typology. This demonstrated how the brochs of the western isles (Skye and the Long Island) and on the mainland opposite, such as those of Dun Telve and Dun Troddan in Glenelg, were smaller than those in Orkney and Shetland. But although smaller, their walls were thicker in construction. Furthermore, whereas those of the west were usually located on sites that were naturally defensive (i.e. on a rock outcrop or island), those of the north were free-standing on open ground. Put in a few words, these areal variations suggest that the brochs of the west were cruder and less advanced than those of the north. This leads on to the conclusion that the latter, being more advanced, must be later in development.[51] Having reached this conclusion, MacKie reasoned that the prototypes of the broch were to be found in the west not the north.[52] The broch itself had emerged by the second century BC and continued in occupation until the second century AD.

Wheelhouses have a distribution identical to that of the broch and have a similar overlap in time. They consist of small stone

[50] J. R. C. Hamilton, *Excavations at Jarlshof, Shetland* (Edinburgh, 1956); idem, 'Forts, Brochs and Wheel-houses in Northern Scotland', pp. 111–30 in A. L. F. Rivet (ed.), *The Iron Age in Northern Britain* (Edinburgh, 1966).
[51] The most comprehensive treatment of this aspect is to be found in E. W. MacKie, 'The Origin and Development of the Broch and Wheelhouse Building Cultures of the Scottish Iron Age', *Proc. Prehistoric Soc.*, xxxi (1965), pp. 93–146 but esp. pp. 105–10.
[52] Ibid., pp. 124–46. See also, E. W. MacKie, 'Brochs and the Hebridean Iron Age', *Antiquity*, xxxix (1965), pp. 266–77.

fortlets, eight to ten metres in diameter, whose interior was subdivided into sections by radial stone piers. In some instances, these radial piers are affixed to the outer wall of the fort. In others, usually tagged aisled wheelhouses, they stop short of it. The piers are thought to imitate in stone the roof-supports which timber-framed buildings possessed. Unlike the thatch or skin-covered roofs of timber dwellings, wheelhouses may even have been corbelled or roofed with stone. Although their distribution overlaps with that of the brochs there are some interesting differences. No wheelhouses, for instance, are to be found on the northern mainland or in Orkney. On balance, it seems likely that whilst their style was beginning to emerge at the same time as the early brochs, most fully-fledged examples were not built until well into the broch period. However, they continued in use for longer, some Shetland wheelhouses still being dwelt in at the time of the Scandinavian settlements in the ninth century.[53]

At the other end of the Atlantic Province, in the south-west Highlands, is another group of settlements known as duns. This is a generic term covering a range of circular and semicircular forts of small to medium size, built in the drystone traditions of the region. Like the brochs, some employ a hollow-wall technique with galleries between the two retaining walls: these are called galleried duns. Before they were more accurately dated, these galleried duns were, in fact, seen as possible precursors of the broch. Such a connection is completely dispelled by the fact that most galleried duns, as well as those duns utilizing a solid wall, were probably not erected until the first and second centuries AD. In some cases, such as the example of Kildonan on Mull, they were not built until as late as the early Christian period.If anything, their relationship to the broch is not one of parentage, but of complementarity. Whereas the latter are to be found from Skye and Tiree northwards, duns are mostly to be found to the south, their main concentrations being in Argyll, Bute, Renfrew, and Ayrshire.[54] Broadly contemporary with them are the

[53] Hamilton, 'Forts, Brochs and Wheelhouses', pp. 111–30; MacKie, 'Origin and Development of the Broch and Wheelhouses Building Cultures', pp. 93–146.

[54] A review can be found in G. Maxwell, 'Duns and Forts—A Note on Some Iron Age Monuments of the Atlantic Province', *SAF* (1969), pp. 41–52. Maxwell reviews, but does not resolve, the varying definitions of duns, leaving the reader with what he calls the currently held view which sees them as 'a large class of small stone-walled forts of differing plan, size and date'.

numerous crannogs—small, artificial-island settlements—now known to exist in the south-west Highlands. Recent survey work has shown a notable string of examples along Loch Awe, with outliers in adjacent lochs like that of Loch Leathan.[55]

The region of Scotland with least definition in terms of Iron-age settlement and society is that of the south-west, or the Clyde–Solway Province. A fairly diverse range of settlements have been recorded. The most distinctive are the timber-framed crannogs. Over forty examples lie scattered across the region, but particularly in Galloway and Ayrshire. Possibly the best-documented sites are those of Milton Loch in Kirkcudbright-shire[56] and Lochlee in Ayrshire.[57] Both proved rich in material remains. Each formed a roughly circular island made of oaks or birch logs laid down parallel to each other, and held down by piles and beams morticed together into a rigid framework. Although timber dug-out canoes were recovered at Lochlee, both sites had access to the mainland via timber-based causeways. Only one hut was found on each island, though both excavation reports note that this solitary hut had obviously been rebuilt a number of times following fire. Despite their insular existence, the inhabitants of these crannogs were farmers. At Lochlee, they grew barley, kept sheep, cattle, pigs, and horses, and hunted red deer, roe deer, and wild boar. The farming economy of Milton Loch was conveyed more dramatically by the discovery during the excavation of a beam or stilt of an ard, one of the earliest ploughing implements yet found in Scotland.

As well as crannogs, Iron-age settlement in the south-west was enriched by outlying examples of brochs, duns, and vitrified forts. A significant number of these particular structures occur strung out along the coast of Galloway. More peculiar to the region itself and more enigmatic are the *birrens or burians*, that lie along the valley slopes and river terraces of upper Annandale, Ewesdale, and Eskdale. These are small, circular enclosures defined by a

[55] RCAM, Scotland, *Argyll*, vol. ii, Lorn (Edinburgh, 1975), esp. p. 94.

[56] The original excavation report is provided by C. M. Piggott, 'Milton Loch Crannog; A Native House of the Second Century A.D. in Kirkcudbrightshire', *PSAS* lxxxvii (1952–3), pp. 134–52. As the title suggests, it was seen as occupied during the sub-Roman period. However, M. Guido, 'A Scottish Crannog', *Antiquity*, xlviii (1974), pp. 54–6, provided a carbon-14 dating of 490 BC ± 100 years for the site's pile and a similar dating for the plough found there.

[57] R. Munro, 'Lochlee Crannog, Ayrshire', *PSAS* xiii (1878–9), pp. 175–251.

stone wall or embankment. One or two contain the remains of rectangular huts, whilst others have scooped platforms similar in character to the scooped settlement sites which lie further east. Excavation of the *birren* at Boonies in Westerkirk parish (Dumfriesshire) has confirmed that such scoopd platforms were the basis for timber-framed dwellings. The dating of this site by carbon-14 suggests it was built and occupied during the latter part of the Iron age, but continued to be occupied during the Roman period.[58] Adding still further variety, to this pattern of Iron-age settlement were the hill forts that dot the region. Some like Walls Hill in Renfrewshire and Burnswark in Dumfriesshire are large enough (15–20 acres or 6–8 ha) to be regarded as *oppida* or hill-top towns. They probably discharged the function of tribal trading centres or even capitals.

The Roman Period

The Roman occupation of Scotland was a partial, fluctuating affair. Although an attempt was made to define a frontier which dissected Scotland into a barbaric north and an Imperial south, the Romans could have had few illusions that their occupation of the area behind this frontier was anything other than a strong military presence, liable on many occasions to be questioned by tribal rebellions. Their penetration into Scotland began in AD 80. In a campaign led by Julius Agricola, they quickly overcame resistance from native tribes whom Roman writers identify as the Selgovae of Roxburghshire, Selkirkshire, and Dumfriesshire, the Votadini of the Lothians, and the Damnonii of the Clyde valley. Their military initiative was strengthened by the immediate construction of strategically-placed forts. The largest was Newstead. This was sited in the lee of the Eildon Hills, on top of which was Trimontium ('Three Hills'), the tribal capital of the Selgovae. It does not surprise us to learn that the Selgovae were the most stubborn of all the tribes which the Roman invasion confronted.[59] Other forts were built guarding the valley route-

---

[58] Jobey, 'Excavations at Boonies', pp. 118–40.

[59] S. Frere, *Britannia. A History of Roman Britain* (London, 1978), pp. 123–36. In respect of the Selgovae, Frere observed that 'the numerous small hill-forts in their territory imply a lack of political centralization which may have proved disastrous when the moment of crisis so swiftly arrived.' The Romans, he went on to suggest, deliberately laid out their roads and forts so as to 'cordon off' the Selgovae from their neighbours, p. 126.

ways that gave vital access to central Scotland, such as those at Gatehouse (Fleet Valley), Glenlochar (Dee Valley), Dalswinton (Nithsdale), and Milton (Annandale). Linking these forts was a network of newly-built roads. Some kept to the valley ground, like those running through Nithsdale and Annandale. Others strode boldly across hill ground, such as the main easterly route which entered Scotland across the Cheviots or the connecting route from Annandale across Eskdalemuir into the Tweed valley.

Once southern and central Scotland had been secured, a large expeditionary force foraged northwards through Strathmore to the north-east Lowlands. Their objectives were altogether more limited than they had been further south. Only marching camps, consisting of large bank and ditch enclosures, were built. The largest surviving example is at Raedykes near Stonehaven which is 93 acres (37 ha) in extent. No doubt aware of the dangers of exposing a long flank to the Caledonii tribes who held the Highland areas to the north and west, they soon pulled back to the line of more permanent forts which they had built between the Clyde and Forth. However, even this line of defence was vulnerable. Indeed, in AD 122, when an attempt was made to define a frontier on the ground, in the shape of Hadrian's Wall, it left not just northern Scotland but the whole of Scotland outside the so-called *Pax Romana*. Within twenty years, though, the entire exercise was repeated all over again with the building of the Antonine Wall across the waist of Scotland from Bridgeness on the Forth to Old Kilpatrick on the Clyde.[60] In its day, and for a long time thereafter, this must have been the most monumental landmark in the Scottish human landscape. It consisted of a deep, dry ditch in front of the wall, then the wall itself, and behind it, a paved road. The actual wall had a foundation of stones with a thick capping of turf. At regular intervals along it were strong points in the form of small forts. The fact that it was built so soon after Hadrian's Wall has caused some to see it as signalling a dramatic change in the political and military situation of central and southern Scotland enabling or encouraging the Romans to reoccupy the areas they had previously abandoned. But recently, D. Breeze has described its con-

[60] Ibid., pp. 165–93; A. S. Robertson, *The Antonine Wall*, Glasgow Arch. Soc. (Glasgow, 1970).

struction as an 'abberration' because it did not reflect a deteriorating situation in Scotland at the time, suggesting instead that it was possibly a sign of the power politics being played out in Rome and the desire in some quarters for a military project that reaped prestige.[61] Whatever the reason, the Antonine Wall was occupied only during two brief periods, one from AD 146 to 155 and another which some date from AD 158 to 165. When it was finally abandoned, the frontier retreated southwards once more to Hadrian's Wall. Apart from outposts at forts like Newstead and Bewcastle in Roxburghshire, and a new military campaign in the early third century which penetrated as far north as Moray and Banffshire, the Roman occupation of Scotland had effectively ended.

Society in southern Scotland was probably organized on a tribal basis throughout the Romano–British period. Each tribe presumably worked out its own *modus vivendi* with the Romans, some experiencing deeper and more far-reaching changes than others. Thus, a tribe like the Selgovae, with its heavy Roman presence, must have been closely supervised, whilst the tribe which occupied the Galloway region, the Novantae, seems hardly to have concerned them. Turning to the actual changes that occurred, tribes in strategic areas, such as the Selgovae, Votadini, and Damnonii, were probably forced to pull down or de-militarize their more heavily defended forts and *oppida*.[62] But in areas like the middle Tweed valley or on either side of Lauderdale, where small stone-built hill forts were fairly numerous, their occupation undoubtedly, continued—if not necessarily without a break into the post-Roman period.[63] On the credit side, the native population must have enjoyed an expansion of trade during the Roman occupation. Judging from the finds which have been made at purely native sites, exotic Roman goods passed freely between native hands. In return for such items, the existence of a large standing army provided the various tribes with a ready market for metal ware, leather goods and, above all, for grain. It has been argued that the native economy

[61] D. J. Breeze, 'The Abandonment of the Antonine Wall: Its Date and Implications', *SAF* (1975), pp. 67–80.

[62] Frere, op. cit., pp. 174–5.

[63] RCAM, Scotland, *Selkirkshire* (Edinburgh, 1957); RCAM, Scotland, *Peebles-shire* (Edinburgh, 1967); R. W. Feachem, *The North Britons* (London, 1965), pp. 196–200.

prior to the Roman occupation was largely pastoral. In a now classic phrase, S. Piggott referred to the tribal communities of the region as 'wandering bands of footloose Celtic cowboys'.[64] Since the Romans preferred to live off local supplies, he went on to suggest that they overcame this deficiency in the local economy by transplanting into the region Belgic communities from south-west England.[65]

However, more recent work suggests that the Celts who inhabited the upland areas of Britain both before and during the Roman period were more skilled in the arts of arable husbandry than Piggott at that time believed. The Milton Loch plough head and stilt, with its date of 400 BC ± 100 years, proves this, as does the dating of the Lochmaben ard beam to 80 BC ± 100 years.[66] So too do the various early field systems to be found in the Southern Uplands. Two types have been identified. On the one hand, there are those comprising small, irregular fields bounded by low banks and clearance cairns, such as the large complex to be found on White Meldon Hill in Peeblesshire. On the other hand, there are those comprising more elongated or strip-like fields, such as Tamshiel Rig in Roxburghshire or Glenrath village in Peebles-shire. Both these types can sometimes be found on the same site, as at Stanshiel Rig in Dumfriesshire, where examples of the latter overlie the former. According to R. W. Feachem, sites possessing small, irregular fields were probably in use no later than 500 BC and were settlements of Bronze-age or early Iron-age communities. Those based on more regular, strip-like fields, meanwhile, probably date from the late Iron age or Romano–British period.[67] This change from one type to another could conceivably manifest the impact of new intrusive communities or the increased local demand caused by the presence of the Roman legions.[68] Alternatively, it may be a case of local, native population growth leading to extra demand and through

[64] S. Piggott, 'Native Economies and the Roman Occupation of North Britain', pp. 1–27 in I. A. Richmond (ed.), *Roman and Native in North Britain* (London, 1958), p. 25.

[65] Ibid., pp. 20 and 25.

[66] Guido, op. cit., pp. 54–6.

[67] Feachem, 'Ancient Agriculture', pp. 340–2. Plans of sites can also be seen in the RCAM, Scotland volumes, such as *Roxburghshire*, vol. ii, p. 943.

[68] See, for instance, W. H. Manning, 'Economic Influences on Land Use in the Military Areas of the Highland Zone During the Roman Period', pp. 112–16 in Evans, Limbrey, and Cleere (eds.), op. cit., pp. 114–15.

this mechanism, innovation.[69] Conceivably, the difference between these two types of field layout could reflect the differing
needs of the spade or ard as opposed to the plough. Feachem's
view is that the shift from one type of layout to the other was
punctuated by a hiatus during the middle of the first millennium
BC when climatic deterioration led to the abandonment of
upland sites like White Meldon Hill and Stanshiel Rig. Their
resettlement during the late Iron age was, he argued, only
accomplished with the use of new and better cultivation
techniques, techniques which could account for their differences
in layout.[70] Whatever their explanation, though, the extent of
cultivation during the Iron age and Romano–British period must
not be overstated or misplaced. Work by paleobotanists like J.
Turner[71] and H. H. Birks[72] on the Southern Uplands has shown
that cultivation was still largely small-scale and temporary in
character throughout these two periods. Only around AD 400 do
pollen profiles suggest that clearances for cultivation became
both widespread and permanent. At the same time, it must be
kept in mind that the early field systems which have survived
have done so in situations which, today, would be classed as
marginal hill ground. Arguably, they may have been just as
marginal when in use. The number of Iron-age settlement sites
that ghost through as crop marks on the low ground of upper
Clydesdale is instructive here, for it suggests that along this and
other similar valleys, early fields may lie beneath or incorporated
into modern field patterns.[73]

[69] Jobey, op. cit., p. 138 talks of population growth at this point. See also, Jobey,
'Homesteads and Settlements of the Frontier Area', p. 13.
[70] Feachem, 'Ancient Agriculture', p. 348.
[71] Turner, 'Post-Neolithic Disturbances of British Vegetation', p. 105.
[72] Birks, 'Studies in the Vegetational History of Scotland II', p. 210.
[73] RCAM, Scotland, *Lanarkshire: Prehistoric and Roman Antiquities* (Edinburgh, 1976),
details a number of crop mark sites, such as those near Covington, Pettinain, and
Liberton.

Chapter 2

Early Medieval Scotland

The early centuries of the historic period form a crucial yet
tantalizingly obscure period of Scottish history. Into a country
already consisting of Britons and Picts, there came cultural
movements involving the Scotti from Ireland, the Angles from
Northumbria, and the Vikings from west Norway. The intrusion
of these disparate cultures clearly added substantially to the
cultural diversity which existed in Scotland at this point. Indeed,
for a time, parts of Scotland, such as Argyll, the south-east, and
the Northern and Western Isles, came within the orbit of cultural
regions which stretched far beyond Scotland's borders as we
know them today. However, for all their initial contrast and
distinction, it was the gradual coalescing of these various cultural
groups, at least in political and dynastic terms, that eventually
formed the basis of the Scottish Kingdom. Given the scarcity of
evidence for the period, the questions we can meaningfully ask
about it are limited. Fortunately, we are in a position to delineate
the probable areas occupied by the different cultural groups and
how these altered over time, but questions directed at their social
organization, economy, and types of settlement receive much
more unsatisfactory answers.

The Picts

Because of the uncertainty surrounding many aspects of their
character, the Picts are usually seen as the most enigmatic of the
cultural groups who inhabited Dark-Age Scotland. They are
thought to be a locally derived culture, compounded out of the
various cultures who existed in central and northern Scotland
during the late prehistoric period. In a carefully circumspect
reference to them, F. T. Wainwright declared that

philologists, archaeologists and historians, differing among themselves
at many points, would probably all agree that the historical Picts were a

heterogenous people and that the antecedents of Pictland should not be sought in a single people . . . the historical Picts represent a number of racial and cultural groups which impinged or were superimposed on one another in the area which we recognize as Pictland.[1]

A more precise statement of origin is still not possible. Indeed, such is the uncertainty over how the Picts came to be, that some would consider it a historical impropriety to talk of them as a discrete or uniform group before their first mention as *Picti* in the written record, an event dated to AD 297. As Wainwright succinctly put it, 'the historical Picts are the only Picts known to us.'[2]

Their hybridized background is still apparent in the earliest references to their political make-up. By the early part of the third century AD, they appear organized into two broad tribal groups or confederacies, namely, the Caledonii and Maeatae. This distinction possibly corresponded to a politico–geographical distinction which had emerged by the fifth century between the Picts who lived north of the Mounth and those who lived south of it. The exact structure of these two provinces is unclear. They may have formed loose groupings of semi-independent regional kingdoms that owed allegiance to a high king. Alternatively, each province may have formed a unified kingdom that was subdivided into large territorial units ruled over by powerful deputies of the king known as *mormaers*. Either way, we must not expect too great a degree of political centralization at this stage: the cultural heterogeneity of the Picts together with the facts of geography would have seen to this. The interpretation accepted has a bearing on the tribal groups and districts listed in sources like the *Chronicle of the Picts* or the *De Situ Albanie* (see Table 1). The most interesting list of the Pictish Heptarchy and its territorial structure is possibly that afforded by the twelfth-century manuscript entitled *De Situ Albanie*: this list divides each district into two parts (see Table 1). Even Caithness has its division into 'this side of the mountain' and 'beyond the mountain'. According to the *De Situ Albanie* itself, this bipartite

[1] F. T. Wainwright, 'The Picts and the Problem', pp. 1–53 in F. T. Wainwright (ed.), *The Problem of the Picts* (Edinburgh, 1955), p. 12.

[2] Idem, 'Picts and Scots', pp. 91–116 in F. T. Wainwright (ed.), *The Northern Isles* (Edinburgh, 1962), p. 91.

Table 1: Pictish Districts

A	B	C	D
Fortiu	Strathearn and Menteith	Hilef (Isla?) to the Tay	Fortrenn
Fothreue	Fife with Fothreff (Kinross)	The Dee to the Spey	Fib
Cirhenn or			
Cirig	Angus with Mearns	The Forth to the Tay	Circinn
Fotla	Atholl and Gowrie	The Tay to the Hilef (Isla?)	Fotla
Catt	Caithness, this side and		
	beyond the mountain		Cait
Ce	Mar with Buchan	The Spey to Druimalban	Ce
Fidach	Moray and Ross	Moray and Ross	Fidach

List A is based on M. O. Anderson's analysis of Pictish districts using the *De Situ Albanie* in her *Kings and Kingship in Early Scotland* (Edinburgh, 1973), pp. 139–45. List B is A. O. Anderson's version of the notable pairing of Pictish districts in the *De Situ Albanie* taken from his *Early Sources of Scottish A.D. 500 to 1286*, vol. i (Edinburgh, 1922), pp. lxvi–lxvii. List C is the gloss provided by the Bishop of Caithness on the location or bounds of the Pictish districts which was incorporated into the *De Situ Albanie*. Critical comment on the value of these bounds is afforded by I. Henderson, *The Picts* (London, 1967), p. 36 and W. J. Watson, *The History of the Celtic Place-Names of Scotland* (Edinburgh, 1926), pp. 107–17. List D is based on the supposed seven sons of Cruithne and their respective tribal territories as evidenced by the Pictish Chronicle, see W. F. Skene (ed.), *Chronicles of the Picts, Chronicles of the Scots, and other early memorials of Scottish History* (Edinburgh, 1867), pp. 23 and 136.

structure of tribal provinces was rooted in the fact that each one had within it a subordinate province or *sub-regio*. Interweaving fact with mythology, it described these seven provinces as held by the seven sons of Cruithne. Under them, there existed in each district an under-king or *regulus*. Logically, each sub-region represented the domain of an under-king. A. C. Thomas has stressed that this bipartite structure of Pictish provinces was not a phenomenon that was unique to them. Indeed, he suggests that this mapping of divided kingship into the territorial structure of early tribal districts may once have been universal in early Europe. However, like other archaic elements, the Picts preserved theirs down into the early historic period simply because they were a 'conserving society' rather than an innovating one.[3] Arguably, such a pattern of territorial organization tells us much about how Pictish society itself was organized. By analogy with modern ethnographic examples, such self-classification was invariably based on simple oppositions and was used to regulate

[3] C. Thomas, 'The Interpretation of the Pictish Symbols', *Archaeological Jnl.*, cxx (1963), pp. 68–9.

intra-tribal marriage alliances, exchange, and ceremonial rank-ings.[4]

At some point during the sixth or early seventh centuries, the northern and southern area of Pictland appear to have passed under the authority of a single over-king. Despite this dynastic and political integration, differences of a sort can still be discerned between its northern and southern parts. Key elements of Pictish culture which can be mapped or discussed in geographical terms, continued to manifest areal differences along these lines, even though they include patterns of distribution that were established after the union of Pictland. Especially informative in this respect are the various types of Pictish standing stones. Dating from the sixth and early seventh centuries are the non-Christian standing stones (or Class I). These early stones have stylized design motifs, based on spiral and zoomorphic patterns, incised on them. But unlike later stones, their symbolism is entirely pagan in character. When mapped, they reveal a concentration in the north-east, particularly the Garioch and Mar areas of Aberdeenshire, with small concentrations further west along the Spey valley and around the shores of the Moray and Cromarty Firths stretching as far north as south-east Sutherland. By comparison, those in southern Pictland are much less numerous. In view of this imbalance between the areas to the north and south of the Mounth, it is commonly believed that the tradition of erecting and designing such stones evolved in the north. When we turn to look at Pictish standing stones displaying Pagan *and* Christian motifs (Class II) or just Christian motifs (Class III), we find a quite different pattern. The distribution of these is weighted more in favour of the southern Pictland area. Although the interpretation is fraught with difficulties, this shift in emphasis from north to south when comparing non-Christian with Christian standing stones has been seen as reflecting a shift in Pictish cultural and political domination from the north to the south following the unification of the two areas.[5]

Pictish standing stones have an undoubted symbolism. The obvious interpretation would be to see them as burial markers for

[4] A. and B. Rees, *Celtic Heritage* (London, 1962), pp. 118–85; E. Durkheim and M. Mauss, *Primitive Classification*, trans. and ed. by R. Needham, 2nd Eng. edn. (London, 1969), p. 68; P. Bourdieu, *Outline of a Theory of Practice* (Cambridge, 1977), pp. 124–58.
[5] See, e.g., I. Henderson, *The Picts* (London, 1967), p. 101.

persons of rank. This, in fact, was the conclusion reached by
Thomas in a review of Pictish symbols and their meaning. He
argued that the various motifs were meant to express the status,
occupation, and lineage of the persons whose burial they
commemorated. In his own words, the stones and their motifs
convey 'a stylized and detailed symbolism, in a non-literate
milieu, which by its very nature is precluded from indicating
any deceased person by his given name . . . must perforce do this
in terms of his status and group-affiliation'.[6] In the case of those
stones which bear a solitary motif, he speculated on whether it
was more than coincidence that the number of different motifs
identifiable—fourteen—equalled the number of tribal divisions
in Pictland as evidenced by sources like the *De Situ Albanie*, since
it is a well-attested fact that primitive tribes often possess totems
or symbols of identity based on animal forms and the like.[7] If
those with no more than one motif do represent tombstones,
then there is the further possibility that they may have boundary
associations. It was customary in early Irish society to bury a
person in the boundary of his land, the spot being marked by a
standing stone.[8] The idea behind such a practice was that it
invested the land with a spiritual defence against strangers, and
thus strengthened the bond between the kinsmen of the deceased
and their patrimony. In this connection, it is surely of interest
that Columba was reportedly buried in the boundary or girth of
his sanctuary around Iona,[9] whilst the girth or sanctuary which
surrounded the monastery founded by Maelrubha at Applecross
(AD 673) is known to have been marked out by stone crosses.[10]

An alternative interpretation of Pictish standing stones is that
they celebrate alliances or marriages between different lineages.
In actual fact, this was considered as a possibility by Thomas.[11] It
is one that focuses on the fact that the Picts were a matrilineal

[6] Thomas, op. cit., p. 87.
[7] Durkheim and Mauss, op. cit., pp. 17–20. C. Levi-Strauss, *Totemism* (Harmond-sworth, 1969), pp. 83–177.
[8] See discussion in T. M. Charles-Edwards, 'Boundaries in Irish Law', pp. 83–7, in P. H. Sawyer (ed.), *Medieval Settlement* (London, 1976), pp. 83–7.
[9] A. O. Anderson and M. O. Anderson (eds.), *Adomnan's Life of Columba* (Edinburgh, 1961), p. 109, offer no support for this tradition.
[10] W. J. Watson, *The History of the Celtic Place-Names of Scotland* (Edinburgh, 1926), p. 125. Despite this tradition, Maolrubha was not buried at Applecross but in Sutherland, see A. N. Scott, 'Saint Maolrubha', *SHR* vi (1909), p. 276.
[11] Thomas, op. cit., pp. 87–8.

society, descent being traced through the mother not the father. Although usually discussed in relation to the descent of the Pictish throne, it affected each and every Pictish tribesman as regards the inheritance of property. However, matrilineage had other implications. It usually meant a prescriptive system of marriage. This was arranged by lineages matching marriage partners with those of like age from another lineage, one providing the daughters and the other, the sons. Conceivably, Pictish standing stones may celebrate such an alliance. Thomas did not reject this possibility, but he did feel that it required the expertise of the anthropologist rather than the historian to vouch for its plausibility. This expertise was provided by A. Jackson.[12] As well as exploring the kind of residential pattern which the Picts probably adopted, establishing a case for it being of the avuncular type, he made the need for marriage arrangements between lineages an explicit dimension of the problem. On the symbols themselves, he stressed that they 'occur in pairs and only in pairs ',[13] the solitary examples being mere fragments. The only admissible exceptions are those which bore a third symbol consisting always of a mirror and comb. In his judgement, the latter signified alliances in which a bride-price was paid.

Using the inscriptions to be found on standing stones, together with evidence of Pictish place-names, K. Jackson has probed into the nature of the Pictish language and produced an interpretation of its underlying character that again contrasts north with south. Altogether, he identifies two broad linguistic zones. Occupying the whole of southern Pictland and extending across the Mounth as far north as the Moray Firth, was a linguistic province in which the language spoken was basically a form of Celtic. However, it was not a Celtic allied with the Goidelic branch of the language as spoken by the Picts' western neighbours, the Scotti, but a type which Jackson calls Gallo–Brittonic. Mixed in with this predominantly Celtic language, though, was a strong pre-Celtic or non-Indo-European element. As one moves northwards into Sutherland, Caithness, and the Northern Isles, this pre-Celtic substratum—which no doubt reflects the contribution to Pictish culture of surviving Bronze-age influences—becomes more dominant. In exposing

---

[12] A. Jackson, 'Pictish Social Structure and Symbol Stones', *SS* xv (1971), pp. 121–40.
[13] Ibid., p. 130.

these areal variations, Jackson's work emphasizes the cultural origin of the Picts as a fusion of surviving Bronze- and Iron-age elements.[14]

His conclusions provide a suitable backcloth for examining the distribution of the place-name element *Pit-* meaning a 'piece of land', 'a landshare', or simply a 'farm'. *Pit-* is easily the most important place-name element which we can associate, albeit circumstantially, with the Picts and their settlements.Its distribution coincides roughly with a so-called Gallo–Brittonic province of Pictland. Obviously, in view of this correspondence with a distinct linguistic province, it would be wrong to read too deeply into its absence from the extreme north. Usually, it occurs in conjunction with a personal name. These personal names, however, are invariably Irish. This may be explained by the fact that before their union with the Picts in AD 843 and the emergence of the kingdom of Alban or Scotia, the Scotti are thought by some scholars to have pushed eastwards into the core areas of Pictish settlement. The roots of this migration may lie in the unsettled conditions which prevailed along the western coastal areas when the Norse, having taken control of the Long Island, began to pressurize the heartland of the Scotti to the south. At first, the Scotti may simply have taken over established *Pit-* place-names, substituting their own personal name for an earlier Pictish one. However, most *Pit-* place-names are thought to have been created *de novo* during the ninth and tenth centuries, possibly during a phase when the Pictish areas were bilingual with both Gaelic and Pictish being spoken.[15] One additional point of interest regarding *Pit-* elements is that if their distribution is compared with that of the Gaelic place-name prefix *Bal-*, the two appear to be geographically complementary. In fact, not only is it likely that the two elements have the same meaning, but some examples of *Pit-* in the central Highlands area may have been replaced by the element *Bal-*. If this was the case, then the meaning attached to *Bal-* by Irish scholars becomes

[14] K. H. Jackson, 'The Pictish Language', pp. 129–60, in Wainwright (ed.), *The Problem of the Picts*, esp. p. 157.

[15] W. F. H. Nicolaisen, *Scottish Place-Names* (London, 1976), p. 176. Nicolaisen talks of most *Pit-* place-names as having 'originated, let us say, in the ninth to the eleventh centuries when Gaelic gradually established itself in the north-east, first in a period of bilingualism when Pictish and Gaelic were spoken side by side in the area'.

relevant, for they see it as connoting settlements inhabited by bondmen or servile groups dependent on a particular lord or freeman.[16] Significantly, Jackson argued that settlements bearing the element *Pit-* were probably the estates or holdings of Scotti freemen or lords, on which were settled communities of bondmen.[17]

In a review of the problem, G. Whittington has introduced new considerations which threaten to undermine some of these ideas. He affirmed that *Pit-* signified a 'share of land', but questioned its exact correspondence with the element *Bal-*. The basis of his point is that *Pit-* had a double meaning, representing not only an estate or holding, but also the settlement within this estate. *Bal-*, he suggests, may have taken over this second meaning, the first being taken over by the term 'davach'.[18] Such an elaborate view, though, seems unnecessary, even if what it proposes is not implausible. There are many examples of place-names whose meaning narrowed as time went by and the conditions under which they were used altered. *Bal-* and *Pit-* could quite easily have begun with the same meaning, as a 'share of land' held by freemen within a wider tribal territory. But as population grew, their meaning would have narrowed from being a substantial estate to being a relatively compact holding around a single settlement. The fact that *Bal-* and *Pit-* elements in central and eastern Scotland were incorporated into place-names at different times should make us wary of trying to read too great a difference of meaning in their use. In fact, work on *Baile-* or *Bal-* elements in Ireland is instructive here. Work by L. Price on its changing usage concluded that the earliest references to it, those dating from the twelfth century, had the meaning of a 'piece of land'. In his own words, 'when first used as a place-name element it meant the territory of a small tribal or family group' and 'cannot here be restricted to its present-day meaning of "hamlet, group of houses", much less "town, village" '.[19] In fact,

---

[16] For a discussion of relevant Irish work see D. McCourt, 'The Dynamic Quality of Irish Rural Settlement', pp. 126–63 in E. Jones and D. McCourt (eds.), *Man and His Habitat. Essays Presented to Estyn Evans* (London, 1971), pp. 152–3 and 157.

[17] K. H. Jackson, *The Gaelic Notes in the Book of Deer* (Cambridge, 1972), p. 114.

[18] G. Whittington, 'Placenames and the settlement pattern of dark-age', *PSAS* cvi (1974–5), p. 105.

[19] L. Price, 'A Note on the Use of the Word *Baile* in Place-names', *Celtica*, vi (1963), pp. 119–26.

in between these two phases of usage, during the thirteenth and fourteenth centuries, it described an estate or holding worked by tenants of bond or dependent status. As noted in the previous paragraph, the latter is a meaning ascribed to it by Jackson. But clearly, in the still earlier meaning attached to it by Price, it is wholly analogous with that of *Pit-*.

On the question of when *Pit-* elements were first used, Whittington tries to create a more open discussion than anyone hitherto engaged on the matter. Generally speaking, its use in place-name formation during the ninth and tenth centuries is based on its restricted distribution, and its association with Gaelic personal names. In reply, Whittington points to the possibility that its confinement to the central and eastern Higlands may be misleading, reflecting what survived rather than what existed. If *Pit-* elements were present elsewhere, but smothered by later substitutes, then logically, the date of its first use would need revision. As support, he points to the presence of *Pit-* elements south of the Forth. How else, he asks, are these to be explained except as fragments of a once more extensive pattern.[20] Obviously to accept such a view would be to ascribe a much earlier origin to the settlement and landholding system depicted by the element *Pit-*.

One of the reasons why the Picts have proved so problematical as a culture is because so few settlement or occupation sites can be linked directly to them. Although souterrains were once seen as inhabited by the Picts, they are now seen as dating from the first and second centuries AD, or the proto-Pictish period. Besides, excavation has also shown that they were not dwellings but food or stock compounds.[21] Another well-trodden trail in the search for Pictish settlements has been the widely held belief that the vitrified forts of central and eastern Scotland were built by them. Again, however, excavation and the application of carbon-14 dating has demonstrated that most were built before the Pictish period began, no matter how generously we define it.[22] However, there are exceptions. A notable one is the large fort at Burghead

---

[20] Whittington, 'Placename and the settlement pattern', pp. 108–9.

[21] F. T. Wainwright, *The Souterrains of Southern Pictland* (London, 1965). This study was largely based on the sites at Ardestie and Carlungie for its detailed conclusions.

[22] E. W. MacKie, 'The Vitrified Forts of Scotland', pp. 205–35 in D. W. Harding (ed.), *Hillforts* (London, 1977), esp. pp. 224–6.

in Moray. It consisted of a vitrified defence wall straddling a headland. Its construction and occupation can be dated to the period AD 400 to 800, thus placing it firmly within the period of the historical Picts.[23] From its size, it can be argued that it must have been a major regional centre, perhaps a tribal capital. Recent work has also shown that one or two smaller vitrified forts, such as those of Craig Phadraig on the edge of Beauly Firth and Cullykhan in Banffshire, although built earlier in the Iron age, were reoccupied during the early Pictish period, or around AD 300 to 400.[24] This squatting in established settlements was typical of Scotland generally at this point. As L. Laing has recently said, the 'settlement types of Early Christian Scotland are those of the Iron age, and there is no category of Late Iron Age settlement (i.e. one occupied in the first to the second centuries AD) that does not appear to have been occupied at least sporadically in the period from the fifth century onwards'.[25] However, before dismissing the Picts as lacking an architectural style of their own, mention must be made of the recent discovery of small, cellular stone-huts at Buckquoy (Orkney) and the Udal (N. Uist). Both were occupied during the Pictish period, but whether they can be instated as typical of Pictish settlement as a whole remains to be seen.[26]

It is a reasonable supposition that, given the assumptions made regarding the place-name element *Pit-*, many Pictish sites now lie buried beneath settlements bearing this element. Obviously, awareness of this will not by itself yield ideas on the layout or form of Pictish settlement. Only excavation will do this. However, it does enable us to examine the siting and general location of Pictish settlement. Such a study has been carried out for the Fife area. The conclusions reached are revealing. Most *Pit-* settlements are located on light, well-drained soils. In some cases, there is a preference for south-facing slopes. As the authors of this study rightly point out, given these site characteristics, it is

[23] A. Small, 'Burghead', *SAF* (1969), pp. 61–8.
[24] A. Small and B. Cottam, *Craig Phadraig*, Dundee University, Department of Geography occasional paper no. 1 (1972); J. C. Craig, 'Excavations at Cullykhan Castle Point, Troun, Banffshire', *SAF* (1971), pp. 15–21.
[25] L. Laing, *Settlement Types in Post-Roman Scotland*, British Archaeological Reports, no. 13 (1975), p. 33.
[26] I. A. Crawford, 'Scot(?), Norseman and Gael', *SAF* vi (1974), p. 9; A. Ritchie, 'Pict and Norseman in Northern Scotland', *SAF* vi (1974), pp. 23–9.

difficult to avoid the conclusion that the Picts were cultivators, with a settled and probably mixed economy.[27]

Another approach to the question of where the Picts lived has been published by A. Small and B. Cottam.[28] Concentrating on southern Pictland, they analysed the associations between drystone forts and symbol stones, as well as the location of both in relation to land quality. Comparing forts with Class I symbol stones (or those of a non-Christian character), they found a high degree of statistical correlation as regards their location. In their own words, 'only in a few instances does a symbol stone lie beyond the territorial compass of a fort, and then not significantly so.'[29] However, when Class II symbol stones (or those with both pagan and Christian motifs) are compared with forts, there appears much less of an association. Whereas forts tend to be linked with hill-ground areas, Class II stones show a distinct preference for low-ground sites. There are also signs of penetration into new areas, or areas with no representation of forts. Most interesting of all, Class II stones suggest signs of nucleation as if settlement itself was becoming nucleated. Small and Cottam see this nucleation as caused initially by political factors, but sustained by religious or agricultural needs. However, if we are dealing with communities who occupied definite territories, and if they practised partible inheritance as they probably did, then nucleation could reflect no more than the straightforward expansion of settlement and the accommodation of this growth into the system of landholding by progressive partition. In a comparable study of Class III stones (or those with Christian but no Pictish or pagan symbols), they found that the preference for low-ground sites and nucleation was intensified. Since forts now had no bearing on settlements, they carried out a comparison between Class III stones and *Pit-* place-names. What they found

[27] G. Whittington and J. A. Soulsby, 'A preliminary report on an investigation into *pit*-placenames', *SGM* lxxxiv (1968), pp. 117–25. Given their persuasive case for the arable basis of the Pictish economy, it is worth keeping in mind the ideas offered by A. Boyle, 'Matrilineal succession in the Pictish monarchy', *SHR* lvi (1977), pp. 1–10, and his mention of the link drawn by anthropologists between matrilineal societies and pastoral farming or fishing, pp. 8–9. This link between matrilineal societies and pastoralism has now been put on a systematic basis by J. Goody, *Production and Reproduction* (Cambridge, 1976).
[28] M. B. Cottam and A. Small, 'The Distribution of Settlements in Southern Pictland', *Medieval Arch.*, xviii (1974), pp. 43 and 64
[29] Ibid., p. 47.

was that both dislayed a preference for good-quality arable land, but that they constituted exclusive sets of distribution. This, they reasoned, could only be explained by seeing them as contemporary but complementary elements in the landscape. Their explanation as to why this should be so is less convincing, but then it is hardly an easy problem to answer. They suggest that *Pit*-elements and Class III stones denoted different types of settlement. The former appear to be located in forested areas, and probably formed scattered holdings or clearings. The latter, meanwhile, are seen by them as settlements of greater pretensions and more urban qualities. Whilst one can accept that there may indeed have been differences between the two as regards function, social status, or origin, to suggest differences of settlement type between the two seems unwarranted given that symbol stones are being used as a surrogate for settlement in too literal a manner. After all, there may be a case for arguing that symbol stones may have been sited peripherally rather than centrally on an estate.

It has been said that if the Scots wish to see themselves as anything more than an Irish colony, then it is to the spirit of the tribes who made up the Picts that they must turn.[30] Such sentiments beg the question of whether there are Pictish institutions which survived after the formation of the Scottish kingdom which might be taken as the Pictish contribution to the Scottish way of life. There is nothing in our understanding of the eventual demise of the Pictish kingdom as a separate political unit to suggest it was accompanied by drastic social and economic disruption. Indeed, the union of the Picts and Scots to form Alba was so uneventful that it puzzles us why a people who enter the historical record like a lion, as formidable warring tribes constantly harassing the Romans, should leave it like a lamb, conceding overlordship so quietly to Kenneth mac Alpin and the Scots. H. M. Chadwick's observation that a dynastic marriage between the Picts, a matrilineal society, and the Scots, a patrilineal society, would effectively confine succession to both kingdoms to a single line, is a plausible explanation.[31] The survival of so many *Pit*- settlements is a good indication of how

[30] I. Henderson, 'The Problem of the Picts', pp. 51–65 in G. Menzies (ed.), *Who Are the Scots?* (London, 1971), p. 65.
[31] H. M. Chadwick, *Early Scotland* (Cambridge, 1949), p. 130.

much continuity we can expect from Pictish institutions. But there are problems of recognition when we consider less tangible institutions like those of landholding and tenure. Much more work needs to be done on the social and agrarian patterns of medieval Scotland before we can decide on those whose confinement to eastern Scotland north of the Forth recommends them as possible Pictish survivals. At present, we have very few candidates from which to choose, but a strong case can be made out for a land measure like the davach.

The Britons

Along with the Picts, the only other cultural group living in Scotland at the start of the Dark Ages was the Britons. These were a Celtic people. Their affiliations though, were not with the Goidelic-speaking Celts, like the Scotti, but with the Brythonic-speaking Celts of Cumbria, Wales, and Cornwall. Modern scholars tend to draw a fine distinction that was employed by the Britons themselves between 'the men of the north' and 'the men of the south'. But such implied differences had much less substance than their shared differences with, say, the Picts or Scots.[32]

The history of the Britons has less of the obscurity that surrounds other early Scottish cultures. We know, for instance, that during the immediate sub-Roman period, southern Scotland was divided between a number of British tribes and that, by the fifth century, these had begun to group themselves into a number of primitive states.[33] Three deserve to be mentioned. In the north-west, pivoted around the lower Clyde valley and occupying an area formerly associated with the Damnonii was an emergent kingdom of Strathclyde, whose capital may have been Alcluith on Dumbarton Rock. By the tenth century, it had become the kingdom of Strathclyde. South of the Forth, and occupying the former territory of the Votadini, was another

[32] See discussion in I. Ll. Foster, 'Wales and North Britain', *Archaeologica Cambrensis*, cxviii (1969), esp. pp. 3–4.
[33] K. H. Jackson, 'The Britons in Southern Scotland', *Antiquity*, xxix (1955), pp. 77–88; D. P. Kirby, 'Britons and Angles', pp. 80–9 in Menzies (ed.), op. cit., pp. 80–1; D. P. Kirby, 'Strathclyde and Cumbria. A Survey of Historical Development to 1092', *Trans. Cumberland and Westmorland Antiq. and Arch. Soc.*, n.s., lxii (1962), pp. 77–94.

kingdom called Gododdin. During the second, third, and fourth centuries, when this area was the territory of the Votadini, their tribal capital may have been the magnificent hill-top town of Traprain Law. This site was abandoned during the early fifth century, and by the time the area was incorporated into the kingdom ruled by the Gododdin, the administrative focus of the region had shifted, *possibly* to Edinburgh. Finally, in the south of Scotland, possibly on either side of the Solway Firth (its exact location being uncertain), was a powerful British kingdom called Rheged whose capital may have been at Carlisle. Apart from Strathclyde, which continued as a separate state until its union with the rapidly expanding kingdom of Alba via a dynastic succession in the early eleventh century, the separate life of these British kingdoms was relatively short.

Attempts have been made to chart the areas held by the Britons through their place-names. An element of particular value is that of *Tref-*, meaning a farmstead.[34] Examples of its use include such names as Traquair (Peeblesshire), Trabroun (East Lothian), and Terregles (Kirkcudbrightshire). Although the latter may not appear very Welsh or *Cumbric*, to use the correct term for the northern dialect of Welsh, when seen in its early form of Travereglys—meaning 'tref yr eglwys' or 'the village with a church'—then its origin is more obvious. When place-names incorporating *Tref-* are mapped, they display a fairly wide scatter over southern Scotland south of the Antonine Wall. Presumably it was an element that was used in place-name formation by all the tribal groups of the region. Other elements can be detected which have a more confined distribution. The element *cair*, meaning a fort or stockaded farm, for instance, is restricted to the territories occupied by the Gododdin and Rheged.[35] The element *pren*, denoting a wood, is confined solely to the Lothians or Gododdin.[36] On the question of when such place-name elements were used, Jackson's work on Cumbria has a great deal of interest. He found that *cair* was used in place-name formation during the first and second centuries AD, but that as settlement became less defensive over the third and fourth centuries, its

[34] W. F. H. Nicolaisen, 'Celts and Anglo-Saxons in the Scottish Border Counties: The Place-Name Evidence', *SS* viii (1964), pp. 148–9.
[35] Ibid., pp. 150–2.
[36] Ibid., pp. 146–8.

place was taken over by *tref-*.[37] Applied to southern Scotland, such a distinction might enable us to trace the adjustment and growth of native society after the withdrawal of the Romans.

Although we are dealing with roughly the same cultural groups who comprised native society during the Roman period, the range of evidence bearing on the character of their settlement and economy is considerably less for the post-Roman centuries. Whatever the impact of the Roman occupation on native society, their withdrawal initiated or allowed changes in the organization and disposition of settlement, with few native settlements of the Roman period surviving much beyond the fourth century. Such settlement sites as do exist do not yet add up to a consistent pattern. In some cases, one had the occupation of small defended forts similar to that excavated at Dalmahoy (Midlothian).[38] Elsewhere, it was a case of small stone huts being built within the shell of an abandoned fort.[39] One or two crannogs, such as that at Buston, were also occupied during this period.[40] Taking a different approach to the problem, we can link settlements bearing British place-name elements to the Britons, such as those using the element *eccles*, meaning a church.[41] Examples can be found throughout southern Scotland. The Britons were of course receptive to Christianity and provided an important medium for its diffusion through southern Scotland during the late Roman and sub-Roman period. The symbolic centre of such activity was Whithorn, or Candida Casa, a church on the Solway Firth that was founded by St Ninian probably during the early fifth century.

The Scotti

Of all the cultures who moved into Scotland during the Dark Ages, the most significant was that of the Scotti from north-east Ireland. Their arrival can be dated to the fifth century.[42]

---

[37] K. H. Jackson, 'Angles and Britons in Northumbria and Cumbria' in H. Lewis (ed.), *Angles and Britons* (Cardiff, 1963), pp. 60–84.

[38] Laing, *Settlement Types*, p. 1.

[39] RCAM, Scotland, *Roxburghshire*, vol. i, pp. 20–1 and 35.

[40] L. Laing, *The Archaeology of Late Celtic Britain and Ireland c.400–1200 A.D.* (London, 1975), p. 37.

[41] Jackson, *Language and History*, p. 227. Its use in Scotland is mapped and discussed by G. W. S. Barrow, *The Kingdom of the Scots* (London, 1974), pp. 60–4.

[42] J. Bannerman, 'The Dal Riata and Northern Ireland in the Sixth and Seventh

Although their initial base was in mid-Argyll or Cowal, they quickly carved out for themselves a much larger territory, equivalent to the whole of modern-day Argyll, which became known as the kingdom of Dalriada. This early association between the Scotti and Argyll has a special meaning because the latter was the area occupied by the Scotti migrants, or the first-generation settlers. However, it must not disguise the fact that they later expanded into areas beyond the strict confines of Argyll. The place-name evidence, for instance, suggests they may have pushed eastwards into the central and eastern Highlands, the very heartland of Pictish power. As noted earlier, the seal on this mixing of the two cultures was set by their political union in the mid-ninth century. Whatever their pattern of relations beforehand, the union of the Picts and Scots was very much to the advantage of the latter. It was a Scottish king who ruled the new kingdom and it was the language of the Scots, or Gaelic, that became the dominant tongue of the Highlands at large. In the early eleventh century, this same kingdom absorbed the Britons of Strathclyde and secured dominion over the Lothians after a battle between Malcolm II and the Northumbrians in 1018. Thus, what had begun as a mere Irish colony, was, by the eleventh century, in command of virtually all the Scottish mainland.

Because the Gaelic language spread with their authority, the value of Gaelic place-names for the study of their settlement is greatly reduced. Indeed, if place-names are to serve any value in this situation then we face the difficult task of isolating place-name elements that were used by the Scotti at different phases in their settlement and rise to dominance. Such a task is at least aided by the fact that their language was not static but changing, so much so, that what started out as similar to Irish Gaelic became, by the tenth century, a distinct branch of the Goidelic language. Fitting into this category of place-name elements whose popularity of use may have altered over time is *sliabh*, meaning a mountain in its original Irish form but used in Scotland to describe anything from a small hillock to a mountain.

Centuries', pp. 1–11 in J. Carney and D. Greene (eds.), *Celtic Studies. Essays in Memory of Angus Matheson* (London, 1968), p. 1; J. Bannerman, *Studies in the History of Dalriada* (Edinburgh, 1974), pp. 1 and 126.

Its distribution shows a concentration in the area which historical tradition has always linked with Dalriada. However, if *sliabh* helps confirm our ideas about Dalriada as a territory roughly coincident with Argyll, it also raises new problems. In addition to its concentration in Dalriada, its distribution reveals a further concentration in the Rhinns of Galloway and Moray.[43] An element which appears to have come into use at a slightly later date than *sliabh* but which continued in use much longer is that of *cill*, meaning a church or holy cell. Its distribution picks out not only the established area of Dalriada and the south-west, but also, the areas of eastern Scotland into which the Scotti may, arguably, have infiltrated during the ninth and tenth centuries. It survives in modern toponymy as *Kil-*, as in Kilmalcolm (Renfrewshire) and Kilbrandon (Argyll).

The presence of Gaelic place-names in the south-west raises the question why. The occurrence of an element like *sliabh* suggests that some originated at an early date. However, when faced with the tradition of an Irish or Scotti settlement in this area, writers like Chadwick dismissed it as improbable.[44] Further work by W. H. Nicolaisen, however, has given the idea more substance. In a survey of Gaelic place-names in the region, he considered the distribution of *Auch-* (Gaelic *achadh*, meaning a field), *Baile-* or *Bal-*, *sliabh* or *slew*, and *cill* or *Kil-*. All these elements are present in the south-west in quantity, but are absent from the south-east. Apart from the very presence of an archaic element like *sliabh*, he felt their sheer number was revealing. The traditional viewpoint is that they were incorporated into place-names during the short period from the union of Strathclyde with Alba in the eleventh century, a union which opened the area to Gaelic influences, and the coming of the Normans in the twelfth. Nicolaisen reasoned that this was far too short a period, especially for an element like *Auch-* which could only have been used by a Gaelic-speaking farming population. As an alternative, he proposed that such place-name elements were the record of a Scotti settlement and its subsequent development. On the basis of their distribution, he used the various elements to structure an evolutionary perspective of the Gaelic influences that bore on the

[43] W. F. H. Nicolaisen, 'Scottish Place-Names: 24. Slew- and sliabh', *SS* ix (1965), pp. 91–106.
[44] Chadwick, op. cit., p. 155.

region. 'From a small beginning in the sixth century in the Rhinns of Galloway (*sliabh*)', he wrote,

> via ecclesiastical activities in the coastal areas of Solway and Clyde from the seventh to the ninth centuries (*cill*), backed by increasing Gaelic speaking settlement, perhaps supported by new incomers from Bute and Kintyre and also Ireland, and making small inroads into Strathclyde from the west and the Lothians from the east, north and north-west from the tenth to the beginning of the twelfth centuries (*baile*)—to the more intensive settlement of Strathclyde and Dumfriesshire after 1018 (*achadh*), our distribution maps give a visible account of the rise of Gaelic in the Scottish south.[45]

Nicolaisen's conclusion that these Gaelic place-names may date back to a pre-tenth-century layer of Gaelic influences have now been endorsed by J. Macqueen's work on the use of spoken Gaelic in the region.[46]

At the time when the Scotti founded Dalriada, the most characteristic settlement form of their homeland was the rath, a circular, drystone fort. Drystone forts of comparable design exist in the south-west Highlands. As pointed out in the previous chapter, however, these forts—or duns—have proved to be mostly pre-fifth-century in date. All that can be claimed is that a few were reoccupied during the period of Scotti colonization.[47] With this possibility removed, we are left with few archaeological structures that can be labelled as the sites inhabited by them during the pioneer phases of their settlement.[48]

An alternative approach to how they lived and organized themselves is to try and tease information out of the small handful of manuscripts which relate to the Scotti. From these, it is evident that Dalriada was divided between three kindreds, each of whom had a chief who, in turn, owed allegiance to the king of Dalriada. These three kindreds were the Cenel Loairn of the north (Mull,

[45] W. F. H. Nicolaisen, 'Gaelic Place-names in Southern Scotland', *Studia Celtica*, v (1970), p. 34.

[46] J. Macqueen, 'The Gaelic Speakers of Galloway and Carrick', *SS* xvii (1973), esp. p. 26. Macqueen concludes that the evidence indicates a 'substantial Gaelic-speaking settlement in Galloway in the period between the sixth and ninth centuries', a settlement which he described as 'church directed'.

[47] Laing, *Settlement Types*, pp. 12–16; H. Fairhurst, 'A Galleried Dun at Kildonan Bay, Kintyre', *PSAS* lxxxiii (1938–9), pp. 185–228.

[48] Laing, *Settlement Types*, pp. 12–16 reviews this problem.

Ardnamurchan, Morvern, Lorn, Coll, and Tiree), the Cenel nGabrain of the south (Cowal, Jura, Bute, Arran, and Kintyre) and the Cenel nOengusa of Islay. By *c.*700, a fourth kindred had emerged, or the Cenel Comgaill of Cowal. These probably originated as a sept of the Cenel nGabrain which managed to assume greater independence as the power of the latter weakened. A valuable glimpse of early Dalriada is provided by the *Senchus Fer nAlban*. This is a document that is likely to have been compiled in the seventh century, but which survives in the form of a tenth-century edition. Its information consists of genealogies and survey data. Amongst the survey data is a list of houses within the territory of each kindred.[49] In the case of the Cenel nOengusa and possibly the Cenel nGabrain, the number of houses given are grouped according to each district or township. Islay, for example, formed the territory of the Cenel nOengusa and was said to contain 430 houses. These were arranged into districts as follows:

Oidech	20 houses
Freg	120 houses
Caled Rois	60 houses
Ros Deorand	30 houses
Ard hes	30 houses
Loch Rois	30 houses
Ath Cassil	30 houses
Cenel nOengusa	30 houses
Non-assigned houses in total for Islay = 80	

In the case of the Cenel Loairn, the houses are grouped according to the leaders or nobles of the different septs. As in Islay, they were assessed in multiples of 5, with 5, 10, 15, 20, and 30 houses being typical.

In a lengthy analysis of the *Senchus*, J. Bannerman concluded that the house-listing was linked to the payment of tribute. This tribute is likely to have been paid by freemen whose status was that of *doer-cheli* or base clients, since a house custom or *bes-tige* was a usual form of tribute owed by freemen in early Irish society. Its predominance in the *Senchus* suggests that such freemen formed the mass of Dalriadic society at this point.[50] The number

[49] Bannerman, *Studies in the History of Dalriada*, pp. 131–46; J. Bannerman, 'Senchus Fer nAlban part II', *Celtica*, ix (1971), pp. 216–65.

[50] Bannerman, *Studies in the History of Dalriada*, pp. 134–8.

of houses assigned to each district or sept probably signified the notional amount of tribute paid by clients of that particular district or sept to its leader or chieftain, but in turn, it also signified the level of tribute owed by the leader or chieftain to the king of Dalriada. The survey, therefore, has two levels of meaning. The way in which tribute was apportioned between the different districts or septs can also yield information on the organization of Dalriada. According to Bannerman, it was a system based on 20-house units. These he equated with the davach or ounceland. Related to the number of houses apportioned to each district or sept, this would mean that each sept tended to hold $\frac{1}{4}$, $\frac{1}{2}$, $\frac{3}{4}$, or 1 whole unit, whilst, in the case of Islay, each district tended to be rated at $1\frac{1}{2}$, 3, or 6 units, the last mentioned being, in effect, the local hundred. It would also mean that the 20-house unit which was later used throughout the western Highlands and Islands for fiscal and military levies can be dated back to the early historic period.

   A. A. M. Duncan has remarked that the *Senchus* listing 'is not a geographer's description but an account of the basis on which a king, perhaps of Dal Riata, might exact tribute. Each group of "houses" is a notional assessment, yet behind such notions must lie the real thing.'[51] If there is a clue to this reality in the listing then it conceivably lies in the relationship between the 20-house units on which it seems based and local land assessments. In part answer to this problem, Bannerman saw the 20-house unit as representing the equivalent of the davach or ounceland, the two largest land measures in the west Highlands.[52] This is certainly a plausible suggestion. The main difficulty with it is that there are reasons for believing that whilst the davach and ounceland may have started out as measures of tribute, it was only later that they were adapted as land measures (see pp. 75–9). If this process of adaptation had taken place by *c.*700, then the 20-house units employed in the *Senchus* can be used as a statement of actual land assessment in Dalriada. If not, then we are left merely with a notional assessment of tribute payment, that tells us little about the actual number of houses, people, or the amount of land in the region.

[51] A. A. M. Duncan, *Scotland: The Making of the Kingdom*, vol. i, *The Edinburgh History of Scotland* (Edinburgh, 1975), p. 74.
   [52] Bannerman, *Studies in the History of Dalriada*, pp. 140–1.

According to A. McKerral, at the centre of early Celtic social and agrarian organization—in Dalriada no less than elsewhere—was a unit known as the *baile* or *bailebetaigh*.[53] Although the term was later used of any sizeable farming community and its land, the *baile* was initially a large parish-like unit. When rentals allow us to see it in detail during the later medieval period, it appears to have lost its original integrity or extent and to have become physically subdivided into halves, quarters, eighths, etc.[54] These shares formed separate townships or clachans strewn across the territory of the *baile*. Attempts have been made by scholars like R. A. Gailey to work back to the early appearances of the *baile* in the south-west Highlands by reconstituting the various fractional shares or clachans to which it had been reduced by the end of the eighteenth century.[55] Although fraught with difficulties, such exercises can serve as a general guide to just how much fission the early *baile* underwent.

Supplementing the *baile* on Islay and in Kintyre was a land unit known as the quarterland.[56] In contrast to his description of the *baile* as a social and agrarian unit, McKerral saw the quarterland as a fiscal unit, being the basis on which the burdens on land were levied.[57] Logically, he presumed that when first devised, four equalled the *baile*. But owing to the break-up of the *baile* into small clachans over time, the quarterland tends to appear in early documents not so much as a subdivision of the *baile* but as a land unit that could itself embrace a number of small settlements or clachans. The obvious analogy to be drawn here is with the quarterland of Ireland, where many a *baile* was divided into quarterlands.[58] When discovered on Islay and Kintyre, therefore, it seemed reasonable to see this very distinct

[53] A. McKerral, 'Ancient Denominations of Agricultural Land in Scotland', *PSAS* lxxviii (1943), pp. 41–3. The role of the *baile* in Celtic landscapes is also brought out by W. Reeves, 'On the Townland Distribution of Ireland', *Proc. Royal Irish Academy*, vii (1857–61), pp. 473–90.

[54] C. G. Smith, *The Book of Islay* (Edinburgh, 1895), Appendix III, pp. 490 ff., provides numerous instances of these fractions of the *baile*. See also, J. Smith, *General View of the Agriculture of the Hebrides and or Western Isles of Scotland* (Edinburgh, 1811), p. 82.

[55] R. A. Gailey 'The Evolution of Highland Rural Settlement', *SS* vi (1962), p. 171.

[56] See, for example, Smith, *Book of Islay*, pp. 48–50 and 88–93; *Origines Parochiales Scotiae*, Bannatyne Club (Edinburgh, 1851), vol. ii, p. 281; Macqueen, op. cit., p. 32.

[57] McKerral, 'The Lesser Land and Administrative Divisions of Celtic Scotland', *PSAS* lxxxv (1950–1), p. 56.

[58] McKerral, 'Ancient Denominations of Agricultural Land', pp. 43–4.

method of *baile* subdivision as a system brought into the area by the *Scotti*.[59] An important reservation to this view was subsequently entered by W. D. Lamont. Whilst accepting that quarterlands were implanted from Ireland, Lamont felt that there was no direct connection between the quarterlands disclosed by rentals and charters of the sixteenth century or later, and the quarterlands originally laid out by the Scotti. Because of a major reorganization of Islay's tax assessment, there exists what he termed a discontinuity between the familiar 'Islay Quarters and Eighths' of more recent times and those of 'ancient Islay' developed around the *baile*. The latter comprised quarterlands which he saw as larger than those of the more modern system.[60] However, even taking Lamont's more elaborate interpretation into account, there are still difficulties in the way of seeing the quarterlands of even 'ancient Islay' as a system imported to the region by the Scotti. Back in the fifth and sixth centuries, the payment of tribute is likely to have been still levied on kin groups rather than land. To infer the existence of a quarterland system for the purpose, therefore, may be premature. If so, there is no lack of reason why such a system could not emerge later. An attractive proposition is an idea mentioned by McKerral,[61] but not pursued by him with any great enthusiasm. The inheritance of property in early Celtic society was based on the four-generation kin-group. The workings of such a system would have made quarter-shares held by the different kin-groups commonplace. Not only would this fit in with the fission of the *baile*, but it would help explain why, when the levying of tribute was eventually transferred from kin-groups on to land, the *quarter*land was chosen as the basis. This would be an even more interesting line of inquiry if it could be established that the quarterland did not embody the notion of a quarter of a *baile*, but merely the proprietary stake of a kin-group within it. This may seem an unnecessary aside, until it is realized that despite all the assumptions, studies of the *baile* in Ireland and the Isle of Man

[59] Reeves, op. cit., pp. 473–90; McKerral, 'The Lesser Land and Administrative Divisions of Celtic Scotland', pp. 55–6.

[60] W. D. Lamont, 'Old Land Denominations and "Old Extent" in Islay', part I, *SS* i (1957), p. 185; ibid., part II, p. 281.

[61] McKerral, 'The Lesser Land and Administrative Divisions of Celtic Scotland', p. 63.

show that it generally contained *more* than four quarterlands![62] Clearly, some other meaning may have been implied by the term than the obvious one of a quarter-*baile*. If we could calculate the number per *baile* in Islay or Kintyre, a similarly enigmatic relationship between the two may well have prevailed there.

The Angles

The expansion of the Angles of Northumbria into southern Scotland began during the opening years of the seventh century. By a series of military successes, they quickly acquired control over most of south-east Scotland. On their western flanks, the kingdom of Rheged was subsequently absorbed through a combination of military pressure and royal marriage, but Strathclyde managed to maintain its independence if not all its territory in the face of their advance. Altogether, Anglian rule over southern Scotland lasted barely three centuries. By the early eleventh century, following the decisive battle of Carham, the Scots secured possession of the region as far south as the Tweed itself, a boundary that was to endure, though not without a change of status, until the present day.

The old assertion that the Anglo-Saxon settlement of Britain involved a large-scale colonization based on the nucleated village and a farm economy based on the two- or three-field system has suffered greatly at the hands of recent writers. Their settlement is now considered by some to have been a small-scale affair, a settlement by a warrior aristocracy who, by taking over the reins of authority and administration, were able to exercise an influence far beyond their actual numbers.[63] Such a reinterpretation must affect the meaning which we attach to Anglo-

[62] E. Davies, 'Treens and Quarterlands in the Isle of Man', *TIBG* xxii (1956, pp. 97–116; F. Seebohm, *The English Village Community* (London, 1896), pp. 224–5.

[63] Typical of this revised view in England is C. C. Taylor, *Dorset* (London, 1970), p. 41. The ideas of G. R. J. Jones are also important here; see G. R. J. Jones, 'Multiple Estates and Early Settlement', pp. 15–40 in P. H. Sawyer, *Medieval Settlement* (London, 1976), pp. 15–40 esp. pp. 39–40. For relevant comment on Scotland see Jackson, 'The Britons in Southern Scotland', p. 84 and his statement that the 'comparative rarity of English place-names in South-West Scotland, contrasted with their much greater frequency in the South-East, does suggest that the English occupation of these widespread western districts was more in the nature of a scattered upper crust of landlords rather than a really thick settlement of peasants'.

Saxon place-names in southern Scotland. A number can be dated to the Anglian period. Amongst the earliest are those incorporating the elements *ingas*, meaning 'the place of the people of' (+ a personal name), and *-ham*, meaning a 'village or farmstead'. Only a small handful of these exist. Like Whittingham (East Lothian) and Coldingham (Berwickshire), they are sited along the fertile coastal plain of East Lothian or the lower Tweed basin.[64] Slightly later and slightly more numerous are place-names using the elements *-ham* and *-ington*, meaning a 'village or hamlet', as in Smailholm (Roxburghshire) and Letham (East Lothian) or Mersington (Berwickshire) and Haddington (East Lothian).[65] Still later in date, but having a much wider distribution, are place-names incorporating the element *-wic*, meaning a minor or secondary settlement. As well as having a much fuller representation in the south-east, with examples like Hawick (Roxburghshire) or Dawick (Peeblesshire), it occurs in Ayrshire (i.e. Prestwick) and north of the Forth (i.e. Hedderwick) in Angus.[66] If we are dealing with sizeable movements of Anglian settlers into the region, then the gradually more numerous and fuller distribution of these placename elements, spreading from the lower Tweed Basin and the Lothian coastal district to other parts of southern Scotland, would depict the growing intensification of their settlement in the region.[67] As the author of these ideas, Nicolaisen, has also observed, the survival of British place-names in the upland areas like the Pentland Hills suggests that the displaced British communities may have taken refuge in such areas. Support of a kind for this idea is provided by current thinking on the impressive, cross-country ditch systems or linear earthworks that traverse parts of the south-east. The manner in which some seem to divide the upper portion of valleys like those of the Tweed, Ettrick Water, and the Teviot from the Merse, coupled with their non-defensive nature, have led some archaeologists to argue that they were territorial markers, perhaps dividing the seemingly pastoral British communities of the west from the more seden-

[64] Nicolaisen, 'Celts and Saxons', pp. 158–61.
[65] Ibid., pp. 161–5
[66] W. F. H. Nicolaisen, 'Scottish Place-names: 28. Old English *wic* in Scottish Placenames', *SS* xi (1967), pp. 75–84.
[67] Nicolaisen, 'Celts and Saxons', pp. 168–9.

tary, arable-based communities of the Anglians on the low ground to the east.[68]

However, if we start with the assumption that the Anglian settlement was no more than an infiltration into the region of a small number of lords and warriors, then our interpretation of the toponymic record, as well as linear earthworks must alter. Instead of recording the establishment of Anglian communities, Anglian place-names would now be seen as tracing the imposition of their authority on existing native settlements or the creation of new native settlements under their lordship. Either way, the discontinuity of settlement history which the Anglians were thought to have effected would disappear. In its place, we would have the survival without too much dislocation of native British communities now subject to Anglian rule. Perhaps the experience of Eddleston in Peeblesshire may hold a wider lesson. It began as Penteiacob, a Cumbric name. By the twelfth century it was known as Gillemorestun, a name incorporating both Gaelic and Anglo-Saxon elements. Finally, by the end of the twelfth century, it had been granted to Edulf, son of Utred, and had become Edulf's *tun*, an English name.[69] Behind these changes of fortune, and overlord, surely lies the possibility of Anglian continuity too.

As regards the form of their settlement, the Anglians are commonly associated with large, nucleated villages, such as those typically found in the Midland counties of England. This being the case, it might be thought a point of some significance for Anglian settlement in Scotland that areas like the Tweed basin and the Lothians should be ones where fairly large nucleated villages existed alongside small fermtouns that are more typical of the Scottish countryside. The lower Tweed valley, an area firmly within the Anglian fold, contains examples like Chirnside, Coldingham, Auchencraw, Greenlaw, Lilliesleaf, and Denholm. We must be careful how we use these villages though. Whether a settlement appears large or small depends on what happened to it over the medieval and early modern periods, not on the form in which it was initially cast. This can be argued even for those settlements in the south-east which appear to have a planned or

[68] RCAM, Scotland, *Roxburghshire*, vol. ii, pp. 479–83; RCAM, Scotland, *Selkirkshire*, pp. 126–8.
[69] Based on RCAM, Scotland, *Peebles-shire*, vol. i, p. 5.

regular layout, such as Midlem, Denholm, and Lilliesleaf in Roxburghshire. Work on similar settlements south of the Border has proved that such villages were not planned at the outset of their formation but much later, possibly as late at the twelfth or thirteenth centuries.[70] As with other contemporary cultures in Scotland, there is little we can say about the Anglian economy. It is unlikely that they introduced a two- or three-field system to the south-east since such methods of farming were probably not developed until the tenth century or later.[71] Besides, later evidence suggests that the south-east had well-developed infield–outfield systems of farming, though whether even these had fully developed before the end of the Anglian period is in doubt.[72] Taking a retrospective view of the period through later documents, it seems likely that the south-east had a fairly complex pattern of landholding already established by the end of the Anglian period, with more small- and medium-sized estates than elsewhere.[73] It would not be unreasonable to suppose that behind this well-developed or fractionated system of landholding, there was a well-established arable economy.

The Norse

Although Viking raiders were familiar around the coasts of Scotland throughout the eighth century, it was not until around AD 800 that actual settlement commenced.[74] The earliest settlements were in the Northern Isles. Over time, they extended

[70] B. K. Roberts, 'Village Plans in County Durham', *Medieval Arch.*, xvi (1972), pp. 33–56; J. Sheppard, 'Medieval Village Planning in Northern England: Some Evidence from Yorkshire', *Jnl. of Historical Geography*, ii (1976), pp. 3–20.
[71] J. Thirsk, 'The Common Fields', *Past and Present*, xxix (1964), pp. 3–29; R. A. Dodgshon, 'The Origin of the Two- and Three-Field System in England: A New Perspective', *Geographia Polonica*, xxxviii (1978), pp. 49–63.
[72] R. A. Dodgshon, 'The Nature and Development of Infield–Outfield in Scotland', *TIBG* lix (1973), pp. 1–23; R. A. Dodgshon, 'Farming in Roxburghshire and Berwickshire on the Eve of Improvement', *SHR* liv (1975), pp. 140–54.
[73] G. W. S. Barrow, 'The Pattern of Lordship and Feudal Settlement in Medieval Cumbria, *Jnl. of Medieval History*, i (1975), pp. 117–38.
[74] F. T. Wainwright, 'The Scandinavian Settlement', pp. 117–62 in Wainwright (ed.), *The Northern Isles*, pp. 126–7; D. M. Wilson, 'The Norsemen', pp. 103–13 in Menzies (ed.), *Who Are the Scots?*, pp. 103–5; A. Small, 'The Historical Geography of the Norse Viking Colonization of the Scottish Highlands', *Norsk Geografisk Tidsskrift*, xxii (1968), p. 3.

themselves south-westwards into the Western Isles, especially Lewis and Harris, and southwards on to the northern tip of the mainland. The unfolding pattern of their colonization can be read from place-name evidence in two ways. On the one hand, we can piece together the progressive extension of their settlement at the regional level. On the other hand, we can trace its local intensification, from the appearance of primary settlements on the better land, through the gradual filling out of the settlement pattern until the less attractive or more marginal sites were occupied.

With regard to the former, the area occupied by the Norse within a few generations of the first arrival of *landnamsmenn*, or 'landtakers', may be depicted by the distribution of the element -*staðir* (or -*stath*), meaning a 'farm'. Place-names incorporating this element, such as Gunnista (Shetland) and Mangersta (Lewis), are mostly confined to Shetland, Orkney, Lewis, Harris, and Skye, with only one on the mainland. Furthermore, except for examples on Orkney, most are coastal. Indicative of the second stage of Norse colonization, or the areas settled by AD 900, may be the element -*setr*. In modern times, this is rendered as -setter, as in Malsetter (Orkney) or, if Gaelicized, as -side or -shader, such as in Linside (Sutherland) or Grimshader (Lewis). When mapped, -*setr* place-names do not reveal a settlement of new areas, but merely the more intensive occupation of existing areas. For some, this marked intensification of settlement during the second half of the ninth century evidences a large influx of new migrants, an influx which has been tentatively dated to around AD 860 to 900. Providing a view of Norse settlement at its peak of expansion may be the element -*bolstaðr*, meaning 'a farmstead' or 'divided farm'. In the present landscape, it occurs in the various forms of -*bister*, -*ster*, -*bost*, -*bus*, -*bol*, or -*pol*. Apart from concentrations in established areas of Scandinavian settlement, the mapping of these elements suggests a southward extension into wholly new areas, both on the mainland and in the Hebrides. Generally speaking, the long-established areas of Norse settlement provide the forms of -*bister*, -*ster*, -*bost*, and -*bus* as in Norbister (Shetland), Scrabster (Caithness), Shawbost (Lewis), and Grobust (Orkney). The newest areas, the southern Hebridean islands of Tiree, Coll, Mull, Colonsay, and Islay together with the straths and coastal areas of Sutherland, tend to provide examples of -*bol* and *-poll* as in Eriboll (Sutherland) or Crossapoll (Islay).[75]

Taking an overview of the distribution of their settlement, the feature which stands out most is that, even at its maximum extent, it did not affect the western edge of the mainland, only the extreme northern tip (Caithness and Sutherland) and eastern coastal areas as far south as Easter Ross. This is not to say that Norse place-names do not occur along the western seaboard of the mainland. However, those which do occur are topographic elements like *-dale*, meaning a 'valley', rather than elements connected with habitation sites. Admittedly some, like Smeasary (meaning 'summer pasture') in Inverness-shire, have become subsequently attached to settlements. One interpretation of this imbalance between the offshore islands and the western edge of the mainland, and one which Smeasary illustrates well, is that the Norse may have used the western flanks of the mainland as a source of summer pasture, timber supplies, or for hunting.[76] In terms of its over-all density, their settlement was probably greatest in Shetland and Orkney and, to a lesser extent, the Outer Hebrides. In the case of the former, it has been argued that virtually every field and settlement name is of Norse origin.[77] In the case of the latter, it has been calculated that at least four-fifths of all major settlements on Lewis carry Norse names.[78] As one moves south, the ratio of Norse to Gaelic names alters in favour of the latter. On Islay, it is around 1:2, whilst on Arran, it is only 1:8. However, as A. Small has observed, this progressive change in the ratio of Norse to Gaelic place-names from north to south may mean very little in terms of the density of their original settlement. The Northern and Western Isles were much less densely settled prior to the Norse settlements than the islands of the southern Hebrides, so that even a relatively small occupation could give a misleading preponderance of Norse to other names. At the same time, the Gaelic reasserted itself more strongly and more quickly in the southern part of the Hebrides than in the

[75] Based on W. F. H. Nicolaisen, 'Norse Settlement in the Northern and Western Isles', *SHR* xlviii (1969), pp. 6–17. For a cautionary note on Nicolaisen's definite chronological framework for place-name elements, see D. M. Wilson, 'Scandinavian Settlement in the North and West of the British Isles—An Archaeological Point-of-View', *Trans. Royal Historical Soc.*, 5th ser., xxvi (1976), p. 103.

[76] Small, 'Historical Geography of the Norse Viking Colonization', p. 12.

[77] H. Marwick, *Orkney Farm-Names* (Kirkwall, 1952), p. 210.

[78] Small, 'Historical Geography of the Norse Viking Colonization', p. 11.

northern part. More Norse place-names, therefore, may have been lost or replaced in the former area.[79]

The problem of using place-names to chart the history of Norse settlement has been tackled at a different scale by H. Marwick.[80] Concentrating his attentions solely on Orkney, he was concerned with trying to disentangle the different stages by which the local settlement was filled out. In contrast to the conclusions of Nicolaisen, Marwick put forward the element -*byr*, meaning a 'farmstead', as a mark of the very earliest Norse settlement. In terms of their site, settlements bearing this element in their name are located on the most fertile ground and, today, represent the most substantial settlements. A sure test of their primary character is the simple fact that they never occur in a position which could be described as subordinate to another settlement. Coming into use at a slightly later date than -*byr*, but still very much a part of the earliest stages of Norse settlement, are those place-names using the elements -*lands*, -*garth*, and -*bister*. Like -*byr*, these are invariably linked to large settlements on the more fertile ground. However, the fact that they tend, in some cases, to be subordinate to -*byr* settlements implies their general usage was later. There is little doubt, though, that their use was widespread during the early pioneer stages of Norse settlement for, like -*byr* settlements, they all relate to sites that were skatted. Skat was an early land-tax imposed by the Norse king. Although levied on arable land, it appears in later sources as a payment for the use of the surrounding pastures or skattald.[81] Logically, settlements which paid skat must date from before the point of its imposition, whilst those free of it must post-date its imposition. The only obstacle to this assumption is that the exact point of its introduction is open to dispute. Marwick thought its imposition date from *c*. AD 900, so that skatted settlements pre-dated this

---

[79] Ibid.

[80] Marwick, *Orkney Farm-Names*, pp. 227–51.

[81] This widely held view that skat was paid for skattald is discussed briefly in the survey of Shetland tenures and landholding, compiled *c*.1772, and published in O'Dell, *Historical Geography of the Shetland Islands* (Lerwick, 1939), p. 243. The payment of skat for skattald, it was said, was 'universally believed to be so'. The existence of arable skatlands, however, questions this idea. The greater likelihood is that skat began as a levy on arable or skatland. At a later date, the use of skattald may have formed the pretext for levying an augmentation of skat, hence perhaps, this confusion with skattald.

point.[82] However, others favour a late date.[83] But such disagreement does not alter the basic principle involved, namely, that the difference between skatted and un-skatted settlements is a valuable measure of relative age. Just as settlements whose name incorporates the elements *-lands*, *-garth*, or *-bister* must pre-date AD 900 or thereabouts, because they were invariably skatted, so also can it be reasoned that townships using the place-name elements *quoy*, as in Quoyness, or *-setr*, as in Inkster and Malsetter, tend to be later foundations because the majority were unskatted.[84] Reinforcing this conclusion is the fact that settlements bearing the elements *quoy* or *-setr* are located mainly in positions which are marginal or peripheral to the main townships.

More so than other cultural groups in early medieval Scotland, the Norse can also be viewed through their actual settlement sites. A number of such sites have been excavated, such as those of Jarlshof and Underhoull in Shetland, Birsay and Skaill in Orkney, Freswick in Caithness, and Drimore and the Udal in the Uists.[85] The typical Norse homestead appears to have been a long house, varying in length from 15 to 25 metres, with a byre at one end, sleeping quarters at the other, and living quarters in the middle. They were constructed with thick, drystone walls, the outer edge of which was probably in-

---

[82] Marwick, *Orkney Farm-Names*, pp. 191–215. A brief reference to the imposition of skat occurs in A. W. Johnston, 'Notes on the Fiscal Antiquities of Orkney and Shetland', *Old Lore Miscellany of Orkney, Shetland, Caithness and Sutherland*, vol. ix, Old Lore Series xi (1933), p. 138. In AD 880, wrote Johnston, 'Harald's first expedition to the West, in which he subdued Orkney, Shetland and the Hebrides. He imposed a skatt or feu duty of one eyrir of gold on each of the existing plogsland, or ploughlands, afterwards called an *eyrisland* in Orkney and Shetland, and a *tirung* in the Hebrides, amounting to about one-third of the rent, of which his feoffees had to pay two-thirds to the crown and retain the other third for the expenses of the government.'

[83] Wainwright, 'The Scandinavian Settlement', p. 136, n. 4, was obviously not convinced of a *c.* AD 900 date. The discussion in W. Sabiston, 'An Analysis of the A.D. 1535 Rental of Birsay', pp. 99–115 in H. Marwick, *The Place-Names of Birsay* (Aberdeen, 1970), goes further and implies a variable date for its imposition, with skat being adjusted as new land was taken in.

[84] Marwick, *Orkney Farm-Names*, pp. 227–51.

[85] R. J. C. Hamilton, *Excavations at Jarlshof, Shetland* (Edinburgh, 1956), pp. 102–6; A. Small, 'Underhoull, Unst, Shetland', *PSAS* xcviii (1967), pp. 225–48; S. Druden, 'Excavations at Birsay, Orkney' in A. Small (ed.), *The Fourth Viking Congress* (Aberdeen, 1965), pp. 22–31; A. O. Curle, 'A Viking Settlement at Freswick, Caithness', *PSAS* lxxiii (1938–9), pp. 71–110; A. Maclaren, 'A Norse House on Drimore Machair, South Uist', *Glasgow Arch. Jnl.*, iii (1974), pp. 9–18; I. A. Crawford and R. Switsur, 'Sandscaping and C14: the Udal, N. Uist', *Antiquity*, li (1977), p. 151.

tercoursed with turf as a protection against the wind. In the case
of sites like those at Jarlshof and Underhoull, their ground-
plan—whilst rectangular—had a distinct bow-shape to it, a trait
which anticipated a design feature of the Hebridean black-house.
Apart from that at the Udal, all these Norse sites were
undefended or of a non-military character. This has prompted
some scholars to argue that, despite their initial appearance in
the historical record as raiders, the Norse colonization was a
relatively peaceful affair,[86] involving family groups.[87] But a note
of dissent to this idea has been expressed by I. Crawford. His
work at the Udal (N. Uist) suggests that the very first act of Norse
settlers there was to throw up a defensive enclosure, so that not all
Norse communities can be said to have integrated themselves
peacefully with existing cultures.[88] In a review of their economy,
Small has emphasized the extent to which early Norse settlements made use of all the resources of their environment, with
cultivation, livestock farming, hunting, and fishing all pursued.
Informed largely by what occurred at Jarlshof, he suggested that
the growth of population gradually induced a greater reliance on
fishing as the main supplement to farming, together with a build-
up of a more clustered settlement in place of the dispersed
settlement which typified the earliest phases of Norse colonization.[89]

During the discussion of Norse place-name elements, it was
mentioned that they display a decreasing density of occurrence as
one moves southwards through the Hebrides, but that there were
good reasons why this may not reflect a decreasing density of
actual settlement. However, there are fewer doubts regarding the
areal differences apparent when we consider the long-term
impact of the Norse on local rural society. In the Northern Isles,
basic and formative institutions like that of land tenure or the
grouping of townships for fiscal purposes into skatlands or

---

[86] Ritchie, 'Pict and Norseman in Northern Scotland', pp. 33–4; Wilson, 'Scandinavian Settlement', pp. 99 and 101–2.

[87] Wainwright, 'The Scandinavian Settlement', p. 140 summarized the basis of this
point when he said that 'raiders may bury their fallen comrades, but only settlers build
permanent houses and farms, and only settlers have their womenfolk with them. Among
the earliest pagan Scandinavian graves in the Northern Isles those of women are as
common as those of men.'

[88] I. A. Crawford, *Excavations at Coileagan an Udail, North Uist. 14th Interim Report* (1976),
no pagination; Crawford and Switsur, op. cit., p. 131.

[89] Small, 'Historical Geography of the Norse Viking Colonization', pp. 9–10.

ouncelands bore the deep and lasting imprint of the Norse. Even if their relationship to some elements of landholding and settlement was more adaptive than creative, the over-all conclusion must still be that their influence in the far north was profound and persistent. However, in the Western Isles, they managed only an ephemeral contribution to the cultural landscape. Indeed, according to Crawford, Gaelic influences had reasserted themselves by the twelfth century.[90] As with all continuity problems, however, cultural survival can occur in a veiled form. A hint of how complex the problem may be is provided by Crawford's plausible suggestion that the units of lordship into which the Western Isles and adjacent mainland appear divided in the twelfth century may denote earlier (or Norse?) units of sub-kingship. Altogether, four such units can be discerned. They comprise (*a*) Lewis, Harris, Skye, and the adjacent parts of the mainland, (*b*) the Uists and the mainland around Glenuig, (*c*) Tiree, Coll, and Mull, and (*d*) the southwest Highlands and Islands including Islay and Kintyre. What makes the ancestry of these units intriguing is that they appear associated with distinct clan groups: thus, the MacLeods and MacDonalds were linked with units (*a*) and (*b*) respectively.[91]

[90] Crawford, 'Scot(?), Norseman and Gael', p. 14.
[91] Ibid., pp. 3-4.

Chapter 3

Early Scottish Society:
Its Patterns of Territorial Order

Despite the ceaseless shift of cultural influences and authority, early Scottish society was not bereft of pattern in its appearance. This was especially true of its relationship to land, which was mediated through complex interlocking systems of territorial order, extending from the level of the individual holding, up through townships, to wider areal units embracing several townships and known by scholars as *multiple estates*.[1] The vital ordering and administrative functions discharged by these systems acted as a powerful preservative. So much so, that their bits and pieces, if not their structured wholes, survived well into the late medieval period, and even beyond. Once we learn how to reconstitute them, and to decipher the information encoded within them, they will surely tell us a great deal about early Scottish society. In looking more closely at these patterns of territorial order, the discussion will concentrate on three aspects. First, it will examine the physical make-up and distribution of multiple estates in Scotland. Secondly, it will review the evidence for their social function. Thirdly, it is proposed to examine the general problem of land denominational units, the building blocks out of which holdings, townships, and even multiple estates were constructed.

Scottish Multiple Estates

Multiple estates were broad, areal units stretched over a number of different settlements. In their variety of scale, they have been likened to a parish, but some were undoubtedly larger. They drew their character from the fact that they were units of lordship, a lordship exercised by a tribal chief, a king, or a feudal

---

[1] G. R. J. Jones, 'Multiple Estates and Early Settlements', pp. 15–40 in P. H. Sawyer (ed.), *Medieval Settlement* (London, 1976), pp. 15–40. Alternative terms are federal manors or discrete estates.

baron. The lord's power was usually focused on a single capital settlement. It was here that he maintained all the trappings of his power and authority. Thus, it was here that his reeve, his appointed representative for carrying out the day to day running of the estate, was located. Here too would be his demesne, a demesne worked by the labour services of the bondmen invariably tied to him. These bondmen lived either in the capital settlement or in the settlements tied to it. Here also would be the lord's court, to which his bondmen were tied for legal purposes and at which any freemen living within the estate paid suit of court and showed their fealty. If the lord himself was not resident within the estate, then his more lordly powers were vested in yet another representative attached to the capital settlement.[2]

The study of Scottish multiple estates can be traced back to the pioneer work of W. Robertson[3] and W. F. Skene[4] in the 1870s on shires and thanages. Despite their early initiative, the problem received little serious attention until G. W. S. Barrow revived the issue in the early 1970s, with two important papers reviewing the current state of ideas on both the thanage and shire.[5] Of course, since Robertson and Skene first defined the problem, its intellectual context has altered significantly. Work in England and Wales by a succession of scholars, but notably J. E. A. Jolliffe[6] and latterly G. R. J. Jones[7] has shown conclusively that multiple estates were not an institution tied to a specific cultural group, but were to be found in different cultural contexts.

Naturally, this must affect our view of the shire and thanage. In particular, it means they cannot be seen as unique forms of territorial order *sui generis*, but as local species of a wider genus.

---

[2] Broad definitions of multiple estates can be found in ibid., pp. 15–18 and G. R. J. Jones, 'Post-Roman Wales', pp. 281–382 in H. P. R. Finberg (ed.), *Agrarian History of England and Wales*, vol. i, part ii, *AD43–1042* (Cambridge, 1972), pp. 299–308.

[3] E. W. Robertson, *Historical Essays in Connexion with the Land, the Church &c* (Edinburgh, 1872), esp. chapter on 'Shire', pp. 112–33 and 'Toschach and Thane', pp. 160–5.

[4] W. F. Skene (ed.), *The Historians of Scotland*, vol. iv, *John of Fordun's Chronicle of the Scottish Nation* (Edinburgh, 1872), Appendix, pp. 441–60. See also, W. F. Skene (ed.), *Celtic Scotland* (Edinburgh, 1872), vol. iii, chapter on 'The Thanages and Their Extinction', pp. 246–83.

[5] Barrow, 'Pattern of Lordship and Settlement in Cumbria', pp. 117–38; idem, 'Pre-Feudal Scotland: Shires and Thanes', pp. 1–69 in *The Kingdom of the Scots*.

[6] J. E. A. Jolliffe, 'Northumbrian Institutions', *English Historical Rev.*, xli (1926), pp. 1–42.

[7] Jones, 'Multiple Estates and Early Settlements', pp. 15–40.

Equally important, once their uniqueness is removed, there is no reason why multiple estates should not be looked for in western and northern Scotland. In short, we need to consider the real possibility that multiple estates were a universal unit of territorial order in early Scotland, but cast in a different terminological guise according to their cultural or regional context.

Clearly labelled as a type of multiple estates were the thanages of eastern Scotland. In terms of their distribution, they were to be found discontinuously scattered from Sutherland in the north, southwards through the north-east Lowlands, the Mearns, the Carse of Gowrie, and Strathmore, to Fife. Of the seventy or so examples so far identified, most are located on the lower ground. Only a few, such as those of Fortingall and Cranach in Perthshire or those of Cromdale and Glenlivet in the Spey Valley and along its tributary, the Livet, included a substantial proportion of hill-ground within their bounds. If we are able to conclude anything from this distribution, then it is that the thanage was an institution that throve best, and survived best, in arable areas. As a unit geared to the extraction of dues, renders, and labour services, this would make sense.

The composition of a few thanages can be reconstructed using land charters for the twelfth, thirteenth, and fourteenth centuries, for even at this late stage, they were conveyed as integral estates. The fact that one or two have the form of later parishes enables us to place and orientate them in the landscape. The thanage of Birse in Aberdeenshire demonstrates the potential of this approach. A charter conveying it to the Bishop of Aberdeen and dated to 1180 × 1184 listed sixteen towns plus a Kirkton and the Forest of Birse.[8] Its equivalence to the parish of Birse hardly needs to be stated. In a brief review of the problem, R. Muir has attempted to chart the approximate boundaries of other thanages in the north-east. Allowing for the fragmented coverage of his sources, his map hints at a continuous estate structure, a reasonable conclusion given the close-packing of thanages in the region.[9] Indeed, if we allow for those thanages which Muir

[8] G. F. Browne (ed.), *Echt-Forbes Family Charters 1345–1727. Records of the Forest of Birse 926–1786* (Edinburgh, 1923), pp. 192–7; G. W. S. Barrow (ed.), *The Acts of William I King of Scots 1165–1214. Regesta Regum Scottorum* (Edinburgh, 1971), p. 286.
[9] R. Muir, 'Thanages', pp. 27–8 and 127 in P. McNeill and R. Nicholson (eds.), *An Historical Atlas of Scotland c.400–c.1600* (St Andrews, 1975).

discounts or overlooks,[10] then the whole of the north-east must once have been divided into a more or less continuous system of multiple estates. Nor can the isolated examples in the Grampians, like Glenlivet and Rothiemurchus, be allowed to deceive us over conditions in upland areas. There too, the problem may be one of non-survival rather than non-existence. Special social conditions factors may have been at work in these Highland areas that militated against their survival.

Writing back in 1872, Robertson sought to impose a formal structure on the thanage as regards the number of townships which it comprised and its total assessment in terms of land units, seeing them as comprising 12 townships and 48 davachs.[11] By contrast, Skene tended to emphasize their variety of structure. The examples he cited had up to 23 townships, as in the case of Arbuthnott thanage (Kincardine) in 1170, and a davach assessment that ranged from as few as 3 up to 18.[12] These differences are not irreconcilable. Basically, Robertson was seeking to discern the normative structure of the system, or the logic by which it was devised. Skene, meanwhile, was concerned with its actual appearances in early charters. Their differences of emphasis may signify no more than the changes absorbed by the system from the point when it was first devised to the point when it comes into view. Its susceptibility to partition, coupled with the easy growth of new townships, could soon throw a disguise over any original layout. Skene appreciated this, for he offered as an example of his 'small' six-davach thanage the clearly partitioned estates of Magna and Parva Blar, each of which equalled three davachs.[13] Alternatively, it could be argued that the system was laid out pragmatically from the very beginning, so that Robertson's quest for order and symmetry is misleading.[14]

Like multiple estates elsewhere, the thanage contained certain

---

[10] For reasons he does not disclose, he discounts some of those listed in Skene, *Celtic Scotland*, vol. iii, pp. 246–83.

[11] Robertson, op. cit., p. 128.

[12] Skene (ed.), *John of Fordun's Chronicle of the Scottish Nation*, p. 450.

[13] Ibid., p. 450. Barrow also talks of the fissionable tendencies of thanages and shires in his 'Pre-Feudal Scotland: Shires and Thanes', p. 39.

[14] This question of symmetry in the pattern of territorial organization is complicated by the confusion between the order prescribed in law codes, such as those outlined by Welsh and Irish law codes, and that which actually prevailed on the ground. The former was not necessarily reflected in the latter.

key components that were essential to its function. The officer in charge of its day to day management as an estate was termed the thane, mair, or *Toiseach*. The principal settlement or *caput* of the estate, or the settlement at which the lord's demesne and his court were located and from which he exercised his authority, was called the Thaneston. This often became incorporated into place-names. The thanage of Fettercairn provides an example of a Thanestone.[15] Most thanages also possessed a Kirkton, where the principal church plus an endowment of land was sited.[16] A further feature of many thanages is that they possessed an area of common grazing shared between the entire inhabitants.[17] Because of the multiplicity of interest in them, these commonties tended to prove durable elements in the local landscape.

Descriptions of the shires of eastern and south-eastern Scotland reveal an unmistakably similar structure to that of the thanage. Each comprised a scatter of different settlements that were bound together as appendages of the shire's capital settlement. Barrow has noted how townships in shires north of the Forth often incorporate the place-name element *Pit-*. In his own words, the 'meaning of *pett*, a portion of something larger, seems peculiarly well suited to a shire consisting in *manerium cum appendenciis*'.[18] By the time they appear in the eleventh or twelfth centuries, shires were usually held from the King by ministerial tenants known as thanes.[19] Within each shire's system of settlements was again a settlement that had a special link with the thane. In Coldingham shire, for example, it was Swinton. Since thanes probably exercised 'a basic civil and criminal jurisdiction on the "king's behalf" as well as acting as reeves for the estate',[20] it was only

---

[15] Skene, *Celtic Scotland*, vol. ii, pp. 258–9. Mention might also be made of W. C. Dickinson's discussion of 'mairtowns' in Fife, since the terms thane and mair were sometimes interchanged. The Sheriffdom of Fife was divided into four quarters, each having a *mair*. Attached to the office of *mair* was land known as *mairsland* or *mairstown*. See W. C. Dickinson (ed.), *The Sheriff Court Book of Fife 1515–1522*, Scottish History Soc., 3rd ser., xii (1928), pp. lxiii–lxiv. In Wales, the officer in charge of the day to day running of multiple estates or *maenorau* was called a *maer* and the chief settlement where he lived was the *maerdref*.

[16] Barrow, 'Pre-Feudal Scotland: Shires and Thanes', pp. 60–4; Robertson, *Historical Essays*, p. 126.

[17] Barrow, 'Pre-Feudal Scotland: Shires and Thanes', pp. 50–3.

[18] Ibid., p. 59.

[19] Ibid., p. 64. See also, Robertson, *Historical Essays*, pp. 160–5.

[20] Barrow, 'Pre-Feudal Scotland: Shires and Thanes', p. 41.

logical that the thane's toun should be associated with both the court and demesne of the shire. Shires also possessed a kirkton. In Coldingham shire, it was Coldingham itself, a settlement which Coldingham Priory held as a large personal demesne *c.*1300.[21] Viewing the problem in a broader perspective, Barrow has highlighted a possible link between the place-name element *eccles* and the principal kirktons of shires, as with Eccles in both Berwick shire and Stirling shire, Eglenamin in Kinrymonth shire and Eaglescarnie in Haddington shire.[22]

As with the thanage, Robertson has raised the issue of whether the shire initially possessed a formal structure as regards the number of its constituent townships and its land assessment. Perceptively, he argued that its structure was analogous to the thanage. 'Such was the Scottish thanage, such the early English shire; a district reckoned at twelve townships, and eight-and-forty ploughlands, or davachs, and either placed under the super-intendence of a royal deputy, or else made over to a leading magnate; whilst in things ecclesiastical, it was under the superintendence of a greater or lesser minister.'[23] To bolster his case, he gave strong emphasis to those examples that still bore the imprint of this twelve-township structure, such as the shires of Coldingham (Berwickshire) and Yetholm (Roxburghshire).[24] As with the thanage, though, the normative structure of the shire is not so easily read from early sources, some having more and others less than Robertson's set figure.[25]

The use of the term thane in the context of the shire begs questions about the latter's origin. It could be argued that as a unit of territorial order to be found in northern England, its presence in Scotland was a spin-off from the Northumbrian conquest of the

[21] Ibid., pp. 28 and 31; Robertson, *Historical Essays*, p. 125; T. Raine (ed.), *The Priory of Coldingham, Its Correspondence, Inventories, Account Rolls and Law Proceedings of the Priory of Coldingham*, Surtees Soc. (1841), pp. xciv–xcvii.

[22] Barrow, 'Pre-Feudal Scotland: Shires and Thanes', pp. 60–4.

[23] Robertson, *Historical Essays*, p. 128.

[24] Ibid., p. 125.

[25] Barrow's reconstruction of the shire of Abernethy in 'Pre-Feudal Scotland: Shires and Thanes', p. 51, suggests it embraced at least 17 vills bearing archaic place-name elements. A rental of the parish of Clatt (Aberdeenshire), dated 1511, rated it as 27 ploughgates; see J. Robertson (ed.), *Illustrations of the Topography and Antiquities of the Shire of Aberdeen and Banff* (Aberdeen, 1862), vol. iv, pp. 486–7. By comparison with the shire of Clatt, Arbuthnott was rated as 54 ploughgates, exactly twice as much, see Skene (ed.), *John of Fordun's Chronicle*, p. 450.

south.[26] Later, in the twelfth century when David I was on the Scottish throne, it may have been extended northwards into Fife and the coastal lowlands of the north-east as part of a scheme to feudalize the area. However, the growing confidence with which historians have equated the shire and thanage, and the increasing awareness of how the shire was itself a Celtic survival rather than an Anglian innovation in northern England, means that there is no need to invoke David I or any subsequent Scottish king as a major innovator here. Changes in tenurial status apart,[27] the apparent extension of the shire system north of the Forth may have involved little more than a new terminology for an institution that was already familiar there. Even this may overstate what was involved. According to Barrow, the mixing of these terms and concepts north of the Forth—as with the shared use of the term thane in relation to both the shire and thanage— may date back to before the eleventh century and reflect a Pictish propensity for borrowing Gaelic and Anglian terms alike.[28]

Once we move away from eastern and south-eastern Scotland, we move into areas where the problem of multiple estates still lacks precision. However, there are strong hints that a comparable system of territorial order existed in the Northern Isles. It is best documented for Orkney. Although their exact number is not known for certain, Orkney appears to have been divided into six separate districts known as 'huseby' districts. At the centre of each huseby, was 'a royal administrative farm of military character'.[29] This central farm or demesne carried the title of Huseby as a place-name, as with Houseby on Stronsay, Houseby on Shapansay, Husabae on Rousay, and Housebay on Birsay. Like the shires and thanages further south, each huseby centre was surrounded by dependent townships. A. Stiennes has proposed a normative structure to their layout, each huseby having a land unit assessment of around 30 to 35 ouncelands.

[26] The north of England shires are discussed in Jolliffe, op. cit., pp. 1–42. Scholars, notably Glanville Jones, have now established the existence of multiple estates in areas outside Northumbria. See, Jones, 'Multiple Estates and Early Settlements', pp. 15–40; G. R. J. Jones, 'The Tribal System in Wales: A Reassessment in the Light of Settlement Studies', *Welsh History Rev.*, i (1961), pp. 111–32.

[27] Barrow, 'Pre-Feudal Scotland: Shires and Thanes', pp. 38–9 and 46 provides comment on the specific tenures associated with shires and thanages.

[28] Ibid., pp. 64–5.

[29] A. Stiennes, 'The Huseby System in Orkney', *SHR* xxxviii (1959), p. 36.

Each ounceland was further subdivided into four skatlands, each of which comprised either a large single township or a cluster of small townships.[30]

The evidence for the former existence of multiple estates is least legible with respect to the western Highlands. Such evidence as exists is largely circumstantial, rather than direct. For instance, territorial toponyms like Morvern, Ardnamurchan, Knapdale, Cowal, and Lorn, embracing groups of settlement, may be diagnostic of such a system. Equally relevant is the fact that these districts possessed territorial assessments. Districts like Morvern, Ardnamurchan, Glenelg, Kintail, and Trotterness all boasted territorial assessments in merklands as if they had some integral meaning in relation to the territorial organization of the Highland region.[31] More conclusive are the various references to *Toschdor*, the Gaelic term for the king's or chief's representative charged with the responsibility of managing a multiple estate. It occurs in relation to the territories—and presumably multiple estates—of Levenax (Lennox), Cowal, Kintyre, Knapdale, Craignish, and Lochaber.[32] Beyond these indirect signs, there are relatively few clues as to the structural configuration of multiple estates in the region. By contrast, when we turn to consider their functioning (see below, pp. 68–73), the evidence for the region is much more revealing.

The same can be said of the south-west. There are no formal references to a system of multiple estates like the shire and thanage. Indeed, Robertson has talked of there being a shadow all but impenetrable resting over Scottish Cumbria as regards this problem.[33] However, there are clues. An obvious one is the organization of the region into what Barrow cautiously called 'secular divisions', such as Kyle Regis and Stewart, Cunningham, Strathnith (Nithsdale), Strathannan (Annandale), Desneasnor, and Glenker.[34] Furthermore, these units appear to have functioned as integral estates, for they can be found being

---

[30] Ibid., p. 42.
[31] See R. C. MacLeod (ed.), *The Book of Dunvegan*, vol. i, *1340–1700*, Third Spalding Club (Aberdeen, 1938), pp. 3–5, 55, and 93; *Geographical Collections Relating to Scotland Made by W. Macfarlane*, vol. i, Scottish History Soc., li (1906), pp. 521–2 and 532.
[32] Skene (ed.), *John of Fordun's Chronicle*, p. 459.
[33] Robertson, *Historical Essays*, pp. 164–5.
[34] Barrow, 'Pattern of Lordship and Feudal Settlement in Cumbria', p. 125.

granted as such during the twelfth and thirteenth centuries.[35] In the case of Carrick and Galloway, the office of *toschdor* also occurs.[36] Finally, as with the western Highlands, if the problem is phrased in terms of the relationships built up around multiple estates, then there is again no lack of relevant material.

No matter which area we are dealing with, there is no direct evidence for multiple estates prior to the eleventh century. And yet, as a system of territorial order, it has greater relevance for the period extending back before the eleventh century. As Barrow put it, the 'historian who searches the record of late medieval Scotland for traces of those earlier, darker centuries stretching back before the days of King David I (1124–53) will soon find himself pondering two unsolved but connected problems, the shire and the thane'.[37] Needless to say, this willingness to endow multiple estates with an antiquity that takes them back deep into the early historic period, and possibly beyond, demands an explanation. There are a number of ways in which the problem can be approached. Skene's contribution was to emphasize its tribal roots. Multiple estates like the thanage and shire were compared with the Irish *tuath* or tribal area. They preserve, he concluded, 'many of the characteristics of the older Celtic tribe'.[38] In other words, when clan chiefs are seen yielding up their territories to the Scottish king from the twelfth century onwards, and holding their land thereafter by Crown charter, what we are witnessing is not the pioneer instatement of a new *form* of feudal administration, but the final stage of an archaic system.

More recently, Barrow has added further to this debate over origins by making a number of pertinent observations on place-names. The use of the element *Pit-* by the dependent settlements of shires (and thanages), for instance, implied a system at least as old as the use of this element. As regards thanages, he also noted how many of them appear to have capital settlements which bear

[35] Ibid., pp. 126 and 130.

[36] Robertson, *Historical Essays*, p. 163.

[37] Barrow, 'Pre-Feudal Scotland: Shires and Thanes', p. 7.

[38] Skene, *Celtic Scotland*, vol. iii, pp. 281–2. Skene made the point that 'thanages had therefore obviously replaced the more ancient *Tuath*', p. 281. Like Robertson, Skene was concerned with the transition from tribalism to kingship, a transition which the history of multiple estates appears to have straddled. See ibid., pp. 281–2 and Robertson, *Historical Essays*, p. 160.

Brittonic or P-Celtic place-names, an association that points to a pre-ninth-century origin. Yet another association is the use of the element *eccles*, the old Brittonic or Cumbric name for a church, in connection with the Kirktons of shires: this too, suggests continuity from the early Christian period. Indeed, Barrow goes further and suggests that early churches may have been founded thanage by thanage, shire by shire.[39] In so far as multiple estates must have formed the activity spaces around which early society revolved, this is plausible. Focusing on individual examples, he traced the early history of the Border shire of Yetholm. Held back in the seventh century by King Oswy, its integrity as an estate was preserved despite its subsequent granting to the Church and the establishment of the Anglo–Scottish border through it, a durability which led Barrow to see it as a 'shire of great antiquity'.[40] Moreover, when the Cheviot farms listed in the seventh-century grant of Yetholm shire are set besides the rich pattern of late prehistoric and Romano–British settlement sites *within* them, it is impossible not to be convinced of this antiquity.[41] Of course, the cross-cultural nature of multiple estates is, itself, a firm indication of its ancient roots. Exactly how ancient must remain an open question, but the important and seminal work by G. R. J. Jones suggests that some probably extend back into the Iron age.[42] This would accord with the tribal origins put forward by Robertson and Skene. If accepted, it would mean that such estates provide a crucial thread of continuity from the prehistoric period through into the historic. More important, it would mean that despite all the disruptions of the early historic period, the new cultural influences that intruded into Scotland at this point did not necessarily sweep all before them, but may have provided a new gloss on basically stable patterns of lordship and landholding. Indeed, a society organized into multiple estates enabled a few to influence the many.[43]

---

[39] Barrow, 'Pre-Feudal Scotland: Shires and Thanes', pp. 63–4.
[40] Ibid., p. 35.
[41] RCAM, Scotland, *Roxburghshire*, vol. i, pp. 15–39 and 156–94, vol. ii, pp. 325–71.
[42] See especially, G, R. J. Jones, 'Settlement Patterns in Anglo-Saxon England', *Antiquity*, xxxv (1961), pp. 221–32; Jones, 'Post-Roman Wales', pp. 380–2.
[43] Jones, 'Multiple Estates and Early Settlements', pp. 39–40.

Multiple Estates: Their Functional Character

The discussion has so far considered multiple estates solely in terms of their structural character, as estates comprising interlinked clusters of settlement. But they were also interlinked clusters of people, with measured or defined relationships and obligations. Most commentators have devoted some space in their definitions of multiple estates to such relationships. Early scholars like Skene, for example, cited a number of early charters in which thanages and the like were conveyed not just as collections of townships held as a single estate, but as a social system replete with bondmen, bondagers, native-men and their followers, tenantry, and the services of the freeholders. Such terms, for instance, were used in the charter by which Robert II granted the thanage of Glamis to John Lyon.[44] Barrow too, has stressed this aspect of multiple estates. Speaking in particular about the shire system, he referred to 'its characteristic features of fee-farm (Scots: feu-ferme), money rents, seasonal ploughing and reaping, wood-cutting and carrying duties, tribute in cattle and pigs and obligatory hospitality (*conveth*, waiting).'[45]

The labour services listed by Barrow survived with little modification or dilution well into the early modern period. Of more immediate interest are the obligations which can be classified as tribute and hospitality or what Skene described as the 'services of the freeholders'.[46] There were five types of obligation or service, types which are conveniently brought together in a charter conveying land from Sir Ewen of Argyll to the Bishop of Argyll in 1240 free of all duties including 'cain et coneueth feact slagad et ich'.[47] Cain was interpreted by Skene as a rent or 'return from land, whether in kind or money', though others see it as a per capita rent.[48] The confusion over its meaning may stem from the tendency for these dues or renders to shift from being initially a burden on persons to being anchored to specific

[44] Skene, *Celtic Scotland*, vol. iii, p. 266.
[45] Barrow, 'Pre-Feudal Scotland: Shires and Thanes', p. 35.
[46] Skene, *Celtic Scotland*, vol. iii, p. 251.
[47] The charter in question is reprinted in A. A. M. Duncan and A. L. Brown, 'Argyll and the Isles in the Earlier Middle Ages', *PSAS* xc (1956–7), p. 219. See also, Skene (ed.), *John of Fordun's Chronicle*, p. 451.
[48] Ibid., p. 452.

blocks of landholding.[49] Linked with cain was an obligation known as *cuid oidche*. This was the hospitality due from freemen or tenants to their chief during his annual sojourn on the estate. It was a hospitality that extended to the chief's household, but whether it also included his warriors as Skene stated is unclear. Much would depend on how the chief's household was defined. On Tiree, it was said that the island 'was wont to quarter all the gentlemen that waited on McLean all winter not under a 100'.[50] The *feact* and *slagad* mentioned in the Bishop of Argyll's grant were the obligations of expedition and hosting which free members of a tribe or clan owed to their chief.[51] The term 'ich' is more usually described as 'cobach', and simply meant a tribute payment.

Although defined here in the context of the thanage, such renders and obligations occurred in association with all multiple estates. Thus, cain and conveth can be broadly equated with the cornage and waiting (or waytinga) of shires.[52] They are often referred to as such in early documents, but as the medieval period draws to a close, they tend to persist as nondescript payments made by tenants in the form of cattle, swine, cheese, malt, barley, meal, and fodder. What is so striking about such payments in kind is the way they were scaled in strict proportion to the arable assessment of touns.[53] In some cases, such as on the Minto estate in Roxburghshire, it is still possible to find token payments of

---

[49] This statement is based on the simple fact that tribal obligations and services were specific to a person's status, whether he was a bondman or freeman. Yet, where such obligations and services survived into the late medieval period, they appeared attached to tenants, or rather they were an integral part of the tenure of their holdings. For comparable changes in respect of Welsh tribal obligations, see T. Jones Pierce, *Welsh Medieval Society*, ed. J. Beverley Smith (Cardiff, 1973), pp. 322–4.

[50] 'Tiree Rental 1662', p. 344.

[51] Skene, *John of Fordun's Chronicle*, pp. 453–4.

[52] Cornage and waytinga are discussed in W. Rees, 'Survivals of ancient Celtic custom in medieval England', pp. 146–68 in *Angles and Britons* (Cardiff, 1963), pp. 160–5.

[53] See, for example, *The Miscellany of the Spalding Club*, iv (1849), pp. 261–319, which reprints the 'Rentaill of the Lordschipe of Huntlye alias Strauthbogye 1600'; SRO, GD44/51/747; A. Macpherson, *Glimpses of Church and Social Life in the Highlands in Olden Times* (Edinburgh, 1893), pp. 503–13, which provides a rental for 'The Lordshipe of Badzenoche', 1603. An interesting survival in the way of tribute is that documented by Dickinson (ed.), *Sheriff Court Book of Fife*, pp. lxv–lxvi. In 1494, the *mair* of Renfrew was said to receive 'from ilk persone haffand ane pleuch within the schir ane thraiff of aitis and ane lam or iiiid. of thaim that has na lammes & Ilk half pleuch a stouk & sa furth accordin to thar malingis'.

'kain' hens being made as late as the eighteenth century.[54]

Given the lack of explicit evidence for a system of multiple estates in the western Highlands, it is significant that the renders and obligations commonly linked with them are readily documented there, albeit through the sources that post-date the period when multiple estates as such prevailed. Thus, a sixteenth-century report on the Hebrides talks about 'white plaiding by their *cuidichies*, that is, feasting their master when he pleases to come into the country, each one a night or two nights about'.[55] The report goes on to mention the discharge of *cuidichies* on both Skye and Mull.[56] A few decades later, an agreement between the chief of MacLeod and one of his tacksmen, after a back reference to a recent Act of Parliament, recorded that since 'the laws of the Kingdom prohibits the former abuse of *sorneing* and *cudeachis* oppression and things usually done in time bypast within the Isle of Skye we shall not crave take or ask any *cuddeaches* or obligatory-meat from any of the said Jon and his men'.[57] Later still, the 1751 valuation of Argyll noted how the proprietor of Knapdale had a servitude of a night's lodging from one of his tenants, with an entry for 'Cuid-vich, 20s'.[58] In fact, remnants of the system even dragged on into the nineteenth century for payment of cain and *cuid oidche* was a matter of complaint to the Napier Commission in 1884.[59]

An interesting aside on this obligation of freemen to provide food for their chief concerns the Macdonald lands in Islay. Tacks for land on the island were said by tradition to have contained the phrase 'I Macdonald, sitting upon Dundonald give you right to your farm from this day till to-morrow, and every day thereafter, so long as you have food for the great Macdonald of the Isles'.[60] That there was substance in this tradition is underlined by a sixteenth-century report about Islay

[54] NLS, Minto MSS, Box 17/112, Tacks of the Minto estate, 1713–53.

[55] Skene, *Celtic Scotland*, vol. iii, Appendix III, 'Description of the Isles of Scotland', pp. 428–40, esp. 429.

[56] Ibid., pp. 432 and 435.

[57] MacLeod (ed.), *Book of Dunvegan*, vol. i, *1340–1700*, p. 183.

[58] A. McKerral, 'The Tacksman and His Holding in the South-West Highlands', *SHR* xxvi (1947), pp. 13–14.

[59] *Evidence taken by the Royal Commissioners of Inquiry on the Condition of the Crofters and Cottars in the Highlands and Islands* (London, 1884), p. 993.

[60] *Origines Parochiales Scotiae*, vol. i, part i (Edinburgh, 1854), p. 26. Compare the statement made by M. Martin, *A Description of the Western Islands of Scotland 1699* (London,

that 'each merk land man sustains dayly and yearly one gentleman in meat and cloth, who does no labour, but is regarded as one of their master's household men, and is sustained and furnished in all necessities by the tenant, and ready to serve his master's aid and advice'.[61] Such an imposition must surely have had its origin in an earlier system whereby chiefs and their retinue were dependent as a matter of practical necessity as well as of kindred spirit on the food provided by their fellow clansmen. It shows how an obligation rooted in a quite different kind of social ethos could be transformed into one of feudal right, outwardly the same but inwardly propelled by a quite different set of values. It is perhaps in this context that we should see the oft-quoted story about the MacNeil of Barra. After the chief had finished his meal, a member of his household mounted the topmost turret of Kisimul Castle and proudly proclaimed that now that the Chief of Barra had finished his meal, the rest of the world could start theirs. Wrapped up in this colourful story is surely the old notion that a tribe or clan supported its chief with food, a notion clearly turned into a first priority by MacNeil and other chiefs.

This functional side to early multiple estates has a more profound significance, for it exposes their background far more effectively than their mere structure could ever do. To understand this background, we need first to grasp the nature of tribal chiefdoms and exchange systems as formally defined by anthropologists like M. H. Fried[62] and M. Sahlins.[63] Put simply, early tribal groups regulated their external affairs either through war or through the exchange of wives, gifts, and goods.[64] The first of these mechanisms is self-explanatory. The second is less so. The basic principle of primitive exchange systems rested on the notion

1716 edn.), pp. 98–9. Talking of the Steward of the lesser and southern islands, Martin wrote that he was 'reckon'd a Great Man here, in regard of the Perequisities due to him; such as a particular share of all the Lands Corn, Butter, Cheese, Fish, etc, which these Islands produce; the Measure of Barley paid him by each Family yearly, is an Omer, as they call it, containing about two Pecks'.

[61] Skene, *Celtic Scotland*, vol. iii, Appendix III,, p. 438.

[62] M. H. Fried, *The Notion of Tribe* (Menlo Park, 1975).

[63] M. Sahlins, *Stone Age Economics* (London, 1974).

[64] Examples of women and slaves forming part of a system of exchange or tribute payment can be found in the *Book of Rights*, an 11th-century Irish source, or M. Dillon (ed.), *Lebor Na Cert*, Irish Text Soc. (Dublin, 1962).

of prestation and counter-prestation, of gift-giving and reciprocal gift-receiving, perhaps with wives moving in one direction and food or material goods like cloth and weapons moving in the other. In time, there might emerge within a tribe a 'big-man' who, acting as a 'tribal banker', assumed supervisory control over the collection and exchange of food and goods as well as over the more delicate matter of intertribal marriage alliances. Out of this trend developed the whole idea of chiefdom and with it, ranked societies. The 'big-man' or chief could extend his personal control over the tribe in a variety of ways, such as the redistribution of food during times of crisis or shortage, thus obligating the members of his tribe more firmly to him. Likewise, he could extend his control by the addition of client groups: these might be minor tribes or clans who received his military protection in return for gifts or tributes of food and goods. Given the exceptionally detailed evidence from the western Highlands for the payment of food renders by tenants to their chief, of tribute payments, of feastings and hostings and of clientship, it is impossible not to be impressed by the similarity which these relationships and obligations had to those of chiefdoms. The one is both a context for, and an explanation of, the other. The same conclusion can be applied to the relationships and obligations that charged multiple estates elsewhere in Scotland.

If this interpretation is valid, then it follows that the relationships and obligations centred on multiple estates were of the essence to their character. This must have a bearing on how we treat units like the thanage or shire. Given their appearances as part of a coherent system, it has always been tempting to see them as designed specifically to scale and localize the various relationships and obligations that seem so intimately connected with them. However, if such relationships and obligations derived from earlier systems of chiefdom, then at the outset, their territorial spread must have ebbed and flowed with the fortunes of the tribal or kinship groups to which they were linked. The need to fix them within a more rigid territorial framework may have arisen only when these different tribal or kinship groups became incorporated into a wider system of kingship, thereby adding a new tier—a new level of expectation—to the hierarchy of relationships and obligations. With such varied histories already behind them, we can hardly expect the formalization of multiple estates in the guise of units like the thanage or shire to have swept aside their innate variety of size and composition in an effort to make reality fit in more closely with notional schemes of territorial order.

Land Denominational Units

The study of Scottish land denominational units has a long and distinguished tradition. Back in the nineteenth century, scholars like Robertson,[65] Skene,[66] and F. W. L. Thomas[67] all made valuable contributions. More recently, the debate has been sustained by such scholars as A. McKerral,[68] D. Lamont,[69] A. A. M. Duncan,[70] and G. W. S. Barrow.[71] Two aspects of the problem have attracted most comment, namely, the size represented by particular land units and their derivation. The discussion which follows takes a slightly different focus. Although some assumptions and ideas on their size will be put forward, this aspect will not be dealt with at length. Instead, the main weight of the discussion will centre on the problem of their derivation and the comparatively neglected issue of whether such land units formed part of a planned system or one put together in a piecemeal fashion.

The geography of Scottish land units is well known. In the south-east were to be found ploughgates and oxgates or their Latin equivalents of carucates and bovates. In addition, there were also to be found touns assessed in husbandlands or, to a lesser extent, merklands. North of the Tay, the pattern alters, carucates and bovates are still to be found in early land charters, but more and more touns are assessed in terms of the davach, a large unit built up out of four ploughs or ploughgates. The

[65] Robertson, *Historical Essays*, pp. 133–41, chapter on 'Scottish Measurements'.

[66] Skene (ed.), *John of Fordun's Chronicle*, p. 450.

[67] F. W. L. Thomas, 'What is a Pennyland?', *PSAS* vi (1883–4), pp. 253–85; F. W. L. Thomas, 'Ancient Valuations of Land in the West of Scotand', *PSAS* viii (1885–6), pp. 200–13.

[68] McKerral, 'Ancient Denominations of Agricultural Land', pp. 39–80.

[69] Lamont, 'Old Land Denominations and "Old Extent" in Islay', part i, pp. 183–204 and part ii, pp. 86–107; idem, 'The Islay Charter of 1408', *Proc. Royal Irish Academy*, 60C (1959–60), pp. 177–83.

[70] Duncan, *Scotland: the Making of the Kingdom*, pp. 311–22.

[71] G. W. S. Barrow, 'Rural settlement in central and eastern Scotland', pp. 257–78 in Barrow, *Kingdom of the Scots*, esp. pp. 264–77.

davach can be traced throughout the north-east, as well as in parts of the central Highlands and the extreme north-west. Further north, in Caithness and across in the Northern Isles, the prevailing units of land measurement alter yet again, those of the ounceland or urisland (Latin, *unciata*) and pennyland being used. In the Western Isles, the situation is more confused. Ouncelands, pennylands, the davach, the tirunga, and merklands were all extensively used, plus a number of more localized measures such as the senemarges (Kintyre), cowlands (Islay and Coll), and males (Tiree).[72]

Sense can be made of this plethora of measures by seeing some as linked together in a graduated scale of assessment (i.e. 8 oxgates = 1 ploughgate) and the difference between others as representing the personalized inputs of different cultures like the Irish or Norse.[73] However, not all problems can be explained away in this fashion. Left unexplained are still problems which are basic to the whole question of Scottish land units. Why, for instance, does one find apparently unrelated land units being used within the same toun in the western Highlands and Islands?[74] Why does the davach adjust itself, chameleon-like, to the size of local measures used alongside it in both the west and east of Scotland?[75] An answer to these sorts of questions can be pieced together by looking at the derivation of land units.

Viewed overall, Scottish land units can be aranged into two broad classes as regards their derivation. Stated simply, those of eastern and south-eastern Scotland appear to have been land measures *ab origine*, whilst those of the far north, the west, and

---

[72] For senemarges, see *Origines Parochiales Scotiae*, vol. ii, part ii, Appendix, p. 2. For cowlands, see Lamont, 'Old Land Denominations and "Old Extent" in Islay', part ii, pp. 86–8. For males, see 'Tiree Rental 1662', p. 344. Lamont, 'The Islay Charter of 1408', p. 178 derives the latter from a Norse grain measure, or *miel*.

[73] Of course, the way the ounceland varies between the Northern Isles and the Hebrides should warn us that the cultural input may only have been a new terminology rather than a case of new land units or measures.

[74] A typical example is provided by the assessment of touns in Ardnamurchan and Sunart. The Crown rental in G. P. M'Neill (ed.), *The Exchequer Rolls of Scotland*, vol. xvii *A.D. 1537–1542* (Edinburgh, 1897), pp. 622–5 computes touns in merklands. By contrast, the 1723 'Anatomie of Parish and Barony of Ardnamoruchan & Swinard' in Sir Alexander Murray, *The True Interest of Great Britain, Ireland and Our Plantations* (London, 1740), Table vi.

[75] Altogether, as many as 3 different sizes can be attributed to it: 416, 160(80), and 96(48) acres. The last two sets of possibilities reflect the difficulties in deciding whether some sources are dealing with whole davachs or half davachs.

south-west appear to have had a fiscal meaning. The agrarian origin of those in the east and south-east is implicit in their very terminology. Terms like oxgate, ploughgate, bovate, carucate, and husbandland are quite obviously measures of ploughing capacity or, in the case of the husbandland, a notional unit of sustenance for the typical peasant family. Such an interpretation is also implied by the manner of their use or treatment. Thus, sources like the *Regiam Majestatem*[76] as well as estate material[77] seem anxious to stress their acreage equivalent, the oxgate or bovate being 13 acres and the ploughgate or carucate being 104 acres. The size of the husbandland seems more equivocal. Early sources ascribed to it a size of 26 acres,[78] but later evidence suggests that the term had displaced the bovate or oxgate as the preferred term for the smaller 13-acre unit.[79] Such a broad consensus over their size suggests these land units were meant to be standardized holdings. More important, it hints strongly at a system of land measure that had definite bounds and limits on the ground. This, in fact, is borne out by early foundation charters for the south-east which refer to ploughgates being perambulated and laid out (see pp. 175–6).

The land units of the north and west pose more difficult problems as regards their derivation. These problems are immediately confronted with a unit like the davach. Its exact derivation is obscure. Three possibilities have been advanced. The first is that it represents a term incorporating the same notion as an oxgate, signifying the amount of land that could be ploughed by one animal.[80] The second is that it is based on the Gaelic word for a vat and signifies the amount that was yielded by a particular amount of land. As one writer has neatly put it, the measures of the south-east were concerned with what went into the soil, or the plough, whereas those of the north-east were

[76] *APS* i, p. 387.

[77] A good source is SRO, RHP2487 which refers to a number of touns, such as the daugh of Foderletter, in which a davach is defined as comprising 32 oxgates of 13 acres each and 4 ploughlands of 104 acres each.

[78] See, for example, *APS* i, Notices of the MSS, p. xxiv, footnote reference on the Monynet MS. See also, I. F. Grant, *The Social and Economic Development of Scotland Before 1603* (Edinburgh, 1930), pp. 44–5.

[79] R. A. Dodgshon, 'The Nature and Development of Infield–Outfield in Scotland', *TIBG* lix (1973), pp 1–23, esp. p. 7.

[80] In the writer's opinion, this interpretation is quite incompatible with its size.

concerned with what was planted or produced.[81] The third possibility and the one favoured by the present author was first offered by W. E. Levie in 1931 but has since been endorsed by scholars like K. H. Jackson. It is that the word davach meant a vat but, as such, expressed the amount of food payable as a food render.[82] Such an idea has a number of attractions. Apart from making sense of the meaning of davach as a term, it is consistent with its scale as a land measure. It tends to be overlooked that by any standards the davach was an extremely large measure. Estimates vary, but there are firm grounds for believing that it constituted 416 acres of arable in the north-east but only 160 or 96 acres in the western Highlands.[83] This does not suggest a peasant holding, but a multi-township measure. Only by seeing it as a food render payable to a superior or chief can sense be made of this large, multi-township character.

Seeing it as a food render would also provide an appropriate backcloth for explaining why the davach was so varied in size. Faced with this variation, McKerral thought it expressed the inevitable growth of townships, with the area covered by the davach being extended in the process from arable to embrace pasture ground as well.[84] Such a view overlooks a point of considerable interest. When we examine the unitary subdivision of the davach in the north-east, it is based on the familiar Anglian units of the oxgate and ploughgate, the whole structure being divided into 32 oxgates and four ploughgates.[85] By contrast, the western davach displayed affinities with Celtic systems of measurement, being divided into units of 48 and 96 acres or 80 and 160 acres.[86] This chameleon-like adjustment to local systems

---

[81] Barrow, 'Rural Settlement in Central and Eastern Scotland', p. 269.

[82] W. E. Levie, 'The Scottish Davach or Dauch', *Scottish Gaelic Studies*, iii (1931), p. 100; K. H. Jackson, *The Gaelic Notes in the Book of Deer* (Cambridge, 1972), p. 116.

[83] The same point can be made by their composition. By the time we can examine them through 18th-century surveys, most davachs consisted of a cluster of touns, some having as many as 10 or more separate touns within them.

[84] McKerral, 'Ancient Denominations of Agricultural Land in Scotland', pp. 52–5.

[85] SRO, RHP2487. See also, *Registrum Episcopatus Moraviensis*, Bannatyne Club (Edinburgh, 1837), p. 433, rental dated 1565, also contains ample proof of the davach equalling four ploughs or 32 oxgates. So too, does the Huntly Lordship rental of 1600 reprinted in *The Miscellany of the Spalding Club*, vol. iv, pp. 261–319.

[86] Celtic systems seem to have been built up out of units of 20, 40, 80, 160, and 320 acres or out of 32, 64, and 128 acres. The davach of 160(80) or 96(48) can be fitted into either scheme. For further comment, see Robertson, *Historical Essays*, pp. 131–51

of measure suggests that it formed an overlay on units of measure that already existed. To see it as a food render that was converted from being levied on people or kin groups to being levied on land, a conversion adjusted to suit local systems of assessment, would accommodate the evident variation in the size of the davach. However, for reasons explored below, there may still be a place for McKerral's assumption that the larger davach was an 'expanded' version of the smaller.

A fiscal origin has also been argued for other land units of the Highlands and Islands. Writing of Orkney, for instance, J. Storer Clouston opined that 'land from ancient times was divided for the purposes of taxation into "urislands", or ouncelands, (each containing eighteen pennylands)'.[87] Further south, Lamont likewise dubbed the pennyland as 'entirely fiscal'.[88] In fact, the system was more elaborate than these bald statements would indicate. Each ounceland was subdivided into four skatlands, each made up of $4\frac{1}{2}$ pennylands in the west and 5 pennylands in the north. Skatlands were almost certainly conceived as the original basis for the payment of skat, the land tax imposed by the Norse kings and composed originally of bere or malt, butter, and fish. Both Marwick and Lamont trace it back to a Norse ship impost, with each skatland being a *leding* that was obliged to supply and support one man for a warship.[89] Their supporting argument, though, is unconvincing. A credible alternative would be to see skatlands as the basis for the levying of a wide range of obligations owed by freemen to their chief or king. The most important was probably a conventional food render, hence the composition of skat as a payment in kind and its linkage—through skat*land*—with arable. However, they probably also included an obligation to attend expeditions and hostings, an obligation which the Norse kings may have defined as a ship impost, but it would be misleading to see this as the primary meaning of skat. The closest analogy would be with the Hebridean touns that were required to sustain one of their chief's household or fighting

[87] J. Storer Clouston (ed.), *Records of the Earldom of Orkney 1299–1614*, Scottish History Soc., 2nd ser., vii (1914), p. xxxv. See also, the discussion in A. W. Johnston, 'Notes on the Fiscal Antiquities of Orkney and Shetland', *Old Lore Miscellany of Orkney, Shetland, Caithness and Sutherland*, ix, Old Lore Series, vol. xi (1933), pp. 53–63, which likewise argues a fiscal basis for land assessments in the far north.
[88] Lamont, 'The Islay Charter of 1408', pp. 177–8.
[89] Ibid., pp. 177–8; Marwick, 'Naval Defence in Norse Scotland', pp. 6–7.

men, an imposition that arose out of a system of *cuid oidche*. Of course, as these early forms of skat dissolved, it seems to have been left with the meaning of a payment made for the use of skattald, the common grazings formerly attached to skatlands.

Ouncelands and pennylands in the Hebrides are thought to have been equally charged with a fiscal meaning.[90] The former generally occurs in its Latin form, *unciata*, or else in its Gaelic form, *tirunga*.[91] In some cases, it had an equivalence to the davach, with estates having an assessment of both. Indeed, one particularly valuable charter for land in North Uist treats the tirunga and davach as one. Without any ambiguity, it refers to 'the davach called in Scotch the terung of Paible, the davach called in Scotch the terung of Pablisgerry, the davach called the terung of Balranald'.[92] They certainly helped to apportion the same obligations. The fiscal origin of the pennyland is strongly hinted at by a charter dated to before 1200 by which Reginald, the son of Somerled, 'granted to that monastery [Paisley] eight cows and two pennies for one year, and one penny in perpetuity from every house on his territories from which smoke issued'.[93] At a later date, the idea of each occupied house paying a penny as an annual due was probably transformed into one whereby each householder who paid it thereby had right to a definite amount of land, or a penny*land*'s worth. In effect, it became a form of rent, a fixed annual amount of money for a fixed amount of land. There is no explicit statement of how much land it contained, but there is a good case for seeing it as a unit of four acres (= four farthinglands). The phrase 'every house ... from which smoke issued' helps clarify the phrase 'a reeking hen' which crops up as a render in a number of sources.[94] Unlike its counterpart in the Northern Isles, the Hebridean ounceland was divided into 20 pennylands. This is stated categorically by a seventeenth-century Tiree rental.[95] What is not so clear is whether there existed between the ounceland and pennyland a unit equivalent to the

---

[90] Lamont, 'Old Land Denominations and "Old Extent" in Islay', part i, p. 191.

[91] 'Tiree Rental 1662', p. 344; *Collectanea de Rebus Albanicis*, ed. for Iona Club (Edinburgh, 1847), p. 22.

[92] *Origines Parochiales Scotiae*, vol. ii, part i, p. 374.

[93] Ibid., p. 2.

[94] See, for instance, V. Gaffney (ed.), *The Lordship of Strathavon*, Third Spalding Club (Aberdeen, 1960), Appendix, pp. 214–15.

[95] 'Tiree Rental 1662', p. 344.

skatland of the Northern Isles. Marwick thought the quarterland of Islay and Coll might have been its equivalent.[96] Doubling for the idea of skat as a due may be the term *quowart* (or *quert*) which occurs in a sixteenth-century Tiree rental.[97] It is noted down in rentals by a payment in meal and cheese over and above that paid as rent. The merkland, a unit used throughout the western Highlands and Islands, has also been charged with a fiscal meaning. As one seventeenth-century source put it, a merkland was 'so callit becaus every sic portoun off land off Old payit a merk of maill'.[98]

Apart from their variety, the other outstanding feature of land units in the western Highlands and Islands is their tendency to duplicate rather than supplement each other. Assessments in different types of land unit can be found juxtaposed for the same toun or group of touns, but they do not always give the impression of forming part of a single, graduated scale of land measurement. This is well illustrated by rentals for the region. For instance, a seventeenth-century rental for Tiree outlines the assessment of the island in terms of the tirunga, males (a grain measure), the pennyland, and the merkland. From the way in which they were equated—with a tirunga = 48 males = 20 pennylands = 6 merklands—it is difficult to see how all four could have formed part of the same graduated scale of assessment.[99] Likewise, on Skye, districts, like Trotterness can be found assessed in terms of the tirunga, davach, pennyland, and merkland, yet not in a fashion which would suggest they were all part of the same scale.[1] The same was true of Kintail and Glenelg. Thus, in 1509, James IV granted to John MacKenzie 'the 40 marklands of Keantalle, namely, the davach of Cummissaig, the davach of Letterfaern, the davach of Gleandrllr, the davach of Glemlik, the davach of Letterchall, the two davachs of Croo, and the three davachs between the Water of Keppach and the Water of Lwyng'.[2] In nearby Glenelg, the situation is more complex. In a land charter

---

[96] Marwick, 'Naval Defence in Norse Scotland', pp. 8–9.

[97] *Collectanea de Rebus Albanicis*, pp. 173–9.

[98] *Reports on the State of Certain Parishes in Scotland 1627*, Maitland Club (Edinburgh, 1835), p. 83.

[99] 'Tiree Rental 1662', p. 344.

[1] MacLeod (ed.), *Book of Dunvegan*, vol. i, pp. 3–5, 55, and 93 for merklands, davachs, ouncelands, and poundlands. Vol. ii, pp. 83–5 for pennylands.

[2] *Origines Parochiales Scotiae*, vol. ii, part ii, p. 392.

of 1334, Glenelg is described as equalling 12 davachs. A late sixteenth-century grant of its lands in life-rent to the wife of Tormot Makcloid suggests a more elaborate system. Each townships was given an assessment in both davachs and pennylands. In each case, townships were assessed as five or ten pennylands, the former being stated as a half-davach and the latter, as one davach. Yet at the end, the entire grant is said to equal 24 merklands.[3] A similar mixing of assessments occurs on Islay. Sources can be found which assess touns in quarterlands, cowlands, pennylands, and merklands.[4] Whilst these different measures must be equated in some way, it does not follow that they formed part of a single, graduated scale of measurement.

Sense of this duplication can only be made by seeing assessments in the western Highlands and Islands as fiscal in origin. It is suggested here that each of the different systems of measurement denoted a different kind of render or due, hence their side by side use and compatibility. Clues as to what they may broadly represent are given by the sources in which the different kinds of assessment were most commonly employed. For example, davachs and ouncelands tend to be cited mainly in charters of conveyance or confirmation. Merklands too, tend to occur as territorial assessments in land charters, the prime (but revealing) exception being the sequence of sixteenth-century Crown rentals for the south-west Highlands.[5] The impression given is that such assessments dealt with liabilities that were seen as incumbent on the estate (and its owner) rather than the individual toun (and its occupier). By contrast, estate rentals deal mostly in pennylands, as if these were the measure that mattered most between landowner and tenant.[6] These differences of usage may reflect no more than the differences of scale, for the pennyland was a much finer and smaller unit of measure than the davach or ounceland and was, therefore, more appropriate for measuring land at the level of the individual holding. Alternatively, they may mean that units like the davach,

[3] Ibid., p. 829; MacLeod (ed.), *Book of Dunvegan*, vol. ii, p. 69.

[4] Islay denominations are reviewed by Lamont, 'Old Land Denominations and "Old Extent" in Islay', part i, pp. 183–204 and part ii, pp. 86–207. Examples of their use can be found in Smith, *Book of Islay*, Appendix.

[5] McNeill (ed.), op. cit., pp. 622–5.

[6] Stanhope, *True Interest of Great Britain*, Table vi; MacLeod (ed.), *Book of Dunvegan*, vol. ii, pp. 79 ff.; *Collectanea de Rebus Albanicis*, pp. 1–3 and 160–79.

ounceland, or merkland were linked with dues paid by the estate holder to his superior or the King, whilst the pennyland was tied to dues paid by tenants to the estate holder. Establishing the fiscal derivation of these land measures does not answer the question of what they represented in terms of acreage. Unlike the oxgate or ploughgate, there are no official statements of how much land they were meant to contain. One way of circumventing this deficiency may be to compare those assessments which equate one land measure with another. Unfortunately, even comparing a handful of such assessments shows that the land measures involved did not necessarily have a constant relationship with each other. For instance, the seventeenth-century Tiree rental mentioned earlier specifically declared 'a Tirunga is a 6 merkland and is divydit into 48 males or 20 pennylands'.[7] By contrast, sixteenth- and seventeenth-century sources for Skye and the mainland areas opposite reveal a different and more varied relationship between the davach and merkland, though there is a hint that four merklands per davach was the rule in a number of districts.[8] As regards the pennyland, there seems more consistency, an average of 20 pennylands per davach being commonplace.[9] There are still exceptions, though, for a 1509 grant of Morvern refers to some touns as being made up of 'pennylands' and others as made up of 'great pennylands'.[10] Clearly, caution is needed before attaching particular acreages to these land measures. Like the davach, which is variously stated or implied as being 48(96) or 80(160) acres in the western Highlands and Islands,[11] the merkland and pennyland were evidently subject to differences of interpretation from one district to another. Yet too arbitrary a situation would defy explanation and run counter to the notion that they were designed to apportion tribute or dues imposed from above. Simplicity they may have lacked, but fairness and logic they must have possessed.

---

[7] 'Tiree Rental 1662', p. 344.

[8] MacLeod (ed.), *Book of Dunvegan*, vol. i, pp. 3–5, 55, and 93; *Origines Parochiales Scotiae*, vol. ii, part ii, p. 392.

[9] 'Tiree Rental 1662', p. 344; *Origines Parochiales Scotiae*, vol. ii, part ii, Appendix, p. 829.

[10] Ibid., vol. ii, part i, p. 191. See also, p. 314.

[11] A comparison between 'Tiree Rental 1662', p. 344, *Origines Parochiales Scotiae*, vol. ii, part ii, p. 829 and T. Pennant, *A Tour in Scotland and Voyage to the Hebrides* (Chester, 1774 edn.), p. 314, is sufficient to bring out this diversity.

What we need to establish in future work are the rules which governed their variation, both in relation to each other and in terms of acreage.

An important aspect of early land assessments is the question of whether they were devised according to a normative system or whether they were laid out pragmatically. This is a question which needs to be answered at two levels: the toun and the district.

Generally speaking, regularity is more easily discerned in the assessments for the north and west than for the south and east of Scotland, whether one is dealing with the district or individual toun. It requires little effort to uncover sources which list territorial assessments for the north and west of the country. Furthermore, in the case of merklands, they seem to have been part of a co-ordinated scheme. Thus, in western Scotland, quite a number of districts were assessed as either 40 or 80 merklands.[12] There are noticeably fewer district assessments in pennylands for western Scotland, but at least one source affirms that the typical cluster of pennylands (= a davach) was further aggregated into larger units of 120 pennylands.[13] As regards the davach, both Robertson and Skene saw the thanage as rated as 48 davachs, citing the 48 davachs of Huntly as a case in point.[14] This would be a plausible figure for a district assessment, if only because it would be consistent with the structure of the Irish *tuath* or Welsh *cantred* which were both subdivided into two paired units of 48 townships, plus two royal townships each, making a total of 100 townships in all.[15] With this in mind, and given the paired nature of early Pictish districts, groupings of 48 davachs would seem a reasonable assumption. Unfortunately, as already noted during the discussion of multiple estates, it has little actual support. In fact, those district assessments which have survived show no apparent uniformity whatsoever, with areas like Glenelg,

[12] MacLeod (ed.), *Book of Dunvegan*, vol. i, pp. 3–5; *Geographical Collections*, vol. i, pp. 521–2 and 532. Other levels of assessment include the 27 merklands of Moidart (*Origines Parochiales Scotiae*, vol. ii, part i, p. 202), 48 merklands of Saddell (Ibid., p. 24), and the 32 merklands of Vaternish (*Geographical Collections*, vol. i, p. 532).

[13] The clearest exposition of pennyland groupings is that offered by 'Tiree Rental 1662', p. 344. See also, the comments of Marwick, 'Naval Defence in Norse Scotland', pp. 8–9.

[14] Robertson, *Historical Essays*, p. 128.

[15] See, for instance, Jones, 'Post-Roman Wales', p. 299.

Durness, and Assynt being variously rated as 12, 10, and 4 davachs respectively.[16] Admittedly, these districts may have been grossed up into wider units of 48 davachs but, as yet, there are no grounds for asserting this. Conditions in the Northern Isles pose a different set of problems. Stiennes has proposed a grouping of ouncelands (the equivalent of the davach) into districts of 30 to 35 ouncelands,[17] but it would be truer to say that there is more agreement over the fact that each ounceland was made of only 18 pennylands in the far north.[18]

By comparison, it is much more difficult to find traces of broad territorial assessments for the south and east, let alone instances of uniformity. Despite Robertson's insistence that shires were rated at 48 ploughgates each, and his citation of examples like Coldingham in support, the evidence is insufficient for firm conclusions to be drawn. More important, the handful of territorial assessments in ploughgates that have been located, such as those for Arbuthnott and Alyth (both in Angus) contain no obvious accordance.[19] What is more, new ploughgates can be seen in the process of creation during the twelfth and thirteenth centuries.[20] Such tinkering with the local pattern of assessment hardly favours a fixed system, one laid out according to a formal plan and subject to no alteration. Unlike the Highlands and Islands, therefore, there would seem no secure grounds on which to argue for an ordered scheme of territorial assessment.

Focusing on the individual toun produces a similar conclusion. Crown rentals for the western Highlands and Islands depict a high degree of regularity between touns as regards their merkland assessments, with toun after toun in areas like the south-west Highlands being rated as either four or two and a half merklands.[21] If, as I would argue, the merkland began as a unit

[16] *Origines Parochiales Scotiae*, vol. ii, part ii, pp. 692 and 704; MacLeod (ed.), *Book of Dunvegan*, vol. i, p. 268.

[17] Stiennes, op. cit., p. 42. See also, Storer Clouston (ed.), *Records of the Earldom of Orkney*, p. xxxv; J. Storer Clouston, *The Orkney Parishes. Containing the Statistical Account of Orkney 1795–1798 (Kirkwall, 1927) p. xx*. The latter provides details of the urislands (ouncelands) and pennylands for all the parishes and townships of Orkney.

[18] Ibid., p. x; D. Balfour (ed.), *Oppressions of the Sixteenth Century in the Islands of Orkney and Zetland* (Maitland Club, Edinburgh, 1849), Appendix II, p. 111; Marwick, 'Naval Defence in Norse Scotland', p. 7.

[19] Skene, *Celtic Scotland*, vol. iii, p. 259; SRO, GD16/27/130 and GD24/1/653.

[20] Barrow (ed.), *Acts of William I*, pp. 241–2 and 303, documents examples.

[21] McNeill (ed.), op. cit., p. 277; McKerral, 'Tacksman and His Holding', pp. 13–14.

of eight acres, then it would mean that the average toun in this area comprised either 20 or 32 acres of arable land. Regularity between touns has also been argued in regard to pennyland assessments,[22] though the case is a little less convincing. However, many touns have undergone extensive fission by the time we perceive them in rentals for the early modern period. To restore the original toun structure, we may need to combine touns into groups. As long ago as 1880, F. W. L. Thomas observed how pennylands were grouped together into units of 18 in the far north and 20 in the west.[23] The variations in pennyland assessment which can be detected in the earliest rentals could be variations only within this basic framework, for touns in the far north were frequently rated as being three, six, or nine pennylands whilst those of the west were commonly rated as four or five pennylands.[24]

The question of whether touns in the south and east had a uniform pattern of assessment is a more difficult one to answer. Viewed solely in terms of ploughgates, then there is a basis for presuming a uniform rating since many early touns consisted of one, or, at most, two ploughgates. But when seen through sixteenth-, seventeenth- and eighteenth-century sources—in which they are invariably assessed in terms of oxgates, husbandlands, and merklands—their uniformity seems more elusive, though certain levels of assessment do recur.[25]

Taking an overview of the foregoing discussion, there would seem a prima-facie case for supposing that assessments in the north and west display positive signs of being a planned system, one guided by normative assumptions, whereas those of the south and east appear more pragmatically constructed. However, there is more to the problem than mere appearances. If there existed different systems of assessment, it cannot be assumed that

[22] McKerral, 'Ancient Denominations of Agricultural Land in Scotland', p. 57.

[23] Thomas, 'What is a Pennyland?', p. 277.

[24] For the former see Stanhope, *True Interest of Great Britain*, Table vi; *Origines Parochiales Scotiae*, vol. ii, part ii, Appendix, p. 829. For more random patterns of pennyland asessment at the toun level, see MacLeod (ed.), *Book of Dunvegan*, vol. ii, pp. 83–5; *Collectanea de Rebus Albanicis*, p. 1. For pennylands in Orkney, see Storer Clouston, *Orkney Parishes*, p. 1.

[25] Lists can be found in *Report on the State of Certain Parishes 1627* and R. A. Dodgshon, 'Towards an Understanding and Definition of Runrig: the Evidence for Roxburghshire and Berwickshire', *TIBG* lxiv (1975), p. 21.

they were all devised or imposed contemporaneously. At the same time, the settlement pattern to which they related was not static. Straightforward expansion in the number of settlements or the splitting of individual touns into pairs or groups of settlements could transform the symmetry of any original pattern of assessment. Bringing these points together means that order, or the lack of it, in the east and south-east could quite easily reflect the point when assessments were devised and the changes subsequently wrought by the expansion and splitting of settlements, not how they were devised. Thus, it could be argued that because they preserve more of their uniformity, merkland ratings may be younger than pennyland assessments. Of course, this much could be guessed from historical evidence, for pennylands have always been interpreted as a Norse impost, dating from before they relinquished the Hebrides in 1266.[26] The merkland, meanwhile, must date from a time after the Hebrides and Galloway became fully incorporated into the Scottish kingdom since it is found in both these areas as well as in the Lowlands. One suggestion is that its links with *Old Extent* imply a thirteenth-century origin.[27] But we need to be wary over what exactly is being dated here. Arable land, replete with its own scale of measures, most certainly pre-dated the creation of pennylands and merklands. The latter merely adopted a unit on this scale as the basis for an impost or valuation, or imposed their own scaling. The imposition of the ounceland especially made little attempt to conceal this fact. As both Marwick and Lamont made clear, its variation between the Hebrides and Northern Isles can only mean that it was adapted to pre-existing land measures.[28] Dating the first appearance of oxgates, ploughgates, and husbandlands in the east and south-east is equally problematical. Their purely agrarian character may mean that

---

[26] Storer Clouston (ed.), *Records of the Earldom of Orkney*, p. xxxv talks of pennylands existing from 'ancient times' by which he meant the early Scandinavian period. By contrast, Balfour (ed.), op. cit., Appendix II, p. 111, has provided the only note of dissent to this view with his suggestion that they were a Scottish measure introduced into the Northern Isles by the Scottish Jarl after the late 13th century.

[27] J. D. Mackie (ed.), *Thomas Thomson's Memorial on Old Extent*, Stair Soc. (Edinburgh, 1946), pp. 77–132 reviews relevant opinion on *Old Extent*. See also, Lamont, 'Old Land Denominations and "Old Extent" in Islay', part ii, p. 92, who dates it exactly to 1266 or shortly after, or during the reign of Alexander III.

[28] Marwick, 'Naval Defence in Norse Scotland', pp. 8–9; Lamont, 'The Islay Charter of 1408, pp. 172–8.

they date back to the very earliest phases of Anglian settlement in the region, though again, to state this is only to date the scheme of measurement and not necessarily the pioneer cultivation of the arable land being measured. Another factor that must be taken into account concerns the functional use made of assessments. If those of the east and south-east were of an agrarian character whilst those of the north and west were of a fiscal character, or bound up with the payment of dues and renders, then the latter were more likely to preserve their formal structure, especially as regards their extra township groupings.

Given all these problems, the only way of deciding whether assessments were imposed on an area as a planned, comprehensive system or simply pieced together randomly toun by toun is to analyse the numerical structure of the different systems of assessment. Putting aside the question of terminology, which tends to confuse rather than to clarify, two *main* systems of assessment can be identified, one based on units of eight acres and the other on units of 13 acres. Although the former is found largely in the west and the latter largely in the east and south-east, there are a number of areas where the two schemes overlap in distribution. Seen simply in terms of acreage, each appears a quite different system and might be interpreted as constituting the contribution of a separate culture. This would also imply that between such cultures, there existed some degree of discontinuity in respect of landholding, a conclusion that runs counter to that reached earlier. However, the problem is not so easily foreclosed. If inspected closely, it can be seen that these two outwardly unrelated systems were, in fact, structured in a similar fashion, their basic or elemental units of eight and 13 acres being used to build holdings and touns that were generally measured in terms of the same scale of multiples, or $4 \times$, $8 \times$, $16 \times$, etc. This could be dismissed as chance or of no importance, if it were not for two telling pieces of evidence that relate to how we interpret land measures.

The first is the tendency for the same terms of description to be used in the different systems of measurement. The most obvious example is the davach, which occurs in the north-east as made up of 13-acre units and in the west as made up of eight-acre units. Less obvious examples are available for the south-east, where land units are labelled as merklands or bovates in one source but husbandlands in another. More pointed is the evidence for Newstead in Roxburghshire. Sixteenth-century evidence reveals it as a toun assessed in terms of eight-acre units, but eighteenth-century sources show it was assessed in 13-acre units, but with no change in their over-all number. Information concerning the toun's acreage shows that the revised definition of what each unit comprised had been accommodated by an extra field of arable.[29] Given that by the seventeenth and eighteenth centuries, touns in the south-east generally consisted of a minority of eight-acre touns set amidst a majority of 13-acre ones, this raises interesting possibilities about their evolution from one to the other.[30] Needless to say, this idea of eight-acre units being expanded (by the addition of five acres) to become 13-acre units would, if applied to areas like the Highlands, help explain why measures like the davach seemingly occur in both the broad systems of land measurement under review.

The second piece of evidence concerns the tangled problem of *Old* and *New Extent*. Despite much discussion, the full meaning of *Old* and *New Extent* has not been resolved. It was undoubtedly fiscal in origin, the current view being that the terms embody an increase (*New*) that was probably imposed during the fourteenth century on the Crown's customary (*Old*) tax levy on land, the levy being a burden on land which the Crown gathered in whenever it had need of finance (i.e. during the Wars of Independence, 1286 to 1371).[31] Yet surprisingly, most reviews of the issue omit to stress that it was an *Extent*, one that was used freely in the assessment or measurement of land. Whatever its implications for the tax burden on land, to use *Old* and *New Extent* in this way is surely to imply that there was an *Old* and *New* assessment of the land associated with it. In other words, when *New Extent* replaced *Old Extent*, there probably occurred a change

---

[29] Typical of this mixing of terms is the use of merklands and husbandlands in relation to SRO, Home-Robertson MSS, Paxton, no. 279, Minits of Agreement of the heraters of paxton anent Division of the Lands, thereoff 18 and 21 Nov 1706; Berwickshire Sheriff Court MSS, Duns, Register of Decreets, Division of lands in Paxton, 26th Oct. 1752. Grant, *Social and Economic Development of Scotland*, p. 46, cites Sir John Skene as saying that the merkland and husbandland were equal in acreage.

[30] Based on J. H. Romanes, 'The Kindly Tenants of the Abbey of Melrose', *Juridical Rev.*, li (1939), pp. 201–16; Roxburghshire Sheriff Court MSS, Register of Decreets, Decreet of Division, The Runrig Lands of Newstead, 17 March and 12 May 1752; Dodgshon, 'Towards an Understanding and Definition of Runrig', p. 21.

[31] Mackie (ed.), op. cit., pp. 77–132.

in the assessment of land. This change is unlikely to have taken the form of an increase in the number of merklands (the measure invariably used in this context), otherwise there would be little purpose in subsequent charters referring so pointedly to the fact the merklands being conveyed were merklands of *New* as opposed to *Old Extent*. Under these circumstances, the change is more likely to have taken the form of an increase in the acreage of merklands.

One can only speculate on what these *Old* and *New* acreages for the merkland might have been. As noted above, merkland touns in south-east Scotland suggest that it was initially a unit of eight acres. This would link it with the merk as a measure of weight or cloth, both of which were units similarly subdivided into eight parts. To complicate matters, there are those touns which occasionally referred to their husbandlands as merklands, a slip of the tongue that would imply a merkland of 13 acres.[32] The widespread use of a 13-acre unit has always struck the writer as an obscure choice for a basic land measure. How much easier it would be if it could be explained as a revaluation of eight-acre units, adding five acres to it. Could it be that when offered reassessment by the Crown in the latter's effort to raise the tax levy on land, landholders exchanged the inspiration of the merk as a unit of weight or cloth for its inspiration as a monetary unit of 13s. 4d? As a problem, *Old* and *New Extent* are not so troublesome in eastern Scotland, because they rarely crop up in charters. It is in the west that the phrases were most widely used, and where this possible reassessment may help explain matters. To envisage an increase from eight to 13 acres is certainly capable of yielding interesting figures. At eight acres, a toun or holding of six merklands would give a davach of 48 acres, whilst one of *c.*13.4 acres would yield a davach of around 80 acres, both credible estimates. At the same time, it affords a basis for explaining why sixteenth-century Crown rentals for the south-west Highlands assess some touns in merklands and others in merks (13s. 4d, 26s. 8d, etc.). They may have been able to do so because there was an element of shared meaning between the two forms.

Considered alogether, the foregoing evidence hints at a possible line of evolution for Scottish land units which would admit their variety but not at the expense of continuity in toun

[32] McNeill, op. cit., pp. 612–14 is typical.

layout or assessment. As touns grew in size or became subject to new cultural stimuli, their over-all assessment may have remained the same, but the basic unit of assessment may have been re-defined. Given its residual character in areas like the south-east and occurrence in widely scattered areas, the earliest system was probably that based on a unit of eight acres. Tentatively, it is suggested that this may have been revised upwards in size to being a unit of 13-acres, in some touns, especially in the east and south-east of the country. It must be emphasized that this is still a largely hypothetical view. It has some support in the evidence but not enough to be conclusive. Its chief merit is that it offers a rational explanation for some of the more awkward problems posed by Scottish land units.[33]

---

[33] To avoid any confusion of meaning, the acreages cited in the foregoing section on land units have not been followed in the text by their metric equivalents. The main conversions are as follows: 4 acres (1·6 ha), 8 acres (3·2 ha), 13 acres (5·2 ha), 20 acres (8 ha), 26 acres (11 ha), 32 acres (13 ha), 48 acres (19 ha), 80 acres (32 ha), 96 acres (39 ha), 104 acres (42 ha), 160 acres (65 ha) and 416 (168 ha).

Chapter 4

Feudal Society
and Its Economy 1100–1650

The centuries immediately following the emergence of the *regnum Scotiae* are characterized in some history texts as a period when feudalism first spread into Scotland.[1] As a concept of social and economic organization, the far-reaching implications of feudalism are undeniable. Under it, all land was held of the King in return for services of a military, judicial, or civil character. The status of men was affected no less than that of land, for in acknowledging the King as their superior, they became his vassals, legally dependent on him to a greater or lesser degree. As the system evolved, it gave rise to a complex hierarchy. At the top was the King. Beneath him, were the larger territorial lords: these were usually invested with a degree of the King's power commensurate with the size of their land grant. In turn, such lords sub-enfeoffed lesser lords, knights, and freemen with land in return for their loyalty and support, though such lesser individuals could also hold directly of the King. At the grass roots of the system were the ordinary husbandmen. Some of these may have been freemen, owing no more than suit of court to a lord and perhaps some specific military services, but many were probably of bond status or servile. Not only were bondmen legally tied to a particular lord, but they were obliged to render labour services and pay a *ferme* or rent for their holdings. Their servile predicament was further elaborated by the levying of a diverse range of dues and fines, such as heriot or wergeld. The ultimate effect of feudalism was to create a system of power, patronage, and property that revolved around, and descended downwards

---

[1] See, e.g., J. D. Mackie, *A History of Scotland* (Harmondsworth, 1964), p. 45, who makes the point that 'under the sway of the House of Canmore, the Celtic monarchy evolved into an organized feudal state and in this development English influences played a great part.' G. W. S. Barrow, 'The Beginnings of Feudalism in Scotland', *Bulletin of the Institute of Historical Research* (1956), pp. 1–27 talks only of military feudalism which he tagged as an 'innovation of the twelfth century'. Idem, *The Anglo–Norman Era in Scottish History* (Oxford, 1980), now provides the most authoritative discussion of the Anglo–Norman impact in Scotland.

from, the King. In order to succeed, it sought to be all-embracing. No man without a lord was the rule of the day. Defined in these broad terms, however, feudalism as developed by David I and his successors must have had a depressing *déjà vu* about it for the ordinary husbandman. Recent work has tended more and more to stress the feudal elements already present in the tenures of early Scotland, vassalage being a reality for some even before the Scottish Kingdom had emerged.[2] Nor can we retreat behind the assumption that what was new was military feudalism or military service as a condition of tenure, for this too had its antecedents in early historic Scotland, as in the case of the Norse imposts of the Hebrides or the obligations of *feachd* and *sluagh* (expedition and hosting) rendered by landholders in the Highlands.[3] In short, the problem can no longer be construed in terms of a discrete concept that was introduced by David I and his Norman followers into a Scotland that was innocent of its meaning.

However, despite these qualifications, it would be quite wrong not to see the spread of Anglo–Norman feudalism as marking an important point of change. Prior to the twelfth century, feudalism—such as it was—fostered a network of vassalage whose extent was prescribed by the independent lordships or earldoms into which the countryside was partitioned. From the twelfth century onwards, these lordships or earldoms were progressively integrated into a single *dominium* under the Scottish King. Nor was this the only change. Because land now passed to the Scottish King and was held of him by charter, the intoduction of feudal tenure provided an opportunity for transforming the pattern of landholding in Scotland, both in terms of who actually held the land and the disposition of estates on the ground. There can be no doubt that this opportunity was taken. Out of the changes made

[2] Jones, 'Multiple Estates and Early Settlments', p. 16; idem, 'The Tribal System in Wales', pp. 111–32; D. Howells, 'The Four Exclusive Possessions of a Man', *Studia Celtica*, viii–ix (1973–4), pp. 48–67; T. M. Charles-Edwards, 'Kinship, Status and the Origin of the Hide', *Past and Present*, lvi (1972), p. 9.

[3] A summary of the sort of obligations the writer has in mind is provided by Marwick, 'Naval Defence in Norse Scotland', pp. 1–11. Initially, such military obligations—or those of expeditions and hostings—were probably part of the relationship between kinsmen and their chief and not a condition of tenure. But by the time the Celtic earldoms or Kingdoms acknowledged the Crown as the superior, they had probably been transformed into an explicit condition of tenure. For extra comment, see Howells, op. cit., pp. 47–50.

emerged some of Scotland's greatest secular lordships, like those held by the Bruces or Stewarts. As Barrow has recently written, the 'setting up of these great lordships profoundly affected, indeed may be said to have determined the feudal landscape of Scotland'.[4] Included in this process was the endowment of vast monastic lordships, a powerful force for change in any European medieval landscape. But although Anglo–Norman feudalism had a strong aristocratic basis to it, there was far more to its character or impact than the mere assumption of lordship. Barrow has also stressed the extent to which Anglo–Norman adventurers and followers—those beneath the rank of lord— were granted holdings, many carved out of the waste as fresh additions to the settlement pattern, so much so that one can regard their implantation into the Scottish countryside as a genuine landtake.[5] Since feudal rights and incidents were anchored as much to specific blocks of land as to individuals, their imposition encouraged a sharper definition of property rights which had enormous influence on how land was used and colonized. Amongst the consequences of this was an institution like infield–outfield farming, which had its roots in the stricter territorial definition of property fostered by feudalism. Finally, we must not overlook commercial feudalism or the control over early burgh foundation and trading privileges exercised by the King. All these factors were an immediate or ultimate consequence of Anglo–Norman feudalism and need to be explored.

The Spread of Feudal De Rege Scottorum

The creation of a single, more exclusive feudal system in which land was held of the Scottish King by Crown charter, and men became his vassals, was a long drawn out process rather than an instantaneous event. If it had a point of beginning, then that point was the late eleventh century, but its pace quickened noticeably under David I (1124 to 1153). David I had been educated in England and had extensive estates there. He was well acquainted, therefore, with a well-developed feudal system based on vassalage and, in particular, with the potential value of

---

[4] Barrow, *Anglo–Norman Era*, p. 64.
[5] Ibid., pp. 48–50.

military service as a prop to his regal power. In fact, he had already experienced the exercise of power in Scotland, for he had been given what was virtually the sub-kingship over part of southern Scotland by his elder brother, Alexander I (1107 to 1124). Taken together, these biographical facts help explain why he advanced the pace of feudalism so much, and why he concentrated his early efforts in the south of the country. The south-east, especially, was heavily feudalized during his reign. During the reign of his successor, Malcolm IV, feudal tenure under the Scottish Crown was extended to the western Lowlands on a large scale, with areas like Clydesdale being brought firmly under its grip.[6] It also made progress in the south-west at this point, though the extreme south-west, or Galloway, managed to preserve its Celtic independence right up until the early thirteenth century.[7] Perhaps Malcolm IV's most notable step towards the feudalization of his kingdom was the granting out of the former royal demesne areas of Fife, Angus, the Carse of Gowrie, and the Mearns by feudal tenure. This was not its first extension north of the Forth. David I had begun the task with the granting of Duffus to a Fleming called Freskin, who later adopted the family name of Moray. Since the rate of feudalization was, in part, determined by the ease with which the King's authority could be asserted, it was inevitable that Highland areas proper should resist its attractions longest, though it has rightly been said that Highland chiefs were just as much interested in the exercise of strong lordship (as opposed to mere paternalism) over their followers as the Anglo–Normans by the thirteenth century.[8]

[6] The geographical spread of feudalism *de rege Scotiae* is best described by Barrow, 'The Beginnings of Military Feudalism', pp. 279–314; idem, 'Scotland's "Norman" Families', pp. 315–36 in Barrow, *Kingdom of the Scots*, pp. 315–36; idem, *Anglo–Norman Era*, esp. pp. 30–60. Although less topographic in its analysis of landholding changes, R. L. G. Ritchie, *The Normans in Scotland* (Edinburgh, 1954), Chs 3 and 4 are still essential reading. His over-all verdict on the geography of Normanization, pp. 292–3, is that the 'appearances are that David's Normans came in considerable numbers into a country which had long been divided into well-marked properties and were accommodated with such scattered estates or pieces of land as happened to be anywhere. Waves of settlement from the South would naturally expend much of their force in Lothian, Cumbria, and Fife. But wherever there was a Royal castle or a burgh, a sheriff or an abbott, there were Norman landowners. By the end of David I's reign it cannot have been appreciably more difficult for Normans to settle in Strathearn than in Fife, or in Moray or Mar than in Angus or the Mearns.'

[7] R. C. Reid (ed.), *Wigtownshire Charters*, Scottish History Soc., 3rd ser., li (1957), pp. xiv–xvii; Barrow, 'Pattern of Lordship and Feudal Settlement in Cumbria', pp. 128–30.

[8] Idem, *Anglo–Norman Era*, p. 137.

After an early start along the southern and eastern fringes of the Highlands, feudal tenure became securely established in the central and west Highlands by the mid-thirteenth century. With the Norse evacuation of the Hebrides in 1266, this area also became part of the King's domain. However, although land was held thereafter by Crown charter, it really meant very little at first. Indeed, when Andrew Og assumed the title of 'Lord of the Isles' during the mid-fourteenth century, the whole of the Hebrides as well as large portions of the mainland opposite became incorporated into a Lordship that was effectively beyond the rule of the King. Only with the collapse of the 'Lordship of the Isles' in 1493 was the Crown's authority asserted over the region in anything other than token form. But even elsewhere, the feudal subjugation of native earldoms to the Crown proved a prolonged affair.[9]

Feudalism gave the Scottish Kings the power to radically alter the pattern of landholding. Indeed, the granting of land to lords and knights who, in return, commended themselves to him as his vassals and fighting men was essential to the Anglo–Norman feudalizing process. It was a process characterized by the establishment of Norman, Flemish, and Breton lords and their followers on fiefs throughout Scotland. They came via a preliminary base in England, mainly Northamptonshire, Yorkshire, and Sussex.[10] Displacing hostile native lords and trading their land for the military backing of Anglo–Norman knights was obviously one way in which the Scottish King ould secure control over the countryside. Many of Scotland's apparently traditional families do, in fact, have their origin in this implantation of Anglo–Norman lords and knights. Families like the Hays, Bruces, and Stewarts of the south-west and the Douglases and De Morevilles further east were all of Anglo–Norman extraction. Although the early lordships granted by the King were quite large (as with Annandale and Lauderdale), smaller fiefs became more common as the feudalizing process continued either by direct grant from the King or by sub-enfeoffment from the larger territorial barons.

[9] Idem, *Kingdom of the Scots*, pp. 374–9. For a recent essay on the Lordship of the Isles, see J. Bannerman, 'The Lordship of the Isles', pp. 209–40 in J. M. Brown (ed.), *Scottish Society in the Fifteenth Century* (London, 1977), pp. 209–40.

[10] Barrow, *Anglo–Norman Era*, p. 106.

Some of these smaller land grants involved established holdings or estates, but others, especially in Lothian proper, upper Clydesdale, Cunningham, and Strathgryfe, involved the creation of entirely new settlements. These new settlements are identifiable through their place-names, combining an Anglo–Norman personal name with the English element *tun(e)*.[11] A fine group occurs in upper Clydesdale, with examples like Lamington, Wiston, Symington, and Roberton.[12] They owe their origin to the granting out of knight's fees by Malcolm IV to Flemish adventurers. As these particular settlements show, it was not uncommon for such knight's fees to be based around a single settlement. The focal point of their power was usually the castle or stronghold built on top of a motte, a motte being a natural or artificial conical mound surrounded by a ditch. Many survive in the modern landscape, such as those of Lumphannan (Aberdeenshire) and the Mote of Urr (Galloway). A recent attempt to map their distribution has shown them to occur in most parts of Scotland outside the Highlands, with notable concentrations in the north-east, the western Lowlands, Dumfriesshire, and Kirkcudbrightshire.[13] In the latter two counties, many were possibly built by Galwegian lords and knights, but elsewhere, they were associated with Anglo–French families.

Not surprisingly, the one major region exempt from this heavy intrusion of Anglo–French families was the Highlands. Some inroads were made into the stock of native landholding around the edges of the Highlands, such as by the settlement of the Freskin family in Moray or the granting of the lordship of Garioch to Earl David, and even within the Highlands proper, such as by the implantation of the de Meyners family (later the Menzies) within the earldom of Atholl. Otherwise, one was more likely to find the native ruling stock surviving the conversion to feudal tenure. Large native earldoms, like those of Lennox, Atholl, Strathearn, Ross, and Mar, as well as the purely Lowland earldom of Fife, all continued in native hands during the transition to feudal tenure, though there was a break of

[11] Ibid., pp. 35–7 provides list and comment on these *new* settlements.
[12] Reid, op. cit., p. xv.
[13] G. C. Simpson and B. Webster, 'Charter Evidence and the Distribution of Mottes in Scotland', *Chateau Gaillard*, v (1970), pp. 16. See also, G. Stell 'Mottes', pp. 28–9 and 128 in McNeill and Nicholson (eds.), op. cit., p. 128.

occupation in one or two cases. In the western Highlands and Islands, the larger clans like the mac Dougalls of north-west Argyll or the mac Donalds of Islay also managed to maintain their landholding during these critical centuries of change. It was of course not only in the Highlands and Islands, or in Fife, that native Celtic lords survived feudalization. Continuity was also to be found in Galloway.[14]

If feudalization under the Scottish Crown involved changes in the landowning structure of major portions of the countryside, did it also lead to a re-drawing of the layout of estates? The accepted assumption has long been that it did, with large estates being created in sensitive areas, like the Borders or along the edge of the Highlands, and smaller estates elsewhere. However, Barrow has now put forward persuasive reasons for believing otherwise. If we survey the broad layout of fiefs in southern Scotland, a distinction will be evident between the south-east and south-west. The former is dominated by small estates consisting of either single settlements, or of a small number of tenements scattered over two or more townships. The latter, meanwhile, was characterized by large, compact fiefs, often with strongly marked natural boundaries such as river valleys and watersheds. More important, these large fiefs appear to coincide with territorial units or *partes* that were granted out by the Scottish Crown without dismemberment.[15]

Feudalism was not a static, unchanging concept. As its circumstances altered, so too did its character. The first significant change was the decline of military feudalism during the reigns of the two Alexanders in the mid-thirteenth century, at least in the Lowlands. In the Highlands, and probably in the Borders, its decline was not so precipitous. Some tenants continued to be under an obligation to provide their clan chief

[14] The most authoritative discussion of this aspect is Barrow, *Kingdom of the Scots*, pp. 374–9 and 328–9; idem, *Anglo-Norman Era*, pp. 61–90.

[15] Idem 'Pattern of Lordship and Feudal Settlement in Cumbria', p. 130. After saying that Galloway, Carrick, and part of Nithsdale remained 'stubbornly unfeudalized', Barrow wrote that change was more rapid in the areas to the east and north. 'David of Scotland seems to have surveyed his great Lordship or principality from the east to the west selecting now this ancient district, now that, to grant one or other of his closest followers to hold as military fiefs. In the east, in the Merse, Teviotdale, and Lothian, the new fiefs were usually single manors, villages or even smaller estates, sometimes made up of tenements dispersed across several miles of country, such as the Whittons, half Chatto and Lilliesleaf granted to Walter of Ryedale', p. 130.

with military support throughout the medieval period, and even beyond. With a frankness that impresses even for the times, Sir Duncan Campbell of Glenorchy granted a lease in 1588 to Donal and Dougall McCarlich for lands in Lorn and bound them to commit slaughter on the Clan Gregor 'till he should be fully satisfied with their diligence in the matter'.[16] On some estates, however, a sharp distinction was drawn between who was to labour the ground and who was to take up arms. The late sixteenth-century reference to Islay that was quoted in the previous chapter bears this out. So too does the comment from the same report to the effect that MacLeod of Lewis could 'raise on this pairt of the Ile callit Lewis 700 men with Rona, by thame that laboured the Ground, of quhilkis nane are chairgit or permittit to gang to ony hoisting or weiris in all the haill Iles, but are commandit to remane at hame to labour the ground'.[17]

Serfdom too, seems to have started its decline early, disappearing completely by the fourteenth century.[18] The significance to be attached to its early disappearance depends on how one chooses to define feudalism. If defined largely in terms of vassalage, a vassalage in which serfdom was of the very essence, then the disappearance of the one signals the disappearance of the other. However, feudalism has also been charged with a much fuller meaning, one that instates it as a mode of production in which the surplus labour of tenants was abstracted through labour services and rents in kind. Seen in the context of this broader definition, serfdom serves as a means of peasant coercion, but it hardly strips feudalism of its essential relationships.

More important, once we focus on these essential relationships, then feudalism must be accepted as a far more durable institution in Scotland than has hitherto been conceded. In fact, both labour services (sowing, ploughing, harvesting, and carriages) and rent in kind (grain, stock, poultry, fish, or cloth) continued to form the basis of landlord–tenant relationships in many areas throughout

---

[16] *Origines Parochiales Scotiae*, vol. ii, p. 145.

[17] Skene, *Celtic Scotland*, vol. iii, Appendix, p. 439.

[18] T. C. Smout, *A History of the Scottish People 1560–1830* (London, 1969), provides a good summary, pp. 39–40, concluding that serfdom 'died a quiet death in the fourteenth century'. A clear statement of the view that the continuance of servile obligations and heritable jurisdictions (both of which continued in Scotland until the 18th century) were just as feudal when stripped of personal bondage or serfdom can be found in J. Blum, *The End of the Old Order in Rural Europe* (Princeton, 1978), pp. 33–4.

the late medieval period. Two examples of their survival can be given. The first is from a particularly fine rental compiled in 1600 for the Huntly Lordship. In it, the toun of Belliehill, like many others, is entered as paying 'maill, ferme, custom and claith'.[19] After specifying the nature and amount of produce to be paid annually, it bound the tenants to perform 'seruice, areadge, caraidge, wsitt and wount'. The second is from the *Register* of Coupar Abbey in which are transcribed numerous fifteenth- and sixteenth-century tacks. Typical of those recorded is one for a quarter of Balbrogy issued in 1472 which required annually from the tenant not only a small amount of money, but also, 'nine hens, 5 bolls of horse corn, 8 bolls of barley and meal, and he shall dig 25 loads of peats, and shall lead 12 loads to the monastery, with one draught in each year for lead, tiles or timber if required'.[20] As will be argued in Chapters 7 and 8, such rents and services even persisted into the early modern period on a significant scale. This is not to say that there are no examples of commutation from as early as the thirteenth century onwards, only that they do not appear to predominate until as late as the sixteenth and seventeenth centuries.

It goes without saying that a systematic study of the whole process of commutation is urgently needed. In anticipation of such a study, the pattern that may be found could turn out to be quite the reverse of expectations. Given that the conversion to money rents drew tenants into a market or transactive economy in order to meet their newly defined obligations, it is the sort of change that 'progressive' arable areas might be expected to pass through first. In fact, the opposite may prove to be the case. Perhaps because they yielded a higher rent in their unconverted form, the more fertile arable areas appear to have responded sluggishly to commutation. More to the point, it is striking how rents in marginal or peripheral areas like the Hebrides or the Northern Isles had undergone a substantial degree of commutation by the sixteenth century. In the case of Morvern and Kintyre, the actual process is documented by a note accompanying a 1541 rental. It records how 'all the marts,

---

[19] *Miscellany of the Spalding Club*, vol. iv, pp. 261–319.
[20] C. Rogers (ed.), *Rental Book of the Cistercian Abbey of Cupar Angus* (London, 1880), vol. ii, p. 207.

cheese, and mail are sold for silver to the tenants of the ground'.[21] Previously, they had been carted across Scotland to Stirling. Commutation, even from Crown tenants, was not always so easy. A sixteenth-century petititon by chiefs in the Western Isles who owed mail and duty to the King lamented that they were 'unable to pay his Majesty's duties of these lands, by reason of the Proclamation Prohibition made within the bounds of Argyll that no merchants or others shall buy any marts, horse or other goods within the West Isles; the said Islemen having no other means of possibility to pay his Majesty's duties but by the sale of their marts and horses'.[22] The reason for this precocious development of peripheral areas possibly lies in the problems of distance and transport. Indeed, even within the confines of a Lowland estate, distance could be an influential factor in the progress of commutation. A diary kept by Patrick, first Earl of Strathmore during the mid-seventeenth century explained away the mixture of money and produce received as rent for touns in the Barony of Tannadyce (Angus) with the words that 'lands lyeing at a greater distance' were 'all converted into money'.[23]

So long as men were regarded as bond tenants or serfs, then they were tied both to their lord and their holdings. Moreover, since it was a hereditary condition, their descendants were equally tied by virtue of 'kin and descent'.[24] As serfdom faded, so also must have the hereditary ties to land. Personal freedom was gained, but at the expense of the peasant's standing on the land. The exact means by which the change took place lies concealed, but the tenants disclosed by rentals and the like dating from the fourteenth, fifteenth, and sixteenth centuries all held land by tack or were tenants at will. Generally speaking, tacks were for relatively short periods of between one and five years, longer agreements being more the exception than the rule. For example, a rental of 1376 for the great Honour of Morton, an estate with property in Midlothian and Dumfriesshire, shows the bulk of its

[21] G. P. M'Neill (ed.), *The Exchequer Rolls of Scotland XVII A.D. 1537–1542* (Edinburgh, 1897), p. 646.

[22] *Collectanea de Rebus Albanicis*, p. 153.

[23] A. Millar (ed.), *The Glamis Book of Record. A Diary Written by Patrick Earl of Strathmore 1648–1689*, Scottish History Soc., ix (1890), p. 48.

[24] See comments of I. F. Grant, *Social and Economic Development of Scotland* (Edinburgh, 1930), p. 75.

tenants held on a year to year basis. The remainder had tacks lasting no longer than five years.[25] On the Coupar Abbey estates, there are signs of a long-term shift in the duration of tacks. Those for the fifteenth century were mostly for five years or less,[26] but those dating from the opening decades of the sixteenth century contain quite a number issued for life.[27] Even so, the conclusion must be that the majority of Lowland tenants generally occupied their holdings precariously rather than securely, with frequent reviews of tenure. In the Highlands, any literal reading of the evidence is clouded over by the intervention of a tacksman between landlord and tenant, reducing the position of the latter to a sub-tenant. Observations on the broad mass of tenures tend to highlight their ephemeral nature, as with the late sixteenth-century comment on Lismore which noted its landholding as 'every year altered or set'.[28] However, the rentals for the region do reveal that tenants could hold land by tack and that, in some cases, quite lengthy tacks were involved.[29] What proportion of these long sets were to tacksmen rather than to the peasants who actually laboured the soil cannot be gauged without a more demanding analysis of the sources. But certainly, we must keep an open mind on the possibility that tacksmen and sub-tenant enjoyed differing degrees of security.

An important qualification to the foregoing discussion is kindly tenure. The exact meaning of kindly tenure remains elusive. It is likely that it did not have a fixed or stable meaning, but varied over time and according to local custom. Whatever its variations, however, its basic implications were more or less the same. Tenants who held by kindly tenure were conceded the right to the unhindered occupation of their holding and the right to pass it on to an heir. Although they are sometimes referred to as kindly in rentals, the basis of their rights are never specified.[30]

---

[25] *Registrum Honoris de Morton*, Bannatyne Club (Edinburgh, 1853), pp. xlvii ff.

[26] Rogers (ed.), op. cit., vol. i, pp. 118–252.

[27] Ibid., vol. ii, pp. 146–57. Grant, *Social and Economic Development of Scotland before 1603*, pp. 253–4 also provides a full discussion of early tacks.

[28] Skene, *Celtic Scotland*, vol. iii, Appendix III, p. 435.

[29] A convenient source of tack length is M'Neill (ed.), *Exchequer Rolls 1537–1542*, pp. 612–45. It may be significant that many Highland rentals do not record tack length. See Smith, *Book of Islay*, Appendix, pp. 484–5; *Black Book of Taymouth*, Bannatyne Club (Edinburgh, 1855), rental 1582.

[30] The best discussion is still Grant, *Social and Economic Development of Scotland before 1603*, pp. 248–52. On p. 249, she talks of kindly tenants having 'strong moral if not legal

Hence the assumption by scholars that such tenure was founded on kindness, a tacit acknowledgement by landowners that where a family had long associations with a particular holding (three generations +) then they had a *de facto* if not a *de jure* right to continue in possession. The term even crept into an Act of Parliament,[31] but was never an unassailable right. Its silent disappearance is proof of this.[32] Its importance depends on how its origins are interpreted. For some, it represents a Lowland phenomenon that developed on a limited scale over the fifteenth and sixteenth centuries, mainly on Church properties.[33] As to the reason why, one is left with the impression that it was gesture of good will.[34] Alternatively, there is the possibility that it represents the decayed outlines of a once more tangible set of rights, rights that had once been more substantial and widespread than late medieval or early modern sources suggest.[35] The references to it in the Highlands, a neglected dimension to the problem, may ultimately prove a fruitful avenue of inquiry here. (See pp. 109–10.)

A more durable form of hereditary tenure which developed during the late medieval period was that of feuing. A feu was a lease of land in perpetuity in return for a fixed annual rent. As a tenure, it existed on Church lands as early as the twelfth century. After spreading slowly at first, the volume of feuing began to increase sharply in the fifteenth century. This expansion was encouraged, but not initiated by, an Act of Parliament passed in

---

claims'. She treats so-called rentallers and kindly tenants as the same. An interesting attempt to define the rights of a kindly tenant occurs in *Hope's Major Practicks 1608–1633*, ed. by J. A. Clyde. Stair Soc. (Edinburgh, 1837), vol. i, p. 232.

[31] *APS* iii, p. 351.

[32] The way it acquired a curiosity status in modern times is a sign of this quiet disappearance. See, A. Geddes, 'The Four Royal Towns of Lochmaben. A Study of Rural Stability', *TDGNHAS* xxxix (1954), pp. 83–101; John Lord Carmont, 'The King's Kindlie Tenants of Lochmaben', *Juridical Rev.* (1910), pp. 323–37.

[33] Discussions, such as Grant, *Social and Economic Development of Scotland before 1603*, pp. 248–52, certainly rest on the kindly tenures to be found on Church lands when one gets back to the 16th century, but this may reflect the greater abundance of material for such estates.

[34] Ibid., p. 249.

[35] Such a view is expressed by I. R. Shearer (ed.), *Selected Cases from Acta Dominorum Concilli et Sessionis 1532–1533*, Stair Soc. (Edinburgh, 1951), p. 128, editor's notes. Shearer defines kindly tenants as 'hereditary *native* landholders possessing their lands by virtue of the old rights of their family'.

1457/8.[36] Over the following century or so, the practice spread rapidly affecting not just Church lands, but also, Crown and lay estates. The Act of 1457/8 spoke of its value in giving would-be improvers absolute security to tenure and therefore guarantees over any investment. For those who feued out property, such as the abbeys, it provided a means of raising capital which, in the short term, was in excess of what could be generated by a normal fixed-term lease.[37] However, over time, it proved to be destructive of their interests; monetary inflation made sure of this. To whom was land feued? It has been argued that the vast extension of feuing during the fifteenth and sixteenth centuries, passed over the heads of sitting tenants and conveyed land to outsiders: thus, the process is conceived as one of disruption for the existing pattern of landholders. Fortunately, this facet of feuing has received closer scrutiny in a recent study.[38] It was shown that out of a large sample of feus granted by the great abbeys, as many as 63 per cent of all recipients were already established tenants on the holdings being feued. The proportion of land being feued to existing tenants was especially high in the cases of Paisley and Scone Abbeys. The former feued 80 per cent out of a total sample of 149 feus to existing tenants, whilst the latter feued 77 per cent out of a total sample of 116 feus. The significance of feuing as a point of discontinuity in landholding, therefore, would seem to have been exaggerated in the past.

The significance of feuing in other directions, though, cannot be overstated. By giving security of tenure, it greatly encouraged the embellishment and improvement of property. The parishes around Glasgow affected by the feuing of the Bishopric lands in the mid-sixteenth century were the very same parishes which late seventeenth-century descriptions represent as containing numerous mansions set down in well-enclosed and well-wooded policies.[39] Such a landscape would not have developed before the eighteenth century if it had not been for the early existence in

---

[36] *APS* ii, p. 49.

[37] An Act of Parliament (*APS* ii, p. 376) talks of feuing of Crown lands being 'to the grett proffitt of his croun'. Seeing it in the long term, Duncan, *Scotland: the Making of the Kindgom*, pp. 410–11 described it as a 'dissipation of resources' given the depreciation of the currency.

[38] M. H. B. Sanderson, 'The Feuars of Kirklands', *SHR* lii (1973), pp. 117–86.

[39] *Descriptions of the Sheriffdoms of Lanark and Renfrew*, compiled in 1710 by William Hamilton of Wishaw, Maitland Club (Glasgow, 1831), pp. 28 and 29–30.

these parishes of large feus. Contemporaries appreciated this relationship between the two. A description of the Barony parish of Glasgow encircling the burgh, noted how since 'the fewing of this parish, it is exceedingly improven by the several heritors' and then went on to describe the new mansions, tastefully planted gardens, and well-laid enclosures which had appeared.[40] The building of substantial farmsteads and mansions also followed the feuing out of Ettrick Forest by the Crown from the early sixteenth century onwards. In fact, it has been argued that Selkirkshire had few durable buildings until feuing provided the incentive.[41] A similar consequence to feuing has been documented for Strathisla in Moray by M. H. B. Sanderson. Holdings and townships in the Baronies of Strathisla and Kinloss, such as Millegan, Kinminit-rie, Balnamoon, Fortray, Crannach, and Auchinhove, were feued out by Kinloss Abbey during the mid-sixteenth century. Not long after, the larger feus had acquired tower houses and their occupiers, the pretensions of bonnet lairds. Their family aspirations though, were relatively short-lived, for by the end of the seventeenth century, the Strath had fallen into the hands of Alexander Duff of Braco.[42]

Feuing had a hand in the preservation of some very large runrig townships. These particular touns were no doubt already large before they were feued. However, the fact that they were feued conferred a stability on their appearances which makes them stand out when we view them later in the changing conditions of the seventeenth and eighteenth centuries. In fact, many of the runrig touns that were underpinned by feu tenure were only eventually removed by legal process. Good examples were to be found in the Tweed valley and the Merse (i.e. Newstead, Blainslie, Darnick, Gattonside, Eildon, Lessuden, Chirnside, and Coldingham), having been feued out by such abbeys as Melrose and Coldingham Priory.[43] A like cluster, including examples like Caputh, Dulgarthill, Furgarth, and Dowally, existed in the Tay valley, feued out as runrig touns by

---

[40] Ibid., pp. 29–30.

[41] RCAM, Scotland, *Selkirkshire*, p. 23.

[42] Sanderson, op. cit., p. 134; See also, M. H. B. Sanderson, 'The Feuing of Strathisla: A Study in Sixteenth Century Social History', *Northern Scotland*, ii (1974–5), pp. 1–11.

[43] The general character of these touns is discussed in Dodgshon, 'Towards an Understanding and Definition of Runrig', pp. 19–25.

the Bishop of Dunkeld.[44] The complex landholding situations which it perpetuated in the landscape are captured by their original feu charter. Coupar Abbey, for instance, not only feued large holdings *en bloc*, like Glentullacht and Auchindory, but also granted feus of smaller runrig fractions such as the 'fourth part of the lands of the eastern portion of the town of Balbrogy'.[45] Similarly, amongst the feus given out by Scone Abbey are examples like the 'quarter of the landis callit the fourth rynrig of the Sandyhill' near Balquhormok (Perthshire), feued in 1585.[46]

The Clan System and Landholding

The earlier résumé of how Celtic earldoms in the Highlands and Islands were converted into fiefs held directly of the Scottish King stressed that such tenures spread into the region slowly. Large areas, including the Lordship of the Isles, retained a high degree of autonomy until virtually the end of the fifteenth century. Furthermore, even after Crown feudalism had spread into the region, it did not have quite the same impact as on Lowland estates. The critical factor was not so much the newly struck relationship between the major landholders and the King—which undoubtedly constituted a major change—but the relationship between these landholders and their under-tenants, for it is through this half-hidden relationship that the great mass of Highland tenures were articulated. Although our understanding of events and trends at this level is decidedly inadequate, it has been argued that tenures at this lower level were regulated by a *Landrecht* quite different from feudalism, a *Landrecht* that reflected the nature of contemporary Highland society with its ordering of relationships on the basis of kinship and clanship. In an elaboration of this idea, A. Cunningham argued that the imposition of feudal tenures by the Scottish King created a conflict between the two tenures, a conflict which ultimately flowered into Highland support for Jacobitism.[47] Her attempt to distinguish so sharply between the two, however, finds less support in recent studies. As explained earlier, the tribal tenures

[44] Sanderson, 'Feuars of Kirklands', p. 128.
[45] Rogers (ed.), op. cit., vol. ii, p. 166.
[46] *Liber de Scon Liber Eccleise de Scon*, Bannatyne Club (Edinburgh, 1843), Appendix III.
[47] A. Cunningham, *The Loyal Clans* (Cambridge, 1932), pp. 17–18.

of early historic Scotland also involved lord–vassal relationships and military service as conditions of tenure, principles that were feudal by any definition. This is what W. C. Dickinson probably had in mind when he saw the growing Jacobitism of the Highlands as a reaction not against feudal tenure *per se*, but against the replacement of feudal tenure under the Earls by feudal tenure *de rege Scottorum*.[48] But whilst admitting that the web of tenurial relationships in the region were partially woven out of feudal strands, even before the twelfth century, it must also be conceded that its real strength was derived from the strands of kinship. No discussion of late medieval tenures in the Highlands would be complete, therefore, without some consideration of kinship and clanship.

It has been argued that as the tribal structure of Highland society began to break down over the twelfth century, the clan groups into which such tribes were segmented came into greater prominence as the dominant social and political units of the region.[49] Clans were large, cognatic groups which traced their descent through the male line from a distant eponymous ancestor. They were usually divided into septs or branches that were known as a *sliochd* or *clann*. The former represented maximal lineages, tracing their descent back ten or twelve generations, whilst the latter were minimal lineages of shallower depth traceable back only four or five generations. According to R. G. Fox, the larger clans were ' "clans of recognition" because they performed primarily ideological rather than behavioural functions'.[50] However, as we focus on the *sliochdan* within the larger clans, or even on the smaller clans, their behavioural functions come more to the fore. These behavioural functions were

---

[48] W. C. Dickinson (ed.), *The Court Book of the Barony of Carnwath 1523–1542*, Scottish History Soc., xxix (1937), p. xvii, fn. 4.

[49] An early statement of this view can be found in Skene, *Celtic Scotland*, vol. iii, p. 287. During a discussion of the *fine* or clan, he argued that 'when by marriage or otherwise, the earldoms passed into foreign hands, the Gaelic population became the subjects of a foreign overlord, the greater tribe became broken up, and they emerged from it in the form of clans or broken tribes'. See also, I. F. Grant, *Highland Folk Ways* (London, 1961), p. 23. In contrast to this traditional view, R. G. Fox has preferred to stress a more diverse social background for clans, see R. G. Fox, 'Lineage Cells and Regional Definition in Complex Societies', pp. 95–121 in C. A. Smith (ed.), *Regional Analysis. vol. ii. Social Systems* (New York, 1976), p. 102.

[50] Ibid., p. 104.

especially important in relation to land. They expressed themselves in two ways.

(*a*) *Territoriality*. First, there was a tendency for clans to map
themselves into landholding by acquiring a dominant control
over a particular area of territory. This territorial expression was
an intrinsic part of their character. A sixteenth-century Act
talked of clans being bound together by 'pretense of blude or
place of thare duelling'.[51] Indeed, the rise and fall of clans can be
measured in terms of their territorial expansion and contraction.
One without land was a 'broken clan' just as a man without a
clan was a 'broken man'. The history of the Highlands affords
numerous illustrations of this changing association between clans
and their territories. On a macro-scale, it underlies the decline of
major clans like the Macdougalls after 1300, or the rise of those
like the Campbells and Mackenzies from the fifteenth century
onwards. At a micro-scale, it is chronicled by those lesser clans
which appear and then disappear from the historical record,
presumably through their failure to survive as landholders.[52]

Territorial control over an area was accomplished in a variety
of ways. An obvious means was the acquisition of land from
dispossessed or outlawed clans by Crown charter. The Mackenzies, for example, profited in this manner from the forfeiture of
the earldom of Ross in 1476 and the Lordship of the Isles in 1493,
building up a clan territory that projected far beyond their native
Kintail, with extensive properties in areas like Easter Ross and on
Lewis.[53] Documenting these windfalls, however, is only half of
the problem. Equally crucial is the process by which clansmen
were infiltrated into the landholding structure of such new
territories. Speaking generally, the procedure followed was for
major portions of such land to be given out as sub-tenancies to
chiefs or captains of the major cadet branches of the clan, or its
sliochdan. These sub-tenancies were then broken up further
between the senior members or families of the *sliochdan*. Beneath

---

[51] *APS* iv, p. 40.

[52] Further comment on changing geography of clans can be found in Barrow, 'The
Highlands in the lifetime of Robert the Bruce', pp. 362–83 in Barrow, *Kingdom of the Scots*;
Bannerman, 'Lordship of the Isles', esp. pp. 217–18.

[53] The ultimate extent of the Mackenzie property is revealed in a 1718 rental
reproduced in *Report to the Secretary for Scotland by the Crofters Commission on the Social Condition
of the People of Lewis in 1901, as Compared with Twenty Years Ago* (Glasgow, 1902), Appendix
o.

them, were to be found others related to varying degrees of kinship, but as the Gartmore manuscript phrases it, as 'the propinquity removes, they become less considered'.[54] Control over an area could also be gained by tactical marriages. Thus, the expanding domain of the Frasers of Lovat over the thirteenth, fourteenth, and early fifteenth centuries has been ascribed as 'primarily due to a sequence of carefully planned marriages'.[55] A systematic analysis of marriage patterns in both the Highlands and Lowlands from 1500 to 1700, by I. Carter helps to emphasize this functional role of marriage. In the Highlands, his review of marriage patterns amongst the senior families of the Macdonalds and Mackenzies suggested a high degree of territorial endogamy, a preference for marrying locally within the Highlands in order to further or buttress their political and territorial ambitions.[56] Another vital mechanism by which clans acquired new territories and new members was by the overtly feudal means of manrent or bondrent. Smaller families of clans commended themselves to a larger, more powerful clan, seeking its protection in return for their political and military backing. In some cases, such client groups even adopted the name of the foster clan.[57] The formal manifestations of the custom can be traced through bonds of manrent or contracts of friendship. Typical of the former is the bond of manrent between Malcolm McDonchie VcIntyre VcCoshen and Ronald Campbell of Barrichibyan in 1612, by which the said Malcolm bound himself 'and all others to be descended of my body to be loyal, true and of old native men in all lowliness and subjection to the said Ranald and his heirs male for ever'.[58] Often, the subjection of such families was marked by the payment of *calpe*.[59] Judged harshly, *calpe* was a form of

---

[54] Cited in Skene, *Celtic Scotland*, vol. iii, p. 318.

[55] C. Fraser, The Clan Fraser of Lovat, (Edinburgh, 1966 edn.), p. 19.

[56] I. Carter, 'Marriage Patterns and Social Sectors in Scotland before the Eighteenth Century', *SS* xvii (1973), pp. 55–7.

[57] *The Highlands of Scotland* in 1750, intro. by A. Lang (Edinburgh, 1898), p. 39, observed that the 'Common Inhabitants of Lewis are Morisons, McAulays, and McKivers but when they go from Home they all who live under Seaforth call themselves McKenzies'. Grant, *Social and Economic Development of Scotland Before 1603*, p. 501 remarks that a document of 1537 lists 59 inhabitants in Duthil parish, none of whom were Grants. By 1569, a list for the parish provided 43 Grants. She cited this information in a discussion on the growth of the Clan Grant, whose growth she described as an 'example of the rapid manufacture of a clan', ibid., p. 501.

[58] *Collectanea de Rebus Albanicis*, p. 206.

[59] An early reference to it occurs in M. Martin, *A Description of the Western Islands of*

protection money, but it could equally well be seen as a means of placing such families on the same footing as the kinsmen of the chief to whom they laid calpe by making them liable for a regular due or render. Illustrating the second form of agreement is the mutual bond of friendship between Kenneth McKenzie and Lachlan McIntosche of Dunachton in 1597 by which they promised that 'they and their kin and friends shall assist each other in all their honest and lawful concerns'.[60] Such agreements lend credence to the view that the 'clan system in general cultivated people, not crops'.[61]

An excellent study of how a small clan grew in size, acquiring in the process a specific association with a definite territory, is provided by A. G. Macpherson's analysis of how the clan Macpherson established itself in the Badenoch area of Inverness-shire. The clan first emerged out of what he calls 'the embers of the old Clanchattan tribe'.[62] The clan traced its descent from an eponymous ancestor who lived during the early fourteenth century. Following his death around 1350, his three sons formed the basis of the *sliochdan* that comprises the clan. Over the period from 1350 to 1700, each *sliochd* managed to entrench itself in a specific part of Badenoch. Thus, *Sliochd Iain* established itself quickly in Pitmean, Bealid, and Garvamore, and from these key pioneer touns spreads outwards into surrounding settlement. The *locus* of *Sliochd Choinnich* was in Cluny township. That of *Sliochd Ghill-Iosa* centred on touns south of the Spey, such as Caraldie, Etterish, Phoness, and Killyhuntly. This gradual mapping of the clan's kin structure into the landholding pattern of Badenoch was achieved by a combination of marriage and successful cattle dealing. By no means unusual is the fact that this growth was entirely at the purely tenant level, most of their property being

Scotland 1699 (London, 1716 edn.), p. 115. A duty payable by tenants, he wrote, to 'their Chief tho they did not live upon his Lands; and this is call'd Calpich: there was a standing Law for it also, call'd *Calpick-Law*: and I am inform'd that this is exacted by some in the main Land to this day.' *Hope's Major Practicks*, vol. i, p. 271 defines it as 'a gift which any other man not a tenant gives to the head and chief of a clan for his maintenance and protection'. Instances of *calpe* being paid by agreement can be seen in *Collectanea de Rebus Albanicis*, p. 197; Grant, *Social and Economic Development of Scotland Before 1603*, pp. 501–5.

[60] H. Paton (ed.), *The Mackintosh Muniments 1442–1820* (Edinburgh, 1903), p. 52.

[61] Fox, op. cit., p. 113.

[62] A. G. Macpherson, 'An Old Highland Geneaology and the Evolution of a Scottish Clan', *SS* x (1966), p. 9.

leased from landholders like the Earls of Moray and Huntly and the laird of Grant.

The territorial extent of a clan could shrink for reasons almost the reverse of those just mentioned. Marriage could take land away from a clan as well as partners.[63] Forfeitures too, could decimate its territory overnight.[64] Tacksmen belonging to a stronger clan could oust those of a weaker clan, and then communicate its fondness of kin to the lower levels of the landholding hierarchy.[65] It was also possible for large clans to break up or segment into smaller ones, as their branches obtained written charters independently from the King, thereby establishing themselves independently of their parent clan.[66]

(*b*) *Tenure*. The second means by which the behavioural functions of the clan system expressed themselves in relation to land was through tenure. This is far from being an easy problem to discuss, for it concerns matters that are scarcely adumbrated in early sources, let alone treated in any substantive manner. It is phrased here in terms of a single theme, and that is, did the so-called tribal tenure with which scholars have typified the early historic period, survive in any form into the latter part of the medieval period, imprinting its values on the relationship between clan groups and their property holdings? Reduced to essentials, the central feature of tribal tenure was the hereditary occupation of land by groups of kin rather than individuals, the latter only holding land through their membership of the former.[67]

Taking the question of hereditary tenure first, this is one area

[63] For instance, the land held by the Mackay of Ugadale in Kintyre passed through marriage via an heiress into the MacNeils. See Grant, *Social and Economic Development of Scotland Before 1603*, pp. 491–2.

[64] Ibid., p. 488 provides a table listing those properties forfeited when the Lordship of the Isles broke up in the 15th century, such as that held by the different branches of the Macleans in Mull, Tiree, Islay, Jura, Scarba, Morven, Lochaber, Knapdale, Glencoe, and Ardgour.

[65] The MacIans of Ardnamurchan, for instance, were gradually ousted by the Campbells, once the Earl of Argyll had acquired the superiority through forfeiture and planted his own tacksmen there. The Macleans on Mull were replaced in a similar way.

[66] Fox, op. cit., p. 106 offers the example of the Macdonalds of Sleat. A relatively minor branch of the Macdonalds, their rise to prominence over the 17th century followed the acquisition of a Crown charter for their property.

[67] Discussion of tribal tenure amongst the Celts is provided by P. Vinogradoff, *Outline of Historical Jurisprudence* (Oxford, 1920), vol. i, pp. 321–43; W. E. Levie, 'Celtic Tribal Law and Custom in Scotland', *Juridical Rev.*, xxxix (1927), pp. 191–208.

of the problem in which we must tread cautiously. Taken at face value, the available evidence suggests that the typical clansman held his land either by temporary tacks or at will. However, it may be misleading to read too literally from early sources. What cannot be gleaned from tacks and rentals, but what is certainly conveyed by more discursive kinds of evidence, is the vaguely defined notion of *duthchas*. Individuals or families were said to have the *duthchas* of a particular holding or toun.[68] Although rarely defined with precision, it means that they possessed the right to its hereditary occupation. The impression given is that whilst it had no force in law, it nevertheless had the force of custom behind it. Whether this distinction between law and custom could always be drawn is difficult to decide, but either we admit the very real possibility that the Highlander once possessed kin-based hereditary tenures comparable to those disclosed by the Irish and Welsh law codes, of which *duthchas* may be a hollow survival, or we face the stiffer task of explaining why not. Offering more potential for analysis are references to individuals and their heirs having the 'right and kindness' of a toun, or the right to their 'kindlie habitatiounes towmes and possessions'.[69] The obvious analogy here is with the kindly tenure of Lowland Scotland. Like the latter, such phrases embody the claim which a person had to a holding by virtue of his family's having possessed it for at least three generations.[70] Stated in this form its meaning can raise few objections. Far more contentious is the unavoidable question of why such tenures were thought to be 'kindly'. Was it because of the tolerance and kindness of the feudal superior? Alternatively, does it embody a somewhat diluted kin-based right to land? After all, it was a term being used freely in a kin-based society. There again, its meaning may be deliberately hybridized. Clan chiefs may have introduced an intended play on words when asserting their superiority over land, conveniently replacing kinliness with kindliness.

Before trying to examine the question of whether land was held

[68] Macpherson, 'Old Highland Genealogy', pp. 12–13; *Burt's Letters from the North of Scotland*, intro. by R. Jamieson (London, 1876 edn.), vol. ii, p. 1.

[69] See *Collectanea de Rebus Albanicis*, pp. 88–9.

[70] This is a common assumption not only as the basis for *duthchas*, but also, for kindly tenure. It is of interest that life tenures were defined in tacks as 57 years, or three periods of 19 years, a length which formed the least possible sub-four-generation period: each 19-year period just failing to make a full generation and the gross just failing to add up to four.

by 'groups of kin', a point of clarification is needed. The tenure of
land by 'groups of kin' does not mean the co-residence in, or the
co-tenancy of, a toun by groups of kin, each having a separately-
defined portion, but the possession of land as a joint- or common-
tenure by such groups. In the case of the former, each person is
linked residentially and agnatically, but not tenurially. In the
latter, the residential, agnatic, and tenurial linkages are insepar-
able. A person's tenure can only be defined in relation to his
agnatic ties, for the one was mediated through the other. It is
insufficient, therefore, to establish that groups of kin held and
worked the same toun. Their joint-tenure must be established.[71]

The need for this point of clarification becomes apparent as
soon as the literature on the problem is reviewed, for the holding
of land in runrig has often been put forward as a specimen of
tribal tenure since it was thought to involve the joint tenure of
land by small, egalitarian groups of kin.[72] Its actual nature is
discussed more fully in Chapter 5. Suffice it for the moment to say
that it was based on a *several* tenure, though there must have been
many touns in which these several tenures were held by related
kin. This is not to deny that there were touns held under a joint
tenure, only to say that they must not be confused with runrig
touns. Focusing on those which can be classed as examples of
joint tenure, most involved no more than two or three landholders.[73] Even disregarding the question of whether they were kin,
their restricted number hardly does justice to a tribal concept of
tenure. Of course, there are many Highland touns whose
territorial· structure cannot be discerned. Of particular interest
are those held by tacksmen, for it was in the nature of the
tacksman system that such touns could be sub-let to the
tacksman's kin. Where the tenure of these sub-tenants was
vaguely defined, then it is conceivable that it might pass for a
joint tenure of land by kin groups. However, such an arrangement would not have been implicit in the tenure of land, but a
choice by the tacksman. Herein lies the key distinction between
the clan system and earlier systems of a tribal nature. In the

[71] Extra comment on this point occurs in R. A. Dodgshon, 'Runrig and the Communal
Origins of Property in Land', *Juridical Rev.* (1975), pp. 189–208.
[72] See, for example, F. D'Olivier Farran, 'Runrig and the English Open Fields',
Juridical Rev., pp. 134–49.
[73] Where explicit, the evidence tends to affirm that most examples of joint tenure
involved brothers or fathers and sons.

latter, individuals within the same kin group had equal status and claim with respect to tenure simply because property rights were first and foremost invested in the kin group of which they were an equal member. Within these property-holding groups, those linked laterally stood in the same relation to tenure as those linked lineally. In the clan system, meanwhile, individuals did not have this equal status and tenure as of right. But its outward appearance approximated to that of the tribal system in so far as those with greater claim to land used their kinship ties to thread together their tenurial ties, sub-letting to relatives and so on. It was a form of patronage in regard to land, with kin always coming first, the consideration becoming more and more attenuated as the degrees of kinship became more and more removed.[74]

To some extent, one of the reasons why the holding of land by groups of kin has become such a persistent theme in Highland history lies in its implicit connection with the concepts of *duthchas* and kindly tenure. Behind these twin concepts was the customary belief that once a family had occupied land for three generations, then the fourth and subsequent generations acquired a secure right to occupancy. Such a belief defined the basis of tenurial right in a way that compares closely with similar customs in Ireland and Wales.[75] In both these areas, the size of the kin groups holding land was restricted to those linked within four degrees. Once groups had expanded beyond this degree of consanguinity, they split up into new groups, provided always that sufficient land was available. The custom of a family obtaining a secure possession of land by the fourth generation can be seen as an application of this four-degree principle, for it is another way of saying that once such a group had taken shape agnatically, then its right of possession was complete. Furthermore, once secure in possession, each member of this four-degree kinship group must trace his right of possession back to the same

---

[74] Consider the comment in *Highlands of Scotland in 1750*, p. 93 that 'throughout all Lochaber and the adjacent Wild countries, the Farms have been always given to the Cadets of the Lesser Families that are the Heads of Tribes, which they possess for Ages without any lease'. For recent comment on the link between kinship and landholding if not tenure, see Bannerman, 'Lordship of the Isles', pp. 209–40.

[75] D. A. Binchy, 'The Linguistic and Historical Value of the Irish Law Tracts', *Proc. British Academy*, xxix (1943), pp. 195–227; T. Jones Pierce, *Medieval Welsh Society*, pp. 289–308 and 353–68.

person, the original family occupier. They are all bound together by this fact. The basic weakness of this sort of point is that it remains largely inferential. As already made clear, there is no sign in early sources of kin groups linked to within four degrees being considered as landholding corporations in any way.[76] If such an idea had once prevailed, then it had disappeared before documents shed light on tenures. There are signs of a circle of kinship being recognized for other purposes, such as the nine degrees defined by the law of Clan Macduff in respect of the blood feud, or that embodied in the idea that clans acknowledged 'kindred to forty degrees, fosterage to a hundred', but none in relation to land.[77]

(*c*) *Conclusion.* To sum up the foregoing discussion, there is a prima-facie case for arguing that the clan system was not underpinned by anything other than a form of feudal law. However, and this may be the essence of distinctly clan-based tenure, tenurial ties were channelled through kinship ties in such a way as to impose on landholding a corresponding network of blood relationships that served to bind it together in a pseudo-tribal fashion. Such a conclusion, however, cannot be the end of the matter, for here and there in the Highlands are signs of a customary law. We can treat these signs in one of two ways. Either they can be dismissed as vestiges of a body of law that had been stripped of its potency, or they can be regarded as glimpses of a customary law which, by relying on consensus rather than any written code, survived more strongly than late medieval documents reveal, the one acting as an invisible hand to guide the other. Seen in this way, the question of when one system gave way to the other becomes almost unanswerable since they functioned in different dimensions, the one being the *pays légal* and the other, the *pays réel*. Nor need we expect the transition from one to the other to have been revolutionary. Compared with Wales, where the tribal system dissolved first into joint proprietary units of *gwelyau* held by groups of kin and then, as land became scarce and the social scale of these kin groups too large, into individual freeholds,[78] the outcome of developments in the Highlands, with

[76] Unless, of course, one concedes the four-generation principle regarding *duthchas* as a tangible right of Highland society.

[77] Duncan, *Scotland: the Making of the Kingdom*, pp. 107–9 offers a summary of the role of kinship generally in medieval Scotland.

[78] Jones Pierce, *Welsh Medieval Society*, p. 342.

its ultimate loss of tribal freeholds, may seem to imply a more radical change, but this is to confuse the processes involved. As B. Malinowski has said of tribal systems elsewhere, the critical question is not the either/or of collective and individual owner-ship but the extent to which elements of both were intermixed and related.[79] If we hypothesize that at some point, the free lineages of the Highlands decided to retain their patrimony undivided so as not to endanger their social standing as major landholders, then this would be no more than what happened in a similar social context in Ireland and Wales. However, the internecine strife that was endemic to the Highlands may have fostered a different second stage of *de*-tribalization. Whereas the Welsh *gwelyau* decomposed into individual freeholds, their Scottish equivalents may have become structured into semi-feudal, patriarchal groups, as their stronger members and families asserted their authority over others. After all, the tribal system itself had focused power and authority on its more lordly members. Out of such a process may have been born that peculiar blend of feudal and kinship ties which so characterized the clan system.

Tenure in the Northern Isles

The one area of the Highlands and Islands where small peasant freeholds can be found during the medieval period is in the Northern Isles. These freeholds were occupied by odallers holding their land by an allodial tenure known as odal tenure.[80] A simple explanation for the presence of such a tenure would be to see it as implanted by the Norse, since they retained control over the area until 1468. Whilst such a view is both convenient and admissible, it may to some extent blur the issues by seeking to emphasize what was distinct about the Northern Isles. Land law was rarely static over long periods, but constantly shaped itself to the pressures and needs acting upon it. What we need to compare is not the two systems at one point in time, but their respective

[79] C. K. Meek, *Land Law and Custom in the Colonies* (London, 1949 edn.), p. 12, note on Malinowski.

[80] The nature of odal tenure can be pieced together from Balfour (ed.), op. cit., p. xxxi; Storer Clouston, *The Orkney Parishes*, pp. xvii–xx; Storer Clouston (ed.), *Records of the Earldom of Orkney 1299–1614*, pp. xxxv–xliii; G. Donaldson, *Shetland Life Under Earl Patrick* (Edinburgh, 1958), pp. 8–10.

lines of evolution. Seen in these terms, it could be argued that the differences between the Northern Isles and the rest of the Highlands and Islands (like those which the latter had with Wales) resulted from similar tribal systems of tenure being detribalized in different ways, the former being decomposed into peasant freeholds of a several nature, under the influence of Norse rule and custom, whilst the latter was transformed into a lord–vassal relationship under the influence of the clan system. Of course, even in parts of the Northern Isles, odal lands were eventually converted to feudal tenure, just as they may have been when Norse control over the Hebrides ceased in 1266.

As with other hereditary tenures, odal tenures acquired much of their character from the way they dealt with the problem of inheritance. Odallers practised partible inheritance. A document entitled 'Complayntis of the Commownis and Inhabitantis of Zetland' dated 1576 declared that 'it is the use and custom of the country when any man or woman dies, having land, goods or gear, to be divided among the heirs, the *Underfowde* (which is the bailie of the parish or isle), accompanied with certain honest neighbours, goes to the principal house where the deceased person lived, called the *Hedbull*, for making the division of the said heirship, called a *Scheind*'.[81] A slightly later declaration, dating from 1610, informs us that all heirs inherited a share, 'sons as well as daughters, allowing always two sister's parts for one brother's part, and being so divided that the elder brother has no further prerogative above the rest of brothers except the first choice of the parts and parcels of lands to be divided'.[82] In fact, the eldest also had right to the head bull of the estate, both its home and lands, but according to Storer Clouston, it was practice for him to receive only the house.[83] Examples of these divisions between kin occur freely in the court records for Orkney and Shetland, such as the 'airf and divisioune' at Ure (Shetland) in 1605.[84]

The long-term operation of partible inheritance had two consequences. First, it led to the progressive disintegration of

[81] Balfour (ed.), op. cit., p. 58.

[82] Storer Clouston (ed.), *Records of the Earldom of Orkney 1299–1614*, p. 184.

[83] Ibid., pp. lx–lxi.

[84] G. Donaldson (ed.), *The Court Book of Shetland 1602–1604*, SRS (Edinburgh, 1958), p. 95. See also, A. Peterkin, *Notes on Orkney and Shetland* (Edinburgh, 1822), vol. i, pp. 36 and 39–41.

estates into smaller and smaller units. It is out of this process that the 'peerie lairds' or small independent landowners with little more than 10 to 25 acres (4–10 ha) emerged. However, it ground down the holdings of many others almost to the point of making them cottagers. In the words of the south Ronaldsway respondent to a survey of Orkney in 1627 'concerning rowms mains or great farms within the Isle of South Ronaldsway there are none such here, only the Isle is divided in to so many *Vrslands*, every *Vrslands* containing eighteen penny lands possessed in small pieces by mean men'.[85] Their plight even by the mid-seventeenth century is dramatically drawn in a comment by Bishop Grahame. 'Their lands by the law of Norway', he reported, 'were equally divided among the children, by an inquest founded upon a warrant of the superior, and now by frequent division from heir to heir, many have not one rig or two, and in some places one rig is divided in four'.[86] The second consequence of partible inheritance was that as estates became increasingly fragmented, there emerged communities bonded together by ties of kin. Storer Clouston labelled these as 'family townships'.[87] Such townships bore the name of the family who formed its inhabitants, such as with Knarston, Corrigall, and Isbister. The emergence of these family groups over the fifteenth and sixteenth centuries created what Storer Clouston saw as an 'odal aristocracy'.[88]

Odal townships were divided into different sectors, each having a separate tenurial status. This sectorization of the toun was not in itself distinctive but the richness of terminology employed for them certainly was. Land conveyances frequently introduce terms like *inskyftis* or *tumals*, tounland, *outchistis*, and quoys. Defined in the same order, such terms probably represent the several tofts on which houses were located, the actual arable land of the toun, the outpasture, and the land taken in for cultivation from the outpasture.[89] Within the toun's complex of

[85] A. Peterkin, *Rentals of the Ancient Earldom and Bishoprick of Orkney* (Edinburgh, 1820), no. iii, 'Documents Relating to the Bishopric of Orkney'.

[86] Ibid., p. 20.

[87] Storer Clouston, *The Orkney Parishes*, p. 146; Storer Clouston (ed.), *Records of the Earldom of Orkney 1299–1614*, p. lvi.

[88] Ibid., p. lvi. Clouston's comment that 'one must look at the family not the individual with odal' is clearly relevant here, ibid., p. lxi.

[89] The best discussion of this is J. Storer Clouston, 'The Orkney Townships', *SHR* xvii (1920), pp. 16 and 21. However, Peterkin, *Notes on Orkney and Shetland*, pp. 5–7 and the

buildings, those which formed the original nucleus or patrimony of an odal family had a special status, being called the head bull.[90] The pasture around the toun's arable, or the *outchistis*, bore the name skattald. It was called skattald not because it was liable for skat but because (as stressed earlier) it was appendent to arable land that was.

It is a reasonable supposition that most land in Orkney and Shetland was once held by odal tenure. However, this situation altered rapidly over the sixteenth and seventeenth centuries. In 1564, the lordship of the two island groups was granted to Earl Robert Stewart. He, and later his son Patrick, proceeded to coerce odallers into accepting his superiority over their land. He did so by setting up 'Courts of Perambulation' in which the odaller's rights were scrutinized and, if possible, challenged. As Bishop Grahame noted, he 'intended to stress the odal lands'.[91] The process did not disrupt occupation, but reduced their tenure to one of leasehold, effectively converting their skat dues into rent. By the end of the sixteenth century, one estimate has put the amount of land held by the Earl in Shetland at 20 per cent. To this must be added a roughly similar amount held by the Bishop. In Orkney, Storer Clouston's analysis of the *Uthell Book* of 1601 shows odal tenure to have been largely confined to the mainland, where it was widespread except in the eastern parishes of Birsay, Evie, Orphir, and St Ola. Most of the North and South Isles, though, with the exception of South Ronaldsway, Sandy, and Rousay, were entirely in the hands of the Earl and Bishop.[92] The Earl's co-equal ranking as a landholder with the Bishop was not to last much longer, for his lands were shortly afterwards forfeited to the Crown.

The pattern of odal land was also transformed by its engrossment in the hands of the more successful odallers or Scotsmen

---

*c.*1772 description of Shetland landholding partially reprinted in O'Dell, *Historical Geography of the Shetland Islands*, pp. 239–40, provide useful cameos of early township structure. For detailed analysis of the layout of an individual toun, see W. P. L. Thomson, 'Funzie, Fetlar: A Shetland Run-Rig Township in the Nineteenth Century', *SGM* lxxxvi (1970), esp. pp. 174–81.

[90] Storer Clouston, 'The Orkney Townships', pp. 25–6.

[91] Peterkin, *Notes on Orkney and Shetland*, p. 124. Peterkin provides a full discussion of this process, pp. 124–7.

[92] Storer Clouston, *Records of the Earldom of Orkney 1299–1614*, pp. lii–liv; idem, *The Orkney Parishes*, pp. 1 ff.; O'Dell, *Historical Geography of the Shetland Islands*, p. 238.

implanted from the mainland. Typical of the many examples of engrossment is the way numerous pieces of odal land in the Orkney parishes of Holm and Paplay were systematically concentrated in the hands of Patrick Smyth of Braco over the sixteenth century.[93] Similarly, in Stromness, the large number of odallers known to have existed in 1601 had disappeared by 1653 when the entire township formed part of the estate of John Graham of Breckness.[94]

The conclusion to be distilled from the aforementioned trends is that landholding in the Northern Isles was undergoing radical change by the end of the medieval period. In particular, whilst the number of odallers may still have been increasing through population growth, the amount of odal land was not. Thanks largely to the efforts of the Earl and Bishop, but also to some amongst their own ranks or to adventitious elements from the mainland, a great deal of odal land was rapidly converted to leasehold or to normal feudal tenure. At the same time, and in keeping with the developments in other parts of Britain during the closing centuries of the medieval period, the fortunes of individual peasant families seem to have diverged sharply. Those still holding strictly by odal tenure suffered most, successive generations inheriting smaller and smaller holdings, reducing many to the ranks of smallholder or even cottager. Others, perhaps the more adaptive or acquisitive, fared better, building up large estates, whose integrity they preserved by the adoption of primogeniture or at least a more flexible approach to the problem of family inheritance, with perhaps one child getting the bulk of the land and the rest, a settlement in money or goods.

The Church and Land

No discussion of Scottish medieval landholding would be complete without a more specific mention of the role played in its development by the abbeys. Monastic foundations like Iona and Old Melrose flourished during the early medieval period. Some, like Old Deer in Aberdeenshire, may even have been fairly

---

[93] Storer Clouston, *The Orkney Parishes*, p. 17.
[94] Ibid., p. 87.

substantial landholders in their day.[95] However, the history of the Church as a really large landholder does not begin properly until the twelfth and thirteenth centuries, when Scotland was swept by a wave of abbey creation. It began in 1094 with a grant of land in East Lothian to the monks of St Cuthbert. Over the next two centuries, as many as thirty-six abbeys were established, together with numerous priories, nunneries, and hospitals. We must also take into account the larger bishoprics, such as St Andrews and Glasgow, which were firmly established as large landholders during this period. Amongst the abbeys, notable examples were founded at Melrose (1136), Newbattle (1140), Coupar Angus (1164), Balmerino (*c.*1227), Culross (1217), and Arbroath (1178), as well as at many other sites. A number of different monastic orders were involved: the Cistercians (i.e. Melrose, Newbattle, and Deer), the Benedictines (i.e. Coldingham and Dunfermline), the Cluniacs (Paisley), the Augustinian Canons (Scone, Holyrood, and Kelso), the Tironensians (Lindores and Arbroath), Premonstratensians (Whithorn and Dryburgh) and the Valliscaulian order (Beauly, Pluscarden, and Ardchattan). In keeping with the traditions of monasticism, Scottish abbeys were offspring or daughter foundations of established monasteries elsewhere. Thus, Melrose and Dundrennan were Cistercian offspring of Rievaulx Abbey in Yorkshire, the Benedictine abbey of Dunfermline was set up by monks from Canterbury, whilst the monks who created Scone Abbey were from Pontefract. The early foundations in central and southern Scotland provided a base for the monastic penetration of areas further north. Melrose, for instance, spawned further foundations at Newbattle, Kinloss, and Coupar Angus. These, in turn, provided a springboard for still further multiplication. Northerly outposts of monasticism, like New Deer, were rapidly being founded during the early thirteenth century by monks from Kinloss, itself a pioneering monastic foundation in Moray.

The abbeys acquired control over vast territories. Their estates were built up by donation both from the Crown and lay landowners. David I was a particularly generous benefactor. As well as being responsible for bringing Cistercian monks from Rievaulx to Melrose, he helped endow the abbeys of Holyrood, Newbattle, Kelso, Cambuskenneth, Urquhart, and Kinloss.

[95] Jackson, *Gaelic Notes in the Book of Deer*, pp. 114–24.

Although lacking the resources of the King, the more important secular lords also made sizeable donations in pursuit of salvation. The de Morevilles and the Earl of Angus, for example, endowed Dryburgh and Arbroath respectively with a great deal of property. Inflating the area of monastic lordship still further were the myriad small donations of lesser landholders, for whom any grant, no matter how small, constituted no mean sacrifice. The lands of Coupar Angus Abbey, for instance, were built up by benefactions from barons like the Hay family, the Earl of Atholl, and Alan Durward (a justiciar of Scotland), as well as grants by landholders of much more modest standing, such as David Ruffus of Forfar who donated to them his lands of Kincref, whilst an Adam White of Forfar gave them a toft within the town of Forfar.[96]

Professor Duncan has recently questioned whether the medieval monks of Scotland were the fine archivists or sharp-minded business men they are traditionally made out to be.[97] What is clear is that their meticulously preserved registers enable the composition of their estates to be reconstructed in detail. We know that Melrose held virtually the whole of Melrose parish. In addition, it also possessed land in the nearby parishes of Lessuden, St Boswells, Elliston, Cameston, Maxpoffle, and Redpath together with property set at a greater distance, in the upper Tweed valley and Teviotdale and in Ayrshire and Dumfriesshire.[98] Nearby Kelso seems to have built up for itself an estate that was equally compounded of land near and far. As well as having land in local touns like Sprouston, Midlem, Hadden, Clarilaw, Mow, Hallydean, and Bowden, it also had property less conveniently situated to the mother house itself, such as in Preston, Innerwick, and Broxmouth in the Lothians, Closeburn and Stabilgordon in Dumfriesshire, and a cluster of holdings in the middle Clydesdale area around Lesmahagow.[99] The lands of Coupar Angus Abbey conformed to the same sort of pattern. In addition to its granges on the rich Carse lands around the abbey,

[96] D. E. Easson (ed.), *Charters of the Abbey of Coupar Angus, vol. ii 1389–1608*, Scottish History Soc., 3rd ser., xli (1947).

[97] Duncan, *Scotland: the Making of the Kingdom*, p. 431.

[98] *Liber Sancte Marie de Melros*, vol. i contains a full list of property held by the abbey.

[99] *Liber Sancte Marie de Calchou 1113–1567*, vol. i. Further discussion on the spread of monastic estates can be found in N. F. Shead's brief review in McNeill and Nicholson (eds.), op. cit., pp. 43–4 and 157.

such as Balbrogy and Keithick, it also acquired property along the valleys which fret the southern edge of the Highlands, like those of the Ericht, Isla, Ardle, and Tay. By the early fourteenth century, its estate totalled around 8,000 acres (3,239 ha), and included both lowland and upland, arable and sheep farms.[1]

The disposition of monastic property was in large measure determined by their benefactors. For instance, where possible, the Cistercians are thought to have preferred sites *in locis desertis*. Whether this was achieved in the case of their eleven Scottish abbeys is open to doubt. One can hardly describe Melrose or Coupar Angus Abbeys as set down in a wilderness. Quite the contrary, they occupied areas which must have been amongst the most closely settled in Scotland in the twelfth century. Perhaps we should keep in mind the stricture which has been levelled against the Cistercians that, in reality, they may have been more inclined to create a desert, by clearances and the like, than to colonize one from scratch.[2] Even in upland areas, their pioneering efforts may need qualifying. There is a strong case, for instance, in arguing that the high pasture ground which Melrose Abbey received in the Cheviots and the Ringwood area of upper Teviotdale were settled areas before the abbey acquired them.[3] Of course, this is not to say that they were not given some land which they subsequently improved or reclaimed. Another principle which is thought to have guided the estate organization of the Cistercians concerns the location of their granges. Granges were arable farms which were managed by the monks themselves or by lay brothers. Ideally, they were supposed to be three miles apart from each other, and no more than a day's journey from the mother abbey. Give the close clustering of property around most Scottish abbeys, this rule was comfortably observed for the bulk of it. However, those like Melrose had land set at such a distance that they could not have been reached within the course of a day's travelling.

Whereas the Cistercians are supposed to have sought the less-

---

[1] The Coupar Angus property-holding can be reconstructed from Easson (ed.), op. cit., vols. i and ii. See also, T. B. Franklin, *A History of Scottish Farming* (London, 1952), pp. 35–40.

[2] R. A. Donkin, 'The Cistercian Order and the Settlement of Northern England', *Geographical Review*, lix (1969), pp. 408–9.

[3] The area held by the abbey has a fair density of late Iron-age and Romano–British settlements, RCAM, Scotland, *Roxburghshire*, vol. i, pp. 156–94 and vol. ii, pp. 325–71.

populated areas, the Benedictines are often portrayed as an order which settled in the more populous districts. In consequence, its holdings are considered to have been more scattered and fragmented. They responded, it is argued, by adopting a vigorous policy of holding reorganization and consolidation. It is impossible to say whether their reputation as estate consolidators is fully justified by their Scottish experience, but it is none the less of interest that a mid-twelfth-century charter of land belonging to Kelso Abbey, a Benedictine foundation which had begun life on a site with decidedly less potential at Selkirk, confirmed the abbey's possession of the church at Selkirk and 'the half carucate of arable which in King David's time lay dispersed through the field. And whereas this arable, so dispersed, was not very useful to the abbey, the king now grants in exchange the same quantity of arable all lying in one piece'.[4] The Kelso monks can also be found exchanging holdings, dividing others into consolidated property, and perambulating the boundaries of their pastoral *vaccaries* elsewhere, especially in the Cheviot district of Mow.[5] However, they were not alone in such activity. Cartularies for other abbeys, such as Dunfermline, St Andrews, Arbroath, and Melrose document their efforts in exchanging and dividing land, and the disputes with neighbours over the precise extent of their pasture rights which the monks were always trying to clarify.[6] Seen in the long term, this had the effect of converting a grazing right into a full property right and was a process of considerable significance.[7]

At first, the abbeys chose to farm their extensive estates themselves or in demesne. However, during the late thirteenth or early fourteenth centuries, their estate economy began to alter radically. Instead of trying to maintain as much as possible in

---

[4] Barrow (ed.), *Acts of Malcolm IV*, p. 227.

[5] *Liber S. Marie de Calchou*, vol. i, pp. 144–6 and 203–15 provides examples.

[6] *Registrum de Dunfermelyn*, Bannatyne Club (Edinburgh, 1842), vol. i, p. 223; *Liber Cartorum Prioratus Sancti Andree in Scotia*, Bannatyne Club (Edinburgh, 1841), vol. i, pp. 104–5, 128–9, and 132; *Liber S. Thome de Aberbrothoc 1178–1329*, Bannatyne Club (Edinburgh, 1848), vol. i, p. 310.

[7] For further discussion see R. A. Dodgshon, 'Law and Landscape in Early Scotland: A Study of the Relationship between Tenure and Landholding', pp. 127–45 in A. Harding (ed.), *Lawmaking and Lawmakers in British History*, Royal Historical Society's Studies in History series (London, 1980), pp. 127–45. Instances of land being perambulated between lay estates can be found in SRO, Airlie MSS, GD16/16/12/201; SRO, Duntreath MSS, GD97/1/2; Paton (ed.), *Mackintosh Muniments*, p. 165.

demensne, they began to lease out property on a large scale and, more and more, to feu it. Early signs of this adjustment are provided by the *Liber de Calchou*. It shows the abbey at Kelso to have leased almost a half of its 3,000 acres (1,214 ha) of arable, including large granges such as those of Sprouston and Harden by 1300.[8] As if to find a use for the stock, materials, and equipment which they had themselves abandoned, they leased their farms by what is called steelbow tenure, providing the tenant with the necessary seed, stock, and implements as part of his tack. A similar system was employed by other abbeys when they too took up the role of *rentiers* and started leasing land on a grand scale. A rental of 1573 for the touns held by Inchcolm Abbey in Fife refers to 'the grange' as 'sett of auld (with steilbow oxin, plewch and graith harrow and harrow grath, horse and laubour the same with scheire dargis out of uther lands ...)'.[9] On the Coupar Angus Abbey estate, the practice of *farming out* land began in the mid-fourteenth century. By the middle of the fifteenth, it was widespread, as the abbey's carefully maintained register of tacks amply demonstrates. By the sixteenth, the trend was towards feuing. The cumulative effects of these trends is to be seen in a rental of 1561, when virtually the entire estate appears leased out, over half of it by feu tenure and therefore irrecoverable.[10] The making of this rental was linked to a request by the Privy Council of Scotland to all ecclesiastical landowners, bishoprics and abbeys alike. Its purpose was to estimate Church income so as to enable government officers to collect a third of it for the upkeep of the reformed clergy. Rentals for other abbeys and bishoprics, like that for Coupar Angus, can be found appendaged to their cartularies or registers. They invariably tell the same story of once vast estates diminished by feuing and, if not feued, leased out to tenants.[11] Of course, by the middle of the sixteenth century, the tide of public opinion was moving strongly against the abbeys. Although the Scottish Reformation treated them more kindly than the fate which befell their sister abbeys south of

[8] *Liber S. Marie de Calchou*, vol. ii, pp. 456–9.
[9] D. E. Easson and A. Macdonald (eds.), *Charters of the Abbey of Incholm*, Scottish History Soc., 3rd ser., xxxiii (1938), p. 221.
[10] Rogers (ed.), op. cit., vol. ii, pp. 181–273.
[11] Other examples can be found in *Registrum Episcopatus Moraviensis*, Bannatyne Club (Edinburgh, 1837), vol. i, pp. 433 ff.; *Registrum de Dunfermelyn*, Appendix II.

the Border, nevertheless, they were soon to disappear as great landholders. Some, however, were given a new lease of life by being converted into temporal lordships or absorbed almost *en bloc* into the estates of those influential families who were fortunate enough to gain from these large windfalls of property. Thus, Deer became the lordship of Altrie in 1587, Coupar Angus became a lordship for James Elphinstone in 1596, Melrose became part of the Morton lordship in 1606, whilst much of the land held by Kelso was incorporated into the expanding estate of Lord (from 1616, the Earl, and from 1707, the Duke of) Roxburghe.

The Feudal Economy and the Lord's Demesne

The patterns of tenure and landholding discussed so far formed the basis for the relationship between lord and peasant, and, therefore, for their respective economies. Our understanding of these economies in the context of medieval Scotland is still sadly deficient. Many vital questions remain to be answered. We need to know far more about the character and gross importance of demesne farming, as well as the chronology of its swings from one period to another. Were these swings induced by changes in profitability or were they consequent upon labour shortages following crises like the Black Death? We also need to know more about the fortunes of the ordinary husbandman. Did he experience phases of extreme deprivation and difficulty? And were these matched by phases of well-being and plenty? An issue as fundamental as the price revolution of the sixteenth and seventeenth centuries has hardly been raised in a Scottish context, yet its impact on the relationship between lord and peasant must have been far-reaching. In seeking answers to these problems, the following discussion has no claim to being definitive. Rather does it seek simply to highlight the issues involved and to map out the limits of their solution.

Turning first to the question of demesne farming, it has already been noted that from their foundation up until the early fourteenth century, the abbeys tended to farm most of their property themselves. This was the great age of demesne farming on the monastic estates and presumably on the larger secular estates. The demesne land of the former was conventionally of two types: the lowland arable farms or granges and the larger, upland pastoral holdings. The former were given over to grain production. Although they were designed ostensibly to make the abbeys self-sufficient, the size and fertility of many granges suggests that a considerable surplus must have found its way to the market place.[12] A straightforward calculation of how much low ground arable they each possessed leaves little doubt over how substantial their grain output must have been. Coldingham Priory, for instance, had 35 ploughgates recorded as *in dominico* in its rental of *c*.1300, a total equivalent to over 3,600 acres (1,457 ha). Virtually all of them were located in low-ground touns. A further feature of the priory's demesne was the way it was apportioned out between touns. Most of its touns had some demesne land. Coldingham itself, for instance, had ten, Swynwoodburn and Swynwood had five, and West Reston two ploughgates *in dominico*. This spread of demesne made it more accessible to the tenants on whose labour services the abbey relied, for all the touns with demesne also had tenant land. Four types are recognizable: bond-land, husband-land, the land held by free tenants, and cottar-land. The full meaning of these tenures is not entirely clear-cut. However, bond-land, or land held *in bondagio*, was probably land still held by a customary tenure of a servile or unfree status. It occured in Coldingham (14 carucates), Swinewoodburn and Swinewood (five carucates), and West Reston (three carucates). Husband-land differed from bond-land in not being charged with this servile status, but nevertheless, it was—in character—a service-bearing tenure. In fact, such a tenure was to be the archetypal tenure of late medieval and early modern Scotland. However, in those touns where it existed on the Coldingham Priory estate *c*.1300 (such as Swinton, Fishwick, Great Ayton, Paxton, and Flemington), tenants mostly paid a money rent. Very few owed services. This may mean that the services owed by husbandmen had been largely commuted, but there is still the chance that some services remained unspecified. The holders of free-land have a more enigmatic tenurial status. They held by what was patently a free tenure and paid a money rent, but any simple definition is clouded by the fact that some owed a few services. At the bottom of the farming ladder were the

[12] Franklin, op. cit., p. 82.

cottars, who held a few acres in return for their labour.[13] As Professor Duncan has pointed out in a fuller discussion of these tenures, their variety and nature suggests that we may be viewing the priory midway through an adjustment, an adjustment that not only involved a reduction in its demesne, but also, the commutation of its labour services or boon works.[14] Other monastic estates had their demesne organized and worked on a different basis, large consolidated granges being the rule. The Carse granges of Coupar Angus Abbey, like Coupar itself, Balbrogy, and Keithok, were of this type.[15] Other estates, like that of Kelso Abbey, mixed touns of both types, with some held exclusively by the abbey and others shared with husbandmen.[16]

In addition to their arable, many abbeys possessed upland grazing land. This was certainly true of those situated in close proximity to the Southern Uplands, like Newbattle, Melrose, Dundrennan, and Sweetheart, or the Highlands, like Coupar Angus, Arbroath, and Kinloss. The exceptions, like New Deer— whose land was confined to the low ground of the parishes of New Deer, Old Deer, Longside, St Fergus, Peterhead, Ellon, and Foveran—were relatively few in number. In addition to their *gerss* or grass touns, some abbeys also had the right of grazing over land to which they did not actually possess the full land right. For example, in the Cheviots, abbeys like Kelso and Melrose were specifically granted the right to graze so-many hundreds of sheep on the waste that surrounded their touns.[17] Elsewhere in the Southern Uplands, the abbeys were sometimes given the right to graze Royal or Baronial hunting forests. Usually, such grants conveyed the pasture rights to the monks but excluded any activity which might interfere with the pleasures of the chase. Melrose, for instance, was given pasture rights in the Lammermuirs by Earl Waltheof which expressly stated 'that moveable folds and lodges for the shepherds shall accompany the flocks of the abbey, so as to avoid any permanent building or settlement

[13] Raine (ed.), *Priory of Coldingham*, pp. lxxxv–cii.
[14] Duncan, *Scotland: the Making of the Kingdom*, pp. 338–42.
[15] Easson (ed.), op. cit., vol. i, pp. xxxiii–xxxiv.
[16] *Liber S. Sancte de Calchou 1113–1567*, vol. i, pp. 456–9. This rental probably records early signs of the swing away from demesne farming. See Duncan, *Scotland: the Making of the Kingdom*, pp. 342–4.
[17] See the collection brought together in *Origines Parochiales Scotiae*, vol. i, pp. 394–410.

within the forest'.[18] A similar grant to Melrose by Richard de Moreville of grazing rights in Wedale restricted settlement for shepherds to a house and the cutting of hay along the edge of the grant area.[19] It was on the strength of such grazing resources that the abbeys built up their reputations as producers of large quantities of wool, hides, and skins.

These products formed the basis of their trading account. An early fourteenth-century manuscript compiled by an Italian, Francesco Pegolotti, details the amount of wool sold by various Scottish abbeys. By far the main producer was Melrose, with an annual yield equivalent to a flock of around 12,500 sheep. Abbeys like Coupar Angus, Newbattle, and Kelso produced only two-thirds of this amount with flocks of around 7,000 to 8,000 sheep. A number of others, like Dundrennan, Glenluce, Kinloss, and Dunfermline, produced around fifteen sacks of wool per year, suggesting flocks of about 3,750 sheep. This must not be taken as a complete listing, for Pegolotti does not assign an annual output to all abbeys: those whose wool was sold as 'mixed' rather than graded (such as Jedburgh and Holyrood Abbeys) were simply assigned a price per sack by him.[20] These flocks, together with their cattle herds, were supported by the combined use of upland pasture and lowland harvest stubble. This integration is typified by Kelso Abbey. Of the 7,700 sheep held by the abbey in 1290, the main concentrations were in the Mow district of the Cheviots (2,800), Spertildon in the Lammermuirs (1,400), and in the barony of Bolden on the edge of the Merse (1,830).[21] Detailed figures for the barony of Bolden show a mixed farming system, with a total of 550 acres (200 ha) of arable and, 1,100 acres (400 ha) of pasture on which were grazed 1,820 sheep and 422 cattle. However, not all the low ground farms worked by the abbeys were balanced between crop and stock in this way. Some of those held by Coldingham Priory appear to have been almost entirely under crop *c*.1300, but this may be because access to grazing was implicit in the holding of arable and did not need

[18] *Liber Sancte Marie de Melros*, vol. i, pp. xiv–xv.
[19] Ibid., p. xv.
[20] Based on a summary and tabulation of Pegolotti's list in Duncan, *Scotland: the Making of the Kingdom*, pp. 429–30.
[21] Franklin, op. cit., p. 81. An extended review of the abbey's property in the Cheviots is provided by Duncan, *Scotland: the Making of the Kingdom*, pp. 417–19.

to be explicitly stated.[22] The efforts of the abbeys to secure more exclusive control over their hill pasture ground gives the impression that they were particularly concerned with the problems of flock management and control. One possibility is that by having more exclusive control over such ground, instead of a right to depasture so-many sheep alongside those of other landowners, the abbeys were able to raise their stocking levels, for with so much low ground arable and pasture, they were well-equipped to exploit the summer potential of the hills to their maximum.

Attention has already been drawn to the way the abbeys began to lease out more and more of their property after 1300, thus bringing this age of demesne farming to a close. The more abundant documentation of their activities after 1300 makes this an easily discerned shift. More difficult to detect are the secular swings which may have occurred prior to 1300. Relying partly on the comparison with England, Duncan has proposed a phase of demesne farming, or 'high farming' as he terms it, during the thirteenth century, when demesne land was expanded to a peak and labour services were exploited to the full. In support, he cited the attempts by Inchaffray Abbey to recover land during the middle decades of the thirteenth century which it had at ferme or leased out for an annual rent.[23] In other words, once we get back to the early thirteenth century and beyond, the extent of demesne farming may recede.

Less well charted by extant documents is the extent and chronology of demesne farming on lay estates. With regard to the pre-1300 period, Duncan has argued that 'high farming' was 'a less marked feature of the economy of a magnate's estate than the careful collection of money rents'.[24] However, he himself would be the first to concede that the evidence for any firm conclusion is thin. His own assessment was based partly on figures for the property of the Earl of Fife, one of the leading landholders of the thirteenth century. These suggest, albeit tentatively, that about one-sixth of the estate's income was derived from demesne.[25] A piece of royal legislation, supposedly dated to 1209 but of doubtful authenticity, required 'the earls barons and freeholders of the realm' to lease out their land and to live off the 'rents and

[22] Ibid., p. 313.
[23] Ibid., p. 414.
[24] Ibid., p. 427.
[25] Ibid., p. 426.

ferms and not as husbandmen or livestock farmers wasting their lands and the country with a multitude of sheep and beast'.[26] This would be a statute of crucial significance if it were not for the doubts over its validity. After 1300, the amount of documentation increases. For this reason, caution must be exercised before translating references to demesne into statements of how much existed. What is certain is that demesne land did not disappear on lay estates. The Morton estate rental of 1376, for example, distinguishes between *Proprietas* and *Tenandria*.[27] Judging from the amount of *Proprietas* in the Baronies of Stabilgordon and Waterstirker in Dumfriesshire, the lordship had a substantial amount of land in its own hands, most of it sheep pasture. Of course, far from reflecting estate policy, this may only signify the decimations of the Black Death. Increasingly though, demesne land was restricted to maynsing or bordland, and directed towards the upkeep of the landowner's household rather than to market production. The 1627 *Report of the State of Certain Parishes* refers to a number of touns as being held *in maynsing*, but it also shows that such land could pass freely from lord to tenant and vice versa.[28] In spite of their expanding role as *rentiers*, however, Scottish secular lords were not divorced from the practical business of handling large quantities of grain and stock. The payments of rent in kind ensured this.

The Feudal Economy and the Peasant

Like that of its lordly counterpart, the history of the Scottish peasant economy has yet to be written in the detail worthy of its significance. Those European countries where its history over this period has been pieced together must surely teach us that it was not one of unchanging relationships and values, whatever else we might adduce about the peasant tradition. Not only did the tenurial status of the peasant alter, but he faced recurrent crises in his economy. Some of these crises were grounded in natural

---

[26] *APS* i, p. 382.

[27] *Registrum Honoris de Morton*, p. xlvii, section entitled 'Extentus Proprietis Baronia de Waterstirker et Tenendrie *c*.1376' and 'Extentus Proprietis Baronia de Stabilgortoun *c*.1376'; SRO, Morton MS, GD150/72.

[28] *Reports on the State of Certain Parishes in Scotland 1627*. For example, p. 48, the East Mains of Dalhousie is described as 'these five or six years bypast was laboured by my Lord in *maynsing* before it was set out for six hundred merks'.

calamities. Others reflected unfavourable swings in the balance between rural society and its resources. Still others reflected unfavourable shifts in the terms of tenure between lord and peasant.[29] These are likely to have been the same components out of which the secular trend of the Scottish peasant economy was shaped. Their precise contribution or chronology pose major problems for the student of rural history.

An immediate question must be whether M. M. Postan's model of the English peasant economy over the twelfth and thirteenth centuries can be applied to Scotland. Stated simply, his model presumes the rapid growth of population over these centuries leading to acute land pressure by 1300, with both a scarcity of colonizable land and an emphasis in the peasant farm economy on grain-cropping at the expense of pasture and stock-rearing.[30] One or two indices suggest that its extension north of the Border certainly warrants our serious consideration. For instance, J. Gilbert has proposed that the disafforestation of land over the thirteenth century may indicate an increasing degree of land pressure.[31] Legislation dated to 1214, but whose exact origin and authenticity is again uncertain, compelled landholders to cultivate more land, either with oxen or their feet (i.e. with a spade).[32] But scrutinized closely, it shows that the problem afflicting the countryside at this point was not an absolute scarcity of land but an insufficiency of cultivated land. In a sense, it needs to be seen alongside the earlier-mentioned statute of 1209—whose background is equally shrouded in doubt—which took landholders to task for 'wasting their lands and the country with a multitude of sheep and beasts thereby troubling god's people with scarcity poverty and utter hardship'.[33] If this evidence is admissible, then it underlines that the main problem may have been the inadequate supply of land being released from

---

[29] The peasant's potential variety of experience is illustrated by Postan's work on England, see M. M. Postan, 'Medieval Agrarian Society in its Prime: England', pp. 548–632 in M. M. Postan (ed.), *The Cambridge Economic History of Europe, II, The Agrarian Life of the Middle Ages* (Cambridge, 1966 edn.), pp. 548–632.

[30] Ibid., pp. 552–6.

[31] J. M. Gilbert, 'Hunting Reserves', pp. 33–4 and 135 in McNeill and Nicholson (eds.), op. cit., p. 34. Gilbert mentions Gala and Leader as disafforested under 'economic pressure'.

[32] *APS* i, p. 397.

[33] *APS* i, p. 382.

demesne rather than a lack of land suitable for cultivation. As with England, the only way of confirming that population growth over the thirteenth century may have given rise to acute land pressure by 1300 is by examining the balance between grass and arable in extents or by plotting the inflation of land values. Neither has yet been adequately studied in a Scottish context. Admittedly, Duncan has sampled the kind of support the argument needs, like the all-arable touns held by Coldingham Priory *c.* 1300,[34] and has linked the outbreak of disease amongst livestock during the late thirteenth century to overstocking.[35] But such evidence is often ambiguous. Early rentals were essentially rentals of arable, and need not have stated the rights of grazing implicit in possession of arable. This may have been the case with the Coldingham Priory touns. Besides, all these touns had rights of grazing over Coldingham commonty, a vast reserve of pasture. Certainly, other abbeys, like Kelso, displayed no evident lack of pasture. As regards the outbreak of stock disease, this was in no way unusual. Natural calamities affecting both stock and crop occurred throughout the twelfth, thirteenth, and early fourteenth centuries. The Chronicle of Holyrood, for instance, refers to a 'very great famine, and pestilence among animals' back in 1154.[36] The Chronicle of Melrose, meanwhile, talks of a frost 'great, and dreadful, and long—in all lands destroyed sheep, and cows, and horses, that were in the open' during the winter of 1205.[37] Yet another 'debt of nature' was settled in 1256, when the Chronicle of Lanercost makes mention of a 'great corruption of the air, and inundation of rain, throughout the whole of England and Scotland, that both crop and hay were nearly (all) lost'.[38] Nor did Scotland escape the famines that afflicted most other parts of Europe during the early fourteenth century. Fordun's Chronicle documents 'a famine and dearth of provisions' in 1310 followed by a 'very hard winter, which destroyed men, and killed nearly all animals in 1321'.[39] It was, in fact, this sequence of poor

---

[34] Duncan, *Scotland: the Making of the Kingdom*, p. 340.
[35] Ibid., p. 421.
[36] A. O. Anderson (ed.), *Early Sources of Scottish History A.D. 500 to 1286*, (Edinburgh, 1922), vol. ii, p. 224.
[37] Ibid., p. 367.
[38] Ibid., p. 587.
[39] Skene (ed.), *John of Fordun's Chronicle*, vol. ii, pp. 338 and 341.

harvests during the early fourteenth century that Postan saw as bringing to an end the rapid population growth of the twelfth and thirteenth centuries, and not the later outbreaks of the Black Death.[40]

The provisional verdict on Scotland *c.*1300, therefore, must be that whilst population had definitely been growing, and whilst this growth had been channelled through into a demand for extra land, there is as yet insufficient support for adding the extra assumption that it had resulted in acute land pressure by 1300. Indeed, before extending Postan's model north of the Border as a working hypothesis, we would do well to keep in mind the qualifications which have been put forward to its application south of the Border. The most serious is that it is based mainly on data drawn from strongly feudalized estates in the south and east of the country.[41] Where contemporaneous data has been examined for estates in the north and west, or across the March in Wales, it reveals a different picture, with larger holdings and no lack of pasture either for stock rearing or for supplementing arable.[42] Needless to add, on both environmental and social grounds, it is to the latter that the Scottish economic historian should turn for his stereotypes when trying to infer what the countryside may have been like *c.*1300.

The comparison with England needs less qualification when dealing with the Black Death. Altogether, two major outbreaks are recorded for fourteenth-century Scotland, though the possibility of others cannot be ruled out. The first was in 1349 to 1350. According to Fordun's Chronicle, there was 'so great a pestilence and plague among men ... nearly a third of mankind were thereby made to pay the debt of nature ... Now this everywhere attacked the meaner sort and common people ... seldom the magnates'.[43] Andrew Wyntoun's *Orygynall Cronykill of Scotland* confirms this death toll, saying that 'off lyward men The Thyrd

---

[40] Postan, 'Medieval Agrarian Society', p. 570. I. Kershaw, 'The Great Famine and Agrarian Crises in England, 1315–1322', *Past and Present*, lix (1973), pp. 3–50.

[41] A general critique can be found in H. E. Hallam, 'The Postan Thesis', *Historical Studies*, xv (1972), pp. 203–22.

[42] C. Thomas 'Thirteenth-Century Farm Economies in North Wales', *AHR* xvi (1968), pp. 1–14; H. S. A. Fox, 'The Chronology of Enclosure and Economic Development in Devon', *EcHR*, 2nd ser., xxviii (1975), p. 193.

[43] Skene (ed.), *John of Fordun's Chronicle*, p. 359.

part of it destroyid'.[44] Another outbreak in 1362, 'like the former one, of the jubilee year, in all respects, both the nature of the disease and the number of those who died'.[45] On the basis of the number who died during these successive plagues, it can be inferred that the relationship between land and people must have become more loose-fitting, more favourable to the peasant. No matter what the pressures were before the Plague, more could now look to being tenants, whilst those already tenants, could look to having more land. The combination of fewer mouths and greater self-sufficiency in the domestic economy of the peasant may have cut back demand, and therefore trade. Altogether, we can expect a century or so when conditions in the countryside remained in some form of steady-state, with neither growth in population nor output, with little incentive for the taking in of new land or the establishment of new settlements.[46]

Putting exact figures to these population movements is another matter. Lacking comprehensive surveys like Domesday Book or poll-taxes to which a conversion factor can be applied, Scottish medieval population estimates are almost an exercise in speculation. Lord Cooper put the total *c*.1300 at 400,000, the vast majority of whom lived in the countryside. Following the Black Death, he envisaged a slow but steady growth up to one million by 1700.[47] Others have tried to fill in the median values by suggesting that during the sixteenth century, the level of population was anything from 500,000 to 700,000.[48] These estimates are admittedly contrived and, to this extent, questionable. However, they help focus attention on how we apportion the weight of population growth after the Black Death. Cooper's assumption of a smooth trend until well into the seventeenth century is unconvincing. Growth is much more likely to have

---

[44] D. Laing (ed.), *The Orygynale Cronykil of Scotland by Andrew Wyntoun* (Edinburgh, 1872), vol. ii, p. 482.

[45] Skene (ed.), *John of Fordun's Chronicle*, p. 369.

[46] It is worth stating here that 15th-century observers were not impressed by the Scots as cultivators. Don Pedro De Ayala (1498) commented that their 'corn is very good, but they do not produce as much as they might, because they do not cultivate the land'. H. Brown (ed.), *Early Travellers in Scotland* (Edinburgh, 1891), p. 44.

[47] Lord Cooper, 'The Numbers and Distribution of the Population of Medieval Scotland', *SHR* xxvi (1947), pp. 2–6.

[48] See the review in S. G. E. Lythe and J. Butt, *An Economic History of Scotland 1100–1939* (Glasgow, 1975), pp. 3–4.

been unevenly distributed. If it is assumed that the century or so after the Black Death was a period of slow growth if not stagnation, then it follows that growth rates over the sixteenth and seventeenth centuries had to be advanced in order to arrive at a population of around one million by 1700. This may still generalize trends too much, for parts of the fifteenth century may have experienced slow growth, due to recurrent famines and wars, whilst the late seventeenth century may not have seen much growth either. However, the idea that *in cumulo* the years from about 1450 up to 1650 saw a sizeable increase in population does accord with the evidence for the expansion of arable and the formation of new settlement. But with a recent authoritative review of modern Scottish population history asserting that 'we cannot know what the long-run trends of population were in the seventeenth and eighteenth centuries',[49] any positive statement about the centuries that stretch back into the medieval period must remain tentative and speculative.

Over the sixteenth and seventeenth centuries, many European countries experienced severe inflation, so much so, that economic historians sometimes talk of it constituting a 'Price Revolution'. The cause of this inflation is still disputed, but the balance of opinion favours the influx of vast amounts of gold and silver from Spanish America as a critical factor.[50] Its impact on societies varied according to circumstances. However, as a time of 'profit inflation', it was those who commanded trade and profits, such as merchants and landowners, who gained most rather than the ordinary peasant or rural labourer. Much depended on how the relationship between the various groups was articulated. Thus, where landowners were dependent, even in part, on rents that comprised a fixed cash payment, then the impact of rapidly rising prices was sufficient to reduce them to bankruptcy. Alternatively, the high profits which the marketing of grain and livestock now held out, encouraged many other landowners to seek ways of augmenting their rents, either by demanding more produce or cash supplements. As regards town–country relationships, the terms of trade swung progressively in favour of the former.

The impact of the Price Revolution on Scotland has hardly

---

[49] M. W. Flinn (ed.), *Scottish Population History* (Cambridge, 1977), p. 4.

[50] P. Burke, *Society and Economy in Early Modern Europe* (London, 1972): H. Kamen, *The Iron Century* (London, 1976), pp. 61–88.

been raised as a problem, let alone discussed at length.[51] This is a major deficiency for it can explain a great deal about the changing relationships of the period. It has long been accepted that Scottish prices underwent a savage inflation over the sixteenth and seventeenth centuries. The few scholars who have mentioned it, however, have tended to treat it as a peculiarly Scottish malaise, so that the wider context of the problem has been ignored.[52] One need only compare the prices of agricultural produce in the early sixteenth century with those prevailing towards the close of the seventeenth century to appreciate the scale of these increases. Items like a wedder or a stone of cheese cost no more than a shilling or so at the outset but were assessed in pounds by the end of the seventeenth century.[53] Two factors were at work. First, there were those increases brought about by the endemically poor performances of the Scottish economy and the recurrent burden of war with the 'auld enemy'. Increases of this sort can be traced back to the mid-fourteenth century. Super-imposed on price increases caused in this way were those triggered off by the impact of the so-called Price Revolution on

[51] This is despite what Devine and Lythe have described as 'masses of contemporary comment on prices and money'. See T. M. Devine and S. G. E. Lythe, 'The Economy of Scotland Under James VI', *SHR* l (1971), p. 95.

[52] During their brief review of currency depreciation, Lythe and Butt, op. cit., pp. 74–5 make no attempt to inform the reader of the wider European debate over this trend, though Devine and Lythe, op. cit., p. 95 do acknowledge this wider context.

[53] The changing price-levels of produce are easily documented, though given the regional variations in the quality of produce, there is really no substitute for the serial analysis of price movements within defined areas, such as in R. Mitchison, 'The Movements of Scottish Corn Prices in the Seventeenth and Eighteenth Centuries', *EcHR*, 2nd ser., xviii (1965), pp. 78–91. However, the following prices abstracted from various sources convey some idea of the scale of increases involved. *Collectanea de Rebus Albanicis*, pp. 173–4: 1*s* per stone of cheese (1588), 8*d* per boll oat meal (1588), 10*s* for a calved cow (1588). Smith, *Book of Islay*, pp. 486, 536, 540, 543, and 553: 16*d* per stone of cheese (1542), 2*d* for a hen (1542), 16*d* for a stone of meal (1542), £4 00 00*d* per gallon of butter (1722), £6 00 00*d* per boll of oatmeal (1722), £12 00 00*d* per stot (1722). Rogers (ed.), op. cit., vol. i, pp. 353–6: 8*s* 4*d* per boll of bere (1561), 8*s* 4*d* per boll of wheat (1561). Easson and Macdonald (eds.), op. cit., p. 226: 12*d* for a hen (1605), 6*s* 8*d* per boll of oats (1605), 10*s* per boll of bear (1605), 12*s* per boll of wheat (1605). 'Rental of Brabster, Caithness, 1697', pp. 46–52 in A. W. Johnston (ed.), *Old Lore Miscellany of Orkney, Shetland, Caithness and Sutherland, IX, Old Lore Series*, xi (1933): £8. 00 00*d* and £10. 00 00*d* per cow (1697), £13. 06 08*d* for a plough ox (1697), £4. 00 00*d* a steer (1697), 2*s* 6*d* a hen (1697), £2. 12*s* 00*d* a wedder and two fleeces (1697), £5. 00 00*d* and £6. 13*s* 4*d* a boll of meal (1697). Floors Castle, Kelso, Roxburgh MSS, Book of Charge and Discharge 1714/1715: £8. 00 00*d* per boll of bear (1714), £9. 00 00*d* per boll of wheat (1714). Ibid., Account Book for Caverton Barony, 1717: £11. 10*s* 00*d* per boll of meal (1717), £6. 10*s* 00*d* per boll of bear (1717), £8. 10*s* 00*d* per boll of wheat (1717). All prices are in Scots currency.

the Scottish economy. Together, the price changes they induced must have sent severe and repeated shock waves through the economy. Out of the constant disequilibrium which they must have engendered, some groups probably enhanced their profits whilst those of others were correspondingly eroded.

It is suggested here that the ordinary peasant found himself in the second category. To some extent, the great mass of peasants were protected against inflation by the fact that they paid rents in kind that were fixed and customary. Inflation, therefore, could not alter the basic equation of how much they paid. Even when tenants paid a customary mail or cash payment as part of their rent, such as those recorded in a rental for the Lordship of Badenoch drawn up in 1603, such mails remained fixed despite inflation.[54] However, tenants in newly-established touns, such as those in former forest areas like Ettrick, were commonly contracted to pay their rents in cash. Moreover, such cash rents had no *customary* levels to act as a brake on inflation.[55] At the same time, there existed a growing body of tenants whose customary multures and services had been commuted to a cash payment. In such instances, the rapid inflation of prices left tenants exposed to avaricious demands, since the checks and balances inherent in a customary system were absent. The rapidly escalating costs of running a large estate and household, coupled with the decline in the value of customary mails and feu-fermes, must have spurred many landowners into squeezing their tenants harder when they could. Some may have forced tenants to abandon their customary mails and multures and to accept a more flexible cash rent in lieu. For reasons discussed earlier, this may have been a strategy adopted in regard to isolated areas, from which the marketing of grain and produce was difficult. To the extent that this brought a tenant into a direct relationship with the market and allowed him to share the benefits of a favourable run of

[54] Macpherson, *Glimpses of Church and Social Life in the Highlands*, pp. 503–15. The broad stability of mail is shown by the equal amount per plough paid by most touns, or £5. 6s 8d per davach. In other rentals, such as Rogers (ed.), op. cit., vol. i, pp. 353–6, the same point is made by the description of money rents as 'auld maill'.
[55] See, for example, G. Burnett (ed.), *The Exchequer Rolls of Scotland*, vol. XI, A.D. 1497–1501 (Edinburgh, 1888), pp. 396–402. In this rental, some touns paid a small number of stock along with their money rents, but these soon disappeared. Nor is there any fixed rate of money rents for stedes, since the latter had no assesment in land units on which it could be levied. Tenants paid for the total resources of the holding.

prices, this was to his advantage, but not if it provided the landlord with a licence for marking up his rent at whim. Alternatively, some landowners may simply have sought to augment customary rents. The many sixteenth- and seventeenth-century rentals which show tenants as paying a customary rent plus an augmentation computed either in cash or extra grain are an adequate testimony of how many took this approach. As will be explained more fully in Chapter 6, the cultivation of non-assessed land, or commonty, may have helped legitimize this enforcement of a non-customary rent. Other types of augmentation took a more disguised form. A submission of 1613 to the Privy Council by tenants on Islay

complained that sir ranald mcsorle knight and his officers and servants in his name have begun to impose upon them very heavy burdens exactions and impositions with which none of their predecessors were hitherto burdened especially by exacting and lifting from them of the duty following for every head of goods which they do hold or pasture upon the waste lands of Islay, viz. *for everie horse, cow and mare four shillings dayly, and for every sheep twelve pennies dayly*, notwithstanding that they do pay his Majesty's duty for the said waste lands.[56]

The payment of skat may have become associated with the use of skattald in the Northern Isles for this self-same reason.

To establish the means by which landowners could stress their tenants does not establish that this is what they actually did. Indeed, where rentals do record dramatic increases in rent levels, such as those for Islay (1509) and for Ettrick (1456 to 1588),[57] it could still be argued that such increases merely kept pace with the inflation of prices rather than exceeded it. To establish that rent formed a greater abstraction of the tenant's labour in 1650 than in 1450 on this basis alone requires a more sophisticated analysis of trends. Reservations might also be entered against the interpretation of the term 'augmentation' in rentals as a sign that

---

[56] *Collectanea De Rebus Albanicis*, p. 160.

[57] Smith, *Book of Islay*, Appendix, pp. 484–5, gives the total money rent for Islay as £167 5s in 1509. By 1696, the money rent (exclusive of multures), was £11,790 16s 4d, p. 520. As regards Ettrick, the broad trend of inflation can be measured by comparing money rents in Burnett (ed.), *Exchequer Rolls of Scotland, XI, A.D. 1497–1501*, pp. 396–402 with the levels of rent recorded in SRO, Buccleuch MSS, GD224/280/1, Rental Books of Ettrick Forest, 1681 to 1719.

tenants were being squeezed harder. After all, any such increase may have simply matched the extra output derived from the cultivation of waste rather than made up for what landlords saw as the shortcomings of customary rent levels. However, some sources leave us in no doubt as to the worsening predicament of the ordinary tenant. The Islay petition mentioned in the previous paragraph is a case in point. The *Complayntis of the Commownis and Inhabitantis of Zetland*, 1576 raised similar grievances. Law-richtmen who spoke for them reported that 'whereas for each three year's *gerssowme* of one *last* of land, they were want to pay five *dolouris*, which is called Eistercowp and Landsettertoun; but now since the Laird began to be Chamberlaine, he has taken for each *last* of land seven *dolouris* and one half, and this from every *last* of land within Zetland.'[58] The *Report on the State of Certain Parishes*, 1627 contains equally relevant observations. In addition to the augmentations of rent that many touns paid, some are specifically described as over-rented, or as being 'at over heich rait'.[59]

An instructive source of evidence on the advantage that accrued to landlords at the expense of the ordinary peasant over this period are various contemporary satirical tracts, whose significance for Scottish rural history deserves wider notice. They depict the Scottish peasant as racked and impoverished by both nobility and burgher alike. Their combined voice make it hard to accept P. Hume Brown's assertion that relations between lord and peasant in Scotland had always been amicable and that the latter 'had little to grumble at'.[60] One of the more eloquent apologists for the plight of the peasant was Sir David Lyndesay (?1490 to 1555). In his *Complaynt of the Commoun Weill of Scotland*, 'Jhone the common weill', was portrayed as one

[58] Balfour (ed.), op. cit., p. 57. Comparable data sets were published by Peterkin, *Notes on Orkney and Zetland*, pp. 124–31. On p. 125, he recites the testimony of Bishop Graham (1642) how Earl Robert (*c.* late 17th century) 'in those days bishop *in omnibus*, and set his rental of teind upon these *udillands* above the avail, yea triple above the avail'. On pp.128–9 he cites a charter of 1587 in which Lord Robert imposed rent increases on various holdings '*in augmentation of rental more than ever the said* lands paid of before'.

[59] *Report on the State of Certain Parishes in Scotland*, 1627, pp. 78–9 and 200. Monktonhall (Midlothian), p. 78, was classed as rented 'at over heich raitt', whilst Stitchill and Home (Berwickshire), p. 200 was classed as 'racket to the hichest'.

[60] P. Hume Brown (ed.), *Scotland Before 1700 from Contemporary Documents* (Edinburgh, 1893), p. xii.

Whose raiment wes all raggit, revin and rent,
With visage lean, as he had fastit lent:
And fordwart fast his wayis he did advance,
With ane richt malancolious countenance[61]

He returned to the same theme in his *Ane Satyre of the Thrie Estaits*, declaiming that the ordinary peasant 'Declynis doun till extreme povertie'. This was because they were 'hichtit sa into thair maill' and 'gentill men thair steadings taks in few'.[62] In what reads like a much more political tract, his *Complaynt of Scotlande* issued in 1549, Lyndesay elaborated further on the peasant's dilemma. In one passage, he has him complaining that 'I labour night and day with my hands to nourish lazy and idle men, and they recompense me with hunger'.[63] Their entire condition was encapsulated in the moving phrase that 'they live through me and I die through them'.[64] Discussing the forces which ensnared him, the peasant lamented how his corn and cattle were taken from him, he suffered evictions, his mails and fermes were raised to unreasonably high levels, and the annual increases of his teinds abused the fertility of his soil.[65] At the core of Lyndesay's ideas was the belief that the problems of Scotland were 'Nother in to the people nor the land' but rather the way it was governed by the three estates of the nobility, Church, and burghs.[66] Of course his view was hardly shared by those he sought to question. The diary kept by Patrick, the first Earl of Strathmore during the seventeenth century castigated the tenants on his Castle Lyon estate in Lyon as 'generally ill payers which indeed was not the fault of the land but the Tenendrie their att that live were a race of evill doers desolate fellowes and mislabourers of the ground'.[67]

However, there were others who shared Lyndesay's sympathies for the peasant. Sir Richard Maitland (1496 to 1586), for

---

[61] *Ane Dialogue Betuix Experience and Ane Courteous Off the Miserabyll Estait of the World*, Compylit by Schir David Lyndesay. English Text Society, ed. F. Hall (London, 1883), pp. 295–8.

[62] Ibid., p. 474.

[63] *The Complaynt of Scotland 1549*, ed. by J. A. H. Murray, Early English Text Society, extra series, xvii (London, 1872), p. 123.

[64] Ibid., p. 123.

[65] Ibid., p. 123.

[66] *Ane Dialogue Betuix Experience and Ane Courteous*, pp. 291–4.

[67] Millar (ed.), *Glamis Book of Record*, p. 10.

instance, was in no doubt as to tragedy of the times. In his *Satire on the Age*, he harked back to a time when 'With luve they did their tennents treat' and the peasant 'wantit nother malt nor wheat'. But now it was all very different. Not only was food scarce, but rents were doubled and landowners had little pity for the peasant's condition.[68] Other writers were especially impressed by the growing disparity between town and country, for whilst the great mass of the peasantry lived their lives out on the edge of poverty, the burghs thrived. An Englishman living in Scotland during the late sixteenth century thought the burghs were amongst those who were gaining at the expense of the nobility, writing that 'methinks I see the nobleman's great credit decay in his country, and the barons, burghs, and such-like take more upon them.'[69] Their gains over the countryside also provoked satirical comment. Robert Henrysoun (*c.*1420 to *c.*1490) wrote a piece entitled *The Tale of the Uponlandis Mouse and the Burgess Mouse.* He first contrasted their standard of living:

> This rural mouse into the winter-tide
> Had hunger, cauld, and tholit great distress;
> The uther mouse that in the burgh can bide,
> Was gild-brother and made ane free burgess—
> Toll-free als, but custom mair or less,
> And freedom had to gae wherevr she list,
> Amang the cheese in ark, and meal in list[70]

Henrysoun then compared their differing fortunes during times of stress, the burgess mouse surviving with far less discomfort than his rural brother. He perceptively ascribed the great welfare of the former to the favours which he enjoyed, favours which helped swing the terms of trade towards the burghs.

---

[68] T. Scott (ed.), *The Penguin Book of Scottish Verse* (Harmondsworth, 1970), p. 178.
[69] Hume Brown (ed.), *Scotland Before 1700*, p. xviii.
[70] Scott (ed.), op. cit., p. 116.

Chapter 5

The Role of the Medieval
Farming Township 1100–1650

The basic social and economic unit of medieval Scotland was the
farming township, a unit known variously as the *baile*, fermtoun,
or simply the toun. Inevitably, differences between one part of
the country and another as regards environmental capability and
cultural heritage nurtured a variety in their shape and appearances. However, through all the welter of local and regional
variation, certain key institutions stand out as shared by all
regions if not all touns. First, there was a predominance of small,
irregularly-shaped, clustered settlements. Secondly, it was commonplace for touns to be held by more than one tenant on a
shared basis, each having an aliquot portion of the whole rather
than a totally separate farm unit within it: this will be referred to
henceforth in the discussion as multiple tenure. Thirdly, where
multiple tenure existed, it was generally the case that each
landholder had his portion of the toun fragmented and dispersed
in the form of intermixed strips or parcels, a system of holding
layout termed runrig or rundale. Lastly, the actual cropping of
touns was organized on an infield–outfield basis, the infield being
an area of intensive cropping and the outfield an area of extensive
cropping under which the land was shifted between grass and
arable in a rotational manner. It must not be thought that these
four institutions necessarily existed together in all touns, or that
they existed throughout the entire length of the medieval period.
However, they were present in all regions of Scotland and, if they
had not already developed by the formation of the Scottish
kingdom, they certainly had by the close of the medieval period.
For this reason, they serve to give coherence and theme to the
study of the Scottish medieval toun and its development.

The Problem of Runrig

If one had to select a characteristic from the foregoing list that
was more basic than the rest, it would surely be the tenure by

which touns were held. Initially, the Scottish toun may have derived its basic definition from the fact that it was an administrative unit.[1] If so, then by the latter part of the medieval period when we are permitted to examine the problem in some detail, this early meaning had shifted or narrowed to a more purely agricultural one.[2] Possible reasons for this change are discussed in the next chapter. Suffice it for the moment to say that the toun had become the unit around which landholding, and therefore much social and economic activity, was developed. Tenants held of the toun: therein lies its meaning. However, the manner in which they did so varied.

We can sense the nature of this variation by looking at early rentals. The Morton estate rental of 1376, for instance, documents tenant numbers for 85 touns in southern Scotland. Of these, approximately 55 per cent were held or shared by more than one tenant. Even amongst those that were held by only one tenant, though, some may have been further sub-let by their tacksman—or the person in whose name the tack or lease was issued—to groups of sub-tenants, whilst others may have carried cottars who worked as herds, ploughmen, etc., to the main tenant. Some entries in this rental have not even got a toun-name, but are noted as being the *Locus de* this or that family.[3] Earlier in date, but less clear and extensive in its coverage, is a rental of *c.*1300 for the Kelso Abbey lands in Roxburghshire: this too gives the impression of a mixed tenurial situation, with some touns held by single tenants and others by multiple tenants.[4] Of similar date (*c.*1300) is a surviving early rental for the Berwickshire lands of Coldingham Priory. Altogether, it lists 22 separate touns, including such examples as Coldingham, Swinton, Ednam, Paxton, and the two Aytons (Great and Little). As mentioned in Chapter 4, although most of these touns had land held in demesne, nevertheless, each could also boast tenant land that was shared between multiple tenants. Most of

---

[1] The author has in mind the situation established by research work on England, whereby *fiscal* settlement groupings recorded by sources like Domesday Book, did not always faithfully reflect actual conditions on the ground. See P. H. Sawyer, 'Introduction: Early Medieval English Settlement', pp. 1–7 in Sawyer, *Medieval Settlement*, pp. 1–2.

[2] The easiest confirmation of this is provided by the way touns were reorganized without restriction. See Ch. 6.

[3] *Registrum Honoris de Morton*, Bannatyne Club (1853), vol. i, p. xlvii.

[4] *Liber S. Marie de Calchou 1113–1567*, Bannatyne Club (1846), vol. ii, p. 456.

these tenants held shares in the form of carucates or bovates, but a few also had land held as so-many acres, presumably the latter formed land which had recently been colonized outside the carucated—or bovated—framework of the toun. Owing to the presence of holdings or tofts described as lying waste in a number of touns, the total number of tenants carried by touns is not always determinable, but touns like Coldingham, Flemington, and Auchencraw can be confidently classed as having in excess of 20 landholders.[5] In other words, they were sizeable touns by any standards.

Sadly, it is not until the sixteenth century that rentals become available in some abundance. A good example of a sixteenth-century rental is that compiled in 1565 for the Bishopric of Moray lands. A major proportion of its touns, notably those in the baronies of Ardclach, Keith, Kinmylies, Strathspey, and Spynie, had already been feued out by this point. Of the 44 touns still in its own hands, some had no recorded tenants but 26 were shown as held by multiple tenants. In some cases, such as Middle Tullibardine, Innerlochty Major and Minor, Kynnedour, and Hiltoun of Birneth, the number of tenants entered in the rental suggests that they too must have been sizeable touns.[6] Elsewhere in the north-east, a 1522 rental for the Forbes estate lands in the parishes of Foveran and Forbes evidences a roughly similar mix of multiple and single tenancy.[7] An excellent breakdown of tenant numbers per toun can be gleaned from a 1600 rental for the Lordship of Huntly, alias Strathbogy. Like other early rentals, there are a number of interpretative difficulties. For instance, there are a significant number of service crofts or allotments tied to fisheries, alehouses, and the like which confuse the number of touns *sensu stricto*. Thus, the parish of Belly alone had eight alehouses, a number which lends support to those early commentators who thought that areas like the north-east devoted no mean proportion of their crop and energies to the brewing of ale and the distilling of *aqua vitae* or *usquebaugh*. A more important deficiency of the rental is its failure to specify the actual occupiers of around one-half of the

[5] *The Priory of Coldingham*, pp. lxxxv–cii.

[6] *Registrum Episcopatus Moraviensis*, pp. 433–9.

[7] Charles XI. Marquis of Huntly (ed.), *The Records of Aboyne 1230–1681*, New Spalding Club (Aberdeen, 1894), p. 45.

touns on the estate. Altogether, only about 80 have their tenants specifically noted down, of which barely 30 were in the hands of multiple tenants. Before deducing from this that multiple tenancy was relatively unimportant in the Huntly Lordship, the reasons why so many touns had not recorded tenants should be taken into account. In the case of those in Lochaber parish, it was because they were patently held by tacksmen. The term tacksman was used in the Highlands for individuals who held a whole toun, or cluster of touns, for which they effectively acted as a sort of estate factor, leasing (or in their case sub-letting) land to the tenants who actually worked the ground, and gathering in rents on behalf of the laird. It was a system that must have thrived before 1600, but it is not until after 1600 that evidence allows us to define the role of tacksmen in full (see pp. 280–5). The fact that Mamore in Lochaber consisted of 40 merklands or 20 touns held by Allane Camerone McOuildowy and that Glenaber comprised a ten merkland of five touns held by Alexander Camerone hints strongly at a tacksman system at work. Beneath the tacksman of these Lochaber touns we might reasonably expect clusters of multiple (sub-) tenants holding of the tacksman as if he were the proprietor. Some touns in the Lordship, however, were entered in the 1600 rental as having neither tenants nor tacksman. We cannot assume they were untenanted, for there are too many, especially in the parishes of Kingussie and Laggan. Instead, we are forced to presume that there was something in the relationship between tenants and the estate which made the latter only interested in recording the rent due from the toun and its occupiers. The logical answer is that tenant numbers in these touns were too complex and arrangements too fluid to be worth recording in detail.[8]

Good sixteenth- and seventeenth-century rentals are available for Orkney and Shetland, though not all are specific about the number of tenants which particular touns may have carried. Those that do have this information leave little room for doubt that multiple tenancy was commonplace.[9] Their rather stark picture can be partly coloured in by contemporary descriptions.

[8] *Miscellany of the Spalding Club*, iv, pp. 261–319. See also, SRO, GD44/51/747.

[9] The most accessible and certainly the most comprehensive source of rentals for the region is A. Peterkin (ed.), *Rentals of the Ancient Earldom and Bishoprick of Orkney* (Edinburgh, 1820), pp. 1 ff.

One such description tells us that before 1614, 'the Earles and Bishops lands were runrig'd through Orkney and Zetland, the former having two and the latter one.'[10] Unless tenants did some skilful double-dealing, such a mixed proprietorship could not fail to produce a mixed tenurial structure in many townships. Endorsing this conclusion is a 1627 report on Orkney which declared many of its *rowmes* to be overburdened with indwellers.[11] A roughly contemporary recollection of Shetland described how there 'are several Towns in Shetland so called, being about eight or ten houses together, where they plow and so corn'.[12] An eighteenth-century description of Shetland, taking a backward glance at earlier conditions amongst odallers, confirms this impression with the comment that 'anciently the number of merk lands in each town were known with the utmost certainty and precision, otherwise when divided as many small towns still are among 7 or 8 proprietors it had been impossible for each to know or instruct his share or interest in it.'[13]

The rental coverage of the western Highlands and Islands does not really begin until the sixteenth century, when a fine series of rentals become available. The most extensive are those covering forfeited lands on Islay and Tiree, and in Kintyre, Ardnamurchan, and Sunart that were held temporarily by the King following the break-up of the Lordship of the Isles.[14] Another, dated 1588, is available for lands on Mull and Tiree which earlier had been held by the Bishop of the Isles.[15] Unfortunately, their value is limited. That for the former Bishopric lands is contained in a royal charter conveying them to Hector Maclean of Duart, and specifies only the rent paid by touns but not their occupants. The Crown rentals are more specific but suffer in their detail from the prevalence of tacksmen. In a study of landholding in the south-west Highlands and Islands using these sixteenth-century Crown rentals, McKerral concluded that all touns were held by

[10] *Geographical Collections Relating to Scotland Made by W. Macfarlane*, Scottish History Society, liii (1908), vol. iii, p. 1.

[11] Peterkin, *Rentals*, No. III, Documents Relating to the Bishoprick of Orkney, p. 72.

[12] *Geographical Collections*, vol. iii, p. 61.

[13] A. O'Dell, *The Historical Geography of the Shetland Islands* (Lerwick, 1939), p. 240. Based on a topographic account of *c.*1772 reprinted by O'Dell, pp. 238–46.

[14] M'Neill, op. cit., pp. 536–9 and 612.

[15] *Collectanea de Rebus Albanicis*, pp. 161–79. Another, less detailed rental for parts of Mull and Tiree and dated 1561 can be found on pp. 1 ff.

tacksmen.[16] Broadly speaking, his point is a valid one. Very few touns in either Kintyre or on Islay had more than one tenant. For instance, a 1542 rental for south Kintyre entered 46 touns, of which 39 were debited to single tenants. Moreover, quite a number of these touns were really groups of touns clustered together to form a single tack, such as Kellalane, Pennagown, Gartloskain, Elrig, and Arinskachar which were all treated as a single tack held by one tenant.[17] All the indications are that these single tenants were tacksmen, the formal representatives of a much more complex landholding structure. Elsewhere, the rental conceals less. On Tiree, for example, 14 out of the 22 touns for which information is provided were shared between multiple tenants.[18] The same is true for other areas covered by this rental. Over half the touns recorded in Strathdee, Cromar, Ross, and Ardmannoch, for example, were in the hands of more than one tenant.[19] Given that such Crown rentals integrated different estates from different areas, it is a fair assumption that these broad differences reflect differences in estate practice, with some areas (i.e. Kintyre and Islay) using a tacksman to mediate between estate owner and working tenant but others, like Tiree, maintaining a more immediate relationship between them.

Whether a toun was held by one tenant or whether it was in the hands of a number greatly affected its character. In the case of the former, the tenant was confronted only with the problem of how best to farm the land. In the latter, the tenants faced a wider range of problems, not least of which was the problem of how best to divide their respective interests in the toun. Two strategies were adopted. Some farmed the township as a single unit and then divided the produce. The majority, however, preferred to divide the land. Again, by far the majority of those who divided the land did so on a strip basis, each tenant having his share subdivided into strips that were scattered across the arable land of the toun, intermixed cheek by jowl with those of his co-tenants. This systematic intermixing of each tenant's strips across the arable of the toun was called runrig or rundale. The earliest

---

[16] McKerral, 'The Tacksman and his Holding in the South-West Highlands', pp. 11–25.

[17] M'Neill, op. cit., pp. 625–33.

[18] Ibid., p. 614.

[19] Ibid., pp. 655–62.

reference to the terms runrig or rundale occurs in a manuscript dated 1428. It refers to land at Haliburton in Berwickshire which was divided 'ryndale' between two landholders.[20] Other references follow fairly quickly: thus, a reference to 'rynryg is made during a dispute over marches at Petfurane (Angus) in 1437, [21] whilst a manuscript dated 1444 refers to land at Primside in Roxburghshire being 'jacentes ad rendale'.[22] Despite this sudden flourish of references, we can hardly doubt that runrig had a history dating back to before the early fifteenth century. Circumstantial support for an earlier existence can be gleaned from two early charters. One, dated 1205, is a grant of land to John Waleram in Ballebotlie (possibly Babbet), Fife, in which the land concerned is described as 'every fifth rig of the whole half of Ballebotlie'.[23] There is nothing obscure about this charter. It simply employs a means of designating a runrig holding by giving it an order in the sequence of allocation. The other charter of interest here is the mid-twelfth-century charter cited earlier, in which half a carucate belonging to Kelso Abbey is described as lying 'dispersed through the field' (*per campum dispersa iacebat*) and which they wanted exchanged for a consolidated piece.[24]

Of course, the intermixture of land in the form of strips was common throughout medieval Europe. This being so, the use of a special term of description, or runrig, to describe open fields in Scotland has led many writers to conclude that there must have been something different about their character to justify such a mark of distinction. A number of possible distinguishing features have been proposed. They range from the parallel alignment of strips or their sequential allocation to the periodic reallocation of strips between the various landholders. The last mentioned has been especially popular, partly because it could be used to reinforce the old notion that runrig was a primitive system of landholding, an institution which relates back to the days when society was organized on a tribal basis and private property did not exist. In such a scheme, runrig seems to capture perfectly the

[20] *Liber Sancte Marie de Melros*, Bannatyne Club (1837), vol. ii, pp. 518–19.
[21] *Registrum de Dunfermelyn*, Bannatyne Club (1842), p. 285.
[22] HMC, *Report on the Muniments of His Grace the Duke of Roxburgh at Floors Castle, by Sir William Fraser, 14th Report*, part III (London, 1894), p. 22.
[23] Barrow (ed.), *Acts of William I*, pp. 423–3.
[24] Idem (ed.), *Acts of Malcolm IV*, p. 227.

midway stage between the decay of communal property and the rise of private property.[25]

There can be no doubt that each of the aforementioned characteristics—the parallel alignment of strips, their sequential allocation, or their periodic reallocation—have some basis in fact. However, none of them is entirely convincing. When estate plans depicting runrig become available in the eighteenth century, they show that not all strips by any means were laid out in a parallel fashion, nor had they been doled out in a strict sequence. At the same time, it is clear from a number of sources that not all runrig systems were subject to reallocation. Many were reallocated only occasionally.[26] More serious, in the case of those examples which involved feuars and landowners, there was an undoubted stability of layout.[27]

A way out of this dilemma over runrig's meaning is to focus on its tenurial background. Briefly, two types of tenure can be recognized in respect of multiple-tenant touns. The least common form was for tenants to hold by a joint tenure, each tenant being 'severally and conjointly' responsible for the management and rent of the entire toun and not just a portion of it.[28] Alongside such touns, but far more numerous, were touns in which each tenant held a separately defined share. These

[25] This is best exemplified by F. D'Olivier Farran, 'Run-Rig and the English Open Fields', *Juridical Review* (1959), pp. 134–49.

[26] How else would we explain the widespread practice of setting the share of a toun by linking it back to the previous occupant, an approach which clearly obviated the need for a re-division and ensured stability of layout?

[27] Those of the south-east, for instance, were stable over generations. In fact, charters of conveyance are available specifying individual strips and shots. See HMC, *The Manuscripts of Col. David Milne Home of Wedderburn* (London, 1902), pp. 197, 214, and 219; HMC, *First Report on the Marchmont Muniments, 14th Report* (London, 1894), Appendix, part iii, pp. 56–8.

[28] Apart from the way such tenants held touns by a single tack, their tenure was often belied by the use of a phrase like 'severally and conjointly'. See, for instance, SRO, Earl of Stair Muniments, GD135/Box 39, tack for Culhorn (1786), which set the toun to John Wallace and John Martin and declared that both 'shall be Conlly and Seally bound for any rent', or C. Rogers (ed.), *Rental Book of the Cistercian Abbey of Cuper Angus* (London, 1880), vol. i, p. 249 which provides a 16th-century tack for the Grange of Airlie in which tenants were set the toun 'coniunctly and severally'. Of course, the fact that such tenants held a toun jointly from a tenurial point of view, did not alter the ultimate need for a division of spoils between them. *Hope's Major Practicks 1608–1633*, ed. J. A. Clyde, Stair Society (Edinburgh, 1938), vol. i, p. 231, helps us with this point. He wrote that 'conjunct persones specifeit in a tack or wther persones quhatsomever conjunctlie named in ane tack, shall make equall division thereof.'

separate shares are manifest either because they held 'per tak partes' each having a separate tack for his share, or because they were each accorded a separate share or portion of rent in a rental.[29] Logically, since runrig was an intermixture of each person's separate holding and not a common or undifferentiated possession of a toun, then it must surely relate to this second form of multiple tenure. Indeed, taking up this view provides a basis for a more searching analysis of its basic nature.

Of fundamental importance to the problem is the fact that where tenants or landholders held a toun in shares, then it invested them with a right to a proportion of the toun and not a holding that was fixed and defined in terms of its layout on the ground. There were two ways in which such shares were measured as quantities. The most obvious system involved the land-unit assessment of the toun. The *c.*1300 rental for the lands of Coldingham Priory, for instance, used carucates or bovates to calculate each tenant's interest,[30] whilst that compiled for the Morton estate in 1376 simply used bovates.[31] A mid-sixteenth-century rental for the lands which belonged to Kelso Abbey lists a number of touns divided into merkland shares: that of Sprouston was held by ten tenants in shares of *VIII, VI, 11½, 11, III, 2, 1, 11, 1 and a ½* merkland.[32] Roughly contemporary rentals available for the north-east, such as those for the Forbes[33] and Huntly[34] estates, show that touns generally comprised a single davach each, or else were divided into so-many 'ploughs'. A tenant's

---

[29] Of the many examples to choose from, a good source is *Registrum Episcopatus Moraviensis*, pp. 433 ff., rental for 1565. Not only does it assign a separate rental statement to each tenant, but it assigns each tenant a specific fractional 'pars' where multiple tenants were involved. For examples of tacks setting shares of a toun, see SRO, Dalhousie MSS, SRO, GD45/16/1544, tack for 'eastmost plough-land of the Mains of Kelly' (1662) and GD45/18/176 which refers to 'quarter of the Mains of Panmure' (1627); SRO, Abercairny MSS, GD24/1/32, tack for 'the just and equall third part of the whole Town & Lands of Achlay' (1756) which bound the tenant to pay 'the just & equall third part of the haill Rents duties Ferms casualities services & others'; SRO, Forbes MSS, GD52/262, tack for 'third of the town and lands of Meickle Funeray' (1677); SRO, Kinross House MSS, GD29/203, tack for one-eighth of lands of Kinasuid (1697); SRO, Leven and Melville MSS, GD26/5/58, tack for 'easterhalf of roume and lands called Pitconmark' (1685). Rogers (ed.), op. cit., vols. i and ii provides numerous 15th- and 16th-century tacks setting only a share of a toun to individual tenants.

[30] *Priory of Coldingham*, op. cit., pp. lxxxv and lxxxvii are typical examples.

[31] *Registrum Honoris de Morton*, vol, i, pp. vii ff.

[32] *Liber S. Marie de Calchou 1113–1567*, vol. ii, pp. 489 ff.

[33] *Records of Aboyne*, p. 45.

[34] *Miscellany of the Spalding Club*, iv, pp. 261–319; SRO, GD44/51/747.

share was computed as either a single 'plough' or as a specific proportion of a 'plough'. On the Huntly estate, some ploughs were subdivided into 'oxingangs', eight 'oxingangs' making up the 'plough'. For example, Over and Nether Formestoune in Aberdeenshire each equalled two 'ploughs' or, if taken together, a single davach: the former was held by five tenants in shares of 6, 2, 2, 4, and 2 'oxingangs', whilst the latter was held by two tenants in shares of 4 and 12 'oxingangs'. A good illustration of a toun held in pennyland shares is provided by a mid-sixteenth-century rental for Castlebay in Shetland.[35]

That each land unit within a toun constituted an equal share of the total resources of the toun is forcibly conveyed by the fact that the use of land units for leasing was sometimes replaced by a system of explicitly stated shares, such as quarters, halves, thirds, or sixths. As argued in Chapter 2 the so-called quarterland system of Islay probably falls into this category. Such quarterlands were said to equal two and a half merklands, but the tenants who shared a quarterland did not necessarily hold merkland shares. Instead, they held *leth* ($=\frac{1}{2}$), *caethramh* ($=\frac{1}{4}$, and *ochdramh* ($=\frac{1}{8}$).[36] One seventeenth-century rental for Islay talks of tenants in some touns having a *carrowran*, which presumably was a quarter-share.[37] The use of explicit shares to lease land was equally well established in eastern Scotland. The rental for the lands of the Bishopric of Moray that was drawn up in 1561 is forthcoming with numerous examples. Typical is the 'villa de Kynnedour' which was held by ten tenants in shares of *VII, XII, XII, VIII, VIII, XVI, XII, VIII, XII*, and *XVI pars*, or Ardivot which was held by five tenants in shares of *quarta pars, quarta pars, sexta pars, sexta pars*, and *VIII pars*.[38] Touns divided into halves, thirds, or quarters are also to be found in the Huntly rental of 1600.[39] If we broaden the problem a little and consider not just tenant runrig touns but runrig touns shared between different feuars and landowners—or those holding land on a hereditary basis rather than by a fixed-term lease—then a great

[35] Peterkin, *Rentals*, Appendix, p. 58.
[36] Lamont, 'Old Land Denominations and "Old Extent" in Islay', part i, p. 183.
[37] Smith, *Book of Islay*, pp. 492–5.
[38] *Registrum Episcopatus Moraviensis*, p. 433.
[39] *Miscellany of the Spalding Club*, iv, pp. 261–319. Further examples can be found in GD44/51/747.

many more examples are available to us. Indeed, it was commonplace throughout many parts of Scotland during the latter part of the medieval period for feuars and landowners to hold a quarter, a half, a third, or a sixth part of a particular toun. An inspection of the many land charters reproduced in the *Register of the Great Seal of Scotland* soon bears this out.[40]

The significance of this *share*holding system of tenure was twofold. First, it meant that tenants or landowners had to divide their notional shares into actual holdings on the ground—to reify them—before they could take up possession and begin farming. This is the reason why runrig holdings give the appearance of being re-divided or re-allocated periodically. Furthermore, linking re-allocation with the need to divide shares into actual holdings at the start of each new lease-set or when new landowners were introduced into a share of the toun helps explain why the frequency of re-allocation appeared to vary so much from toun to toun. Thus, if the shares of a toun were held on a year to year basis, then it was possible for re-allocation to take place every year, as some definitions suppose of *all* runrig touns. However, where shares were held on a long tack, or where feuars and landowners were involved, re-allocation would occur less frequently, perhaps only at the outset of the tenure and no more.[41] However, in many parts of the Lowlands, the formal division of shares into holdings on the ground did not always accompany their leasing or conveyancing. Instead, the problem was circumvented by tenants or landowners being given shares already laid out as holdings and identified through the name of their previous occupier.[42]

[40] Every volume contains numerous examples. Some abstracted by the author can be found in R. A. Dodgshon, 'Runrig and the Communal Origins of Property in Land', *Juridical Review* (1975), p. 196.

[41] Instances of allocation taking place where touns fell into the hands of two or more heritors are given in R. A. Dodgshon, 'Scandinavian Solskifte and the Sunwise Division of Land in Eastern Scotland', *SS* xix (1975), pp. 1–14. Instances of re-allocation at the start of a new tack-set are documented in R. A. Dodgshon, 'Towards an Understanding and Definition of Runrig: the Evidence for Roxburghshire and Berwickshire', p. 19; idem, 'Law and Landscape in Early Scotland: A Study of the Relationship Between Tenure and Landholding'. A fine example also occurs in SRO, Abercairny MSS, GD24/1/32, Articles of Agreement between James Moray of Abercairny & Robert Maxtone in Bellnollo 1765.

[42] See, for example, Rogers (ed.), op. cit., vol. i, pp. 170–1. Typical of the phrasing used in SRO, Abercairny MSS, GD24/1/32, Agreement between Abercairny and Patr. & John Taylors for ½ of Drummy Easter (1763) 'as presently possessed by Robert Murray there'.

A second consequence of shareholding was that it defined property in an open-ended way, specifying an amount but not a precise layout. Inevitably, this meant that the layout of shares was a matter for interpretation. There is a charter of 1572 for a sixth part of Knokkorth in Angus which gave the grantee a choice of having his share either as a consolidated holding or as one disposed in the form of runrig.[43] The implication is clear: his charter accommodated either possibility. That a choice existed can also be demonstrated by comparing two documented divisions between co-heirs. In the sixteenth century, Sir Murdo Menteith, the Laird of Rowiskich, was killed and his lands went in division among his three daughters 'whose heirs do to this day possess them divided by ridges'.[44] Seeking a different solution to an identical problem was an agreement drawn up in 1498 regarding the female co-heirs of William Turnbull of Hassindean in Roxburghshire. The agreement arranged for their marriage and for 'the lands of Hassindean lying in Teviotdale to be evenly divided between the said Lord Drummond Comptroller and John Elphinstoun', their husbands:[45] the outcome was not two runrig holdings but Over and Nether Hassindean.

These evident differences of result beg the question of what criteria guided the division of shares. Being shares, and open to interpretation, it was inevitable that they should be seen as equal, measure for measure. This is often borne out by tacks and charters, for even when being set or conveyed, shares were often designated as 'just' or 'just and equal' shares. Typical is a fifteenth-century Instrument of Sasine concerning the 'Just and Equall half of . . . Tolland Begg' in Argyll.[46] Where documents shed light on the actual mechanics of division, the stress on equality becomes even more marked. The partition of the Lordship of Lennox in 1485, for example, proceeded on a declaration by Council and Session that two of the three heirs involved 'should divide the foresaid lands in two even parts as they best may be parted and divided'.[47] A century or so later, in

[43] J. M. Thomson (ed.), *The Register of the Great Seal of Scotland 1546–1580* (Edinburgh, 1886), p. 771.

[44] *Geographical Collections*, vol. ii (1907), pp. 610–11.

[45] *Registrum Honoris de Morton*, vol. ii, p. 250.

[46] Sir Norman Lamont (ed.), *An Inventory of Lamont Papers 1231–1897*, SRS (Edinburgh, 1914), p. 24.

[47] M. Napier, *History of the Partition of Lennox* (Edinburgh and London, 1835), p. 123.

1592, a division of Harray in Orkney, 'the whole *rendallit* land, as well infield as outfield', proceeded with a court ruling that those involved should 'make an equal division thereon, and give unto every one of the said parties according to their *yarramanna* and *malingis* and no other way'.[48] On a smaller scale still, but with no difference of principle, a division of two merklands in Ayrshire in 1682 was again guided by a court declaration that the 'said parties shall divide the said two merklands between them equally'.[49]

Particularly valuable are those divisions which elaborate on how this equality was achieved. The fine cluster of fifteenth-century tacks for the Cupar Angus Abbey estate are especially forthcoming on how it should be done. A 1468 tack for the Grange of Balbrogy required the toun to be divided into two lots, and 'where the lot shall fall better, that part shall recompense the worse, until they shall be equal'.[50] Another tack, dated 1470, for 'a half of Fortar' stipulated that the 'land shall be equally divided in all its commodities . . . as well as in arable land as in pasture land'.[51] Perhaps the most revealing extracts are those which demonstrate that the definition of equality could have a double edge to it, embracing both quantity and quality. Thus, at Buay in Shetland in 1612 to 1613, the toun officers were called on to meith and march two merks out of the toun lands, and 'the said two merk land to be designated, meithed and marched, as much in quantity and quality with all priviledges and commodities as the two merk Odal lands which lay rig and rendall before'.[52] Comparable evidence linking a runrig layout to the interpretation of shares as equal in both extent and value is provided by the proprietary-runrig touns of Auchencraw and Whitrig in Berwickshire. In both cases, the implicit assumption held is that shares had to be equal in both extent and value, for how else could it be a runrig layout.[53]

[48] Clouston (ed.), *Records of the Earldom of Orkney 1299–1614*, p. 167.
[49] *Archaeological and Historical Collections Relating to Ayrshire and Galloway* vi (Edinburgh, 1889), p. 215.
[50] Rogers, op. cit., vol. i, p. 144.
[51] Ibid., p. 157.
[52] R. S. Barclay (ed.), *The Court Book of Orkney and Shetland 1612–1613* (Kirkwall, 1962), p. 18.
[53] Information for both touns was abstracted from Berwickshire Sheriff Court, Duns, Register of Decrees, and is discussed in Dodgshon, 'Towards an Understanding and Definition of Runrig', p. 289.

This suggestion that runrig developed from the strict interpretation of equality between shares, one that stressed value as well as extent, is not alien to what has been written about it in the past. Several discussions have already proposed that the intention behind runrig was to endow each person with a portion of all the different types of land in a toun.[54] However, there is a difference of context. Previously, this all-pervading sense of equality has been linked to vaguely defined feelings of common welfare that were underpinned by a common or communal tenure.[55] Such a viewpoint is one in which runrig's presumed tribal origins were at least implicit if not explicit. Here its context is seen as being quite different, being related to a tenure of aliquot shares that were held in severalty. Being open to interpretation, they were defined to the limit of each person's right so that shares became equal in both extent and value. It was a concern for maximizing personal interests rather than a sense of common good will that promoted runrig layouts. Of course, as some of the examples cited above showed, not all landholders were prepared to push the interpretation of shares to the very limit and to insist on an equality of both extent and value. Some, but a minority, were prepared to compromise on their rights in order to enjoy consolidated holdings.[56]

A consequence of shareholding is that land held by it had a special status. If one imagines the situation after the division of shares into runrig, we can well understand how each landholder must have viewed his scattered strips and parcels as his share of the toun converted to known property. Only after such a division did he know the precise composition of his holding. Early Scottish law texts do, in fact, talk of the need to 'ken any man to his part',[57] whilst evidence for one or two touns in the extreme south-east actually defines land as runrig precisely because it was 'known property'. The same idea of shares being cast into known and

[54] W. Grant and D. M. Murison (eds.), *Scottish National Dictionary* (Edinburgh, 1968), vol. vii, p. 445 summarize this view with their definition that runrig was a 'system of land tenure in which each tenant was allocated several detached portions and rigs of land by lot and rotation so that each share in turn in the more fertile areas'.

[55] Farran, op. cit., p. 149.

[56] Generally speaking, consolidated holdings were more likely when a toun was shared between different heritors rather than different tenants.

[57] See, for instance, Sir Philip J. Hamilton-Grierson (ed.), *Habakkuk-Bisset's Rolment of Courtis*, STS (Edinburgh, 1920), pp. 297–8.

several property would seem to lie behind the extract from the Court Book of Shetland published by Professor G. Donaldson. The extract refers to six 'honest neighbours' who were instructed to 'part' the lands of Skelbury so that 'ilk awner be possessed with thair awin pairt according to use of neighbourhood'.[58] Considered in relation to the shareholding tenure of such land, it captures what may be the basic meaning of the term runrig.

Before leaving the problem of runrig, some comments are called for on the methods by which a runrig division was executed, since on the results hangs much of the character of the medieval Scottish landscape. Built into the design of a runrig layout was the notion that each landholder should have a share or interest in all the toun's 'commodities'. This was most easily achieved by using a systematic method of division. Although eighteenth-century estate plans show few signs of a comprehensive order in the layout or allocation of strips, this does not preclude the possibility that systematic methods of division had once been employed. In fact, early land charters and the documentation generated by divisions are extremely illuminating on how divisions were executed. Three types of procedure can be identified. Each brought the landholders and his share together by means of a lottery, or, in the phrasing of the times, 'be cut and quavyl' or 'be cavillis drawne and cassine'.[59] Their main differences lay in how shares or their prospective landholders were identified in the lottery. A common approach was for land to be divided into the required number of shares, each of which was then given a token, such as a piece of wood or a particular shape of turf divot. Each landholder would then draw equivalent tokens from a lottery to decide which share or strip would be his. Another method involved drawing lots to establish the sequence or order in which strips would be doled out. In this case, tokens were used to identify the landholders. Hints of this system can often be found in the designation of shares. The 1205 grant of 'every fifth rig of the whole half of Ballebotlie' in Fife that was quoted earlier is a good example. Others include a 1585 tack in the *Liber de Scon* for the 'fourt rynrig of the Sandyhill'

[58] G. Donaldson (ed.), *The Court Book of Shetland 1602–1604*, SRS (Edinburgh, 1958), p. 26.
[59] Dickinson (ed.), *Sheriff Court Book of Fife*, 1515–1522, p. 343.

(Perthshire)[60] and a reference of 1498 to a landholder who possessed the 'thrid rig and part of the landis of the barony of Murthlye' (Perthshire).[61] The meaning of such grants is simple: the landholders concerned were to have the fifth, fourth or third rig in every sequence of allocation as the division worked itself around the townland. The third and last method is possibly the most interesting. It involved the use of a form of sun-division. By it, landholders were given the sunny or shadow share of a toun. If a man was given the sunny portion, then he was allocated those strips which lay to the east or south during each sequence of allocation. If given the shadow portion, then he was given the strips lying to the west and north. In keeping with its systematic approach to the problem of division, the allocation of land began in the east or south of the toun at dawn, and proceeded westwards and northwards with the passage of the sun across the sky. Like the previous method of division, a sun-division intruded into the designation of shares. Numerous early leases and land charters are available from the fifteenth century onwards in which a landholder is said to possess either the sunny (*solarem*) or shadow (*umbralem*) portion of a toun. That such references signify the use of a sun-division to cast shares into runrig is confirmed by early Scottish law texts. Indeed, the description of the procedure involved contained in Sir Thomas Craig's *Jus Feudale* (1635) is quite explicit, leaving no doubt that it could produce runrig.[62] An illustration of the point by example is provided by the division of land at Haliburton (Berwickshire) in 1428. There, the two landholders concerned in the division, Melrose Abbey and Walter of Haliburton, drew lots to decide who held the sunny and who the shadow portion. This being done, the land was then divided 'ryndale be four ryggs & four till aythir pt', that is, each was doled out four rigs alternately.[63] Other sources are equally unambiguous. Even charters of conveyance provide enough information to link sun-division with runrig, such as a charter issued in 1586 for land in Keithok Barony in Angus which

---

[60] *Liber de Scon*, Bannatyne Club (Edinburgh, 1843), Appendix III, pp. 231–2.

[61] G. Neilson and H. Paton (eds.), *Acts of the Lords of Council in Civil Causes, vol. II, A.D.1496–1501* (Edinburgh, 1918), p. 198.

[62] Sir Thomas Craig, *Jus Feudale* (compiled 1603, printed 1655), ed. J. Baillie (Edinburgh, 1732 edn.), p. 425.

[63] *Liber Sancte Marie de Melros*, Bannatyne Club (Edinburgh, 1837), vol. i, pp. 518–19.

described the land concerned as 'terrarum &c. dimediatatem per sortem at divisionem, incipiendo ad solem, per *lie rinrig*'.[64] In some cases, the terms east and west, nether and upper, or fore and back were substituted for sunny and shadow. For instance, when the writer James Bannatye, set the Kirktoun of Newtyle in 1577, he did so by leasing 'the west rig of said lands through the whole town of said Kirktoun both outfield and infield' to one group of landholders, and the 'east rig' to another.[65] The meaning of such terms was no different from that of the terms sunny and shadow.[66]

The Field Economy and the Medieval Township

Most medieval touns were divided territorially into three sectors: infield, outfield, and common grazings (see Fig. 5.1). The infield was an intensively cropped area, usually situated in close proximity to the house sites of the toun. Although there were examples that were put under a single crop each year, the common practice was for it to be divided into two or three breaks, each break being cropped on the same two- or three-year rotation. The actual crops used to build up these rotations were relatively few in number. A convenient overview is provided by rent payments in kind. Most show a permutation of the same five crops: barley or bere, oats, beans, wheat, and peas. Towards the north and west, the mix becomes more elemental with only barley or bere and oats being paid as rent.[67] Towards the east and south, one was more likely to find rentals naming three crops, with wheat and peas or even beans included.[68] Accounts drawn up in connection with the *Thirds of Benefices*, 1561 to 1572, a crop levy on Church lands, confirm this broad geography of crop combinations. Northern benefices, such as those of Inverness-

---

[64] J. M. Thomson (ed.), *The Register of the Great Seal of Scotland 1580–1593* (Edinburgh, 1888), p. 349.

[65] *The Bannatyne Manuscript by George Bannatyne*, ed. and intro. by W. Tod Ritchie, STS (Edinburgh and London, 1934), pp. lxxxii–iv.

[66] See discussion in Dodgshon, 'Scandinavian Solskifte and the Sunwise Division of Land in Eastern Scotland', pp. 10–12.

[67] See, e.g., *Collectanea de Rebus Albanicis*, pp. 173–9; Smith, *Book of Islay*, Appendix III, pp. 487–90, rental for 1614; A. Macpherson, *Glimpses of Church and Social Life in the Highlands in Olden Times* (Edinburgh and London, 1893), pp. 503–15, rental of *Lordshipe of Badzenoche* 1603.

[68] See, for instance, D. E. Easson and A. MacDonald (eds.), *Charters of the Abbey of Incholm*, Scottish History Society, 3rd ser., xxxii (1938), pp. 219–21.

FARMING SYSTEM IN EARLY FERMTOUNS

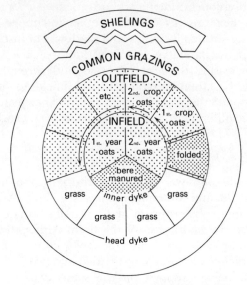

SHIELINGS

COMMON GRAZINGS

OUTFIELD

etc   2nd. crop oats

1st. crop oats

INFIELD

1st. year oats | 2nd. year oats

folded

bere manured

grass   inner dyke   grass

grass   grass

head dyke

FIG. 5.1.   The Farming System in Early Touns

shire, and western benefices, like those of Wigtonshire, had rather
sparse regimens of oats, barley, and meal. Those of Fife, the
Lothians, and the Merse boasted a more diverse range, with not
only oats and barley (undoubtedly the main crop), but also,
wheat, rye, peas, and beans. Areas like Aberdeen and Angus
stood in between, large amounts of oats and barley being levied
together with a little wheat, but no rye, peas, or beans.[69] Some
insight into early cropping patterns is also provided by a
succession of government legislation that was passed during the
fifteenth century. Anxious to counter what seems to have been a
neglect of arable, an Act of 1426 required that owners of a plough
team should sow at least one firlot of wheat, half a firlot of peas,
and 40 beans.[70] A few decades later, the Scots parliament passed
a further law which not only insisted on the cultivation of wheat,
peas, rye, and beans, but even stipulated a rotation.[71] Such a

[69] G. Donaldson (ed.), *Accounts of the collectors of the Thirds of Benefices 1561–1572*, Scottish
History Society, 3rd ser., xlii (1949), pp. 29–44 and summary on p. 49.
[70] *APS* i, p. 13.
[71] *APS* ii, p. 51.

course of cropping, though, could not have been practised everywhere. As already noted, wheat was certainly cropped on the more fertile soils of the Lowlands, and peas and beans did become more widespread as the medieval period wore on. Otherwise, the basis of cropping was barley or bere and oats. Infield was maintained in a state of permanent cultivation by the addition of large amounts of manure. Indeed, in the Highlands and south-west, it was called the 'mukitland'.[72] The most important source of this manure was naturally that of stock. Part was applied directly by stock grazing the harvest stubble. As soon as the last stook had been brought in, a symbolic occasion in the farming calendar of old Scotland, the stock were allowed to wander over the infield and to remain there till spring. We can glimpse this practice through the controls placed on stock movement by the local Baron Court or tacks. To give an example, a mid-sixteenth-century tack for Petlorchy on the Coupar Angus Abbey estate bound the tenants not to 'introduce sheep into the corn until every one shall have made a full leading in of the harvest', whilst, at the other end of the farming calendar, they were also required to remove all calves from amongst the 'blade corn' or stubble by the feast of the Nativity of St John the Baptist.[73] Supplementing the manure provided in this way was that which had accumulated in the kail-yard over the winter months: this was applied to the infield in spring. It was not spread over the entire infield, but was usually reserved for a single break, generally the barley break: the entire infield being manured in this way once during the course of each rotation.[74]

In addition to animal manures, the early Scottish tenant exploited a range of other manures. A popular manure in coastal districts was seaweed. It 'fattens the ground and makes it yield plentifully' wrote a writer on Buchan.[75] Monro extends its use back to at least the late sixteenth century for he describes how the husbandmen of Lewis and Harris 'gudes it [land] weill with sea

---

[72] See, for instance, *Archaeological and Historical Collections Relating to Ayrshire and Galloway* 6, p. 255; *The Black Book of Taymouth*, Bannatyne Club (Edinburgh, 1855), p. 352; R. W. Munro (ed.), *Monro's Western Isles of Scotland 1549* (Edinburgh, 1961), pp. 60, 64–5, and 87.

[73] Rogers (ed.), op. cit., vol. i, p. 129.

[74] This is made explicit by a number of descriptions. See, e.g., *Geographical Collections*, vol. ii, p. 133.

[75] Ibid., vol. i, pp. 45–6.

ware'.[76] A sixteenth-century description of Orkney also observes how they 'guid ther land with Sea Ware'.[77] Another sixteenth-century description, this time of the Hebrides, tells how, on Bernera, many fish were caught but that the inhabitants 'saltis na fisches, but eittis thair staiking and castis the rest on the land'.[78] A widely available manure, but one whose exploitation had serious consequences for the environment, was that of turf. In the Highlands and Islands especially, large areas were skinned of their turf cover using a broad-bladed spade called the flauchter spade. A measure of how widely it was used is supplied by the frequency with which Baron Courts passed acts controlling where and how turf was to be lifted.[79] A still more fundamental solution was to apply fresh soil. An entry in the Baron Court book of Glenorchy for 1621 required tenants of the Barony to spread 'thrie scoir leadis of earth' over 'their middingis for guiding of ilk merkland'.[80] Further west, a similar technique of land improvement was employed on the island of Lismore, with peat soils being used 'to guidis the teillit earth thairwith'.[81] A particularly important manurial supplement in Lowland areas was lime. Judging by the very detailed evidence contained in the *Reports on the State of Certain Parishes in Scotland* (1627), its use spread during the latter part of the sixteenth century.[82] The main area affected was the Lothians, but instances of its use are given for scattered touns in the Clyde valley and Stirlingshire. Its impact on farm output is well conveyed by the Reports. In the parish of Tranent, 'Langniddrie . . . paid before the liming and extraordinary gooding and labouring thereof of stock 21 chalders. And of teind 7 chalders. And which toun of Longniddrie by the liming and extraordinary labouring is now

[76] Munro, op. cit., p. 87.

[77] *Geographical Collections*, vol. iii, p. 324.

[78] Skene, *Celtic Scotland*, vol. iii, p. 431.

[79] D. G. Barron (ed.), 'The Court Book of Urie', Scottish History Society, 1st ser., xii (1892), pp. 111–12 and 125; J. M. Thomson (ed.), 'The Forbes Baron Court Book 1659–1678', pp. 205–321, in *Miscellany of the Scottish History Society*, 2nd ser., xix (1919), pp. 254–5.

[80] *Black Book of Taymouth*, p. 355.

[81] Skene, *Celtic Scotland*, vol. iii, p. 435.

[82] *Reports on the State of Certain Parishes in Scotland 1627*, pp. 37, 44, 52, and 91. A good summary of the early spread of liming is available in T. C. Smout and A. Fenton, 'Scottish Agriculture Before the Improvers', *Agricultural History Review*, xiii (1965), pp. 82–4.

valued of stock to 30 chalders and of teind to 10 chalders'.[83] Such increases in rent based on increases in output are also vouched for by the entries for other touns.[84]

Beyond the infield, at a greater distance from the farmstead, was an area under a more extensive system of cultivation and known as outfield. Its cultivation involved the taking in of pasture ground on a partial and temporary basis. As a rule, that part of the toun that formed the outfield was divided into a number of breaks, some having as many as ten. Each year, one of these breaks would be brought into cultivation and cropped for anything up to five years. During any one year, therefore, between a third and a half of the outfield would be under crop. Within this cultivated portion, one break would be under its first crop, another its second, and so on. Invariably, the only crop sown on outfield was oats. When not in cultivation, breaks were allowed to revert to grass naturally. There is no evidence that they were ever seeded. The only manure that outfield received was that provided by the tathing or folding of stock during summer on the break that was scheduled for cultivation the following spring. The practice of tathing created the need for stock control. This was achieved by the building of small folds made of turf walls. When the tath break had been manured, these turf walls were then spread over the ground and ploughed in.

Early descriptions of outfield which might serve to flesh out this barebones statement of its character are sadly rare. Donald Monro's rather pithy comment about the husbandmen of Lewis and Harris to the effect that 'where he wins his peats this year he sows his bear the next year',[85] whilst capturing the spirit of outfield in a phrase, does little to enlarge our understanding of its early form. References to the term 'outfield' date back to the late fifteenth century.[86] If we make the assumption that terms like 'outset' are outfield by another name, then we can push the date of its first mention back a little further in time, to the early fifteenth century.[87] Slightly more explicit references to outfield

---

[83] *Reports on the State of Certain parishes in Scotland 1627*, p. 135.

[84] Ibid., p. 135.

[85] Munro, op. cit., p. 87.

[86] The earliest reference, dated 1483, is that to be found in J. B. Paul (ed.), *The Register of the Great Seal of Scotland 1424–1513* (Edinburgh, 1882), p. 327.

[87] The earliest reference so far located by the author is ibid., p. 124. Frequent references

breaks, faulds or 'tathit land' begin to occur regularly only during the sixteenth century.[88] Linking these points together in the form of an outfield cropping system is a wadset of 1597 for Hobbister (Orphir parish, Orkney) which granted the wadsetter the 'power to make outbreaks, to rive out corn land and grass, and to alter, flit, and remove dykes, quoys and faulds from one part to another within the proper bounds of the said lands'.[89] Only during the seventeenth century can we start to pencil in the details of its practice. Because it called for collective controls, the folding of stock became, understandably, the first aspect of the system to generate really detailed documentation. Local court records, both barony and regality, show through a succession of acts or fines how tenants were required to keep their stock in the common fold at night and to maintain the fóld dyke.[90] The labour of outfield folding, which is no doubt how the average farmer saw it, is well illustrated in a series of extracts dated 1511 to 1513 from the *Rentale Dunkeldense*. The extracts relate to the baronies of Dunkeld and Aberlady, and refer successively to making the 'flakis for my Lord's sheep', the building of 'dykes for the cattle and sheep folds', the labour of 'keeping and changing (*mutatione*) the sheepfold', and of 'pulling down dykes (*distruentes fossas*) for ploughing'.[91] Obligations exacted from the tenants in this respect also begin to appear in Baron Court records.

Apart from the grass provided by their outfield, grazing was

---

to outsets, though, do not occur in the *Register of the Great Seal* until the early 16th century. See ibid., pp. 706–8 and 778.

[88] Amongst the more interesting of the references available during the mid- and late 16th century are J. M. Thomson (ed.), *The Register of the Great Seal of Scotland 1546–1580* (Edinburgh, 1886), p. 458, which refers to the 'quartem de Outfeild de Byris (excepta the fauld vocat. Cragingurs-fauld' in Fife, and idem (ed.), *The Register of the Great Seal of Scotland 1593–1608* (Edinburgh, 1890), p. 325, which refers to one outfield having 'commoun fauldis'.

[89] Clouston (ed.), *Records of the Earldom of Orkney 1299–1614*, p. 322.

[90] Barron, op. cit., p. 70; *Black Book of Taymouth*, p. 352; *Miscellany of the Spalding Club*, v (Aberdeen, 1852), 'Court Book of the Barony of Leys 1636–1674', p. 232. The latter consists of an act which bound tenants and cottars in the mains to 'fald thair haill guidis, both nolt and scheip, nichtlie dureing the season; and ilk of thame, according to the number of thair guids, to walk the fald thair nicht about, least the guids, for want of attendance, brak the fald.' The Baron Court for Menzies also provides instances of Acts dealing with tathing, such as one which required 'the tennentis in everie towne [to] sett ther fauldis in order conform to use and wont and putt ther goods therin for tatheing their ley land . . .'—SRO, GD50/135, 11 July 1660.

[91] R. K. Hannay (ed.), *Rentale Dunkeldense 1505–1517*, Scottish History Society, 2nd ser., x (1915), pp. 117, 164, and 186.

also provided by commonty or common grazings. In some cases, these common grazings may have been common only to the tenants of one particular toun. In other cases, they were common to a number of touns and therefore subject to a much more complex pattern of regulation and usage. Yet a further variable was that, whilst most touns probably began the medieval period with locally available common grazings, the same was not true at the end of the medieval period. Many Lowland touns must have found themselves increasingly with no on-the-farm grass other than that of outfield and no *locally* available common grazings to act as a substitute. The Merse touns faced this predicament no less than other Lowland touns. By the seventeenth century, many of its touns had little permanent pasture actually on-the-farm. Instead, they were forced to rely on large Lowland commonties, whose use was shared between numerous touns and landowners, or on the grazing potential of the Lammermuirs, the Southern Uplands, and the Cheviots. In the case of the former, some touns, such as Ayton and Auchencraw, had legal access to former shire muirs such as that of Coldingham.[92] Others were able to tap the resources of a few large low-ground commonties whose infertility or poor drainage had inhibited colonization. Falling into this category were examples like the commonties of Hassendean, Stockstruther, and Fogo.[93] A more select group of touns had access to upland grazings which surrounded the Tweed valley. Thus, the toun of Chirnside beside the Tweed, possessed a very large muir some miles to the north on the southern slopes of the Lammermuirs.[94] The parish of Hilton also had common grazings removed some distance from it on the edge of the Lammermuirs, at Otterburn, and Wedderlairs in the parish of Longformacus, whilst the toun of Horndean had grazings at Dirnington.[95] The existence of these detached muirs may date back to the practice of some form of transhumance, when stock were sent away to the summer shielings for part of the year. Shielings certainly existed as the prevalence of the place-name element -*shiel* testifies.

[92] SRO, Home-Robertson MSS, GD227, Billie no. 621, Decreet of Division of the Commonty of Coldingham, 1772.

[93] SRO, Marchmont MSS, GD158, Box 4, Division of Fogo, 1739.

[94] J. Hewat Craw, 'Chirnside Common', *Proc. Berwickshire Naturalist Club*, xxiv (1922), pp. 423–50.

[95] Ibid., p. 423.

Alternatively, some detached muirs may reflect little more than the vagaries of estate-building. Both Chirnside and Longformacus, for instance, were held by the Home family back in the fifteenth century, so that the grazing of the latter by tenants of the former may only have begun at this late date. In fact, there are good reasons for believing that the *large-scale* use of distant shieling grounds by low-ground touns died out fairly early in the south-east, perhaps as early as the twelfth or thirteenth centuries. Large areas of the Southern Uplands and the Lammermuirs became Royal or baronial hunting forests. Furthermore, when they were eventually deforested, they were divided up into stedes or large self-contained pastoral holdings. In the Cheviots, the growth of a shieling system was almost certainly inhibited by the fact that a well-developed toun structure existed *within* the Cheviots as early as the seventh century, which would surely have resisted the penetration of the area by low-ground touns in search of summer grazings. Indeed, there is a pertinent eighteenth-century manuscript concerning the Cheviots which tells how 'three or 400 years ago the most Considerable heretors of that part of the East Border ... Set out their Lands to their Vassals of their own Surname with Considerable Commonty.'[96] Such grazing resources that did exist within the Cheviots then, were used by local touns. The Lammermuirs may have been a part exception to this early decline of shielings. On the one hand, there is the document cited in the previous chapter which gave Melrose Abbey rights of pasturage in the Lammermuirs but expressly forbade them to erect anything other than temporary 'Lodges', which is all many shieling sites were.[97] On the other hand, there is the detailed work by M. L. Parry showing that traces of settlement and colonization dating from around 1150 to 1250 can be found in the Lammermuirs, but that they were generally of a permanent nature rather than part of a shieling system.[98]

Further north and west, and particularly in the Highlands, arrangements were simpler. Around infield and outfield, there

---

[96] Floors Castle, Roxburgh MSS, Repr. Davidson of Summerdean agt. Pringle of Cliftoun, 1713.

[97] *Liber Sancte Marie de Melros*, vol. i, pp. xiv–xv.

[98] M. L. Parry, 'Secular Climatic Change and Marginal Agriculture', *TIBG* lxiv (1975), pp. 5–11.

was built a large turf dyke known as the head dyke:[99] beyond lay the muir, an area of common grazings that might be measured in hundreds of acres and, in some cases, even thousands of acres. Logically, where touns had access to vast areas of mountain pasture, and where there was no competition from alternative users, then such land was usually incorporated into the toun economy as shielings. The use of shielings and hill pasture as a vital source of grazing seems to have been particularly well developed along the eastern and southern edges of the Highlands where the juxtaposition of Lowland arable touns and upland waste seems to have been critical. The Barony of Urie (Kincardineshire) was in this position. Its reaction was typical of other baronies in the same circumstances. A Baron Court Act passed in late spring 1618, declared that it was 'statute and ordained by the common consent of the whole tenants of the barony of Wry, and in particular the tenants of *Mountquheiche*, that their whole goods shall pasture upon the Mounth and out bounds'.[1] Gordon of Straloch summarized the position in Moray in the mid-seventeenth century by saying that so 'much of the soil is occupied by crops of corn .. that pasture is scarce; for this whole district is devoted to corn and tillage. But pasture is found at no great distance, and is abundant in the upland country, a few miles inland, and thither the oxen are sent to graze in summer, when the labour of the season is over'.[2] In many cases, shielings acquired sufficient status for them to be recorded as a definite appendage of a particular toun. Mention of them is quite common in surveys and land charters. Typical is a mid-seventeenth-century disposition of the 'town and lands of Kinchurdie [Duthil parish, Inverness-shire] with sheilling called Third of the Wein lying in braes of Glenkernie near Water of Dullan formerly part of sheallings of lands of Aviemore'.[3] In a general study of the shieling system in Scotland, V. Gaffney refers, amongst other evidence, to a mid-seventeenth-century survey of the Forest of Atholl which details as many as 60

---

[99] Good early references to the head dyke occur in *Black Book of Taymouth*, p. 352; Donaldson, *Court Book of Shetland 1602–1604*, p. 118; SRO, GD50/150, 6 June 1622.

[1] Barron, op. cit., p. 26.

[2] *Registrum Episcopatus Moraviensis*, p. vii.

[3] D. C. Murray, 'Notes on the Parish of Duthill', *Trans. Gaelic Soc. Inverness*, xliii (1960–3), p. 26.

different shiels.[4] Roughly contemporaneous land charters can be used to fill in the gaps and to produce a fairly detailed picture of shiels in the area.[5]

The toun economy obviously required co-operation between tenants if it was to work smoothly. Most were assisted in this task by the oversight of a Baron or Birlaw Court, though a few were administered by a Regality Court. The authority and influence of such courts varied widely. Regality and Baron Courts naturally had the greater power, a power which they exercised through a whole series of acts of court on the husbandry or good-working of touns, levying fines and penalties for defaulters.[6] Such fines mostly took the form of money payments or the confiscation of goods, though a few courts seem to have applied a more retributive kind of law, such as the nailing of lugs for stock theft,[7] or one based more on the public humiliation of offenders, such as the wearing of placards proclaiming their transgressions outside the kirk on Sundays.[8] However, for all their power, such courts tended to be responsible for a group of touns, not just one, and for this reason may have seemed somewhat remote to the ordinary husbandman. By contrast, Birlaw Courts were more immediate since they functioned on a toun basis. Moreover, they were a court run by the toun community, passing judgement on itself. The air of self-help displayed by Birlaw Courts is well brought out by a sixteenth-century Coupar Angus Abbey tack which compelled tenants to 'hold a *byrlay* court among themselves'.[9] Its *ad hoc* character must have contrasted sharply with the powers vested in courts like the Melrose Regality Court, which acted as overseer to a number of large, runrig touns in the mid-Tweed valley that were shared between feuars, such as Eildon and Gattonside. Of course, Birlaw Courts did not necessarily function alone, as the only form of toun administration. In some cases,

[4] V. Gaffney, 'Shielings of the Drumochter', *SS* ii (1967), pp. 91–9. See also, Gaffney (ed.), *Lordship of Strathavon*, pp. 3 and 28–32.

[5] Atholl examples, for instance, are cited in land charters in SRO, *Calendar of Charters and Other Documents of E. J. Ferguson Esq. of Balemond*, nos. 1–293, 1328–1811, p. 94.

[6] The most readily available C. S. Romanes (ed.), *Selections from the Records of the Regality of Melrose 1605–1661*, Scottish History Society, vi (1914); ibid., *1662–1676*, Scottish History Society, viii (1915); ibid., *1547–1706*, Scottish History Society, xiii (1917).

[7] See, e.g., Cramond, *The Court Book of the Regality of Grant* (Banff, 1897), pp. 13, 14–15.

[8] W. A. Gillies, 'Extracts from the Baron Court Books of Menzies', *Trans. Gaelic Soc. of Inverness*, xxxix–xl (1942–50), p. 111.

[9] Rogers (ed.), op. cit., vol. i, p. 000.

they operated in conjunction with higher Baron Courts, in which case they can be seen as a delegation of the latter's power on a toun basis. The implementation of court acts was invariably carried out by appointed toun officers known as birlawmen, *ourmen* or, in the western Highlands and Islands, as constables or *Maor gruinnd* (or *am Maor beg*). The role of these toun officers is defined for us by an entry in the Forbes Barony Court book (Aberdeenshire). '. . . the birlamen', it said, 'is ordained upon a call by any tenants where there is any controversy either in march setting or in any other thing that is at odds . . . that upon the said call they shall go and settle the said business'.[10] Being a birlawman could not have been an easy task. At Forbes, the Court book records a warning that if 'any of the tenants of Tomades does scold or cross any of the *birly* men while they go about deciding controversies', they will be fined.[11] At Leys (Aberdeenshire), meanwhile, a court ruling of 1629 gave the birlawmen the power of the laird 'to take order with all *flytters* [quarrellers] and *bakbytters* as they find the fault'.[12] In some areas, such as the endemically unsettled area of Rannoch, it appears that tenants refused to be birlawmen.[13] Their reluctance is surprising, for the Barony Court book of Menzies indicates that, as part of their job, they were to 'take trial of all sorts of liquor, brandy and *acqua vitae* that shall happen to be proven, drunk and sold in the country' in order to decide its fair price.[14] When one goes on to read that, on one occasion, the Minister at Weem was seen 'so far drunk that when he came home he was dancing and louping over the bee skeps in his yard',[15] one can only speculate on whether it was his duties as a birlawman rather than a weakness of the flesh that gave rise to such athleticism. Needless to say, tenants were capable of similar excesses. A Die Scot who took the tack of Syokis on the Coupar Angus Abbey estate in 1466

---

[10] Thomson (ed.), 'Forbes Baron Court Book', p. 230. See also 'Corshill Baron Court Book', pp. 65–249 in *Archaeological and Historical Collections Relating to Ayrshire and Wigton* iv (Edinburgh, 1884), p. 72, which describes the role of 'birlaymen in redding of martches, pryseing of anything poyndit within the lairdshipe, and decideing of anything debaitable betwixt nychbour and nychtbour'.

[11] Thomson, 'Forbes Baron Court Book', p. 253.

[12] *Miscellany of the Spalding Club*, v, p. 224.

[13] Gillies, op. cit., p. 113.

[14] Ibid.

[15] Ibid., pp. 114–15. A full transcript of the Barony Court book of Menzies is available in SRO, GD50/135.

did so only on the condition that he 'shall be sober and temporate, preserving more strictly a kindly intercourse with his neighbours and relatives'.[16]

Two general areas of control were particularly important for the smooth working of touns: the orderly cropping of land and the seasonal movement of stock through the various sectors of the toun. Both came under the heading of a code of toun law known as 'the keeping of good neighbourhood', 'or good and sweet neighbourhood' as the Coupar Angus Abbey tacks phrased it.[17] This was a broadly defined concept which obliged landholders with 'land lying together in runrig . . . to concur in keeping of good neighbourhood one with another, in tilling, labouring, sowing, shearing, pasturing, and dyking, and in all other things pertaining to good and thrifty neighbourhood'.[18] In short, landholders had to do all things together or at least harmoniously. Where touns were supervised by a Barony or Regality Court, the various aspects of good neighbourhood were made the subject of special acts or orders and their infringement was punishable by fine. For instance, an entry in the Baron Court book of Belladrum (Ross and Cromarty) reaffirmed that it was 'statute that neighbours assist and concur one with another when they are required to comprise corns biggings grass and the like' and laid down a series of fines for any defaulter.[19] Likewise, at Godscroft in Berwickshire, the Barony court made it statute in 1629 that 'no goods be out of the folds or houses in the night, from when the sowing of corn begins till the corn yard *stoke* be stacked; pain, before midsummer, one night's lair in corn, one firlit corn, out of the corn being out of fold or house, half firlit corn; after midsummer being no corn, whole boll corn; out of corn, one firlit'.[20]

Needless to say, stock were affected by a wide range of other toun regulations. Their seasonal movement was always tightly controlled, often by acts of court. Typical is the declaration by the Glenorchy Barony Court book in 1631 that all stock was to be

---

[16] Rogers (ed.), op. cit., vol. i, p. 154.

[17] See, e.g., ibid., p. 187.

[18] Sir James Balfour, *Practicks 1469–1579* (Edinburgh, 1754), pp. 536–7.

[19] A. MacDonald, 'Old Highland Records: A Miscellany of', *Trans. Gaelic Soc. Inverness*, xliii (1960–3), p. 9.

[20] HMC, *Manuscripts of Col. David Milne Home of Wedderburn*, p. 85.

'outwith the head dyke from the 1st May and from the 8th day of June to pass to sheilings'.[21] At Selkirk, a court ruling of 1521 required all stock, except those needed for labouring, to be out of the infield and on the common grazings even earlier, or by the 9th of March.[22] In most cases, landholders were also required to put their stock to a common herd. For example, at Crail in Fife, a declaration of 1556/7 informed landholders that 'John Youll is chosen common herd . . . and that each neighbour that has beasts within the toun put them to the same herd'.[23] Suggestive of more complex arrangements is the way tenants on the Forbes estate who resided within the parishes of Kearne, Clatt, Forbes, and Achedor were bound to 'have one common herd among them' on their common grazings.[24] Signs of inter-toun agreement also emerges from a document concerning the commonty of Bordland and Shiprig in Peeblesshire. It mentions how the

pasturage of Bordland and Shiprig is estimated to feed yearly seven score soums grass, of which seventy-two kine are to be in milk soums and sixteen score milk cows and the rest to be yeld soums, viz., thirty-two yeld nolt, sixteen score yeld sheep, and eight horses or mares . . . A common herd is to be feed for each division by the respective heritor and tenants, each paying a proportional share, while those of Harcas and Northsheill are to cover the peat haggs yearly as they cast to prevent the drowing of their cattle.[25]

This last reference to peat haggs underlines that common grazings were a resource complex, exploited for a variety of products and not just grass. But, as it also makes clear, not all these uses were compatible. Indeed, the conflicting interests of grazing, peat-cutting, turfing, and 'firholling' were recurrent problems in Baron Courts generally.[26] Finally, as the aforemen-

[21] *Black Book of Taymouth*, p. 364. See also, GD50/159, 1 Nov. 1723.

[22] J. Imrie, T. I. Rae, and W. D. Ritchie (eds.), *The Burgh Court Book of Selkirk 1503–1545, part I 1503–31*, Scottish Record Society (Edinburgh, 1960), p. 61.

[23] J. E. L. Murray, 'The Agriculture of Crail, 1550–1600', *SS* viii (1964), p. 93.

[24] Thomson (ed.), 'Forbes Baron Court Book', p. 318.

[25] HMC, *Report on Manuscripts in Various Collections*, v (London, 1909), p. 25. Compare the problem raised at Fintry in Aberdeenshire, where the inhabitants of various touns who had abused their mosses were 'ordained to fill up their pots, levell their lair behind them and mend all former abuses'. See J. Cruickshank, 'The Court Book of the Barony of Fintray, 1711–1726', pp. 1–66 in *The Miscellany of the the Third Spalding Club* i (Aberdeen, 1935), p. 45.

[26] See, for example, *Miscellany of the Spalding Club*, 'Court Book of Skene, 1613–1687', p. 219.

tioned example of Bordland and Shiprig illustrates, stocking densities were controlled by the fixing of soums. The principle followed was that a landholder should only be allowed to graze on the 'outgerss' or common grazings what he could soum and roum on the 'ingerss' or infield in winter. A convenient equation of the two in practice is provided by the soums fixed for the Barony of Edindonyng in Stirlingshire, in a document of 1540, with landholders having the same level of soums in both.[27]

The Medieval Scottish Township: Its Settlement Form

Rural settlement in late medieval Scotland was based on the fermtoun or clachan, just as it was in the eighteenth century when estate plans provide us with the first graphic record of its precise form and layout. Early rentals do, in fact, use the term 'toun' quite often, but whether it described simply a township territory or a cluster of farmsteads is not always clear. Certainly, the settlements to which it was applied in early rentals stand out as the larger units from the point of view of the number of landholders. The term clachan also occurs quite early. It is even used in an Act of Parliament of 1581.[28] The idea that it was used initially to describe the distinctive stone-built dwellings associated with ecclesiastical sites is given a fragment of support by an early seventeenth-century observation on the parish of Houston in Renfrewshire: 'a pairt thereof being sett with Steillbow gear lyming multitude of houses and other extraordinarie industrie made be the inhabitantis and having ane Claghan towne att the kirk thairof'.[29] Although the size of settlement can be inferred from contemporary rentals, it is rarely possible to say anything about the layout of such settlement. Later cartographic evidence suggests they were dominated, but not overwhelmingly so, by an irregular, unplanned appearance and a location in the contact zone between the toun's arable and pasture.[30] There are

[27] HMC, *Third Report* (London, 18729, p. 406.

[28] *APS* v, p. 113.

[29] *Reports on the State of Certain Parishes in Scotland 1627*, p. 193. The idea of it being something different from a normal toun is also conveyed by the phrase 'intra lie Clachane et villam de Cumnok' in a charter of 1580, see Thomson, *Register of the Great Seal of Scotland 1580–1593*, p. 6. There is also the comment by Bishop Leslie about Carrick that 'mony thair clachans, bot mony mae villages', see P. Hume Brown, *Scotland Before 1700 from Contemporary Documents* (Edinburgh, 1893), p. 118.

[30] Their irregular, untidy appearance impressed Edmund Burt, an Englishman who

exceptions to both these generalizations, especially in the more fertile areas, where settlement sometimes had a more orderly plan and a more centrally located position in regard to its arable land.[31] However, they do express the basic form of the majority of settlements. Whether they apply equally to earlier forms remains to be seen. Field archaeologists have carried out valuable work on a number of sites, but their sample so far is still relatively small when considered in the context of medieval Scotland as a whole. A major investigation into the nature of medieval rural settlement is currently in progress in the Uists. As in other parts of the Hebrides, the Uists have seen considerable changes of settlement layout during the last few centuries. These layers of recent change have to be stripped from the problem before we can isolate those sites which, on excavation or by detailed ground survey, may yield positive clues of the nature of early domestic settlement. Guided by estate plans and rentals, I. A. Crawford established that in the selected study area of North Uist, only ten *bailtean*, out of fifty-five, can be both located on the ground and dated back with confidence to before the eighteenth century: those of Sollas, Balelock, Tigharry, Balranald, Clachan Sand, Griminish, Balillery, Penmore, Weilist, and Dunamich.[32] The isolation of these settlements as pre-1700 touns guided the excavations which are now being carried out at Coileagan an Udail or Veilish. Preliminary reports of the excavation suggest the choice was a wise one, with a sequence of occupation that embraces the late Iron Age, the Pictish period, the Norse, the medieval period, and the nineteenth century. With regard to the medieval period, one of the most telling conclusions so far reached is that Gaelic culture had reasserted itself fully by the twelfth century. Of Norse culture, only the rectangular ground-plan of its dwellings remained as a visible sign of its contribution to the culture of the region. However, in case it is assumed that

---

visited the Highlands in the 1720s. He described Highland touns as 'composed of a few huts for dwellings, with barns and stables, . . . all irregularly placed, some one way, some another, and at any distance look like so many heaps of dirt'. See *Burt's Letters from the North of Scotland*. With intro. by R. Jamieson (Edinburgh, 1876 edn.), vol. ii, p. 130.

[31] The writer has in mind the hints of order apparent at settlements like Duncanstown (SRO, RHP 5199/7), Old Flinders (SRO, RHP 5199/2), and at Kelly (SRO, RHP 2153) when they were surveyed in the mid-18th century.

[32] I. A. Crawford, 'Contributions to a History of Domestic Settlement in North Uist', *SS* ix (1965), pp. 34–65.

the long, low, rectangular-shaped black house or *tigh dubh* of today, preserves—by direct descent—the general style of the original Norse dwellings, two other conclusions by Crawford are of interest. First, with one or two exceptions, the buildings on the uppermost or present-day layer of occupation date back to the nineteenth century. Secondly, 'the later sequence at the Udal indicates changes in design in the 16th and 17th centuries, interrupting any possible longer term Norse continuity.'[33]

Excavation, however, is not always productive of answers about the earlier phases of settlement. At Lix in Perthshire, where a fermtoun has been excavated on a large-scale, numerous changes of layout were evidenced for the eighteenth and nineteenth centuries, but there was no trace of pre-1700 occupation sites. The excavator, H. Fairhurst, negotiated this problem by arguing that building materials before this date may have been of a more perishable kind and therefore less easily detectable than the stone walls or footings of more recent structures.[34] As a rule, the typical peasant house within the central and northern Highlands area was either turf- or wattle-walled around a timber frame.[35] Only towards the northern and western seaboards was stone a common building material for peasant houses before the eighteenth century. Quite apart from the perishable materials used for early domestic dwellings, there are other factors which Fairhurst does not mention. An important one is that precisely because they were perishable, early dwellings were subject to changes of site. The pulling down of dwellings, the removal of their timbers or roof couples, and their reconstruction or replacement by new dwellings meant there was an ongoing metamorphosis of settlement layout.[36] Such a process could quite easily have led to new sites and not just new alignments. Arguably of even more relevance to Lix is the fact

[33] Crawford, 'Scot(?) Norseman and Gael', p. 1.

[34] H. Fairhurst and G. Petrie, 'Scottish Clachans II: Lix and Rosal', *SGM* lxxx (1964), pp. 152–6.

[35] Early references to turf- or wattle-walled houses are available in Sir Arthur Mitchell, 'James Robertson's Tour Through Some of the Western Islands, ETC, of Scotland 1768', *PSAS* xxxii (1897–8), p. 14.

[36] Relevant comment can be found in *Burt's Letters*, pp. 28–9 where he talks about the ruins of houses to be found at the edge of towns. 'When one of these houses was grown old and decayed' he wrote, 'they often did not repair it, but, taking out the Timber, they let the Walls stand as a fit Enclosure for a Kale-Yard (i.e. a little Garden for coleworts) and that they built anew upon another Spot.' Baron Court records are also helpful. At Skene,

that it represented a split settlement, with a West, Mid, and East Lix. The splitting of the toun into these three portions almost certainly shifted the focus of settlement in a way that may disguise the site of any original nucleus (see also pp. 195–204). The settlement sites in southern Scotland which have been dated to the medieval period are largely in upland or moorland edge situations. Their significance, therefore, needs to be handled with a certain amount of care. Falling very much into this category are sites like that at Lour, near Slibo in Peebleshire. This consists of a series of one- or two-roomed rectangular houses disposed on an irregular plan within a semicircular enclosure. Their occupation has been dated to the sixteenth and seventeenth centuries.[37] Rectangular house plans have also been reported at Douglas Burn (Selkirkshire), Dunrod (Kirkcudbright), and Galtway (Kirkcudbright). Each of these three sites represents a small clustered settlement which, at some point, has been abandoned. Although one of the houses at Douglas Burn has been excavated and dated to the medieval period, the sites at Dunrod and Galtway are only presumed from historical references to have been occupied during the medieval period.[38] Given that all three sites display fairly good surface detail, it is a pity they have not been surveyed. On a longer-term basis, their complete excavation would tell us a great deal about the living conditions of the medieval Scots peasant. Possibly less typical is the settlement which has been excavated in Manor parish (Peebleshire). It comprises a group of circular or semicircular huts set within a scooped enclosure and bounded by a drystone wall.[39] Like the settlement at nearby Lour, its occupation has been dated to the late medieval peiod. For comparison, circular huts of medieval date have been reported at Muirkirk (Ayrshire), but there, they existed alongside houses of rectangular shape.[40]

'persones that ar infamous' in the toun of Cragidarge were banished the barony, the court preventing their return by declaring 'thar houses to be cassin doune and to be removed'. See *Miscellany of the Spalding Club*, v, p. 135. So scarce was timber in the Highlands, that it was common for tenants to remove doors and roof couples or tails at the end of their tack. See ibid., pp. 218–19 and ibid., 'Court Book of Barony of Leys 1636–1674', p. 223.

[37] J. G. Dunbar and G. D. Hay, 'Excavations at Lour, Stobo, 1959–60', *PSAS* xciv (1960–1), pp. 196–210.

[38] L. Laing, 'Medieval Settlement Archaeology in Scotland', *SAF* (1969), pp. 69–77.

[39] R. B. K. Stevenson, 'Medieval Dwelling Sites and a Primitive Village in the Parish of Manor, Peeblesshire, *PSAS* lxxv (1942–3), pp. 91–115.

[40] Laing, 'Medieval Settlement Archaeology in Scotland', p. 72.

Chapter 6

The Medieval Farming Township
and its Dimensions of Change 1100–1650

Traditional perspectives on the old Scottish fermtoun emphasize its archaic or primitive character. Whether construed as an occupied site, a collectively-conscious group of farmers, or in terms of institutions like infield–outfield and runrig, the toun is seen as developing early, possibly during the closing centuries of the prehistoric period, and then surviving without radical change up to the eighteenth century. Such a view does little justice to the evidence at our disposal or to the medieval farming community. In place of it, the argument to be expounded here favours a much greater degree of change and innovation during the medieval period. Indeed, far from being a self-effacing interlude of stagnation, the late medieval period may need instating as a vital one in the history of the Scottish rural society, a period when many important features of rural organization were first conceived. Altogether, three aspects will be examined, each of which expresses the different ways in which the early Scottish township expanded and developed. First, there is the straightforward increase in the number of settlements. Secondly, there is the way in which established settlements expanded outwards to fill up the landscape. Thirdly, there is the problem of how growth was absorbed once the opportunities for new settlement or further growth had been exhausted. In each of these possible dimensions of growth, the late medieval period witnessed considerable activity.

The Expansion of Settlement

If we could re-create the pattern of rural settlement at the point when the Scottish kingdom first came into being, it is likely we would find most areas already occupied but with a pattern of settlement that was still elementary and immature when compared with that of later centuries. On the lower ground, both in the central valley and the lowlands of eastern and north-eastern

Scotland, the occupation of land must have worn a patchwork appearance. What were to be the larger touns already existed: early land charters say as much. So do place-names. However, around them must have stretched large areas of lowland waste whose colonization was still a matter of prospect rather than retrospect. As one moves into the more hilly or mountainous ground, though much more so in the Highlands than in the Southern Uplands, settlement was probably still very sparse with a great deal of the settlement pattern, as it came to be, not yet formed. Beyond, in the coastal areas of the extreme north and west and in both the Northern Isles and Hebrides, the situation must have been similar to that which prevailed in the Lowlands, with the basic framework of settlement already established, but with much interstitial settlement still to develop.

The study of how the settlement pattern filled out over the next four hundred to five hundred years requires a flexible approach, for only in a relatively small number of cases do land charters proclaim their pioneering nature. Especially valuable amongst the latter are those dating from the twelfth and thirteenth centuries, a period of unquestionable colonizing activity, but one which is poorly documented. Some betoken the expanding settlement of the countryside through their reference to land units being newly laid out. Of this type is one dated 1173 to 1177 which conveyed a ploughgate of land in Mow (Morebattle parish, Roxburghshire) to Paisley Priory (later Abbey) 'by the marches measured and perambulated, with pasture for 500 sheep and for as many animals as are allowed with one ploughgate in that toun'.[1] The closing phrase 'in that toun' suggests that there was already settlement in Mow and that this particular land grant expanded its arable without actually creating a new settlement. However, as their cartularies graphically demonstrate, most abbeys with property in the Cheviots were inclined to hold their land as separate touns.[2] Further north, across the Forth and Tay, references to ploughgates being 'measured out', such as a ploughgate in a clearing at Burgie (= Burgin, Moray) 1153 to 1165

[1] G. W. S. Barrow, *The Acts of William I*, pp. 241–2.
[2] A valuable review of the way the abbeys built up their holdings in areas like the Cheviots can be found in Duncan, *Scotland: The Making of the Kingdom*, pp. 416–19. Documented perambulation agreements are to be found in *Liber S. Marie de Calchou*, vol. i, p. 144 and *Origines Parochiales Scotiae*, vol. i, pp. 394–5, 410, and 426.

or the two ploughgates at Kennethmont (Aberdeenshire) 1189 to
1190, again have an air of newness about them, and cannot easily
be taken as merely old-established landholdings being re-phrased
in terms more familiar to the Scottish Crown.[3] Here and there
amongst these, the earliest of Scottish land charters, are further
clues on the pioneering nature of the times. Thus, one of 1165 to
1174 refers to men settled or about to settle on the muir at
Leuchoruer (Loquhariot) above Borthwick (Midlothian). As if
to bring them within the orbit of Church and civil administration, it ordered them to render teinds and other obligations.[4]
Likewise, another dated 1189 to 1196 refers to the transfer of
tenants from Elrehope to what the grantor, William the Lion,
called 'my waste land in Selkirk'.[5] A few years earlier, land in the
same forest had been granted to Glasgow Cathedral Church,
with permission to 'plough, sow and cultivate everywhere within
the fence which was erected on the day this charter was made' (21
October 1179).[6] A few charters conveyed land in 'clearings', like
the grant of land at Burgie (= Burgin, Moray) mentioned above or
at Blainslie (Roxburghshire) in 1189 to 1190, the latter eventually growing into the large and complex toun cluster of Nether,
Upper, Middle, South, and New Blainslie.[7] Finally, there is a
small handful of charters which declare themselves unam-
biguously as grants of new land, such as that dated 1200 to 1214
which endowed Melrose Abbey with 'new land' at Harehope
(Eddleston, Peeblesshire).[8]

Moving forward in time, a late burst of settlement formation
seems to have occurred during the late fifteenth, sixteenth, and
seventeenth centuries. Some heralded the invasion of disafforested areas. However, in areas already well settled, much of it was of
a peripheral or subsidiary nature, the final pieces in the jigsaw of
local landholding. This is apparent from its description and
treatment. For instance, a number of settlements were outsets
carved out of the adjoining waste by established touns which then
shrugged off these associations to become independent touns.

[3] *Liber S. Thome de Aberbrothoc, vol. I, 1178–1329*, Bannatyne Club (Edinburgh, 1848), p.
55.
[4] Barrow, *Acts of William I*, pp. 203–4.
[5] Ibid., p. 363.
[6] Ibid., p. 263.
[7] Ibid., p. 318.
[8] Ibid., pp. 425–6.

They are manifest in charters or rentals by still being tagged as outsets but are otherwise treated as separate touns with their own names, such as Suyford and Longford in Clatt parish (Aberdeenshire) which began life as outsets of Overknockespack.[9] Others are described as pendicles of Auchinory in a rental of Kinloss Abbey, 1574.[10] Their subsidiary nature is often disclosed by their names, for many used prefixes like 'Newtoun of. . .' or 'Muirtoun of . . .', or else incorporated strong topographic elements, as Stockwood, Claypotts, Burnside, and Woodhead, which were labelled as outsets of Stobhall Mains (Stirlingshire) in a charter of 1582.[11] Even when such new growth is not labelled as an outset or pendicle, place-names can still assist. Little imagination, for example, is needed to discern the colonizing history behind the reference in 1600 to 'lands in Edinsmure cum lie Inland' (Aberdeenshire),[12] or that in the Kinloss Abbey rental of 1574 to 'the Newlands of Millegin called Jonsettis Scheill'.[13] Supporting the same conclusion but in a manner that is itself short on imagination, is the reference in 1555 to 'terras de novo moro erupto, vulgo the New-revin-oute-mure' (Stirlingshire).[14] Providing a slightly more elaborate course of development are those outsets which developed into outfield systems and which, having been cultivated as such by one toun, were detached to form the arable basis of another. At Dalhousie (Midlothian), for instance, an early seventeenth-century source said that the toun 'wanted a great muir called Dalhousie outfield which it had of old. The muir is now set out to David Ramsay for one hundred pounds yearly.'[15] Using an eighteenth-century estate plan as his base map, Whittington has attempted to reconstruct the later settlement history of the Pitkellony estate in Perthshire. His conclusions suggest it affords a convenient illustration within a single context of the various processes just discussed, with outsets and

[9] J. Robertson (ed.), *Illustrations of the Topography and Antiquities of the Shires of Aberdeen and Banff*, Spalding Club (Aberdeen, 1862), vol. iv, p. 500.

[10] Ibid., p. 238.

[11] J. M. Thomson (ed.), *Register of the Great Seal of Scotland 1580–1593* (Edinburgh, 1888), p. 136.

[12] Robertson, op. cit., vol. iv, p. 505.

[13] Ibid., p. 238.

[14] Thomson (ed.), *Register of the Great Seal 1546–1580*, p. 191.

[15] *Reports on the State of Certain Parishes in Scotland 1627*, p. 48.

outfields acquiring separate settlements and independence.[16]

The only major areas where settlement was delayed until well into the late medieval period were the Royal Forests and baronial hunting grounds. In aggregate, they consumed a considerable amount of land. In the Southern Uplands, large Royal and baronial forests were to be found in Ettrick, Annandale, Eskdale, and Dalquhairn. Further north, sizeable forests were to be found in the Clyde valley, such as that of Lesmahagow. The cores of both the Pentland and Moorfoot Hills were once Royal forests, as were substantial areas on either side of the Forth in Stirlingshire and Clackmannanshire. Numerous scattered Royal forests were also to be found disposed around the eastern Highlands, from the Braes of Angus in the south to the fairly large Darnaway Forest in Nairn and Moray.[17] Such forests were not simply areas of waste, but legally protected hunting grounds within which the rights of hunting were jealously guarded for their lords and from which all activities inimical to hunting were excluded. Sometimes grazing was permitted by special licence but nothing that would disturb the animals of the chase. A clear illustration of this is the grant made of grazing rights in Eskdale Forest from the Avenal family to Melrose Abbey. It reserved to the Avenal family 'hart and hind, boar and roe, the aeries of falcons and tercels . . . The monks were expressly excluded from hunting with hounds or nets, from setting traps, except for wolves, and from taking the aeries of hawks.'[18] Settlement, in particular, was strictly forbidden as the grants of pasturage which Melrose Abbey received in the forests of Ettrick and the Lammermuirs bear out.[19] The earliest hunting forests were established as such during the twelfth and thirteenth centuries. But during the fourteenth and fifteenth centuries, the process was reversed as many areas were disafforested and opened up to settlement again. This reversal, however, was not a consistent trend. As large parts of the Southern Uplands and the north-east Lowlands lost their legal status as forest land, the King

[16] G. Whittington, 'Field Systems of Scotland', pp. 512–79 in A. R. H. Baker and R. A. Butlin (eds.), *Studies of Field Systems in the British Isles* (Cambridge, 1973), pp. 552–67.

[17] Based on J. M. Gilbert, 'Hunting Reserves', pp. 33–4 and map 21 in P. McNeill and R. Nicholson (eds.), *An Historical Atlas of Scotland c.400–c.1600* (St Andrews, 1975).

[18] *Liber Sancte Marie de Melros*, vol. i, p. xvi.

[19] Ibid., pp. xiv–v.

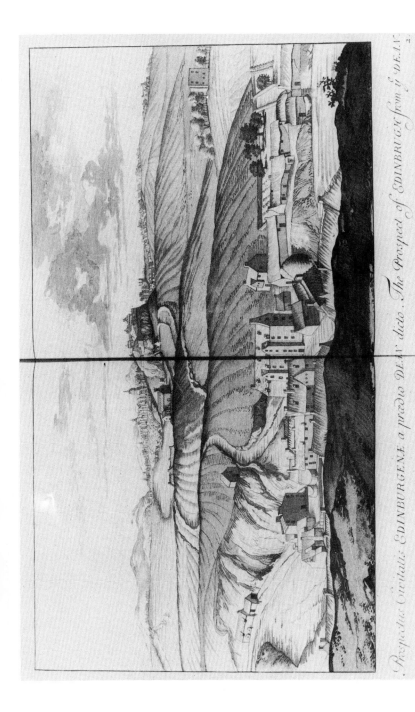

Prospectus Civitatis EDINBURGENÆ a prædio DEAN dicto. The Prospect of EDINBURGH from it DEAN.

1. Prospect of Edinburgh from J. Slezer, *Theatrum Scotiae* (London, 1693), no. 34

2. Runrig Lands of Aberdour (Fife), *c.* 1750. Based on SRO, RHP 1022

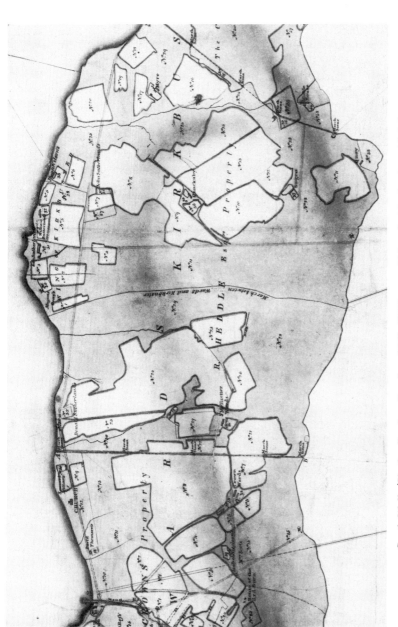

3. South Walls (Shetland), 1823. Based on SRO, RHP 2393. Although this plan is entitled the run-rig lands of South Walls, it does not record the intermixed strips of the various landholders, only the arable shots on which they were based (arable = light shaded areas, pasture = dark-shaded areas).

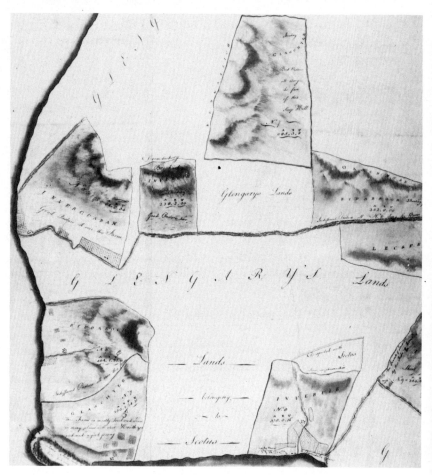

4. Part of Barrisdale, 1769. Based on SRO, RHP 112

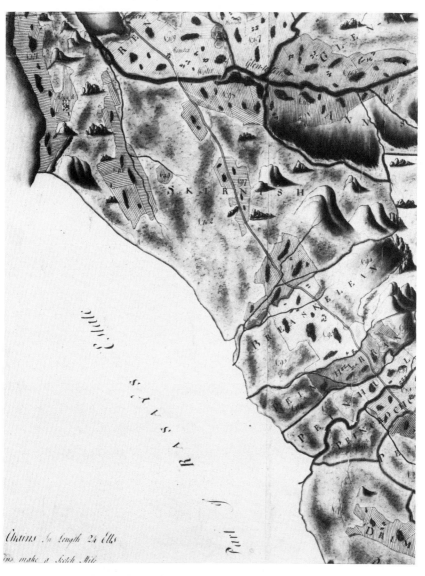

5. Part of north Skye, 1766. Based on SRO, RHP 5993

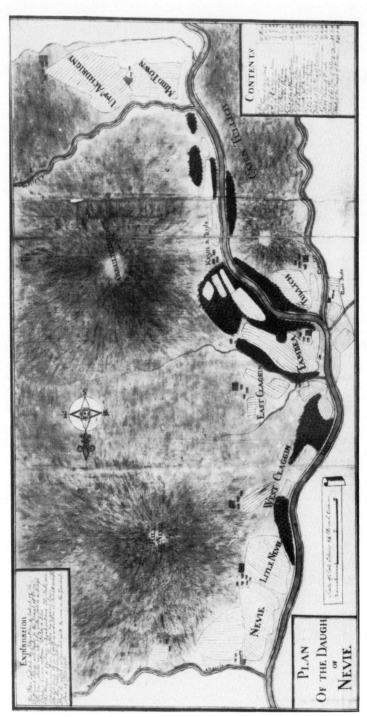

6. Daugh of Nevie, Glen Livet, 1761. Based on SRO, RHP 2487

established new hunting forests in the southern Highlands, such as those of Glenfinglas and Mamlorne, during the fifteenth century.[20]

These broad changes in the over-all budget of forest land, an increase over the twelfth and thirteenth centuries followed by a decrease over the fourteenth and fifteenth centuries together with a shift in the geography of those that remained, meant that land which had hitherto been devoid of settlement was progressively opened up to colonization as the late medieval period wore on. This dramatic revaluation and its implications for settlement can be traced with some degree of clarity in the Southern Uplands, where the large districts of Ettrick, Liddesdale, Annandale, and Eskdale were stripped of their forest status in the century or so that followed their point of maximum coverage in the thirteenth century. The Morton estate rental of 1376, for instance, records a number of pasture farms or stedes, like Todistede, Alcokstede, Gumerstede, and Carryschelis in Liddesdale and on Eskdale-muir, that had conceivably been forest land not long before. More suggestive still, under the heading of 'foresta', it lists 42 touns, including such large and notable Border farms as Braidlie, Gorrenberry, Ladlawhope, and Sougden. It is possible that these stedes existed within Eskdale forest rather than replacd it. If so, then by their collective extent, they must have formed a very broad swathe running through Scotland's premier forest at this date in time. More realistically, we can see them as holdings created out of the forest during the preceding fifty years or so.[21] The colonization of Ettrick forest needs to be seen over a longer time span. Erected into a forest during the twelfth century, small encroachments were already being conceded to ecclesiastical landowners like Melrose Abbey or Glasgow Cathedral church by the end of the thirteenth century.[22] But apart from these concessions, the only settlement to be found within its bounds at this stage was that belonging to the foresters responsible for its management as a hunting forest, but even this was restricted in nature with no cultivation allowed by them.[23] The first signs of a

---

[20] Gilbert, op. cit., p. 34.

[21] *Registrum Honoris de Morton*, pp. xlvii ff.

[22] See, for instance, *Liber Sancte Marie de Melros*, vol. i, p. 94.

[23] A Forester was restricted from having on 'his steid haggar, flegeour, turnour, barcar, colebyrnar, pelar of bark, scab, pikar, wrychtis, swne, nor gait' and were bound to hav 'na

radical change in this situation appeared in the fifteenth century, when Crown rentals record the presence of 'sheep stedis' in the Forest.[24] Over the next century or so, their number increased dramatically, the whole area being put under a network of sheep stedes. Indeed, by the early sixteenth century, the whole of the Border country was famed for the impressive size of both its sheep farms and flocks.[25] Comparable processes of relatively late colonization are to be found in Forest areas outside the Southern Uplands. The Forest of Drimmie in the Braes of Angus, for example, experienced an increasing amount of settlement from the fourteenth century onwards.[26] Further north, A. S. Mather has documented the late colonization of Glen Strathfarrer (Inverness-shire), an east–west-running glen just north of the Great Glen which joins Strathglass about ten miles upstream from the mouth of the River Beauly. For most of the medieval period, its settlement was restricted to Culligan at its mouth and various scattered shielings used by touns in the Aird. Beginning in 1589, this pattern changed with new permanent settlements emerging, such as Deanie and Archuilk, as a tide of colonization moved westwards up the Glen. In some cases, this new growth probably involved the upgrading of shieling sites into permanent settlements. Thus, Inchvuilt, almost at the head of the Glen, appears to have come into existence initially as a shieling for Belladrum in the Aird.[27]

Opportunities exist for placing this whole problem of settlement growth during the late medieval period on a more systematic footing. This can be done by the simple content analysis of contemporary charters and rentals. The survival of thanages and shires as integral estate units after the twelfth century is extremely relevant in this context. In a few cases, it has meant that charters afford a comprehensive, if not a complete view, of a multiple estate and its constituent settlements at a very

telin, sawin, delfyne or ony mauer of corne within the forsaid forrest'. See G. Burnett (ed.), *The Exchequer Rolls of Scotland. vol. XI, A.D. 1497–1501* (Edinburgh, 1888), pp. 394–5.

[24] The earliest detailed view of the unfolding pattern of 'stedes' in Ettrick is in ibid., pp. 397 ff.

[25] Brown, *Scotland Before 1700*, p. 48.

[26] The charter in Easson (ed.), op. cit., vol. i, pp. 52–7 and 93–8 should be compared with Rogers (ed.), op. cit., vol. ii, pp. 195–201.

[27] A. S. Mather, 'Pre-1745 Land Use and Conservation in a Highland Glen: An Example from Glen Strathfarrar, North Inverness-shire', *SGM* lxxxvi (1970), pp. 163–4.

early date. Set beside later evidence, such as rentals, the comparison can be revealing. Thus, a charter of 1180 × 1184 conveying what probably formed the thanage of Birse to the Bishop of Aberdeen can be compared with a rental drawn up three hundred years later in 1511.[28] Likewise, the charter issued by King Edgar in 1095 for Coldingham shire might be compared with the rental covering roughly the same territory compiled by Coldingham Priory *c.*1300. In each case, the comparison points to a general increase in the number of touns.[29] Of course, this simple faith in early land charters as a complete record of settlement is questionable. But arguably, their reliability increases with time. Serial analysis of later charters and particularly rentals dating from the fifteenth century onwards suggest they are quite sensitive indicators of the appearance of new settlement. Used as such, they affirm the point made earlier that a burst of settlement formation seems to have occurred during the late fifteenth, sixteenth, and seventeenth centuries. For example, a list of touns comprising the six davachs in Glenelg held by the MacLeod chief during the mid-sixteenth century specifies 17 touns.[30] By the late seventeenth century, rentals for the estate show their number had increased to 33.[31] Increases, but on a less dramatic scale, are also evident for Islay, 1509 to 1686,[32] Tiree, 1542 to 1768,[33] and in Sunart, 1542 to 1718,[34] and Morvern, 1496 to 1751.[35] According to Crawford, an increase is also detectable in rentals for South Uist over the same period.[36] However, in Ardnamurchan, a slight decrease is apparent, 1542 to 1718.[37]

[28] Both the late 12th-century charter and the 16th-century rental are printed in G. F. Browne (ed.), *Echt-Forbes Family Charters 1345–1727: Records of the Forest of Birse 926–1781* (Aberdeen, 1923), pp. 192–7.

[29] The 11th-century charter is mapped by Barrow, 'Pre-Feudal Scotland', p. 31. For the *c.*1300 rental see *Priory of Coldingham*, pp. 1–122.

[30] The 1583 list is given in *Origines Parochiales Scotiae*, vol. ii, part ii, p. 829.

[31] MacLeod, op. cit., vol. ii, p. 85.

[32] Smith, *Book of Islay*, pp. 490–520 and 584–5.

[33] M'Neill (ed.), op. cit., p. 614 and E. Cregeen (ed.), *Argyll Estate Instructions (Mull, Morvern, Tiree) 1771–1805*, Scottish History Society, 4th ser., I (1964), list on plan in rear folder.

[34] M'Neill (ed.), op. cit., pp. 624–5 and Stanhope, *True Interest of Great Britain, Ireland and Our Plantations*, Table vi.

[35] *Origines Parochiales Scotiae*, vol. ii, part i, pp. 190–1. Later information abstracted from P. Gaskell, *Morvern Transformed* (Cambridge, 1968), pp. 127–8 and 130–66.

[36] Crawford, 'Contributions to a History of Domestic Settlement in North Uist', Table I.

[37] M'Neill, op. cit., p. 622.

Moving across the country to the east and south, comparable increases over roughly the same period can be researched systematically through rentals and toun lists for areas like Aberdeenshire[38] and the Southern Uplands.[39]

A potentially valuable approach to the problem of settlement growth, and one that offers further scope for systematic analysis, is through land assessments. Land assessments relate to different layers of influence. If their chronology of inception can be unravelled even in general terms, it may tell us much about the settlements to which they are attached. For example, in 1962, Barrow pointed out that although the carucate was pre-dominantly a land unit of south-east Scotland, nevertheless, a number of charters 'speak unblushingly and without hesitation of carucates north of the Forth'.[40] He also made the observation that the treatment of these northern carucates was similar to that of the davach in the sense that each one had a separate toponym. This contrasts with their use south of the Forth, where they are generally referred to as so many carucates in the 'toun of . . .'. To Barrow, this difference in the manner of their use suggested that north of the Forth, the carucate was simply another name for the davach, the 'most respectable term available to the latinizing clerks who wrote our documents. Thus, northern "carucates" might not be the same as southern, though they would have borne some relation to them.'[41] Seen in this way, the use of the carucate says nothing about when such settlements were founded. However, Duncan has taken a different line of argument. He has proposed that the occurrence of carucates between the Forth and Mounth denotes settlements established following the spread of Crown feudalism into the area over the twelfth and

---

[38] Comparison, for instance, can be made between a 1424 list of farms in Aberdour parish in Robertson, op. cit., vol. iv, pp. 380–1 or the 1511 list of farms in Chapel of Garioch in ibid., p. 376 with the 1696 lists in J. Stuart (ed.), *List of Pollable Persons Within the Shire of Aberdeen 1696* (Aberdeen, 1844), vol. i, pp. 291–307; vol. ii, pp. 63–76. Not all such comparisons reveal change. A comparison, for example, between the 1552 rental of the Forbes estate in Huntly, *Records of Aboyne*, pp. 45 ff. with a 1740 rental (SRO, GD52/285) suggests no real change.

[39] Comparison between the Ettrick rentals in *The Exchequer Rolls of Scotland*, vi, 1455–1460 (Edinburgh, 1883), pp. 223–4 and ibid. xi, 1497–1501 (1888), pp. 457–60 with rentals in SRO, Buccleuch MSS, GD224/280/I, Rental Books of Ettrick Forest 1681–1719 show considerable change.

[40] Barrow, 'Rural Settlement in Central and Eastern Scotland', p. 266.

[41] Ibid., p. 266

thirteenth centuries.[42] His reasoning centres on the fact that some touns have land assessed in davachs alongside land assessed in oxgates, a sub-unit of the carucate. In such circumstances, he argued, their distinction must be meaningful, otherwise they would surely have been put in common form. In searching for this meaning, Duncan concentrates on a point which Barrow has sympathy with, namely, that the davach or its sub-units formed consolidated holdings (hence its identification as a separate place-name), whilst the carucate was usually part of a large open field complex (hence its tendency towards anonymity south of the Forth). With this in mind, he concludes that some carucates north of the Forth must 'represent the spread of the open field and open field agriculture beyond the Forth, with all that that implies in terms of breaking out new arable to link up the small fields represented by the davach'.[43] If accepted as valid, such an idea would provide a *terminus post quem* for dating those settlements north of the Forth that were computed in carucates.

A similar opportunity for discriminating between different phases of settlement formation exists for the Northern Isles. The imposition of skat tax on settlements during the Norse period means that subsequent growth can be gauged by plotting unskatted holdings. As noted earlier, a major difficulty is deciding on when skat was introduced. Estimates range from c.AD 900 to the twelfth century whilst one recent suggestion is that it was subject to an ongoing adjustment to incorporate new land throughout the Norse period.[44] Such differences of opinion greatly affect the relative dating of skat and unskatted settlements. Working on the assumption that it was imposed c.AD 900 and that its pattern of imposition remained fixed thereafter, O'Dell has mapped skatted and unskatted settlements in Shetland. What he found was that unskatted settlements did not open new areas but merely intensified or filled in the gaps in the existing pattern of skatted settlements.[45] The distinction between settlements with merklands and those without in the Northern Isles also provides a bais for discrimination. Again, however, there are problems in trying to give this distinction an absolute

---

[42] Duncan, *Scotland: the Making of the Kingdom*, p. 320.
[43] Ibid., p. 320.
[44] See p. 55, fn. 83.
[45] O'Dell, *Historical Geography of the Shetland Islands*, p. 274.

chronology, but those settlements without a merkland assessment are unlikely to date from the thirteenth century or before.[46] O'Dell's study of settlements without such an assessment in Shetland conformed to the same pattern as unskatted settlements, intensifying the main areas of settlement rather than adding new ones.[47]

The Formation of Outfield

Perhaps the most self-evident change of the medieval period consisted of the outward expansion of existing settlement into the surrounding waste. Even in the Lowlands, most settlements must have begun the medieval period as detached pockets of occupied land surrounded by waste. Their progressive absorption of this waste was not a straightforward affair. In fact, the process has much to tell us about the character and institutional structure of the early Scottish toun.

The crux of the problem was not so much the legitimacy of a toun's colonizing the surrounding waste, but its inability to absorb such land smoothly or neatly into the existing framework of the toun. The rigidity of touns in this respect stemmed from the fact that they generally possessed a fixed assessment of land units. Whether these land units were davachs or carucates, husband-lands or pennylands, merklands or bovates, they each constituted a fixed or measured amount of land. Often the evidence steps aside from the task of using these land measures as if their value as quantities was understood and tells us exactly how much they do contain. Thus, the Earl of March was said to have 'caused his servant Sim Samond to divide the whole lands in the Merse in husband lands, each husband land xxvi acres where plough and scythe may gang'.[48] A 1761 survey of the Gordon estate, meanwhile, informs us that an oxgate equals 13 acres and that 32 oxgates = one davach = four ploughlands.[49] However, it matters not whether the size of particular land units was absolutely consistent either between settlements or over time.

---

[46] Johnston, op. cit., p. 61 dates this form of assessment to the 12th century. Balfour, op. cit., Appendix II, p. iii implies a 13th-century origin.
[47] O'Dell, *Historical Geography of the Shetland Islands*, p. 275.
[48] *APS* i, p. xxiv.
[49] SRO, RHP 2487.

What was more important was that within each individual toun, they were held to be of a certain size. Peterkin showed awareness of this in his work on Orkney. 'None of these penny lands, or other terms', he wrote, 'indicate any definite extent of ground; and they are of different extent in different touns. But all the pennylands, marks and cowsworth in the same toun are of equal value.'[50] For this reason, the total assessment of a toun can be seen as imparting a precise definition to the amount of land which it contained.

This definition of how much a toun contained was only part of the problem. It would have had little consequence for the question of toun expansion if, as this expansion took place, the new land thereby taken in was incorporated into the toun as so many extra or additional land units. Up to a point, this probably did occur. However, from as early as the thirteenth century onwards, the assessments of most touns probably remained fixed. The parish of Arbuthnott in Angus provides a convenient check on this point. Assessed as 54 ploughgates in the thirteenth century, it was still assessed at that figure in the eighteenth century, five hundred years later. In the meantime, the number of touns had increased from 24 to 47.[51] One cannot, therefore, excuse this stability of assessment by presuming that perhaps nothing had happened to warrant a change. The famous toast by farmers in the north-east—the 'auld aucht and forty o' Huntly—affords further testimony for it refers to the 48 davachs into which Huntly or Strathbogy had been divided of old and which had remained unaltered despite considerable activity in the landscape. Other parts of the Highlands can be found described as comprising so many davachs. For instance, the parishes of Kirkmichael (Banff), Dunballoch (Moray), and Coneway (Moray) were reported to consist of 10, 9, and 11 davachs respectively.[52] Again, the impression given is that these were fixed assessments, an impression which is hardly surprising in view of the archaic nature of the davach and the fact that its use as a means of assessing newly settled land died out by the twelfth century. A comprehensive source of assessment ratings is the *Reports on the State of Certain Parishes in Scotland* (1627). Whether

[50] Peterkin, *Notes on Orkney and Shetland*, p. 6.
[51] Skene, *Celtic Scotland*, vol. iii, p. 259.
[52] *Origines Parochiales Scotiae*, vol. ii, part ii, p. 692; Lewie, op. cit., p. 103.

dealing with husbandlands, merklands, or oxgangs, the over-all conclusion to be drawn from the various parish reports is that whilst rents or *fermes* altered, land unit assessments did not. For instance, in the parish of Temple (Midlothian), it was declared that the tenant land of Clerkington consisted of 'sextein husband landis it payed of auld to vumquihill Sir James Forrester of Corstorphing ten merkis and everie husband land payes presentlie to Sir George Forrester . . . ffoure scoir merkis'.[53] Merklands, no less than husbandlands, appear stable. The parish of Kirknewton was 'divydit merklands so callit becaus every sic portioun off land off old payit a merk of maill, . . . Off thir Merk landis they ar six score and eight in the parochine . . . Leitifhead is a fyiftene merk land lyand runrig.'[54]

It needs to be appreciated that this freezing of assessments, probably from as early as the twelfth or thirteenth century, was not occasioned by the cessation of colonization. Its cause lies rather in the inelasticity of assessments when faced with a situation of change. This in turn relates to changes that were taking place in the nature of lordship. In fact, considerable colonization did take place subsequently. However, the land so colonized was absorbed not as so many extra land units but as so many extra acres. In effect, one had the emergence of a line of cleavage running through the geography of touns, the older core being assessed in land units, and the newly reclaimed land in acres. This cleavage expressed itself in other ways. In some touns, it was reflected in the composition of their rents. The older, assessed core of touns was conventionally held for a customary rent paid in kind. Up to a point, these customary rents or *antiquae firmae* were stable in both content and amount. As at Nesting (Shetland), land was 'rentallit of old at a certane rate quhilk is not changeabill'.[55] New land taken in, however, lay outside this

---

[53] *Reports on the State of Certain Parishes in Scotland 1627*, p. 97.

[54] Ibid., p. 83.

[55] Ibid., p. 227. Instances of farms held for 'antiquam firmam' can be found in *Registrum Honoris de Morton*, vol. i, pp. xlvii ff. It is also worth mentioning that quite a number of the touns listed in the *Reports of the State of Certain Parishes in Scotland 1627* for the Lothians show a fixed relationship between the number of land units and ploughs they contained and the amount of grain (or number of chalders) paid as rent *before* augmentation. Further examples of rents (both fermes and multures) being apportioned to assessments on a fixed basis can be found in Macpherson, *Glimpses of Church and Social Life in the Highlands*, pp. 503–15, 'Rentall . . . Lordshipe of Badzenoche 1603'; *De Rebus Albanicis*, pp. 161–79, rental of lands formerly belong to Abbot of Iona, 1588.

nexus between assessed land and customary rents, and offered an opportunity for forging new relationships. It need occasion no surprise, therefore, to find it treated as an arrented supplement to customary rent that was paid in money not kind. Many rentals, covering estates from the Outer Isles to the Lowlands, contain instances of this cash augmentation of customary rents. Since we are dealing with rents that had previously been paid in kind, such augmentation cannot be ascribed to monetary inflation, for the value of rent in kind rose with the currency. Rather it must be put down to an expansion into non-assessed land. In fact, some sources make this relationship explicit. At Mowir and Feal in Orkney, tenants were required in 1565 to 1566 to pay for their 'ut tylling' in accordance with their set of the 'inlands'.[56] Even in the eighteenth century, tenants on the Mey estate in Caithness were paying cash supplements to their ordinary rents for 'outbreaks' in the muir.[57]

In some touns, but especially those shared between two or more landowners such as one had in areas like the Tweed Valley or the north-east Lowlands, the cleavage between assessed and non-assessed land was given still greater meaning by the fact that, whilst the older core was treated as severalty, the newer land retained some of its character as a former commonty. This is particularly manifest in the way new land was treated as an appendage to the land units which made up the core.[58] For this reason, one sometimes finds the assessment of a toun, an assessment which *sensu stricto* refers only to the older core, used deceptively as if it also embraced new land. The point is nicely made by a comment of Gordon of Straloch. Talking about Strathbogy, he said the area was originally 'divided into 48 davachs, each containing as much land as four ploughs . . . could till in a year. But now, the wood being cut down, the arable land is more than double.'[59] What Gordon of Straloch is trying to

---

[56] Storer Clouston (ed.), *Records of the Earldom of Orkney 1299–1614*, pp. 373–4.

[57] J. E. Donaldson, *Caithness in the Eighteenth Century* (Edinburgh, 1938), p. 77.

[58] Clouston (ed.), *Records of the Earldom of Orkney 1299–1614*, p. 373. Further examples of new land being treated as dependent on old or assessed land can be found in Paul (ed.), *Register of the Great Seal of Scotland 1424–1513*, p. 706 (this consists of a reference to land 'cum le outsettis communibus dependen. et pertinene.'); J. M. Thomson (ed.), *The Register of the Great Seal of Scotland 1609–1620* (Edinburgh, 1882), pp. 45 and 60; J. M. Thomson (ed.), *The Register of the Great Seal of Scotland 1634–1651* (Edinburgh, 1897), p. 519; Dodgshon, 'Nature and Development of Infield–Outfield in Scotland', pp. 3–5.

[59] Robertson, op. cit., vol. iv, p. 173.

say here is that by the mid-seventeenth century, one had the original 48 davachs plus new land appendaged to them. A. Edmonston too, has somethinng to say on the matter in regard to Shetland. When 'a part of the common is enclosed and farmed', he wrote, 'the enclosure is called an "outset", but the outsets are never included in the numeration of merks of rental land.'[60] What he is saying is that the assessment of a toun, its *rental land* as he pointedly calls it, was not adjusted to accommodate new land. The latter simply became a half-concealed appendage of the former. The same conclusion has been drawn from mid-eighteenth-century evidence for touns like Newstead and Eildon in the mid-Tweed Valley. At first, their husbandlands assessments are said to embrace both their 'Infield & outfield'. However, if we probe deeper, we find that each landholder really held so many husbandlands of infield, plus a proportionate share of outfield acres.[61]

This last example introduces what must surely have been the most important by-product of this cleavage between assessed and non-assessed land, namely, the formation of infield–outfield. Put simply, infield was the old assessed core of a toun and outfield, its acred or non-assessed land. Around this institutional rigidity in its spatial organization was developed the farming system which we more familiarly recognize as infield–outfield. The very terms *in*field and *out*field do, of course, evoke a sense not just of mere arrangement but of territoriality, which is what the distinction between assessed and non-assessed land was in essence. Some of the substitute terms put the point more forthrightly. For example, a survey drawn up in 1718 of the vast Buccleuch estate in the Southern Uplands, one of the earliest estate surveys in Scotland, divided land into either 'infield' or 'common'.[62] A charter of 1641 for land in Clydesdale refers to a holding which comprised 'nynscore aikers' of infield and 'of outside called the Mure above six score aikers'.[63] Around Perth and Aberdeen, land was sometimes divided into inland or infield and *forland*: the

[60] A. Edmonston, *A View of the Ancient and Present State of the Zetland Islands* (Lerwick, 1809), vol. i, pp. 147–8.
[61] Dodgshon, 'Nature and Development of Infield–Outfield in Scotland', pp. 3–5.
[62] SRO, RHP 9629.
[63] W. Craige (ed.), *A Dictionary of the Older Scottish Tongue* (1931–), vol. iii (H–L), p. 250.

meaning of *forland* was land outside.[64] An interesting form of mixed phrasing that was used on the Monymusk estate was *intoun and outfield*.[65] Elsewhere, the phrase 'intoun man' was sometimes used in conjunction with that of 'out-toun man' to describe someone with, as opposed to someone without, rights in a toun.[66] In one Banffshire toun, the infield was called the 'intill' and equated directly to the 16 bovates of the toun.[67] Finally, we must not overlook those incipient forms of outfield or outsets. Peterkin defined an outset as 'a peace of land newly win without the dyke'.[68] Linguistically, it means the land beyond or outside that which was set.

If Scottish touns formerly consisted solely of the land which later formed their infield, and if outfield constitutes the land which they colonized from the surrounding waste at some point during the time period from the thirteenth to the eighteenth century, then how can the distinctive character of infield–outfield farming be explained? Given what has been said, the logical explanation for the intensive nature of infield lies in the fact that it must have formed the defined extent of the toun. Indeed, only when it was intensively cropped, is the case for the cultivation of the surrounding commonty likely to have been made. A possible explanation of outfield's character can be developed by looking at the resources available to the Scots farmer at the point when he was contemplating the cultivation of the waste which surrounded the toun. As already proposed, the infield at this point was probably being cultivated on a fairly intensive basis, otherwise the need to encroach on the surrounding waste would not arise. To judge from later evidence, it was maintained in crop by the addition of all the manure produced by stock during the winter half of the year, from the time they grazed the harvest stubble to when they were put back on the

[64] J. G. Burnett (ed.), *Powis Papers 1507–1594*, Third Spalding Club, (Aberdeen, 1951), pp. 173–5.

[65] H. Hamilton (ed.), *Selections from the Monymusk Papers (1713–1755)*, Scottish History Society, 3rd ser., xxxix (1945), pp. 39 and 43.

[66] W. C. Dickinson (ed.), *The Court Book of the Barony of Carnwath 1523–1542*, Scottish History Society, 3rd ser., xxxix (1937), p. cii; Imrie, Rae, and Ritchie (eds.), *Court Book of Selkirk 1503–1545*, p. 7.

[67] J. G. Mitchie (ed.), *The Records of Invercauld MDXLVII–MDCCCXXVIII*, New Spalding Club (Aberdeen, 1901), p. 472.

[68] Peterkin, *Rentals*, part ii, p. 2.

surrounding common pastures. In a system which depended heavily on stock manure for the maintenance of fertility levels, then the *unused* manure produced during the summer period when stock grazed the common pastures was obviously a weak link (see Fig. 6.1). Logically, any attempt to expand beyond the

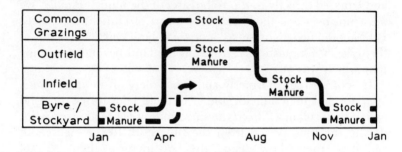

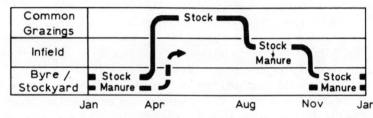

FIG. 6.1. Movement of Stock Within (a) an Infield–Outfield System and (b) Infield–Only System

limits of assessed land would try to exploit this summer wastage of manure. The obvious solution was to concentrate stock on a part of the common pastures for part of the summer, enabling them to dung or tath it ready for cropping. Of course, once in cultivation, this tathed break was automatically removed from further tathing during the one time of the year when the stock were on the common pastures. Almost inevitably, therefore, the stock were moved to prepare a new tath break in readiness for cropping. In other words, the appearance of outfield as a system of temporary cropping can be explained by relating it to the practical problems of tathing.[69]

[69] This argument was first elaborated in Dodgshon, 'Nature and Development of Infield–Outfield in Scotland', pp. 1–23.

Whether this explanation of outfield's character is deemed sufficient in itself or not, ample evidence for touns encroaching on the surrounding waste or commonty during the late medieval period is available. If forced to be more specific, we might say that this evidence become more voluminous round about the mid-fifteenth century. It expresses itself at first in the growing number of references to 'outsets'.[70] From the late fifteenth century onwards, we also start to get mentions of outfield itself, as well as to its counterpart, or infield. The very first reference to outfield occurs in 1483 when a land conveyance refers to 'le Owtfeld de la Kyrktown de Kerymur' in Angus.[71] For comparison, the earliest-known mention of infield occurs in a manuscript ten years earlier and relating to the nearby farm of Abirbrothy.[72] Following these pioneer references, the terms infield and outfield appear with increasing frequency in the next century or so.

Viewing the problem from a slightly different angle, we can sense the process through the not inconsiderable evidence for the division or absorption of commonty land. It is well known that an *Act anent the division of Commonties* was passed by the Scots Parliament in 1695. Less widely appreciated is the fact that this Act did not permit the division of commonties for the first time, but merely allowed such divisions to be brought about by only one of the heritors or landowners involved. The division of commonty land had long been possible before then provided all heritors directly affected were in agreement. Exactly when this invasion of waste began is impossible to say, but we must presume that there was a stage when commonty was not so easily engrossed. After all, the fixed assessment of touns would have had little or no meaning if it gave them the unbridled power of absorbing the commonty around them. In the property law of the feudal period, it was an area for depasturing stock, gathering wood, cutting turf, and extracting peat. Slowly but surely, the restraints on its actual appropriation must have been worn down.

---

[70] This is best shown by a comparison between J. B. Paul and J. M. Thomson (eds.), *The Register of the Great Seal of Scotland 1513–1546* (Edinburgh, 1883) with J. B. Paul (ed.), *The Register of the Great Seal of Scotland 1424–1513* (Edinburgh, 1882) or J. M. Thomson (ed.), *The Register of the Great Seal of Scotland 1306–1424* (Edinburgh, 1902). The *1513–1546* volume has numerous references, the *1424–1513* a few, and the *1306–1424* volume none.

[71] Paul (ed.), *Register of the Great Seal 1424–1513*, p. 327.

[72] Rogers (ed.), op. cit., vol. i, p. 174.

The abbeys may have played a critical role in this process. Being interested in pasture as a resource that was crucial to their commercial activities, it is easy to understand why they may have wanted to assert more control over it. This they did through numerous perambulation agreements with adjacent landholders over the thirteenth and fourteenth centuries, agreements which effectively divided out their grazing rights on a more exclusive basis.[73] In this way, their touns acquired two boundaries, one embracing assessed land and the other, assessed land plus grazings. Other landholders later followed their example, though with less publicity. Conceivably, charters which con-veyed land 'by all their boundaries ancient and divided' were possibly trying to put words to their double boundary problem.[74] Of course, to acquire exclusive control over the grazing land around touns did not mean that it was or could be cultivated at this point. But it must have facilitated the process when rising demand eventually made its cultivation a matter of necessity. We know from the better-documented conditions of England that the late fifteenth, sixteenth, and seventeenth centuries were certainly a phase of growing land pressure in the north, or in those areas which can be compared most closely with Scotland. However, what evidence is there from within Scotland itself that pressure over this period pushed touns outwards on to their commonty land or grazing?

The gathering build-up of references to 'outsets' over the fifteenth century, and with them, the slightly later appearances of outfield, is of course one sign. But for most touns, it was probably a relatively discrete, undocumented affair, in which landowners permitted their tenants to cultivate adjacent commonty land pro-vided it did not bring them into conflict with other landowners. The permission given by the Huntly estate to the tenant of Auchinhabrick (Bellie parish, Banffshire) in 1643 to 'rive out new land upon the Commonty of the said Town' must have been typical of these private encroachments.[75] Had conflict with other landowners arisen, the legitimacy of their trespass would have been easily challenged in the courts. There is an intriguing Act of

---

[73] Typical are those in *Liber Sancte Marie de Melros*, vol. i, pp. 104 ff.

[74] Instances of charters incorporating this phrase can be found in Paton, op. cit., p. 9.

[75] SRO, Gordon Castle Muniments, GD44, Feu charter issued by the Marquis of Huntly for Auchinabrick, 1643.

Parliament that was passed in 1592 concerning the 'validities of new bounding evidentis'. It pointed out that many landowners who held their land by Crown charter were suffering from the practice of adjacent landowners having new charters issued for their property in which new bounds were defined, bounds that surreptitiously embraced *extra* land. In particular, it seems their new charters were defining former commonty land as their property to the great prejudice of other landowners with whom it was supposed to be shared.[76] Perhaps in this Act, we are witnessing how the progressive encroachment of commonty land led ultimately to relative or local scarcity, making landowners much more attentive of their rights in the matter. There is an old legal jingle that was certainly in existence by the seventeenth century and which was probably in the mind of many a landowner, or his agent, when casting an eye over the layout of his estate:

> All landis, quherevir they be
> in Scotland partis, hes merchis thrie
> heidrowme, wattir, and mouthis borde
> as eldron men, hes maid recorde
> zoure heidrowm, to the hill direct
> frae zoure hauch teilled in effect
> Betuix two glennis, and mouthis borde
> Devydis they glennis, I sall stand forde
> wattir cummand fraem ane glen heid
> devydis that glen, and stanches feid
> Thortrom burnis in mouthis hie
> Sall stope nae heidrowm, thocht they be.[77]

The application of these principles of toun layout, encouraging and endorsing the occupation of all land as a severalty, no doubt had some bearing on the events that lay behind the 1592 Act. However, for all their air of timelessness, it is unlikely that they had a long history. If applied in the context of the twelfth or thirteenth centuries, they would have overturned the strict territorial basis of feudal tenure and the prevailing notion that landholders held the full property right of assessed pockets of land but not the intervening commonty. Interestingly, O'Dell cited an

[76] *APS* iii, p. 570.
[77] *Habakkuk Bisset's Rolment of Courtis*, p. 296.

extract from a deed of 1554 which defined the natural boundary line to be drawn between the commonties or skattald of two adjacent touns in Shetland. It makes for a revealing comparison with the aforementioned jingle. O'Dell's extract reads 'fra den effste stein i fielde till dan neste i fioren' or, to translate it, 'from the highest stone in the hill to the lowest on the beach'.[78] Even allowing for the fact that they are drawn from distinct legal contexts, the differences between these two extracts—the one concerned with toun boundaries and the other with commonty— is a measure of how far the independence of commonty was worn down and how far the law tried to justify it.

At a more localized level, we can see the process at work in the case of specific areas of commonty. Thus, in 1535, James V granted to his royal burgh of Selkirk the right 'to rive out, break and till yearly one thousand acres of their common lands'.[79] The expansive policy of the Selkirk burgesses was part of a more general trend. A few years earlier, the burgesses of Lauder were given like permission 'to break up and plough their common lands for their greater convenience and profit'.[80] After exercising the King's favour in 1535, the burgh of Selkirk was forced into a different process when it had the remainder of its commonty divided in 1679. The large expanse of commonty to which it still had access lay astride the Selkirkshire–Roxburghshire border and was shared between not only the burgesses of Selkirk, but also, the feuars of Midlem in Roxburghshire and various touns on the Roxburgh ducal estate. The entire commonty was divided by the sheriff courts in 1679.[81] Similar legal processes were used to divide other commonties. In 1505, for example, the commonty of Inchinnan (Stirlingshire) was divided between the farms of Barnys, Bernhill, and Awelandis by an indenture drawn up between the different owners.[82] In 1594, the commonty shared between the touns of Culloch, Lethnotts, and Corsmiles in Angus

[78] O'Dell, *Historical Geography of the Shetland Islands*, p. 53. See also, A. W. Johnston and A. Johnston (eds.), *Orkney and Shetland Records vol. II. Orkney and Shetland Sasines* (Shetland Sasines 1623–1628), ed. by H. Paton and H. M. Paton, i (London, 1942), p. 115.

[79] British Parliamentary Papers, *Municipal Corporations in Scotland, Reports From Commissioners* (London, 1836), IUP Series, no. 9 (Municipal Corporations), p. 395.

[80] Ibid., p. 197; F. W. Maitland, *Township and Borough* (Cambridge, 1898), p. 200.

[81] Floors Castle, Roxburgh MSS, Memorial for His Grace the Duke of Roxburgh Concerning Clarilaw Mosses, 1781.

[82] HMC, *Third Report* (London, 1872), Appendix, p. 392.

was divided out between them.[83] Nearby, the commonty of Hedderwick was divided in 1602.[84] In the far north, a court decision of 1603 ordered that the ness of Scatnes 'shall be equally divided amongst the owners of the lands of Scatnes, each one according to their portions'.[85] In the extreme south of the country, the commonty of Abercorn (Peeblesshire) was divided in 1662,[86] whilst those of Bordland, Shiprig, Harcase, and Northsheil were divided in 1539. The latter was precipitated by the 'unbridled liberty the tenants and possessors of the said lands assumed to themselves in pasturing such multitude of goods as both the property and commonties of the said lands were not able to feed the same'.[87] Such divisions must be seen as the more publicized examples of the long process by which the modern ground plan of touns was unfolded and their surrounding commonty or waste converted into toun property.

The Splitting of Touns

Another dimension through which Scottish touns expressed their growth and changing character was by subdivision. If we survey the modern landscape of Scotland, a feature which would impress would almost certainly be the widespread grouping of farms into what appear to be related pairs or groups. They are recognizable by the fact that they share a common surname, but are distinguished from each other by the use of place-name prefixes like East, West, Nether, Upper, and Lower or by affixes like Mor and Beg. The common belief is that such farms represent the divided portions of once runrig touns and are therefore a product of eighteenth-century improvements. However, one need not search too long amongst early or pre-1700 rentals and land charters to realize that many have a much earlier origin for they are commonplace as early as the fifteenth and sixteenth centuries. What then was their origin?

[83] SRO, Airlie MSS, GD16/4/24.
[84] SRO, Benhom and Hedderwick MSS, GD4/262.
[85] G. Donaldson, *Shetland Life Under Earl Patrick* (Edinburgh, 1958), p. 38.
[86] Sir James Dalyell and J. Beveridge (eds.), *The Binns Papers 1320–1864*, STS (Edinburgh, 1938), p. 51.
[87] HMC, *Report on Manuscripts in Various Collections* v (London, 1909), p. 24 (section on MSS of Robert Morduant Hay). Further examples of pre-1695 commonty divisions are cited in Whyte, *Agriculture and Society in Seventeenth-Century Scotland*, pp. 98–107.

Their origin lies in a process of toun subdivision or splitting which began as early as the written record itself, but which gathered momentum over the fifteenth, sixteenth, and seventeenth centuries. The earliest references to split touns display a vagueness of style. It is not uncommon, for instance, to find them referred to as 'duabus villis de Kynmilies' (Moray, 1384),[88] 'Duas villas nomine Luschar' (Dunfermline, twelfth century)[89] or 'tribus Malgaskis' (Fife, 1196 × 1201).[90] In addition, it is not uncommon for the names of these settlements to alter over time. What appears in one charter as 'over' and 'nether', appears in a later charter as 'easter and wester'.[91] The reason why such prefixes were used, and why they had this capacity to alter over time, is explained by the fact they are the language of a division. As the earlier discussion of subdivision sought to show, terms like east, west, nether, or upper all correspond with each other as distinguishing parts of a division. However, whereas the terms sunny and shadow tend to be used of shares that were intermixed with each other by way of runrig, terms like east, west, nether, and upper tend to be used equally of shares divided into consolidated holdings, or split touns. To give some idea of how common the latter were, a source like the *Register of the Great Seal 1593–1608* lists almost 1,000 touns whose names were prefixed by East, West, Nether, Over, Upper, Little, or Meikle.[92] Occasionally, landholders tried to break away from this tyranny of custom. In a rental of 1561 for touns in Fife, one finds reference to Beith Murtoune, Beith Stewart, Beith Keir, Beith Trumbill, Beith Stenetoun, Beith Sell, Beith Danyell, Beith Bonala, and Beith Parsonne: they are clearly the divided portions of Beith, each portion adopting the name of its occupier as a mark of identity.[93] Another personalized split was that of Linplum in Peeblesshire which became divided into Maxwellis Quarter,

    [88] *Registrum Episcopatus Moraviensis*, pp. 194–5.
    [89] *Registrum De Dunfermelyn*, p. 5.
    [90] Barrow (ed.), *Acts of William I*, pp. 393–4.
    [91] See Robertson, op. cit., vol. iv, pp. 499–500; J. Anderson (ed.), *Calendar of the Laing Charters* (Edinburgh, 1899), p. 210; SRO, Airlie MSS, GD16/13/77.
    [92] See discussion in R. A. Dodgshon, 'Changes in Scottish Township Organization During the Medieval and Early Modern Periods', *Geografiska Annaler*, 58B (1977), pp. 52–3.
    [93] *Registrum de Dunfermelyn*, pp. 435–7.

Boydis Quarter, Makdougallis Quarter, and Hayes Quarter.[94] In some cases, landholders started off with standard off-the-peg prefixes like East, West, Nether, and Upper, but then changed them for more personalized forms. For example, in 1592, we find a reference to 'Middil Persey callit Bawgray' in Forfar,[95] whilst a seventeenth-century source gives us 'Over or Easter Markinch called Kirk Markinch'.[96] A fine sequence of name changes can be traced for Kinmyly in Moray. Referred to as Kinmyly in 1232, it had become subdivided into 'duabus villis de Kynmilies' by 1384. Later documents show that one portion was called Wester Kinmylies, and later Achnabodach, and later still, Ballahelich. Easter Kinmylies, meanwhile, was later known as Muirtown or Baile an fhraich.[97]

We can approach closer to this process of toun splitting by comparing toun or farm lists contained in rentals or conveyances. The series of rentals for Islay over the sixteenth and seventeenth centuries shows a number of touns, such as Cragapols and Dawachs, becoming subdivided into two separate touns or *bailtean*.[98] Comprehensive rentals for the 'stedes' which developed in the Ettrick and Liddesdale areas of the Southern Uplands support a similar trend: those of Mountbenger, Fauldshope, and Kershope, for example, were seemingly split between successive rental statements over the sixteenth century.[99] In a few cases, rentals alone are insufficient. Their use has to be supplemented by land charters. Thus, an early twelfth-century deed in the *Registrum Episcopatus Moraviensis* refers to 'terram suam de Tulibardyn ... terram suam de Kellys'. By the time of a 1545 rental, they had both been split: the former becoming Easter, Middle, and Wester Tullebardine, and the latter Easter and Wester Kelles.[1] Again, early charters refer to touns like Sprous-

[94] C. C. H. Harvey and J. Macleod (eds.), *Calendar of Writs at Yester House 1166–1625*, Scottish Record Society (Edinburgh, 1930), p. 303.

[95] *Liber S. Thome de Aberbrothoc*, vol. ii, Appendix, p. xxxix.

[96] SRO, Leven and Melville MSS, GD26/3/950.

[97] *Registrum Episcopatis Moraviensis*, pp. 26–7, 194–5, 211, and 223; H. Barron, 'Notes on the Ness Valley', *Trans. Gaelic Soc. Inverness*, xliii (1960–3), pp. 150–71.

[98] Smith, *Book of Islay*, pp. 254, 485, 487–8, and 498–500.

[99] See *Exchequer Rolls of Scotland* vi (1455–1460), pp. 223–4; ibid., xi (1497–1501), pp. 457–60; ibid., xxi (1580–1588), pp. 344–9. The picture is brought more up to date by looking at SRO, Buccleuch MSS, GD224/280/1, Rental Books of Ettrick Forest 1681–1719 which shows splitting continued over the 17th century.

[1] *Registrum Episcopatus Moraviensis*, pp. 19, 441–3, 465, and 467–9.

ton and Caverton in Roxburghshire as if they were integral
wholes, yet later seventeenth-century charters and rentals show
them to have become split.[2]

In a surprising number of touns, we can even see the process of
splitting in operation thanks to documents associated with it.
Amongst the most explicit descriptions are those provided by the
Register of Coupar Angus Abbey. During the fifteenth century,
the abbey instructed its tenants to split a number of touns. A tack
for Keithock issued in 1473, for instance, required the 11 tenants
to 'divide the toun at the following whitsunday evenly into four
touns, or at least three'.[3] The Grange of Balbrogy, meanwhile,
was split into 'touns east and west'.[4] The Registers for one or two
other abbeys suggests that they too were engaged in the splitting
of touns.[5] Documented examples are also extant for lay estates. In
Perthshire, the toun of Drummy was divided into three separate
units, called Easter, Wester, and Middle Drummy, in 1573,[6]
whilst mention has already been made of how Hassendean in
Roxburghshire was divided into Over and Nether Hassendean in
1498.[7] A not unusual example of a double division can be pieced
together for Moniack in Inverness-shire. At some point between
1491 and 1519, Moniack was divided into an Easter and Wester
portion. A century later, we then find the Easter portion being
divided yet again into separate East and West portions.[8]
Excellent examples of splitting are also provided by seventeenth-
century court records for Shetland.[9]

[2] Barrow (ed.), *Acts of William I*, pp. 166–7; HMC, *Fourteenth Report*, pp. 13–14 and
23–5; J. Thomson (ed.), *Register of the Great Seal of Scotland 1306–1424*, pp. 191 and 439;
idem (ed.), *Register of the Great Seal of Scotland 1634–1651*, pp. 589, 625, and 640; Floors
Castle, Roxburgh MSS, Rentals 1699–1700.

[3] Rogers, op. cit., vol. i, p. 188.

[4] Ibid., p. 181. See also, Dodgshon, 'Changes in Scottish Township Organization', p.
61 for other examples.

[5] Examples can be found by comparing early charters of conveyance with the 16th-
century rental lists available for most of the main abbeys. See, for instance, *Registrum De
Dunfermelyn*, pp. 173 and 287 with its references first to 'villam de Hales' and, then, 'Halis
estir & westir'.

[6] SRO, Abercairny MSS, GD24/1/146.

[7] *Registrum Honoris de Morton*, vol. ii, p. 250.

[8] SRO, *Inventory of the Title Deeds of the Estate of Easter Moniack belonging to Edward
Satchwell Fraser*, 1796, xerox copy, p. 31.

[9] The author has in mind the various 'schones' or 'scheinds' by which land was divided
between co-heirs and which are well documented by court records for Orkney and
Shetland, see Clouston (ed.), *Records of the Earldom of Orkney 1299–1614*, pp. 83–4, 112–17,
167, and 180; Donaldson, *Court Book of Shetland 1602–1604*, p. 95; Peterkin, *Notes on Orkney*

The fact that these divisions took place, and the fact that they form a small sample out of many hundreds that must have been executed, begs the question by what legal process they were so divided. This is not a problem as regards those touns which involved only tenants holding land by fixed-term lease, or tenant–runrig touns. The landowners of such touns had every right to alter their layout as they saw fit when leases expired. However, it might be considered a problem where more than one landowner was involved. Part of the answer lies in the shareholding basis of tenure. As already made clear, shareholding was open-ended as a title to land. For this reason, a person's share of a runrig toun was such that he could hold land anywhere within the territory of the toun without a change of title. This point needs stressing for it means that the splitting of touns need not have generated much in the way of documentation. The whole process may have been a relatively silent affair. Indeed, because of its shareholding basis, a runrig layout was never regarded as final or fixed before the law. A process or procedure existed as far back as the fifteenth century by which 'any portioners of lands having and occupying the same in third parts, fourth parts, sixth parts, eighth parts, and so furth, and any contention arise between them, any of the parties which thinks himself hurt and scathed in the occupation' was able to apply to the courts for a re-division of the lands.[10]

It must be stressed that the splitting of touns cannot be reduced to a single cause. A number of factors were involved. One was the inheritance of touns or estates by co-heirs. Needless to say, this was an especially potent factor in the Northern Isles. In fact, as long ago as 1918, Storer Clouston perceived the connection between partible inheritance and toun splitting when inquiring into the origin of the prefixes East, West, Nether, and Upper in Orkney. He cited a number of examples which he thought had been produced in this way, such as Nether, Over, and West Linklater in Sandwick.[11] Its link with splitting can also be

---

and Shetland, pp. 36 and 39–41. Some of these divisions almost certainly led to runrig layouts, but others led to split touns and farms. See Clouston, 'Orkney Townships', pp. 39–43 for a discussion of split touns in Orkney.

[10] *Habakkuk Bissset's Rolment of Courtis*, p. 297.

[11] Clouston, 'Orkney Townships', p. 37, offers the view that touns in which individual farmsteads carry distinguishing prefixes like East, West, Mid, etc., stand out from those

vouched for elsewhere in Scotland. Despite the fact that most estates were subject to the rule of primogeniture, instances of partible inheritance can still be uncovered, especially when an estate fell to female co-heirs. For example, in 1522, the estate of Achinbothy–Langmure was divided between seven heirs.[12] In 1679, the touns of Sandwatt, Alishesbeg, Alisheormoir, Ardbeg, Ardmore, and Kinlochbervie in Strathnaver was divided into two 'just and equal' halves as part of a family settlement.[13] Such partitions, however, did not always produce split touns, and care is needed when isolating those that did. Some led to a division based on the allocation of whole touns as shares. In other cases, a runrig division resulted. The division of land between the three daughters of Sir Murdo Menteith was of this type. So too was the division of Achnagathill (Keig parish, Aberdeenshire) in 1596 between the two sons of William Leith, Alexander and Adam Leith, one of whom had the sunny half and the other, the shadow half.[14] However, some did produce split touns. The Hassendean division mentioned on p. 152 is one such example.

Other examples of splitting were rooted in the desire by landowners to rid their land of its runrig intermixture with the property of other landowners. When Easter Moniack was divided or split in 1608, for instance, the entire process was prefaced by the declaration that 'to prevent disputes . . . the parties agreed to have the Old mode of possessing by runrig, laid aside.'[15] Likewise, when Culcairny in Fife was split in 1611, it too was prefaced by a declaration that 'as the said toun and lands has been in times bygone occupied by the tenants and labourers thereof by Rin Rig which has oftimes moved and raised commotion and trouble amongst them'.[16] Before seeing these examples of splitting as divisions of runrig and no more, we

---

touns which carry a single name for the entire toun. Speaking of the former type, he argues that knowing 'the effect of the old odal laws in cutting up land among the heirs, there can only be one rational explanation of such names. A single large manor farm or "bu", embracing the whole township, has been divided into three among the sons of the family. And, in confirmation, one knows that the whole town of Linklater was actually once the property of the Linklaters, and the town of Grimbister, of the Grimbisters.'

[12] SRO, Craigans MSS, SRO 148/103.
[13] SRO, Reay MSS, GD84/1/17/B, 17/9B and 17/10B.
[14] SRO, Leith Hall MSS, GD225/40.
[15] *Inventories of the Title Deeds of the Estate of Easter Moniack*, p. 31.
[16] SRO, Lindsay of Dowhill MSS, GD254/78.

should bear in mind that they only removed proprietary runrig, or the intermixture of property between heritors. Because of the early date at which they were carried out, the possibility that tenant runrig layouts were re-created on the divided portions cannot be ruled out. In fact, the appearance of tenant runrig on the divided portions of a toun split under these circumstances can be vouched for.[17]

An important cause of splitting was the problem of growing scale. Such an explanation is the only way in which we can reasonably explain the splitting of touns which did not involve proprietary runrig and which had tenant–runrig layouts created immediately on their divided, but albeit, smaller portions. The examples of splitting on the Coupar Abbey estate would seem to fall into this category. A late, but extremely relevant illustration is contained in an eighteenth-century survey of the Netherlorn section of the Breadalbane Estate. The survey tells how some 'years ago the greatest part of the Country was divided by Stone Dykes or Ditches into divisions and Two Tenants placed into each of these Divisions. These Tenants Occupy those lots or Divisions in run ridge as They did before the lots took place with only this differences that in place of Eight Tenants in run Ridge there is only Two.'[18] Without doubt though, the most informative comment on the problem and one which has considerable significance for the history of the Scottish landscape is that provided by Gordon of Straloch. In his own words:

Here also I desire to warn my reader that though our Kingdom is, generally speaking, populated with few villages, paucity of inhabitants must not to be inferred. The reason of this state of matters is as follows. Husbandmen eager for tillage thought from the very first that they were restricted in villages, and that when they had so many neighbours, too little provision was made for agriculture; for at first the districts were divided into village settlements. To each of these so much of arable land was allotted as could be tilled with four ploughs. These sections of lands were called in the ancient language *daachs*, which signifies village settlements . . . But when the woods had been cut down four ploughs

---

[17] Typical is the example of the toun of Drummy. In 1573, it was divided into Easter, Wester, and Middle portions (SRO, Abercairny MSS, GD24/1/146). Yet, in the 18th century, Wester Drummy at least was in the hands of multiple tenants (ibid., GD24/1/653).

[18] SRO, RHP972/5, Robertson's Report on Netherlorn 1769.

were no longer sufficient. Wide extent of bounds was inimical to agriculture ... The proprietors therefore, dividing the fields, fixed for each his own bounds according to his means, so that the settlements were continuous but not contiguous; consequently, there was a migration from the villages into the fields, wherever veins of fertile soils invited farmers; and here their abodes were fixed, and with more house-room and without quarrelling, one was not any longer an annoyance to his neighbour.[19]

Gordon of Straloch's extract is worth setting beside a recent statement by Duncan, which drew attention to the way fractions of the davach appear to have separate names—as if they were separate holdings—by the twelfth century. He went on to propose that perhaps

we should see a landscape of small enclosed units of arable often not marching with each other ... but separated by areas of moor and moss. Such small fields would suit dispersed settlement, so that the large village of Lothian was uncommon in the zone of the davach where the unit of settlement was the small hamlet or isolated farmstead grouped around or beside the arable. To establish whether or not this was so is of prime importance for the social and economic history of early Scotland.[20]

Eighteenth-century estate plans show that this dispersed and fragmented character of the davach—if not its enclosed nature—was certainly a feature then. But as Gordon of Straloch's comment helps to underline, behind this apparent stability between the twelfth and eighteenth centuries was a background of important changes brought about by progressive toun split-ting. The contrast between the large villages of Lothian and the smaller, dispersed settlement of the north-east may be explicable in terms of toun splitting, and not just in terms of environmental opportunities, for splitting was endemic in the north-east and must have acted as a regulatory check on any excessive growth in the size of settlements there.

As the foregoing discussion has implied, the splitting of touns could precipitate radical changes in settlement layout. A divided portion might create its own settlement site away from the older

<hr />

[19] *Geographical Collections*, vol. ii, p. 272.
[20] Duncan, op. cit., p. 319.

nucleus, or each of them might migrate to a new site leaving the old focus of the settlement as a deserted site. The former process can sometimes be detected from estate plans. In the Aberdeen-shire parish of Clatt, an eighteenth-century estate plan records details of a toun known as 'Netherknockespack called the Newtoun of Knockespack'. The complementary toun to Nether-knockespack was one known simply as Knockspack. If we probe back through earlier rentals, we find that Knockspack was originally called Over Knockespack.[21] Putting this information together, it could be argued that Nether and Over Knockespack were a split toun, and that the former acquired a new farmstead site, hence the name Newtoun of Knockespack, whilst the latter took over for itself the old nucleus, thereby earning the distinction of being called Knockespack for short. In some cases, each of the split portions may have acquired new settlements. To give an example, when the Grange of Kethok was divided by the monks of Cupar into four separate touns, the tenants were instructed to remove to their separate portions with their cottars.[22] Strongly suggestive of a similar move are early estate plans which display split-toun arrangements with, at their centre, signs or traces of an old, abandoned settlement site. A 1769 plan of Easter and Wester Blairno can be used to demonstrate this point, for between the two touns lies what may have been the nucleus of settlement when Easter and Wester Blairno were simply Blairno.[23]

Even the modern landscape provides scope for testing these ideas. Thus, the farm grouping of East and West Fisk, East and West Kinwhirrie, East and West Carsebank, East and West Cullicudin, and East and West Suddie all have abandoned church sites located in between them. On the assumption that the church is a conservative element in the landscape, it may depict for us the old focus of these settlements. In other cases, a pointer to the old focus of settlement is provided by the prefixes Old or Mains, where they are used in proximity to settlements of the same surname which bear prefixes like East or West. Thus, between East and West Blairordens, we find Oldtown, whilst between Easter and Wester Cultmalundie, we find a farm called simply Mains. Some old sites do not speak so readily for

---

[21] SRO, RHP14753; Robertson, op. cit., vol. iv, pp. 499–500.
[22] Rogers, op. cit., vol. i, p. 188.
[23] SRO, RHP1667/3 and 6.

themselves. This is so with East and West Kinnear, whose old
nucleus is possibly marked by the ruins which now lie between
them. Clearly, such changes must form a backcloth to any work
on deserted settlement in Scotland.[24] Toun-names may have a
seemingly long history in the records, but the precise disposition
of such touns in terms of holding layout and the siting of the
farmsteads may have undergone quite dramatic changes.

[24] Available discussions of medieval settlement by archaeologists ignore the impli-
cations of splitting. See Laing, 'Medieval Settlement Archaeology', pp. 69–77; H.
Fairhurst, 'The Study of Deserted Settlements in Scotland (to 1968), I. Rural
Settlement', pp. 229–35 in M. W. Beresford and J. G. Hurst (eds.), *Deserted Medieval
Villages* (London, 1969), pp. 229–35.

Chapter 7

Rural Society and Economy in the
South and East 1650–1760

As the seventeenth century progresses, there occurs a gradual increase in the volume and quality of evidence bearing on Scottish rural society and its economy. This fuller documentation could not be more timely. The patterns of life and landscape which had emerged during the medieval period began to disappear rapidly during the closing decades of the eighteenth century, first in the south and east (from 1760) and then in the Highlands and Islands (from 1780). Before this happens, we are provided fortuitously with an eleventh-hour opportunity for viewing them in a detail which had previously not been possible. What we see is a country still overwhelmingly rural and agricultural in character and organization. Its agriculture remained bound by systems of landholding and husbandry that were *ab origine* a response to medieval conditions, whilst farm output was largely geared, but decreasingly so, to subsistence needs rather than those of the market economy. Overseas trade was equally confined. It had a well-developed and long-standing trade with the Baltic, the Low Countries, and France, but no official share before the 1707 Act of Union in the vast commercial empire which England was building out of its colonial dependencies. Accentuating Scotland's comparative lack of opportunities for commercial profit was the harsh fact that her predominantly rural and domestic industries had not yet the finance, technology, nor the market potential that were to be the basis of their later growth. However, although still a society whose basic institutions were of a medieval rather than a modern genre, rural Scotland was not without a capacity for change before what is popularly known as the Age of Improvement. This is not meant as an oblique reference to the estate-embellishing activities of the pioneer Improvers of the 1720s, 30s, and 40s, important though their activities were. Rather does it refer to more widespread changes in the nature of farming enterprise and in landholding, the roots of which lay in the seventeenth century.

These were changes, though, that worked themselves out within the framework of existing social and economic institutions. Only as the eighteenth century entered its third quarter does one get a type of change so fundamental and widespread in its effects that it led to the creation of entirely new patterns of order in both countryside and town.

Addressing the theme of rural Scotland during the late seventeenth and early eighteenth centuries, it will help if a firmer distinction is maintained between the Highlands on the one hand and the south and east on the other, than was the case in earlier chapters. Quite apart from the increased volume of evidence now facilitating such a distinction, long-standing cultural and political differences prevailed between these two, indelible divisions of the Scottish realm.[1] Of this there can be no doubt. Moreover, even though an impatient central government strove more earnestly and successfully during this period to curb the cultural and political freewill of the Highlands, such efforts did not lessen the region's differences with the Lowlands or Southern Uplands as regards the organization and economy of its rural communities. When we focus on these problems, the differences between the two areas, such as they were, probably increased at this point. As will be explained, the cause of this pulling apart lay in their contrasting response to the pressures slowly being exerted on them, with the Lowlands and Southern Uplands starting to seek out solutions but the Highlands compounding its problems to the point of crisis.

The Farming Township: Its Scale

An Important documentary gain of this period is the increase of data on the scale of rural Scotland's most basic unit, namely the farming township or fermtoun. Its scale can be measured in two ways. First, it can be assessed in purely landholding terms, or in terms of the number of tenants, sub-tenants, cottars, and the like. Secondly, it can be assessed in terms of mere physical size.

(a) *Landholding* Like so many other problems in Scottish rural history, the landholding structure of touns is something which

---

[1] The socio–political division of Scotland into Highlands and Lowlands appears to have emerged by the 14th century. See Smout, *A History of the Scottish Nation*, pp. 42–3.

deserves a much more detailed analysis than has been accorded to it in the past. On the basis of the small sample of rentals and surveys which the writer has examined, it would seem likely that, whatever the local variations, the over-all balance between multiple and single tenancy was swinging in favour of the latter by the opening decades of the eighteenth century.

In what is regrettably still the only extant study of this aspect in the south or east of Scotland, the writer inspected rentals relating to over 200 touns in Roxburghshire and Berwickshire during the period 1680 to 1766.[2] The conclusion reached was that 54 per cent were, at some point but not necessarily throughout, held by multiple tenants on a fixed or short-term basis. Where, and when, such multiple tenancy did exist, the average ceiling on tenant numbers was around four or five, with larger touns, such as the thirteen tenants who held Crailing (Roxburghshire) in 1689 or the nine who occupied Eckford (Roxburghshire) in 1714 being exceptional. Closer examination of those for which a sequence of rental statements was available led to the further conclusion that multiple tenancy was on the decline over these years and that this decline was accomplished mostly by a reduction in the number of tenants per toun rather than by a division of each person's share into a separate holding. There is more than a strong hint that upland pastoral or gerss holdings in the south-east shifted sooner and more fully into single tenancy than low-ground arable touns in the Merse. On the Buccleuch estate, for instance, rentals for 1708 and 1716 show that its large arable touns in Eckford parish (Roxburghshire) were almost entirely in the hands of multiple tenants. The same rentals, meanwhile, show that its gerss holdings in upper Teviotdale, Ewesdale, Liddesdale, and, to a lesser extent, Ettrick, had already begun to shift into single tenancy. Even in the 1760s, when the latter had passed almost completely into the hands of single tenants, the majority of the former were still shared between multiple tenants. A similar contrast between upland and lowland touns can be detected on the Roxburgh ducal estate, with its Cheviot hill farms being in the hands of single tenants by the 1720s, but multiple tenancy persisting on low ground touns in the Baronies of Roxburgh, Caverton, and Sprouston until the 1740s and 50s. For comparison, B. M. W. Third found a similar contrast when working further north on the Clerk of Penicuik estate. In her words, 'it had been customary at Penicuik during the latter half of the seventeenth century, and perhaps before that, for large pastoral farms to be run by one or two tenants and Baron Sir John Clerk considered one tenant sufficient for the management of what he termed his wild sheep rooms.'[3] In fact, according to Butt and Lythe, this early appearance of single tenancy on sheep farms in the Southern Uplands may date back to the early rather than late seventeenth century, and have as its cause the increased profitability of the wool trade following the Union of Crowns in 1603 and the pacification of the Borders.[4] Putting aside the problem of when it began, there can be no doubt that the reduction of tenant numbers in the Southern Uplands, as well as those examples on the lower ground, signifies the adjustment of the area's landholding structure to market pressures long before the mid-eighteenth century. The logic behind the process was simple. Tenant reduction meant much larger working units for those tenants who survived this filtering process and, almost inevitably, a more commercialized farming system.

Scattered across the south-east were also a number of large proprietary runrig touns, involving hereditary landholders. As many as 49 were to be found in the region. Some, like Eildon, Coldingham, and Smailholm, were held by more than 20 heritors (mostly feuars). Beneath them, and holding land from them, were probably an even greater number of tenants. Because they involved hereditary rights, proprietary runrig touns tended to be fairly rigid in terms of their landholding structure. Indeed, most of them were eventually divided out of runrig by a decreet in the local sheriff court, each landholder being given a separate and consolidated holding in lieu of his share.

The aforementioned study of Roxburghshire and Berwickshire was based on the analysis of various rentals and court records. A much more complete overview is available for Aberdeenshire

---

[3] B. M. W. Third, 'The significance of Estate Plans and Associated Documents', *SS* i (1957), p. 50.

[4] For the increased profitability of sheep farming after 1603, see Smout, *Scottish Trade on the Eve of the Union*, pp. 215–16; Devine and Lythe, 'The Economy of Scotland Under James VI', pp. 91–2. Instances of single tenancy in the area during the late 16th century can be seen in *Exchequer Rolls of Scotland*, xxi (1580–8), pp. 344–9.

thanks to the 1696 *List of Pollable Persons* for the county.[5]
Although compiled ostensibly for tax purposes, the *List* specifies
whether a person was a heritor, tenant, sub-tenant, cottager,
servant, or tradesman. A simple aggregation study revealed that
out of 1,000 touns, approximately one-third were in the possession of multiple tenants (see Table 2). This may seem a low
figure. However, we must reckon with the fact that parts of
Aberdeenshire were probably affected by the tacksman system.
In these circumstances, it seems reasonable to assume that some
of the 'sub-tenants' recorded by the list may not have been of
cottar status, holding an acre or so in return for providing the
main tenant(s) with their labour, but holders of a substantial
proportion of the toun. For this reason, there may be a strong case
for presuming that many of the touns recorded in the *List* as held
directly from the landowner by only a single tenant, but with a
number of 'sub-tenants' holding of this tenant, are realistically
seen as further examples of multiple tenancy. If, guided by this
presumption, such touns are included in the calculation of
multiple tenancy, then the proportion of such touns increases to
over two-thirds of the total. A valuable feature of the Aberdeenshire Poll List is the way it highlights local variations as regards
multiple and single tenancy. Thus, parishes like Fintray, Glen-
muick, Echt, Tullich, and Glengarden appear to have a fairly
high proportion of multiple tenancies, whilst those of Deer,
Methlick, and Monquhitter had fairly low proportions. Some,
like Bourtie, Slains, Skene, and Peterculter, had few multiple
tenancies if the calculation is confined solely to those recorded as
tenants, but high proportions if it is extended to embrace those
entered as 'sub-tenants'. In many instances, we can tie these
variations down to differences in ownership and the manipul-
ative hand of estate policy. For example, in the parish of Coull,
there seems to be a distinction between the touns owned by the
laird of Drum and those held by the laird of Craigevar, the former
being held by single tenants in all but three instances, and the
latter largely held by multiple tenants. However, if we take into
account the 'sub-tenants' on the Drum estate, the distinction
between the two estates is effectively removed. The *List* is also
illuminating on how many tenants were carried by multiple
tenant touns. Broadly speaking, the majority had fewer than six

[5] Stuart (ed.), *List of Pollable Persons Within the Shire of Aberdeen*, 2 vols.

Table 2: A Sample of Landholding in Aberdeenshire, 1696

Parish	Predominantly Single- (S) or Multiple- (M) Tenant Touns or Equally Balanced (E)	Large Nos. of Sub-tenants (or an over-all average of more than one per toun)	Large Nos. of Cottars, Grassmen, and Herds (or an over-all average of more than one per toun)
Aboyne	E	No	No
Birse	M	No	Yes
Bourtie	S	Yes	No
Clunie	S	No	Yes
Coull	S	Yes	No
Crimond	S	No	Yes
Culsalmond	M	No	Yes
Deer	S	No	Yes
Echt	M	No	No
Fintray	E	No	Yes
Forbes	S	No	Yes
Forgue	E	No	Yes
Fyvie	S	No	Yes
Gartly	E	No	Yes
Glengarden	M	No	No
Glenmuick	M	No	No
Glentaner	M	No	No
Keig	S	No	Yes
Kinbetach	M	No	No
Kinernie	E	No	Yes
Kinkell	S	No	No
Kinnoir	M	No	Yes
Leslie	E	Yes	No
Methlick	S	No	No
Montwhiter	S	No	Yes
Monymusk	M	No	Yes
Peterculter	S	Yes	No
Pitsligo	E	No	Yes
Ruthven and Botarie	S	No	Yes
Slains	S	Yes	No
Streichen	S	No	No
Tullich	M	No	No
Tyrie	S	Yes	No
Skene	S	Yes	Yes

Based on Stuart (ed.), *List of Pollable Persons Within the Shire of Aberdeen, 1696*, 2 vols. A generalized rather than an exact presentation of the *List* data was chosen owing to the difficulties associated with its use, difficulties which make the classification of some entries debatable. The main area of uncertainty concerns those individuals entered only as tradesmen, but who may also have had the status of tenant, sub-tenant, or cottar. One further point is that parishes whose touns were predominantly in the hands of multiple tenants were—as a rule—the smaller parishes with fewer touns.

tenants, even when 'sub-tenants' are included. However, most parishes had one or two exceptional touns with more, whilst there were parishes, like Kinbetach, Tullich, and Glengarden, in which numbers were generally higher with six to ten tenants being more of a norm than the exception.[6] By sampling a number of scattered rentals for other parts of southern and eastern Scotland, a generalized picture of tenant numbers can be obtained which at least provides the basis for a provisional if not a definitive conclusion. As in the case of the extreme south-east and Aberdeenshire, when taken together, these rentals make it clear that there were quite a number of estates on which multiple tenancy still prevailed during the late seventeenth and early eighteenth centuries, and others, where it was close to disappearing. For instance, out of 136 touns noted in 1736 rental for the Bargany estate lands of Bargany, Glenassil and Daltippen, Ardstinchar, Knockdaw, and Troweir in Ayrshire, only 13 were set down as held by more than one tenant.[7] Likewise, in the Baronies of Baglillie, Raith, and Cardon in Fife, only three out of 23 touns were in the hands of more than one tenant.[8] Further north, out of 31 touns making up the Baronies of Navar and Lethnot in Angus, only eight were shared between multiple tenants in 1727.[9] On other estates, the situation appears more evenly balanced. For example, in a 1692 rental for the Barony of Corlochie (Angus), 17 touns or crofts were held by multiple tenants and 19 by single tenants.[10] Alongside such estates, however, were some on which multiple tenancy accounted for the majority of touns. Thus, in the south-west, where single tenancy appears to have been fairly widespread by the late seventeenth century, one can still find estates on which it was

[6] Further analysis of the 1696 List is provided by K. Walton, 'The Distribution of Population in Aberdeenshire, 1696', *SGM* lvi (1950), pp. 17–26 and A. Geddes and J. Forbes, 'Rural Communities of Fermtoun and Baile in the Lowlands and Highlands of Aberdeenshire 1696, *Aberdeen Univ Rev.*, xxxii (1947), pp. 98–104. Since this section was written, Whyte, *Agriculture and Society in Seventeenth-Century Scotland*, p. 146, has now mapped the information on single and multiple tenancy provided by the 1696 list. Generally speaking, it suggests that single tenancy prevailed in lower, more fertile areas, such as Garioch, around Aberdeen, and along the Ythan and Deveron valleys.
[7] SRO, Bargany MSS, GD109/3622.
[8] SRO, GD45/5/266.
[9] F. Cruickshank, *Navar and Lethnot* (Brechin, 1899), Appendix, pp. 338–40, 'Rental Book of York Building Company, 1722–6'.
[10] SRO, Airlie MSS, GD16/30/11.

absent or insignificant. The Hay or Park estate lands in Ayrshire and the Corshill estate lands in Renfrewshire are cases in point. The former had nine of its 13 touns held by multiple tenants at the time of a rental drawn up in 1729 to 1730,[11] whilst a list of tenants in Corshill Barony compiled in 1666 suggests that all of its 10 touns carried multiple tenants.[12] Work by J. E. Handley on rentals for the Morton and Delvine estates in Fife and for the Blair Drummond estate in Perthshire confirm this variation in the ratio of multiple to single tenancy.[13]

To establish that single tenancy was a significant element in the south and east of Scotland before the mid-eighteenth century is only to reaffirm what has already been established using fifteenth- and sixteenth-century rentals. There had never been a time when multiple tenancy was overwhelmingly predominant. More pertinent, therefore, is the question of whether single tenancy increased its share of touns over these decades prior to the start of the Improvers' Movement. On balance, it would seem as if single tenancy was better represented in some areas. It has already been mentioned that tenant reduction can be detected at work in the extreme south-east and in the Southern Uplands before the mid-eighteenth century. The conclusions reached by Lebon in his work on Ayrshire and the western Lowlands are also relevant here. 'It is not to be supposed', he wrote, 'that co-tenancy continued to the date of enclosure. From the various sixteenth and seventeenth century documents, it becomes apparent that division of townlands into individual farms was quite common; and probably lands held jointly by a number of tenants were steadily diminishing throughout the two centuries before 1750.'[14] An attempt to monitor trends in Aberdeenshire during these decades before improvement can be made by comparing the 1696 Poll List with eighteenth-century rentals. The two rentals used, though, or one dated 1732 to 1736

[11] SRO, Hay of Park MSS, GD72/541/19.
[12] *Archaeological and Historical Collections Relating to the Counties of Ayr and Wigton*, iv (Edinburgh, 1884), pp. 68–9.
[13] J.E. Handley, *The Agricultural Revolution in Scotland* (Glasgow, 1963), pp. 19, 25, and 62. Whyte, *Agriculture and Society in Seventeenth-Century Scotland*, pp. 143–5 confirms the importance of single tenancy in the Lowlands by the late 17th century.
[14] J. H. G. Lebon, 'The Process of Enclosure in the Western Lowlands', *SGM* lxii (1946), p. 105.

for the Monymusk estate[15] and another dated 1740 for the Forbes estate, evidence no clear-cut trend.[16] In fact, on both estates, the small number of touns which had shifted from multiple to single tenancy since 1696 were balanced by a few which had later moved in the reverse direction. This tendency for tenant numbers actually to increase on even low-lying touns in the north-east marks the start of a process that was to continue unabated throughout the eighteenth century. It involved either the subdivision of touns into a greater number of shares, or the creation of new smallholdings on waste or mossland. Behind it lay a growing demand for land coupled with a willingness amongst landowners to pack their rent rolls. In its over-all effect on landholding, it tends to separate parts of the north-east from trends in the Lowlands and aligns them more with what happened in the Highlands.[17]

Tenants holding a toun directly from the landowner were not the only element in the landholding structure of touns. As in earlier centuries, there were also sub-tenants, cottars, and cottagers. As already noted during the earlier discussion of tenurial conditions in Aberdeenshire, any definition of sub-tenants depends very much on the area we are dealing with. In the areas fringing the Highlands, but particularly in the broken country which divides upland from lowland in Perthshire and the north-east, sub-tenants were often part of a well-developed tacksman system which had overflowed from the Highlands. Sub-tenants in these areas could be substantial holders of land, renting a major share if not the entire toun from the tacksman. However, the term could technically be used of a quite different category of landholder, or the small cottars or cottagers who held small parcels of land in return for their labour. Aberdeenshire may not be a typical county for a number of reasons, but the 1696 *List* certainly testifies to the continued importance of cottars and

---

[15] H. Hamilton (ed.), *Monymusk Papers (1713–1755)*, Scottish History Society, 3rd ser., xxxix (1945), pp. 55–7. See also, Stuart (ed.), op. cit., pp. 373–88.

[16] SRO, Forbes MSS, GD52/285. Whyte, *Agriculture and Society in Seventeenth-Century Scotland*, pp. 151–2, provides further comment on the extent of tenant reduction by the late 17th century.

[17] Late 18th-century commentators discuss at length the smallholding systems which mushroomed on wasteland in the north-east over the late 17th and early 18th centuries. See, for example, G. Keith, *A General View of the Agriculture of Aberdeenshire* (Aberdeen, 1811), pp. 143–54 or *OSA* iii (1792), p. 49.

cottagers at the base of the landholding system. In the north-east, such groups graded smoothly into smallholders and lesser tenants, and helped to provide an easy gradient for the farming ladder, from the meanest cottar to the more substantial tenants who held large touns and saw themselves as bonnet lairds or even 'yeomen'.[18] Further south, as toun size became larger, the number of genuine sub-tenants diminishes but the number of cottars and cottagers increases. Their numerical importance is disclosed by the large number of retrospective references to them in the *Old Statistical Account* of the late eighteenth century. For many contributors to the *Account*, the eventual demise of the cottager system was one of the more noteworthy, as well as one of the more regrettable, side-effects of the Improvers' Movement.[19] The substantial contribution which cottagers and their like must have made to the social character and scale of early touns in the Lowlands is disclosed most sharply by the 1696 *List of Pollable Persons in the Shire of Aberdeen* (see Table 2).[20] A less detailed list of toun inhabitants, one compiled for a different purpose, is available for Galloway.[21] It too, suggests that the non-tenant element on early ferm touns—the servants and tied cottagers— was significant. They ensured that even single-tenant touns could constitute sizeable social units.

(*b*) *Fermtoun and Holding Size* Surveys compiled during the early and middle decades of the eighteenth century, many of which were designated to facilitate their reorganization, suggest their was no absolute uniformity of fermtoun size in the Lowlands and Southern Uplands. However, different *upper* limits can be detected in the various sub-regions. Thus, in the north-east, only

[18] Stuart (ed.) op. cit., vol. ii, pp. 276–317.

[19] Amongst the many such references available see *OSA* i (1792), pp. 173 and 345; ibid., iii (1792), p. 473; ibid., viii (1793), pp. 463 and 471; ibid., ix (1793), pp. 39, 199, and 442.

[20] The parish of Clunie, for instance, had 50 tenants listed, and 57 grassmen (Stuart (ed.), op. cit., vol. i, pp. 217–30). That of Leslie, had 33 tenants plus 68 sub-tenants and herds (ibid., pp. 231–9), whilst that of Keige had 34 tenants entered plus 23 cottars (ibid., pp. 453–63).

[21] *Parish Lists for Wigtownshire and Minnigaff 1684*, SRS 1916. As with Aberdeenshire list of 1696, there is again variety in the way these lists have been compiled. However, in the case of the parishes of Glastoun and Penighame, the number of cottars can be calculated. In the case of the former, there are 90 recorded cottars (pp. 7–10), spread across roughly one half of the 28 touns in the parish. In the latter, 11 cottars and 31 serving men and women were listed (pp. 48–52), spread over the 41 holdings in the parish.

the exceptional toun exceeded 300 acres (121 ha). Beneath this upper limit, there existed a pyramid of touns whose number increased as size decreased. Exemplifying this spread are two surveys covering touns in the parish of Clatt (Aberdeenshire). The first details touns belonging to the Forbes estate. Altogether, nine are listed, the smallest being 26 acres (10 ha) and the largest 301 (122 ha), with a general average of 113 acres (46 ha).[22] The second survey details the touns belonging to James Gordon of Moorplace. It lists a total of 26 touns. Although examples like Auchmenzie and Newbigging exceeded 300 acres (121 ha), the majority were less than 300 acres (121 ha).[23] This tendency for touns to be under 300 acres (121 ha) continues southwards into Angus. However, further into the central Lowlands and across the Tay, in Fife, larger touns start to appear with more frequency. For instance, a survey of the Barony of Ballencriech in the parish of Flisk (Fife) records six of the fifteen touns as over 400 acres (162 ha), the largest being 766 acres (310 ha).[24] Further south still, in the Lothians and the Merse, large touns were fairly commonplace, but not to the exclusion of small ones. Thus, in the Merse, whilst estates like that of Dunglass were characterized by relatively small touns of less than 150 acres (61 ha),[25] others were possessed of more generously endowed touns. Over half the low-ground touns on the Roxburgh estate, for example, were in excess of 400 acres (162 ha).[26] In fact, one or two of its low-ground touns, as well as a few proprietary runrig touns in the area, such as Eildon, Gattonside, Smailholm, Auchencraw, and Coldingham, extended to over 1,000 acres (405 ha).[27] Naturally, towards the higher ground of the Cheviots and westwards into the main body of the Southern Uplands, large touns become even more prevalent. A survey of the 20 touns comprising the

[22] Based on SRO, RHP260/2.

[23] SRO, RHP14753.

[24] SRO, RHP6100.

[25] Reading University Library, Dunglass MSS, MS entitled 'Runrig ground of Dunglass Barrony and Barrony of Colesbrandspath', *c*.1745.

[26] Floors Castle, Roxburgh MSS, Abstract of the Measure of Barony of Sprouston, 1769, and Barony of Roxburgh, 1769.

[27] Based on material drawn from the register of decreets in the Sheriff Court Papers of Roxburghshire (Jedburgh) and Berwickshire (Duns). For details see Dodgshon, 'Towards an Understanding and Definition of Runrig: the Evidence for Roxburghshire and Berwickshire', pp. 19–24.

Roxburgh estate Barony of Primside, most of which lay along
Bowmont and Kale Waters, shows 16 of them as over 400 acres
(162 ha), with nine over 1,000 acres (405 ha).[28] An excellent
opportunity for examining upland toun size is afforded by a 1718
survey of the vast Buccleuch estate possessions in upland
Roxburghshire, Selkirkshire, and Dumfriesshire. The section
covering Liddesdale has been taken as a sample, embracing as it
does both high-ground store and low-ground dale touns. Out of
49 touns mentioned, 15 exceeded 1,000 acres (405 ha), the largest
being a trio of touns over 2,000 acres (810 ha). Only 13 were
under 300 acres (121 ha).[29] Of course, further west still, in the
Lowland area that skirts the Solway Firth, toun size falls away
sharply. For instance, out of 72 touns in the parish of Canonby
(Dumfriesshire), only 15 exceeded 400 acres (162 ha).[30] Extant
surveys for Galloway show a similar balance. Interestingly, as one
moves north onto the lower ground of Ayrshire, toun size does not
really recover, those over 400 acres (162 ha) being very much the
exception.[31] Indeed, their differences of toun size forms a major
point of contrast, between the agrarian structure of the western
and eastern sectors of the Lowlands.[32]

From what has been said regarding tenant numbers per toun
and toun size, it follows that considerable variety must have
existed over what each tenant actually held or *holding size per
tenant.* Clearly, where single tenants held an entire toun, then it
must be accepted that such tenants were in command of quite
substantial holdings. At the upper extreme, it was possible for a
tenant in Fife, Lothian, or the Merse to have an arable toun of
over 300 acres (121 ha), whilst in the Southern Uplands, it could
not have been unusual for single tenants to possess a gerss holding
of 500 to 1,000 acres (185 to 405 ha). In fact, these large
entrepreneurial holdings were regarded by one passing observer
as a feature of the Southern Uplands as early as the mid-

---

[28] Floors Castle, Roxburgh MSS, Computation of the Lands adjacent to the Waters of
Bowmount and Kail with the Barony of Primside, 1769.

[29] SRO, RHP9629.

[30] SRO, RHP52/3.

[31] J. H. G. Lebon. 'The Fate of the Countryside in Central Ayrshire during the 18th
and 19th Centuries', *SGM* lxii, (1946), pp. 7–15.

[32] This contrast is well brought out in Sir John Sinclair's review of holding-size, see
General Report on the Agricultural State and Political Circumstances of Scotland (Edinburgh,
1814), vol. i, pp. 180–1.

seventeenth century. Even in areas like the north-east, where toun size was more likely to be under rather than over 100 acres (40 ha), it could still be argued that such touns offered a comfortable living for a single tenant, his cottars included. Given the broad figures presented earlier showing some Lowland estates had over 50 per cent of their touns in the hands of single tenants, it could still be reasoned that a similar proportion must, at the very least, have constituted viable subsistence units and that many must have been capable of yeilding a marketable surplus.

Of course, on those touns which still carried multiple tenants, the situation was quite different. With at least a half of all Lowland touns still held by multiple tenants in most regions, and with an average number of tenants per toun of between four and six, it follows that the bulk of tenants continued to live their life out in such touns. This needs stressing because the predicament of multiple tenants could be quite different from that of single tenants. We need only take a middling-sized toun of 200 acres (81 ha) divided between five tenants, their cottars and servants, to realize this. In short, even large and substantial touns could be cast into quite modest holdings when occupied by multiple tenants. At a guess, and we can only guess, short of an extensive analysis of early surveys and rentals, the majority of multiple tenants must have held less than 30 to 40 acres (12 to 16 ha) *each*. In areas like the north-east, parts of Perthshire, and possibly the south-west, the ceiling for the majority of multiple tenants may have been significantly less, perhaps only 20 to 30 acres (8 to 12 ha). However, whether we treat the position of such tenants as comfortable or precarious must not be determined on the basis of their holding-size alone. As will be elaborated on later, the question of whether the living of such tenants gave them adequate margins for subsistence was greatly affected by a variety of other factors.

The Farming Township: Its Layout

Estate surveys and plans compiled from the early eighteenth century onwards enable us to examine the layout of early touns in some detail, particularly such aspects as the disposition of runrig, of infield–outfield, and the character of settlement.

Plans depicting runrig are the more scarce. Indeed, in view of the many thousands of runrig touns that once existed, the comparative handful of runrig plans drawn up, and the even fewer which have actually survived, provide us with only the briefest glimpse of runrig's disposition or layout on the ground. Yet all our visual impressions of what runrig looked like must be built up from these plans. Space allows the reproduction of only two examples, those for Auchencraw (1714) in Berwickshire, and for the west part of Duffus parish (1771) in Moray (see Figs. 7.1 and 2). Taking an overview of these and other surviving runrig plans, the conclusion we are forced to reach is that whilst systematically laid-out strips or selions were present to a greater or lesser extent in most cases, part of their layout usually comprises irregular parcels or blocks of land. This does not mean that the methods of land division described earlier were in-effectual. Rather should we bear in mind the special nature of those touns for which runrig plans were compiled. Most involved hereditary rights. Thus, Auchencraw and the west part of Duffus parish were both examples of proprietary runrig. The former held by fourteen heritors and the latter by two, the Duke of Gordon and Robert Chalmers. A few, and only a few, were long-standing and stable tenant–runrig touns, whose layouts were accepted by landowners as the basis for the reorganization of landholding. In the vast majority of cases, however, landowners exercised their right of ignoring the complex web of tenurial interest when seeking to remove tenant–runrig layouts during the eighteenth century. Indeed, the widespread tendency for runrig to be removed by the simple process of tenant reduction is proof enough of this.[33] However, this same point means that tenant–runrig touns for which plans were drawn up probably possessed layouts which, like those of proprietary–runrig touns, were not continually re-cast whenever new tenants entered the toun. In such circumstances, we can expect private excambions and strip amalgamations to have thrown some disguise over the once regular pattern of strips and to have imparted a more evolved and organic appearance to the layout of landholding.

It has been argued that in areas like the Carse of Gowrie, some

---

[33] Apart from the author's work on the south-east in Dodgshon, 'The Removal of Runrig in Roxburghshire and Berwickshire, 1680–1766', pp. 121–7, relevant comment can be found in *OSA* iii (1792), pp. 51 and 384; ibid., viii (1793), pp. 42–3, 88, 255, and 310.

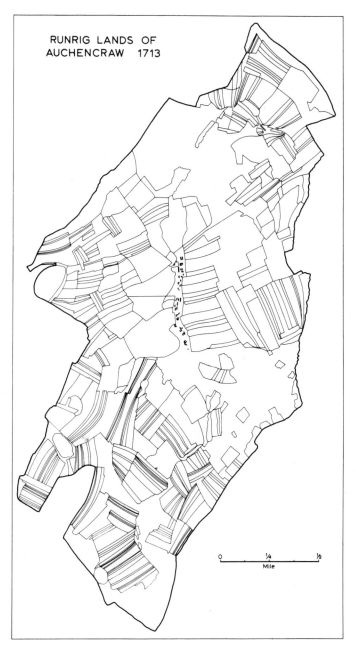

RUNRIG LANDS OF
AUCHENCRAW 1713

0   ¼   ½
Mile

FIG. 7.1. Runrig Lands of Auchencraw (Berwickshire), *c.*1713. Based on SRO, RHP
14788

Runrig lands in west part
of Duffus parish
C. 1773

Fig. 7.2.　Runrig Lands in the West Part of Duffus Parish (Moray), *c.*1773. Based on
SRO, RHP 2004

of the more progressive touns re-cast their entire runrig layouts during this period so as to create a pattern of intermixed parcels rather than strips. Such a pattern is variously referred to as one of rundale or of kavels. Whether such systems were designed as a later compromise between pure runrig and consolidated holdings is difficult to say. Certainly, there can be no doubting that some touns consisted almost entirely of intermixed parcels or 'kavels'. An example cited by A. N. L. Hodd is that of Inchyra in Perthshire.[34] It consisted of a toun 400 to 500 (162 to 202 ha) in extent shared between two landowners. Altogether, it was parcelled out into around one hundred separate kavels, the majority of which did not exceed 5 acres (2 ha). For comparison, the runrig toun of Eyemouth in Berwickshire extended to 747 acres (302 ha). These were parcelled out between 30 different feuars in 612 strips or parcels, exactly two-thirds of which were one acre or less.[35] The full landholding history of Inchyra is, in fact, well documented by a *Session Case* of 1876. The case concerned the problem of fishing rights on the Tay. In an effort to resolve them it probed back into how the rights had come to be shared in the first place. In 1655, it seems, the owner of Inchyra, Sir Alexander Blair, had sold to William Blair 'the just and equal sunie half of all and haill the town and lands of Inchriff, now commonly called Inchyra'.[36] In the same year, he sold the other half to his brother, Andrew Blair. Each share was made up of 'an equal number of these—a kavel belonging to one party always alternating with a kavel belonging to the other party, after the fashion of runrig or rundale'.[37] In 1782, an attempt by the then holder of one of the halves to have the lands divided under the 1695 *Act anent lands lying runrig* failed on the grounds that the Act did not apply to parcels over 4 acres (1.6 ha) in size. In case it be thought that this was giving official definition to 'kavels', it should be added that most runrig touns contained some parcels of this size but the matter was overlooked during their division. The hesitancy of the Perthshire Sheriff Court to proceed with the case is the surest sign

---

[34] A. N. L. Hodd, 'Runrig on the Eve of the Agricultural Revolution in Scotland', *SGM* xc (1974), pp. 130-3.

[35] SRO, Home-Roberstson MSS, GD267/2063, Mensuration and Valuation of the Runrigg Lands of Eyemouth by David Mather, 1763.

[36] Baroness Gray v. Richardson and others, pp. 1031-78 in *Session Cases*, 4th ser., iii (1875), esp. pp. 1047-50.

[37] Ibid., p. 1048.

we have that Inchyra was not an average toun. In fact, when it was eventually divided out into two separate holdings in 1794 to 1795, it required the consent of both proprietors.

To a contemporary observer, the existence of runrig would not have intruded too much, if at all, into what could be seen on the ground. Whether they were held by different landholders or not, the vista stretched out before him would still have been dominated by narrow, gently curving rigs (see Plate I). Such rigs were not a function of runrig or intermixed ownership, even though they sometimes formed the units of ownership, but were bound up with the technical constraints of using a fixed mouldboard plough. The old Scotch plough(s) fell into this category. The commonest type in the Lowlands was infamous for its heavy, cumbersome nature. As well as occupying the efforts of three to four persons to keep it in the ground and on the right course, it was pulled by anything from six to ten oxen, two abreast. In the north-east, plough-teams of twelve oxen were needed. To complicate matters, teams were often shared between a number of different landholders. The self-evident ungainliness of such teams was ridiculed by numerous eighteenth-century writers. Visiting Aberdeenshire in 1778, Andrew Wight recorded how he

saw, for the first time, sometimes 10 oxen, sometimes 12, yoked to a plough, but not all drawing at the same time. To increase my wonder, I saw this long train of oxen ploughing a ridge not much above twice the length of the draught, the foremost oxen turning at the one end of the ridge when the plough was not far advanced from the other, and on wet ground too.[38]

In addition to this type of plough, A. Fenton has identified a lighter implement that was pulled by four horses, all abreast. On the eve of the Improving Movement, it was to be found only in parts of the south-west, though it may once have been more widespread.[39]

If runrig revealed itself at all, then it would only have been in

---

[38] A. Wight, *Present State of Husbandry in Scotland* (Edinburgh, 1784), vol. iii, part ii, pp. 703–4.

[39] See discussion in A. Fenton, 'Plough and Spade in Dumfries and Galloway', *TDGNHS*, 3rd ser., xlv (1968), pp. 152–64.

the grass balks that were sometimes used to divide one man's strip from another. However, the weeds which infested many an arable rig in poorly-farmed touns would have made the distinction between rig and balk an academic one. Reference was made earlier to the way in which 'gule' or corn marigold was actually outlawed by the authorities in an effort to control it. The measures they took were still acted upon during the late seventeenth century as one or two Baron Court proceedings testify.[40] Other weeds were equally troublesome. In 1740, a Mr Bethune of Kilconquhar (Ayrshire) sought Robert Maxwell's advice on the problem of his infield or 'mucked land' which, when dunged, ran 'excessively to Runches, Skellochs, &c. and is full of Quickens and Couch Grass; which are so injurious, that last year they quite overcame his Barley while it was in the Brier or Braird, and so stifled its Growth . . .'.[41] Not all tenants were apt to complain about their weeds. In the south-west, weeds mixed with the bear crop, such as darnel or roseager, were thought to strengthen the ale brewed from it and even to add a 'narcotick' effect.[42]

Arguably the prime value of early estate surveys is the light they shed on the layout of a toun's infield, outfield, and common pasture. The popular image of infield–outfield stresses three attributes. First, it is assumed that infield occupied the better land close to the farmstead. Secondly, it is believed that infield occupied a smaller acreage than outfield. And thirdly, the arable land which made up the infield and outfield is thought to have comprised small, irregular blocks or shots of land that were often discontinuously spread across the fermtoun. The pre-Improvement plans which become available in quantity during the eighteenth century enable us to put these ideas to the test. Broadly speaking, they are valid assumptions. Only in exceptional circumstances was infield not located in close proximity to the farmsteads of a toun. As regards the ratio of infield to outfield, it was also the norm for the latter to be of greater acreage than the former. However, exceptions can be found. Thus, whilst touns in

---

[40] Wight, op. cit., vol. i, p. 35, for instance, talks of the custom of 'riding the guild' and 'guild law', with tenants still being fined for neglecting it.

[41] R. Maxwell, *Select Transactions of the Honourable The Society of Improvers in the Knowledge of Agriculture in Scotland* (Edinburgh, 1743), p. 80.

[42] *Geographical Collections*, vol. ii, p. 103.

the parish of Clatt (Aberdeenshire) had outfields that were anything up to four or five times more extensive than their infields,[43] the reverse was true of touns in the Barony of Ballencriech (Fife): there, infield was fractionally larger than outfield on all but three inland touns that were appendaged to the Barony in the survey of 1759, namely, Ballingry Northside, Southside, and Forgan.[44] The ratio of infield to outfield, however, reflects only the amount of land assessed at the point when the addition of land units step by step with colonization ceased. Generally speaking, the disposition of arable took one of two forms. In the more fertile areas, the small, compact, irregular shots that constituted the basic field units of a toun's arable were joined together to form a continuous cropping area. The plans of Dalmahoy in Midlothian (Plate 2), Roxburgh Barony in Roxburghshire (Fig. 7.3), and Gerrie in Aberdeenshire (Fig. 7.4) illustrate layouts of this type. Alternatively, where land was less fertile or poorly drained, arable was more broken and fragmented, often extremely so. In between, lay patches of moss or bog. Plans of John Forbes's estate (c.1771) in the parish of Clatt in Aberdeenshire and part of Navar parish (1766) in Angus typify this sort of layout (see Figs. 7.5 and 6).

Turning to the question of settlement layout or morphology, the seemingly casual, unplanned style with which some early plans locate farmsteads and their outbuildings might be taken as casting some doubt on whether they really offer a reliable or credible representation of settlement form. In fact, the shapelessness which they portray was in the nature of much Lowland settlement, with no common focus or design in the layout of farmsteads or outbuildings. Amongst the causes of this dishevelled layout may have been the constant renewal cycle which affected early farm dewellings, with tenants often building a new farmstead on their entry to a toun. This was still practised in parts of the Lowlands in the decades before Improvement, though it was more common in the Highlands.[45] Another noteworthy

---

[43] See SRO, RHP260/2 and 14753.

[44] SRO, RHP6100.

[45] An illustration is provided by Barron (ed.), *Court Book of the Barony of Urie*, which, in 1730, ordained that 'no tenent or inhabitant whatsoever within the baronia shall pull down any of their houses at their removeall, after the inventar of the biggings is fulfilled and satisfied', p. 130.

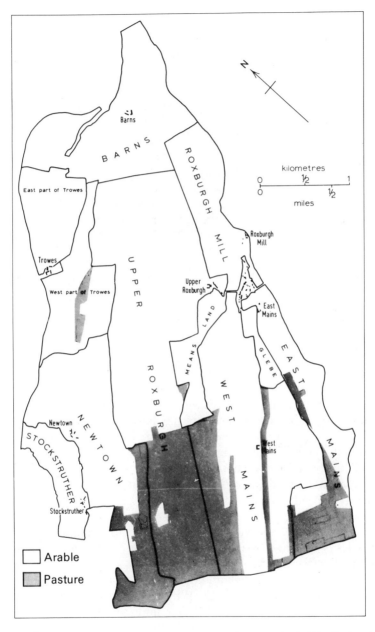

FIG. 7.3.   Roxburgh Barony (Roxburghshire), 1769. Based on plan held by Roxburgh
Estates, Kelso

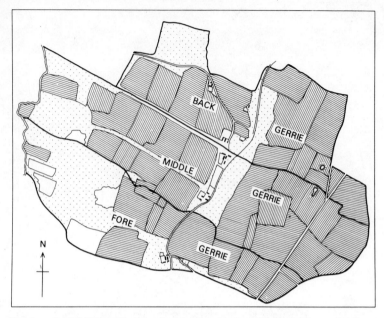

FIG. 7.4.   Back, Mid, and Fore Gerrie (Aberdeenshire), 1761. Based on SRO, RHP 2223

feature of this type of settlement form was its frequently marginal or peripheral nature. Instead of being set in the midst of the toun's arable, such farmsteads were often located at the edge of it, on an adjoining patch of muir that had been avoided by the plough. Elsewhere, settlement has a more central location within the toun, being firmly placed within, not without, the arable. As well as being more central, this type of settlement usually displayed more deliberation, more order, in its layout, with neatly laid-out farmsteads and cot-touns. In some touns (such as Midlem, Lilliesleaf, and Sprouston in Roxburghshire), farmsteads were even set within tofts, whose regular alignment on a single- or two-row basis imparted a definite and long-surviving plan to settlement layout.

The character of Lowland house-types during this period has been well reviewed by I. D. Whyte.[46] Altogether, he distinguished two broad types. The commonest form of dwelling

---

[46] I. D. Whyte, 'Rural Housing in Lowland Scotland in the Seventeenth Century: the Evidence of Estate Papers', *SS* xix (1975), pp. 55–68.

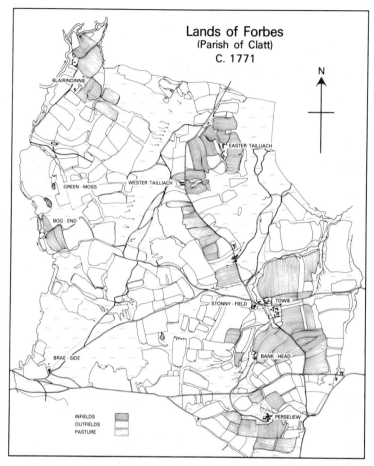

FIG. 7.5.   John Forbes's Estate in Clatt Parish (Aberdeenshire), *c.*1771. Based on SRO, RHP 260/2

amongst the peasantry was that of the long-house, with dwelling, barn, and byre under the same roof. Its walls were built of stone, clay, or turf. Its roof was usually supported by cruck-trusses and covered with either broom, straw-thatch, or turf. An important conclusion of Whyte is that over the seventeenth century, the use of lime mortar in wall-construction became more and more prevalent. Such walls had a much greater load-bearing potential. The effect of this was to encourage the building of two- or three-

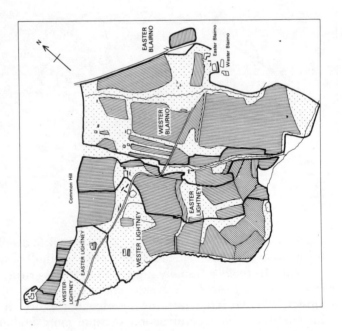

FIG. 7.6 Blairno and Lightney in Navar Parish (Angus), 1766. Based on SRO, RHP 1667/3 and 6

storey dwellings, particularly amongst the lesser gentry and larger tenants. Seen in perspective, it was the start of Scotland's 'Great Rebuilding', a movement that was to continue throughout the eighteenth century and which produced the fine, commodious dwelling houses that are such an attractive addition to the farming landscape of the Lowlands.

Farming Systems in South and East Scotland, 1650–1760

The farming system practised by fermtouns poses one major problem, that of infield–outfield. One can discern other systems of farming, notably the system of grass parks and enclosures which developed initially around mansions or policies for partly ornamental reasons and which then spread to areas like the south-west during the late seventeenth and early eighteenth centuries as a regular farming system. Such alternatives, however, were never as widespread or as important as infield–outfield. This does not mean that the farming landscape of the period was without any real variation in cropping, even though one or two eighteenth-century writers did remark on its uniformity of such. As argued in an earlier chapter, infield–outfield started out primarily as a distinction in the basis of landholding. Around this distinction, there developed two separate cropping systems, the one intensive and arable-based, the other extensive and mixed. Within this broad, loosely fitting definition, it is possible to find quite varied cropping patterns that must have contributed considerable texture to the pre-Improvement landscape. Extant descriptions of infield–outfield from this eve-of-change period afford a glimpse of this variety within.

A particularly graphic description of infield–outfield cropping organization is that provided by J. Anderson's oft-quoted discussion of infield–outfield in Aberdeenshire. He describes infield as divided into three breaks, two of which were under oats and one under bear. The tathed area of outfield, meanwhile, was divided equally between grass and arable. During any one year, the half in cultivation was arranged into five breaks, one of which was under its first crop, another its second, another its third, and so on. Within the half under grass, there was a further break being tathed in readiness for cultivation the following spring.

Thus, each break was in turn tathed, cropped for five years, and then abandoned until its turn for tathing came round again. Beyond the tathed area was a portion of outfield known as faugh land. This too, was cultivated but instead of being prepared by tathing, it was fallowed.[47] In all probability, it was an attempt to extend cultivation beyond the limits set by tathing. The essentials of Anderson's description are vouched for by an account drawn up in 1683 of the system as it was practised in Buchan. In addition to endorsing the division of infield into three breaks and their continuous cropping with oats and bear, it explains how husbandmen sustained the constant cropping of infield 'by dunging it everie thrie years, a third yearly with what dung his Cattle afford in Winter'.[48] The specification of outfield is identical to Anderson's except that it allows for only four crops to be taken after tathing. In its own words, 'our grounds for keeping our cattle in the night time we enclose in summer and before the later end of the harvest they dung this enclosed ground, so that it is fruitful for the first and second crops as the best of our Intowns and it will bear four crops before it need lye in grass.'[49] Other portions were presumably treated as faugh land for they were brought in without manure. There is certainly no doubt that faughing was extensively used in the north-east as a supplementary preparation on outfield. As well as being mentioned in other descriptions of infield–outfield, it occurs in tacks and Baron Court proceedings.[50] Occasionally, the practice manifests itself in field names, portions of outfield being referred to as faughs in contradistinction to the folds which form the tathed area of outfield.[51]

An equally informative description of the system in the Lothians is available from a late seventeenth-century text on farming by Lord Belhaven. As regards infield, it suggests that a more complex and intensive four-break system was employed,

[47] J. Anderson, *General View of the Agriculture of the County of Aberdeen* (*Edinburgh, 1794*), pp. 55–6.

[48] *Geographical Collections*, vol. ii, p. 140.

[49] Ibid., p. 141.

[50] Hamilton (ed.), *Monymusk Papers* (*1713–1755*), p. 24. Other contemporary descriptions or references to faughing occur in *Geographical Collections*, vol. ii, p. 140; Sir Archibald Grant, *A Dissertation on the Chief Obstacles to the Improvement of Land* (Aberdeen, 1760), p. 53; Wilson, op. cit., p. 80.

[51] SRO, RHP5199/9.

that was cropped with wheat, barley, peas, and oats. A further point of contrast with the north-east, was that less outfield (usually only a third) might be under cultivation during any one year. Again, it was prepared by tathing, but where large quantities of pasture existed, faughing was sometimes used. In a detailed comment on tathing, Lord Belhaven informs us of how the stock were penned in small folds built of earth or turf 'that the Sheep and other Bestial may dung them the more equally; tho' it be no where so much practised as in the Lothians and in the Merse'.[52] Also worth mentioning is an eighteenth-century reference to the system as it was practised on the farm of Rossie beside the Southesk in Midlothian. It puts the difference between the manurial resources of infield and outfield in a sentence. 'The infield', it said, 'got nothing save the Winter-dung, and the Outfield the Summer-dung, with a little wreck and Sea-ware cast into the side of the Island.'[53]

South across Lammermuir, accounts of infield–outfield cropping have been culled from the division proceedings of proprietary–runrig touns and from mid-eighteenth-century tacks. For instance, during the division of the proprietary–runrig toun of Chirnside (Berwickshire), a young tenant testified that 'the outfield lands of Chirnside are Laid out into Seven Breaks That Two of these Seven are allways in Tillage by their Turns in Course; And a Third lyes in Faugh every year for Two years, Intermitting the third year: That the Rest Remains in Grass for pasture.'[54] The faugh break mentioned here could denote one of two possible strategies. Either it could indicate a practice similar to that already noted for the north-east and the Lothians, with faughing being used in place of tathing to prepare a newly riven-out piece of outfield for cropping. Such a practice is, in fact, documented for nearby Auchencraw.[55] Or it could indicate a practice documented for other touns, in which faughing was used to prolong a cropping phase that was initiated by tathing. Evidence for other parts of the region confirms that the cropping

[52] J. Hamilton, 2nd Lord Belhaven, *The Countrey-Man's Rudiments of Advice to the Farmers in East Lothian, how to Labour and Improve their Ground* (Edinburgh, 1699), p. 16.

[53] Maxwell, op. cit., p. 32.

[54] Berwickshire County Library, Decreet of Division of the Runrigg Lands of Chirnside and Commonty, p. 33.

[55] Berwickshire Sheriff Court, Duns, Reg. of Decreets, vol. 1713–16, Feb. 1715.

of between a quarter and a third of outfield was fairly general. Tacks for estates like the Lothian and Roxburgh estates, for example, show that tenants were bound by management clauses to crop only a third of their outfield during any one year.[56] A valuable comment on the matter was made by a Roxburghshire tenant farmer. Presenting evidence during a lawsuit in 1758, he informed the court that

> he has occasion to know the practice amongst the tenantrie of that part of Tiviotdale which lyes north of the Tweed particularly the parishes of Edname Stitchill Smaillholm McKerston & Kelso with regard to the management of their outfield and it is a prevailing custom for them to keep at least two parts of their outfield in grass and only one third in corn of the arable outfield.[57]

In the same case, a tenant on the Buccleuch estate lands in Eckford (Roxburghshire) gave his support by saying that all the tenants of the Buccleuch-estate lands in Eckford, as well as the Lothian-estate tenants in the Baronies of Eckford and Oxnam, likewise ploughed only a third of their outfield each year.[58] On the Scott of Harden estate, a late eighteenth-century tack for Bewlie Mains (Berwickshire) restricted the tenant to cropping only a fifth of his outfield, and required that it should be 'foalded and tathed or pastured at least every five years previous to its being plowed'.[59] Other tacks for the same estate, though, such as that issued in 1793 for Oakwood and Huntly (Selkirkshire), set a more generous limit.[60]

Judging from tacks examined for touns scattered throughout the south-east, and from published references, infield was commonly arranged into four or five breaks. Where a five-break system operated, it was based on a rotation of fallow, wheat, pease, bear, and oats.[61] Where only a four-break scheme was

[56] See SRO Lothian MSS, GD237/66, Tacks &c The Marqs. of Lothian. Roxbr.shire, nos. 1–13. The Roxburgh tacks are unclassified, but a good example is Floors Castle, Roxburgh MSS, Tack for Easter Muirdean to John Penman, 1761.

[57] Floors Castle, Roxburgh MSS, Act and Commission John Hood, agt. Robert Davidson, 1758.

[58] Ibid.

[59] SRO, Scott of Harden MSS, GD157/1172, Tack for Bewlie Mains (1795).

[60] Ibid., Tack for Oakwood and Huntly (1793).

[61] Floors Castle, Roxburgh MSS, Tack for Cliftonburngrange (1751), Gallalaw (1748), Fettershaws (1751), Stodrig (1742); SRO, Lothian MSS, GD237/66/3 Tack for Newton, Kersfield and Stirkrig (1753), and 66/4 Tack for Westfield of Nisbet (1753);

adopted, it tended to comprise one of fallow, pease, bear, and oats or wheat, pease, bear, and oats.[62] Although there are fewer references to them, more elemental systems involving only three or even two breaks are also evidenced for the region.[63] Although the use of a four-break system on infield has a fairly long history in the more fertile areas of Scotland, it is difficult to avoid the conclusion that the predominance of four- and five-break systems over the more elementary systems in the south-east was due in large measure to the use of a faugh break. This was probably a major innovation of the period 1750 to 1760. An entry in the *Baron Court book of Stitchill* to the effect that no one was to have the fourth break off the infield provides a strong hint as to when it was first adopted.[64] Likewise, early eighteenth-century tacks whose only specific management clause was to insist on the insertion of a faugh break on infield leave one with the impression that here was something that landowners were trying to establish.[65]

Across the Southern Uplands, a *c.*1700 account of infield–outfield is available for Galloway. Perhaps intentionally, it begins by implying that only outfield really mattered. Thus, we are told that local farmers

divide their arable land into eight parts at least, which they call cropts, four whereof they till yearly. Their first crop they call Lay, and this is that on which the bestial and sheep were folded the summer and harvest before and teathed by their lying there . . . The fourth is that which was their third cropt the foregoing year, however good husbands till, but little of this; and then these cropts or parts remain four years at least untill'd after this so that the one halfe of their arable land is only till'd yearly, the other halfe bearing only grass . . . Thus much for their tilling of their oatland.[66]

SRO, Hume of Marchmont,, GD158/795, Tack for Humehall (1760); Wight, op. cit., vol. ii, p. 343; Berwickshire Library, Duns, Folio 5, no. 6, Tack for 8 husbandlands in Whitsome (1726).

[62] SRO, Lothian MSS, GD237/66/13, 20, 25, 27, and 30.

[63] Floors Castle, Roxburgh MSS, Tack of Hownam to John Riddell, 1752; D. Ure, *A General View of the Agriculture of the County of Roxburgh* (London, 1794), pp. 25–6.

[64] C. B. Gunn (ed.), *Records of the Baron Court of Stitchill 1655–1807*, Scottish History Society, l (1905), p. 110.

[65] See, e.g., SRO, Lothian MSS, GD237/66/1, Tack for Muirhouselaw (1753). Whyte, *Agriculture and Society in Seventeenth-Century Scotland*, pp. 215–17, has now provided valuable comment on the spread of fallow and legumes in the more fertile parts of the eastern Lowlands over the latter part of the 17th century.

[66] *Geographical Collections*, vol. ii, p. 102.

In case it be concluded from this that only outfield cropping existed, the writer goes on to refer to 'beirland', the character of which clearly labels it as infield. 'They sow their Beir', he said,

in the same place every year, and without intermission, which is also peculiar, in a peece of ground lying nearest their house, and this peece of ground they call their Beir-Fay. On which they lay their dung before tilling but their dung will not suffice to cover the same yearly, yea they think it sufficient if in three years space, the whole be dunged, and this I suppose is peculiar to this country.[67]

The slight incredulity of the writer here is a little difficult to understand, for while the mono-cropping of 'beirland' certainly is 'peculiar', its full dunging only once every three years was no different from the predicament of touns in other regions. At least his reference to the mono-cropping of local infields would seem to be reliable. Indeed, one or two instruments of sasine can be found which refer to land as 'barley land' or 'beir land', such was its status within the toun economy.[68]

A more conventional description, and one rich in vernacular terminology, is available for early eighteenth-century Ayrshire. It begins by drawing a distinction between *Crofting* and *Outfield-land*. The former

consisteth of four Breaks; whereof one, after the Year's Rest, is dunged for Bear, the second is Bear-leave, the third Oat-leave, the fourth ley, one year old; so that each Break in its Turn hath one Dunging in four Years: After which, they take three Crops, generally all of the vossing kind; for they sow few Pease and Beans; and they have one Years's Grass.[69]

The most interesting feature of this infield system is its one-year ley, which the reporter is prepared to describe as providing 'one Year's Grass', even though it was probably seeded naturally rather than artificially. In view of the semi-ploughed nature of faugh land, we should not prehaps draw too sharp a contrast between such 'ley' land and the faugh breaks of the south-east. As

[67] Ibid., pp. 103–4.
[68] Reid (ed.), *Wigtownshire Charters*, pp. 127–8; SRO, Earl of Stair MSS, GD135/39, Tack Memoranda Bk. 1771–1810.
[69] Maxwell, op. cit., pp. 213–14.

regards *Outfield-land*, the writer of this account offers a general-ization which may apply elsewhere, saying that it was 'managed differently in Places of the Country; some plowing four Years, others three, and giving it Rest as many. Some take two Crops after one Year's Rest, others three after two years Rest. But most commonly, Where the Management is thought best. There are four breaks of the *Outfield* in Tillage.'[70] To judge from subsequent remarks on the value of outfield grass, each break remained out of cultivation for only three or four years. If this were so, it would suggest a fairly intensive system for an outfield.

Taking a wider view of infield–outfield practice, the more abundant documentation of the late seventeenth and early eighteenth centuries allow us to probe into vital issues like the movement of stock and the use of their manure. For infield, an important source of manure was that provided by the direct dunging of stock when grazing the harvest stubble, or roaming over the infield during part of the winter months. A lawyer representing the Duke of Roxburgh in a lawsuit of 1728 regarding grazing rights in the Barony of Roxburgh, after observing how tenants throughout the Barony, even though belonging to different estates, had depastured their sheep 'in winter time upon the stibbles of the lands of the Barrony of Roxburghe pertaining to the Duke', went on to say that it 'is a common thing in the country that neighbours in the winter time pasture promiscosly upon the grounds of one another'.[71] His point is given some endorsement by evidence for nearby touns. For example, at Kelso, stock had grazed 'since time out of mind thro' all the lands' during the winter,[72] whilst at Chirnside, landholders pastured their sheep over the arable 'from the time the corns are led off the ground to the time the oats are sprung up again'.[73] As a guide to how widespread the custom was, an Act of Parliament passed in 1686 'against Winter herding' stipulated that because of uncontrolled 'promiscuous grazing', stock must be herded, especially at night.[74] In fact, many touns already had

[70] Ibid., p. 214.
[71] Floors Castle, Roxburgh MSS, Memoriall and Claim His Grace John Duke of Roxburghe Against the Lady Chatto, 19 July 1728.
[72] Ibid., Decreet of Division of the Runrigg Lands of Kelso, 1751.
[73] Berwickshire County Library, Duns, Decreet of Division of the Runrigg Lands of Chirnside and Commonty, 1740.
[74] *APS* viii, p. 595.

strict controls over winter grazing, either through tacks or by Acts in their local Baron Court.[75] The amount of stock which landholders could keep in winter, or *rowme*, was subject to particularly tight controls. Many runrig touns had an agreed system of soums or stents regulating the precise number of sheep, cattle, and horses each landholder had the right to graze. To cite examples, at Gattonside (Roxburghshire), it was declared that each 'husband lands stent is twenty sheeps two nolt and one horse',[76] whilst at West Reston (Berwickshire), 'the usual stent of a husbandland was twenty-five sheep five nolt and two horses.'[77]

In addition to the manure which it received from the direct grazing of stock, infield also received the manure which had accumulated from the byre. In the words of a late seventeenth-century commentator on the practice in Buchan, infield was kept constantly in tillage 'by dunging it everie thrie years, a third yearly with what dung his cattle afford in Winter'. His suggestion that the dung available was concentrated on one break per year is borne out by other early descriptions.[78]

During Spring, stock were removed to the outfield grass or common grazings, where they were folded at night on that portion due to be cultivated the following year. Given that it was merely a husbandry practice, the tathing or folding of outfield is surprisingly well documented. General descriptions, such as those quoted earlier, invariably mention it as the means by which outfield was manured. Occasionally, its practice creeps into early tacks. Thus a tack of 1655 for the West Mains of Erlestraithdictie, near Dundee, required the tenant to 'dyke, dung and teath' the several intakes of outfield 'be course and time about' and not to take more than three crops of each intake.[79] Comparable eighteenth-century tacks for estates like the Minto[80] and Lothian

---

[75] See, for instance, J. Dunlop (ed.), *Court Minutes of Balgair 1706–1736*, SRS (Edinburgh, 1957), p. 21; Romanes (ed.), *Selections from the Records of the Regality of Melrose 1605–1661*, p. 194.

[76] For Gattonside see Roxburgh Sheriff Court MSS, Jedburgh, Decreet of Division of the Runrigg Lands of Gattonside, 15 Sept. 1750.

[77] SRO, Home-Robertson, GD267/22/1 Decreet of Division of the Runrig Lands of West Reston, 1775.

[78] *Geographical Collections*, vol. ii, p. 133; Wight, op. cit., vol. i, p. 3; Kemp (ed.), op. cit., p. 149.

[79] HMC, *Report on the Manuscripts in Various Collections*, v, p. 209.

[80] National Library of Scotland, Minto MSS, Box 117, no. 112, Tacks 1713–53, no. 13.

estates[81] (Roxburghshire) contained similar clauses restraining tenants from ploughing outfield without first tathing it. Understandably, court records are a convenient quarry for references, for the failure to observe bye-laws about folding was a common abuse. For instance, an entry in Fintray's Baron Court book for 1720 enacted 'that all sub-tenants in Lamington or elsewhere shall fold their cattel (especially with respect to kine), and that every night, the whole summer time, unless relevant reason can be given by the owners'.[82] With a similar purpose, an entry of 1675 in the Forbes Baron Court book ordained 'that all persons who are lyable in neighbourhood to one another, or anie sub-tenant, who is obliged to fold with his nighbour and maister, sall pey fortie pennies Scotie for each beast nolt for each night they detain them out of the fold, and tuelff penies for each beast sheip'.[83] Elaborating on Lord Belhaven's brief comment on how these folds were constructed, a Berwickshire source informs us that they were made using

turf walls, provincially feal dykes, about five feet high and these were secured on the top by whins, short stakes or straw ropes. This temporary fold was then divided into a series of small folds proportioned by cross walls. During the season, the stock would be brought into these folds for the purpose of manuring it every night. Then the turf walls were dismantled except perhaps for the outermost walls and the turf thrown onto the field which was then ploughed to undergo a course of crops.[84]

Although not so explicit, other references to 'the bigging of the fold dyke' confirm the widespread use of temporary, turf-based folds.[85]

[81] SRO, Lothian MSS, GD237/66, esp. 1–4. Typical is the tack for the Eastfield of Nisbet (1753) which bound the tenant to 'plow no outfield, But what is dunged or folded in the ordinary way'. Other instances of tacks specifying the tathing of outfield are SRO, Abercairny MSS, GD24/1/32, Articles of Agreement between James Moray of Abercairny & Robert Maxtone in Bellnollo, 1765–1773; Hamilton (ed.), *Monymusk Papers (1713–1755)*, pp. 43–4.
[82] J. Cruickshank, 'The Court Book of the Barony of Fintray 1711–1726', pp. 1–66 in *Miscellany of the Spalding Club* i, Third Spalding Club (Aberdeen, 1935), p. 39.
[83] Thomson (ed.), 'Forbes Baron Court Book 1659–1678', p. 299.
[84] R. Kerr, *A General View of the Agriculture of the County of Berwick* (London, 1809), p. 209.
[85] A Monymusk tack, for instance, ordained that 'as the said Whitehill is to be divided the said John Forbes & James Scott are to build a fold upon the outfield, betwixt ymselves as the saids William Ray, Peter Elmsly, Robert McRay, Robert Johnston & Jannet Shuan are to put up another amongst them. And all parties are to have sufficiency of herds conform to their equal proportions to keep their cattle for dunging the said folds.' See Hamilton (ed.), *Monymusk Papers 1713–1755*, p. 44.

In view of the importance attached to their manure and the adopted pattern of stock movements over the farming year, it was inevitable that touns should ease their organizational problems by compelling tenants to subscribe to a common herd. At Ulston (Roxburghshire), it was said that the landholders 'possess in runrig and pasture in common, one herd keeps their cattle in the infield and they have an other herd for the muir'.[86] At Forbes, it was reaffirmed in 1678 that 'the whole tennents within the parochens of Kearne, Clatt, Forbes and Achendor shall putt ther goods to the hill of Curreyne for pastureing, and every parochen to have ane common herd among them'.[87] Failure to abide by the common herding of stock was, in fact, a familiar issue in local court proceedings. A court book relating to Newtyle, Keillours, Cowty, and Bendochie (Angus) passed an Act in 1725 stipulating that 'tenants in use to have common herds for sheep and cattle are not to take on them to separate their flocks, or to refuse to join in the common charge of keeping herds, and that they have their respective proportions of grass, meal and teathing of their own field, according to their proper share'.[88] Not all touns had common herds though. Individual herding seems to be implied by an entry in the court book of Balgair (Stirlingshire), near Fintry, which reminded that 'tenants and possessors with the lands keep no more sheep in the winter tyme that hes not herding for them'.[89]

Although the most important, livestock manure was not the only support of infield–outfield cropping. Other manures were exploited. The use of lime[90] and seaweed,[91] for example, both continued during the late seventeenth and early eighteenth centuries. Some areas also made considerable use of muck-fail and turf cuttings. Their heavy use in the north-east can almost be described as infamous. To some extent, it is difficult to disentangle the use of these manures from the general custom of spreading old thatch or roof turf and abandoned fold dykes from

[86] SRO, Lothian MSS, GD237/89/5, Memorial Concerning the Farm of Ulston, 1758.

[87] Thomson (ed.), 'The Forbes Baron Court Book 1659–1678', p. 318.

[88] HMC, *5th Report* (London, 1876), part i, Appendix, p. 623.

[89] Dunlop (ed.), 'Court Minutes of Balgair 1706–1736', p. 21.

[90] See comments of A. Fenton, 'Scottish Agriculture and the Union: An Example of Indigenous Development', pp. 75–93 in T. I. Rae (ed.), *The Union of 1707* (Glasgow, 1974), pp. 80–1; Whyte, *Agriculture and Society in Seventeenth-Century Scotland*, 198–208.

[91] *Geographical Collections*, vol. ii, pp. 24 and 275.

outfield over arable. However, as developed in the north-east, they involved the casting of turf or the gathering of soil for immediate application to infield or outfield and this was much more extensively employed than in other parts of the Lowlands.[92] In fact, so widespread was it and so deleterious were its effects on the environment, that an Act of Parliament was passed in 1685 specifically against its practice in Aberdeenshire. 'Labourers', the Act declared, 'have introduced a Custom of Delving teiling and casting up great quantities of Corn ground, meadow ground and Suarded ground which they lay in heaps to rott, for making fulzie [turf or soil + dung] or maner to their Land which custom has in great part destroyed the Land in diverse parts of the Kingdom'.[93] Addressing itself to the farmers of Aberdeenshire, where the practice was deemed to be most prevalent, it sought to remedy the problem by forcing tenants to sow a fixed quantity of peas and beans. The reasoning behind this was that such areas were only in need of manurial supplements because they had failed to vary their rotations by adopting such crops, crops which 'doth contribute for improving and fatning of the Ground and for intertainment of people that labour it, and the labouring beasts'.[94] The Act did not succeed in abolishing the practice. The difficulties it faced in attempting to do so are brought out by the contrary actions of the Baron Court at Urie (Kincardineshire). In 1701, an act forbade tenants from 'casting' any ley, sward or meadow ground.[95] Yet in 1726, the court not only gave permission for tenants to 'cast turffs' on commonty land, the source of turf for most touns, but acknowledged its practice on other grounds by asserting that 'no personal shall cast turff or earth whatsoever upon the ground continuous to his neighbours corn, if his neighbours incline to improve the same for corn ground.'[96] Similarly, although early eighteenth-century tacks for the Monymusk estate barred tenants from casting up 'marsh meadow nor corn ground wt foot or flaughter spade',[97] a tenant in Cowly toun was still found guilty of 'casting up with foot or

[92] Examples can be found in Thomson (ed.), 'The Forbes Baron Court Book 1659–1678', p. 318; Hamilton (ed.), *Monymusk Papers (1713–1755)*, pp. 19, 21, and 32.
[93] *APS* viii, pp. 494–5.
[94] Ibid., pp. 494–5.
[95] Barron (ed.), 'Court Book of the Barony of Urie', pp. 111–12.
[96] Ibid., p. 130.
[97] Hamilton (ed.), *Monymusk Papers (1713–1755)*, pp. 27 and 32.

flaughter spade corn and brunt land ground' in 1714.[98] Perhaps the final word should be that of Wight. Seeing the practice at Kinburck near Dunblane, he said their 'manure is the dung they can gather, mixed up with earth; which fills the eye, but cheats the land'.[99]

The Reference to 'brunt land' at Cowly belies another husbandry practice that was fairly common in parts of the north-east. It consisted of the burning of turfs as a preparation for cropping. In a sense, it can be regarded as an early form of paring and burning. A description of its use in Buchan tells how in 'New Deer and neighbouring parishes, the tenants formerly burnt their dry faughs, which were ribbed the beginning of summer, the turf set in heaps, kindled, and, when reduced to ashes, spread over the ridges and plowed in for corn, to be sown the following spring; after which three and sometimes four crops are taken.'[1] Although by the time this comment was written, or 1759, it was said to be dying out on faugh land, it was still vigorously practised on 'out-worn mosses'.[2] Its continuing use on moss land is left in no doubt by a farmer from Achry in Aberdeenshire. Reporting to the Gordon Mill farming club, he informed them how in 'summer 1750 he observed all the country in a smoke, and concluded that the mosses would be exhausted, although they had great plenty, and their leyes would be reduced to a *caput mortuum*, unless the custom of burning was stopped'.[3]

Although not connected with the preparation of arable land, a husbandry practice worth recording is that of water-meadowing. This involved the systematic flooding of meadow land during the winter months so as to encourage an earlier growth of grass in spring. In other words, it helped to foreshorten the so-called hungry-gap over winter. According to E. Kerridge, water-meadowing spread to many parts of southern England during the sixteenth and seventeenth centuries, and formed an improvement which helped make his case for an agricultural revolution at this point.[4] Its early appearance in Scotland has a more modest

[98] Ibid., 'Minutes of the Court of the Lands of Monymusk and Barony of Pitfichie 1713–53', p. 193.

[99] Wight, op. cit., vol. i, p. 125.

[1] Wilson, op. cit., p. 83.

[2] Ibid., p. 83.

[3] Ibid., p. 84.

[4] Kerridge, op. cit., pp. 251–67.

claim for attention, with a mere handful of references to its use in the Howe of Mearns and others for the low ground of Perthshire. One of the former, a source dated 1722, and referring to Fetteroso parish, seems to imply that it was an exceptional form of husbandry, observing that 'one thing remarkable in this parish is they have very ingeniously imployed the many springs they have to the watering of their land'.[5] There are, however, documented examples of its use nearby.[6] A near contemporary instance is provided by the Baron Court records of Urie where a tenant reportedly cast up new water furrows there and thereby interfered with the supply of water to someone else's furrows.[7]

The Farm Economy: Progress or Retrenchment?

The nature of the Lowland farm economy presents a paradox. On the one hand, the decades following 1650 have rightly been linked with an expanding trade in both stock and crop.[8] Yet on the other hand, the majority of tenants were still obsessively concerned with the needs of their household rather than the market, and any suggestion that there were major improvements in husbandry which funded this expansion in marketed produce must be treated with reserve. Resolving this paradox requires an appreciation of two key aspects of the farm economy during this period. The first concerns the question of who was responsible for the increasingly vigorous trade in grain. As tenant numbers fell, and holding-size per tenant rose, there must have been more and more tenants who found themselves with a marketable surplus. However, the main dealers for much of this period were still the landowners, who marketed the grain acquired by them as rent in kind. As such, it was a trade entirely consistent with a farm economy still largely geared to subsistence and the payment of rent rather than market needs. The second aspect concerns an important sectoral shift in farm production over the period 1650 to 1760, a shift which gave greater emphasis to livestock. At the outset, the main stock producers in the south and east of the

[5] *Geographical Collections*, vol. i, p. 249.

[6] See, e.g., SRO, Abercairny MSS, GD24/1/32 which contains numerous references in tacks to water lands.

[7] Barron (ed.), 'Court Book of the Barony of Urie', pp. 161 and 165–5.

[8] Smout and Fenton, op. cit., pp. 80–1.

country were the tenants who held the large gerss holdings in the Southern Uplands. However, as demand from south of the Border rose, their ranks were joined by tenants and landholders in the central and eastern Lowlands and the south-west. Their shift into commercial livestock production was achieved by striking a more equal balance between stock and crop in their farming system or, as in areas like Galloway or around the expanding towns of Glasgow and Edinburgh, by shifting wholly into grass. The resultant growth of stock production is best seen as a sectoral shift rather than a husbandry improvement, though where cropping was moderated to support more stock, then an increase in crop yields may have taken place as arable was given both more rest and more manure.

The over-all impression of agricultural growth, therefore, must not be used to cast Lowland farming over this period into an improving or progressing mould.[9] The growth in output and market responsiveness was brought about largely by tenant reduction and sectoral shift, trends that were grafted on to a buoyant grain trade that was sustained more by rents paid in kind than tenant's surpluses. Once this is established, then the study of the farm economy from 1650 to 1760 becomes an examination of two contrasting types: the one geared to subsistence and hemmed in by its constraints, and the other, an expanding commercial sector, propelled along by market demands and inducements.

(*a*) *Constraints on the Farm Economy.* Taking a closer look at low-ground arable touns, the almost obsessive concern with grain-cropping which guided the farming strategy of many—at least at the start of this period if less so at the end—was a function of the circumstances in which the average tenant found himself. At the root of the problem were the constraints of holding-size per tenant. From what was said earlier on the question of toun size, it will be clear that a substantial number of low-ground touns were 200/300 acres (81–121 ha) or less. In some areas, such as the north-east, they were much less. Considered in relation to a tenant structure which might involve a number of tenants, *plus* their cottars, this invariably meant that what each person and his

---

[9] See discussion in G. Whittington, 'Was there a Scottish Agricultural Revolution?', *Area*, vii (1975), pp. 204–6.

family actually possessed was more limited. Even the really large touns of Fife, the Lothians, and the Merse could be in no better position owing to the sheer number of tenants which they sometimes carried. Reducing the quantity of arable available to each tenant still further was the fact that outfield commonly constituted a major proportion of his share and that during any one year, only a half at most would be cultivated.

Drawing the resources of the average tenant closer to the margins of subsistence were the chronically low yields on all but the best land. Estimates by eighteenth-century commentators put the returns from infield at around four- or fivefold, rising to eight or more on the more fertile and heavier soils.[10] Returns on outfield seed, though, were as low as three- or fourfold.[11] Where farm accounts enable us to check these figures, they would appear to be reasonable. A detailed account put before a meeting of the Gordon's Mill farming club breaks down the returns derived from infield, outfield, and faugh land on a farm beside the Ythan in Aberdeenshire. The most productive sector of the farm was the manured break of infield that was sown with bear: this gave a fivefold return on seed. The remaining breaks of infield yielded only a fourfold return. When first cropped after being tathed, outfield managed a four and a half-fold return, but this fell progressively until by the time it was cropped for the fifth time, returns on seed were only threefold. As one might expect, the most barren part of the farm was faugh land. Yields from here amounted to a two and a half-fold return.[12] Equally specific evidence is available for the Monymusk estate. According to information for 1716, barley gave a threefold return and oats just over twofold. By 1744, no doubt as a result of Sir Archibald Grant's early improvemnts, barley was giving almost a sixfold return, the same as wheat, whilst oats produced a fourfold increase on seed.[13] By the standards of the county, these were good yields. Perhaps to underline his own efforts, Grant suggested that the average local yield from *infield* was less than threefold.[14] Comparable figures for the Minto estate lands of

[10] Wight, op. cit., vol. i, pp. 4–5; Maxwell, op. cit., p. 214.
[11] Wight, op. cit., vol. i, pp. 4–5; Maxwell, op. cit., p. 214.
[12] Wilson, op. cit., pp. 80–1.
[13] Hamilton (ed.), *Monymusk Papers (1713–1755)*, pp. xxxix–xl and 135–7.
[14] Grant, *Dissertation on the Chief Obstacles to the Improvement of Land*, p. 15.

Minto, Craigend, and Churchhead in Roxburghshire can be inferred from accounts for 1691/2. Returns appear to have been sixfold for wheat and bear, but only four and a half-fold for oats and pease.[15]

Yet another factor to be weighed by tenants in decisions over their economy was the grain or meal appropriated as rent by landowners. This continued to be a widespread feature of landlord–tenant relationships in the Lowlands until well into the eighteenth century. Proof of its survival is freely available from estate records. For instance, the Monymusk estate rental of 1741 that was mentioned earlier shows 737 bolls of meal and 96 bolls of bear to have been paid along with other kinds of farm produce in part payment of rent.[16] A rental drawn up in the late seventeenth century for the Barony of Tannadyce in Angus details the payment of 253 bolls of bear and 394 bolls of meal as part of the rent paid by tenants, together with substantial payments of farm products from the Lordship of Lyon and Kinghorne portion of the Glamis estate.[17] In Fife, a 1750 rental for the touns of Strathkiness and Balone records an annual payment of over 300 bolls of grain between them,[18] whilst in the extreme south-east a 1713 rental for a small estate in Eyemouth (Berwickshire) debited 243 tenants with a combined rent of 198 bolls of bear and 34 of oats.[19] Where available, tacks usually enlarge on how such payments were made. For instance, a tack of 1702 for Strathkiness bound the two tenants to pay annually 16 bolls of oats and 10 bolls of bear for the first three years, 14 of bear and 16 of oats for the next 13 years, and 18 of oats and 16 of bear for the last three years of the tack.[20] Likewise, a 1741 tack for Cundry Mains (Ayrshire) required the tenant to pay 12 bolls of 'good and Sufficient meal all Eight Stone and a half the Booll and six Boolls

[15] NLS, Minto MSS, Box 18/124, Farming Accts. of Lands of Minto 1692. For further valuable comment on yields see Whyte, *Agriculture and Society in Seventeenth-Century Scotland*, pp. 74–8. His figures are broadly similar to those cited here, but have more range and detail. One of his more important conclusions is that yield probably increased over the latter part of the 17th century where new cropping systems based on fallow and legumes were adopted.

[16] Hamilton (ed.), *Monymusk Papers (1713–1755)*, p. lxxiv.

[17] A. Millar (ed.), *The Glamis Book of Record*, Scottish History Society, ix (1890), p. 48.

[18] SRO, Balfour–Melville MSS, GD126, Rental of Strickinen and Balon 1750.

[19] SRO, Misc. Rentals and Valuations, Rental of Eyemouth, 1713.

[20] SRO, Balfour–Melville MSS, GD126, Box 1, Tack to Robert Lord, 1702.

Good and Sufficient Bear'.[21] The stress in this last tack on grain having to be of good quality was not exceptional. On the Monymusk estate, tacks stipulated that a portion of the grain paid in had to be that grown on infield.[22] Other estates were more particular still. On the Dalhousie estate, a 1758 tack for Easter Panlathy (Angus) was set for 'Eleven Bolls Bear, Thirteen Bolls Eight peck Oat Meal And fourty Seven pound Seven Shilling and Sixpennies Scots . . . All the Said Victual being good and Sufficient Merchant Stuff and of the best grain growing upon the said lands'.[23] At Strathkiness too, grain had to be 'best Victual Growing on the Ground'.[24]

Closely allied with the payment of rent in kind was the system of steelbow or sharecropping. The main difference between the two was that under the steelbow system, the landowner provided the seed, stock, and farm equipment needed for the farm in return for a share of the produce. In a sense, the condition of the times were favourable to such a system, for as tenant numbers contracted and farm-size per tenant grew, steelbow enabled the more ambitious tenant to reach beyond his immediate circumstances and to stock a really large holding. Hints of its continuing use during this period can be gleaned for scattered parts of the central Lowlands. However, the main area of its survival was the Southern Uplands and adjacent arable areas like Teviotdale. Here, it went under the name of 'thirders and teinders', and was used to frame the relationship not only between landlords and tenants, but also, between tenants and their farm servants where the latter were given responsibility for a led farm. Its character is brought out by an agreement dated 1742 for a farm in upland Roxburghshire. The agreement was between a tenant and the person he had put in as manager of a led farm in his tenancy, a William Legetwood. The agreement obliged Legetwood 'to sow 40 bolls of oats, bear and peas, whereof his master is to have the third and teind shorn and set up'.[25] In other words, the tenant

---

[21] SRO, Bargany MSS, GD109/3647.

[22] Hamilton (ed.), *Monymusk Papers (1755–1755)*, p. 29. Other estates wanting 'infield' corn include Huntly Lordship, see *Miscellany of the Spalding Club*, 4,, pp. 261–319.

[23] SRO, Dalhousie MSS, GD45/18/1944.

[24] SRO, Balfour–Melville MSS, GD126/1, Tack to Robert Lord, 1702.

[25] Anon., 'On the Ancient Husbandry of Roxburghshire', *Farmer's Magazine*, viii (1807), pp. 166–8. See also, NLS Minto MSS, Box 18/124, Farming Acts. of the Lands of Minto 1692.

was to receive a third of the entire crop plus the teinds owed by the farm. Legetwood was also to answer for all the carriages and dargs (or day's work) owed by the farm to the landowner. As regards pasture, Legetwood was himself allowed only a third of the hay crop in return for mowing and leading the entire hay crop to the stack yard, as well as the right to graze so many sheep in return for managing the tenant's stock on the farm.

As in earlier centuries, the payment of grain as rent continued to be used by landowners to fund a very active grain market which often led to its export out of the country altogether. The fuller documentation of this period leaves no doubt over the link between rent payments in kind and this grain trade, for tenants were frequently compelled to deliver it to the market or port themselves. For example, the tenants who took the tack of Kinaldie and Melgum in Coldstane parish (Aberdeenshire) in 1709, and who had to pay victuals or grains as part of their rent, were required 'to carry and transport the said victuals upon their own charge to Aberdeen or any place of like distance'.[26] Tacks issued for touns like Drumaluchie and Gallowgate on the Mar and Kellie estate (Aberdeenshire) also compelled tenants to transport their grain to Aberdeen.[27] Similar conditions bound the tenant who took a tack of Tillydovie (Angus) in 1768, with bear and oatmeal which he paid having to be delivered *either* to the laird's granaries and from there direct to Forfar, Kirriemuir, or any other place of like distance, *or* to the sea ports of Arbroath or Montrose and there loaded on board ship at the tenant's expense.[28] Just how conditional a tenant's tack might be on this issue is best illustrated by those given to tenants on the Monymusk estate during the early part of the eighteenth century. Typical is a tack of 1734 for the toun of Pitmuny. As well as a fixed sum of money, the tenant had to pay

twenty bolls, two firlots, one peck and one half peck of ferm meal, at eight stone per boll good and sufficient unhote or hum'd, made of totch vald and intown corns, without dust, stones, or refuse, payabale betwixt Yool and Candlemas yearly, with the number and quantity of two bolls, three firlots, two pecks and one third part peck of good and sufficient

---

[26] J. G. Mitchie (ed.), *The Records of Invercauld 1547–1828*, New Spalding Club, (Aberdeen, 1901), p. 93.

[27] SRO, Mar and Kellie MSS, 124/130/1 and 17/130/6.

[28] Cruickshank, op. cit., pp. 12–13.

merchant stuff bear and such as will please a merchant payable yearly betwixt Pasch and the Roodday; and to carry the said quantity of meal and bear to Aberdeen or any place of the like distance upon his own horses, sacks, charges and expences and deliver the same to any person or persons having warrant to receive it.[29]

Evidence generated by the actual sale or shipment of such grain underlines the vast amounts that must have been syphoned out of the local market economy in this way. The *Glamis Book of Record* is especially helpful on this aspect. Entries for 1681 tell how the diarist, the first Earl of Strathmore, had 'freighted a ship for Dunkirk for exporting to that place my wheat remnant of bear and pease to the number of six hundred bolls'.[30] In the event, the exact figures were 249 bolls of wheat, 232 of bear, and 56 of peas. In 1684, he was lamenting that having sold his anticipated crop to Glasgow merchants, 'the tenants fell short of the deliveries'.[31] Later, in 1689, he can be found selling 250 bolls of wheat, 200 of oats, and 50 of peas to Bailie Arbuthnot in Dundee.[32]

Such grain payments must have been a serious drain on a tenant's resources, especially in a countryside where yields were low and holding-size restricted. According to T. C. Smout and A. Fenton, the volume of grain marketed probably rose over the seventeenth century. This they ascribed to better marketing facilities and more grain actually being sent to market. In trying to explain why more grain was reaching the market, they favour improvements in output but are careful not to overstress the point.[33] To this can be added the effect which falling tenant numbers per toun may have had on the viability of holdings and their capacity to generate a surplus over and above on-the-farm needs. However, a further possibility is that landowners were abstracting more as rent, so that whilst the amount being traded was increasing, the average tenant may have been just as far removed from direct market involvement as ever he was. Smout and Fenton did, in fact, give due prominence to the role of landowners in the expansion of the grain trade, asserting that this was

[29] Hamilton (ed.), *Monymusk Papers (1713–1733)*, p. 29
[30] Millar (ed.), *Glamis Book of Record*, p. 63.
[31] Ibid., p. 86.
[32] Ibid., p. 102.
[33] Smout and Fenton, op. cit., pp. 77, and 82–3.

certainly true of the grain trade on coastal estates on the east side of the country, where examination of rentals and other papers shows that there was hardly a considerable family on such lands north of the Tay which was not shipping grain or meal either coastwise or abroad: the Earls of Glamis, Kincardine, Seafield, Buchan, Panmure and Sutherland may be taken as typical of this group.[34]

What is really important is that such rentals show that more grain was being shipped because more grain was being collected as rent. As explained in Chapter 4, grain formed the basis of customary rents. This meant that the amount paid was fixed and inflexible by custom. Where tenants cultivated non-assessed land or outfield, however, it was practice to impose an augmentation of rent, an augmentation that took the form of extra grain or a supplementary cash payment. The choice between these two forms of augmentation may well have been determined by the proximity of the estate to a market or port. The 1627 *State of Certain Parishes*, for example, lists quite a number of Lothian touns whose customary rents had been augmented by extra grain payments, an increase which was put down to 'extraordinary labouring' and which probably reflects an expansion into outfield as much as the use of lime on existing arable.[35] Likewise, the tenant who took a tack of Oueryeards of Auchterhouse in 1686 had to pay 'ten bols wheat ten bols bear ten bols oats and ten bols meal which is thrie bols augmentation of the rental'.[36] Such augmentations must have contributed greatly to the increasing flows of grain that reached the market over the seventeenth century. There is even a possibility that such augmentations may have been more exploitive relative to customary rents, as landowners tried to capitalize on the then rapidly expanding European grain market. As a trade centred on the Baltic and Holland, Scottish merchants and their trading contacts would have given landowners a ready access to it.[37] This would have

---

[34] Ibid., p. 80.

[35] *Report on the State of Certain Parishes in Scotland 1627*, pp. 44, 51, 67, and 91. Smout and Fenton, op. cit., pp. 82–4, present valuable data on both the spread of liming and the extension of the cultivated area over the 17th century.

[36] Millar (ed.), *The Glamis Book of Record*, p. 1. Further examples of rents being paid in grain and other produce during this period are provided by Whyte, *Agriculture and Society in Seventeenth-Century Scotland*, p. 34.

[37] Again, the best review of this is Smout and Fenton, op. cit., p. 88.

meant that as the trade in Scottish grain gathered pace, the lot of the average tenant may have worsened. As well as grain or meal, rent payments in kind often comprised fixed numbers of sheep, hens, and geese. Naturally, these too diminished the tenant's available resources. In addition, there was the thorny problem of labour services. The more obvious obligations placed on tenants in this respect were ploughing, harrowing, and harvesting (both shearing and loading), with each tenant's liabilities being calculated as so many dargs or day's labour. Tenants were also required to discharge carriages or so many carting journeys of a fixed maximum distance: these could involve leading peats to the laird's house, carrying timber for the estate, or taking the laird's corn to market. Such services fill out many a tack or estate account-book during this period. One example only need suffice. In 1752, a Thomas Turnbull was granted a lease of Cleughead and Craigend on the Minto estate. His services were listed as

38 loads peats from Sheilswood or yoaking of twa plows 6 shearers 2 servants to win hay on Day 2 men 2 horses 4 days to lead hay 2 men 2 horses to lead corn and if corn and fodder needed to furnish 8 men and 8 horses to carie it from any part of the neighbourhood of Minto to furnish three horses to carie wheat to Jedburgh and 5 horses to carie bear or other grain to Jedburgh Hawick or Selkirk or to any place of the like distance 4 horses to help home with timber for repairs and to lead on 1000 diviots for my Lord's houses yearly or straw in leu of them 2 horses to lead flags and 2 to lead fairns on Day 4 horses to lead peats to the House if needed 2 men on day to the Baillses Moss and to lead 14 loads of the peats. All the above to be Don yearly if required and if not required nothing mony to be paid in leu of those services.[38]

To a greater or lesser extent, Turnbull's burdens were the same as the majority of tenants in southern and eastern Scotland until well into the eighteenth century. Not unexpectedly, reference to such labour services overflow into the local courts, for they frequently led to a conflict of interest. For instance, at Balgair in Stirlingshire, a case brought before the court charged the tenants of the Hill of Balgair with refusing to harrow their master's peas according to agreement. Because it disrupted their own farm

---

[38] NLS, Minto MSS, Box 17/112, Tacks of Minto estate 1713–53, no. 1, tack for Cleughhead and Craigend (1752).

routine, when called upon to do so, they had refused and set their horses loose on the common.[39] Such conflicts and disruptions were the price the farming community paid for labour services.

Yet another aspect of feudalism which survived strongly until the eighteenth century was that of thirlage. Generally speaking, the majority of estates in the Lowlands forced tenants to grind their corn at a local, estate-controlled mill. Not only was a levy of grain paid to the miller for such work, but tenants were also required to pay dues for the upkeep of the mill itself. Tenants bound in this way were said to be thirled, astricken, or sucken to a particular mill. Again, examples abound during this period. J. E. Handley has documented a number for Nithsdale and for estates like that of Blair Drummond in Perthshire.[40] The types of evidence which he used, court records and tacks, are forthcoming with examples for most other parts of the Lowlands. Thus, a 1659 entry in the Baron Court book of Stitchill (Berwickshire) ordained 'that non within the Barrony sell their grinding cornes in the Mercat or uther ways in prejudice of the possessor of Stitchell Myllne. But that they bring their haill grinding corne for the use of their famillies to the Mylle and pay Mylle dewties use and wont'.[41] In Roxburghshire, tenants on the Roxburgh ducal estate were invariably thirled or astricted to the estate's own mills at Roxburgh, Ancrum, Kelso, Sprouston, and Caverton by clauses inserted in their leases.[42] Leases for other estates in the region, such as for the Ladykirk[43] and Home–Robertson estates,[44] contain similar clauses. As well as testifying to its long survival, the *Old Statistical Account* also provides extensive reference to the custom.[45] The many comments on it also confirm that it was one of the most detested of obligations falling on the farming communities of old Scotland. More than one writer talks of millers being alienated from the community because of

[39] Dunlop (ed.), 'Court Minutes of Balgair 1706–1736', p. 6.

[40] Handley, *Agricultural Revolution in Scotland*, pp. 154–60.

[41] *Records of the Baron Court of Stitchill*, p. 16.

[42] Floors Castle, Roxburgh MSS, Tacks for Nether Roxburgh (1740), one fourth part of Nether Ancrum (1744), 'Quarter of the Mains of east Sprouston (1732), the Newtoun of Caverton (1756).

[43] NLS, Ladykirk MSS, no. 999.

[44] SRO, Home-Robertson MSS, GD267 (ex Paxton) 237/10, tack Patrick Home Esq. of Wedderburn to William Johnston, 1766.

[45] *OSA* xiv (1794), p. 80.

thirlage, and of the constant frustration which tenants felt, especially the poorer ones, over their dealings with them. In addition to thirlage, tenants on some estates were restricted in other ways. On the Abercairny estate in Perthshire, for instance, tenants were not only tied to particular mills but also to particular blacksmiths.[46] On others, they were tied to particular brewers or maltsters.[47]

The foregoing discussion has tried to highlight those factors which guided the farming strategy of lowland tenants. The combined effect of these factors was probably such as to reduce the economy of many lesser tenants to one of risk as regards its sufficiency. There was an old saying among Scottish tenants: 'One to eat and one to sow and one to pay the laird withaw'. One would be guilty of overstatement to see this as applicable to all tenants, great and small. However, it does capture the essence of what is to be argued here for those tenants whose lives were played out on the lower half of the farming ladder, and that is, that many had little or no regular surplus beyond the three basic necessities of seed, rent, and subsistence. Of course, what constitutes a regular surplus needs to be generously defined to accommodate the vagaries of climate. As in earlier centuries, the Scottish peasant was often confronted harshly with the 'debts of nature'. The most notable occasion was during 'King William's dear years' when a sequence of bad harvests, from 1695 to 1702, brought deprivation and famine to many parts of Scotland. Contemporary estimates put the number who died at a third of the population, but this was probably true only in a few localities where crop failure was most acute and alternative supplies of meal could not be purchased.[48] Nor should we simply take note of poor harvests. Stock losses due to a hard winter could have an equally catastrophic effect owing to the fact that it diminished

---

[46] SRO, Abercairny MSS, GD24/1/32 provides the example of a tenant in Dowald Wester (1763) who had to grind his grain at Millivab Mill and to take all his smith work to the smith at Milltown of Abercairny.

[47] Extracts from the 'Court Book of the Baronies of Newtyle, Keillours, Cowty and Bendochie 1725' in HMC, *Fifth Report*, part i (London, 1876), p. 623 banned tenants from brewing or selling ales, from setting up malt barns, and from establishing smiddies. Furthermore, the official brewers, maltmen, and smiths were to be preferred to all others in their service and attendance.

[48] J. Anderson, *General View of the Agriculture of the County of Aberdeen* (Edinburgh, 1794), pp. 49–50 claims heavy mortality for parts of Aberdeenshire. However, for a critical view of the 'dear years' see Smout and Fenton, op. cit., p. 73.

the role of livestock as suppliers of the manure with which arable was maintained. As one rather elemental farming proverb put it, 'when the muck runs out, the barley seed is done for',[49] meaning that returns would cover rent and subsistence but not the seed needed for the following year. The peasant response to this situation was logically to secure his subsistence at the very least and, if necessary, at all cost. Early commentators make it clear that subsistence was a matter of grain-growing not stock-rearing. Even in Galloway, an area long renowned for livestock production, a late eighteenth-century writer could talk about cropping earlier in the century as having been almost exclusively concerned with oats for human consumption, and how in some parishes it still accounted for over three-quarters of the crop. He goes on to say that the dependence on oats for subsistence was so great, that 'the failure of the oats was looked to with horror, being considered the next thing to a famine in the country and occasioned every possible shift till a return of another crop.'[50] Not without some insight then did Dr Johnson, in his celebrated dictionary, describe oats as a crop fed to horses in England but to people in Scotland.[51] In short, on many farms or touns, everything was subservient to the business of feeding people.

This concern in some touns with cropping as much as possible can best be illustrated with evidence for the north-east. Thus, an early eighteenth-century source portrays the parish of Coull in Aberdeenshire as 'very fertile in Corn as all the other Parishes of Cromar viz. Tarland, Coldstane and Logie, to which some add Aboyne, but straitned much for Pasturage'.[52] The parish of Drumblatt was also described as 'exceeding fertile of Corns, and well provided with Moss, but straitned for Pasture'.[53] Similar observations on the general condition of Aberdeenshire farming were made by Sir Archibald Grant in 1754. The habit amongst

---

[49] Instances of stock loss in early modern Scotland are given in C. Scott, 'Wintering Hill Sheep', *Trans. Highland & Agricultural Soc.*, xviii (1886), p. 125. After citing examples from the Southern Uplands, he recalls James Hogg's assertion that the great storms formed the 'various eras in the shepherd's calendar; the remembrances of the years and ages that are past—the tablets of memory by which the ages of his children, the times of his ancestors, and the rise and downfall of families can be ascertained.'

[50] J. Webster, *General View of the Agriculture of Galloway*, (Edinburgh, 1794), p. 12.

[51] S. Johnson (ed.), *Dictionary of the English Language*, vol. ii (London, 1833 edn.), p. 215. The author is grateful to Dr John Lewin for drawing this reference to his attention.

[52] *Geographical Collections*, ii, p. 32.

[53] Ibid., p. 36.

farmers of 'puting their whole dependance on oats', he wrote, 'renders their situation extremely precarious and at best very confined'.[54] A few years later, a submission to the Gordon's Mill farming club castigated farmers in the area for 'depending too much on grain' and went on to bemoan the 'great scarcity of Grass. The common tenant takes every way to skimp himself in this article; he throws his best swards for muck fail, he plows to far and over crops.'[55] A Mr Douglas of Fechil beside the Ythan endorsed these sentiments. 'The greatest fault and want of all is scarcity of grass, occasioned, amongst other things, by their having too much land in tillage.'[56]

(*b*) *Inducements to Change in the Farm Economy.* Alongside the constraints outlined in the previous section were forces working in the opposite direction. When these forces acted in combination, their effect was to create a more viable farm structure and a shift in the nature of farming enterprise towards a more market-orientated system.

Acting as one form of inducement were changes in tenure. Already, by the outset of this period, the spread of feu tenure and of wadsetting had given some elements of the landholding structure a degree of permanency. Less boldly delineated in the literature, but no less significant in the long term, are changes in the character of leasehold, which appeared to have taken place after 1650. The most contentious of these changes is the spread of written agreements or tacks amongst tenants. Written tacks exist for some leasehold tenants long before 1650, the Coupar Angus Abbey *Register of Tacks* being an obvious proof of this.[57] However, their frequency of occurrence increases dramatically over the late seventeenth century. This could mean either that they were surviving in greater numbers or that greater use was being made of them by estates. The balance of evidence favours the latter as the explanation. There is too much uniformity over the way tacks suddenly become available in quantity as the seventeenth century draws to a close for it to be other than part of a new

[54] Hamilton (ed.), *Monymusk Papers (1713–1755)*, p. 161.
[55] Wilson, op. cit., p. 87.
[56] Smith (ed.), *Gordon's Mill Farming Club*, p. 84.
[57] Rogers (ed.), op. cit., vols i and ii.

fashion.[58] By the early eighteenth century, very few touns were not held by written tack. The exceptions, such as those noted as having 'no tack' in a 1735 rental for the Bargany estate lands in Carrict,[59] or 'written tack' in early eighteenth-century rentals for the Roxburgh ducal estate,[60] formed a very small percentage of the total. An equally crucial change, but one weighted more towards the early eighteenth than the late seventeenth century, was an increase in the duration of tack agreements. Previously, short agreements of between three and nine years were the rule for the majority of touns.[61] But as the eighteenth century progressed, estates began more and more to issue tacks for 19 or 21 years. The Scott of Harden estate in Berwickshire, for example, had almost half of its larger touns on 15- or 21-year tacks by 1725.[62] The Balfour–Melville estate was also issuing tacks for 21 years by the opening decades of the century.[63] Others, like the Minto estate in Roxburghshire[64] or the Monymusk estate in Aberdeenshire,[65] were slower to make the adjustment, with short leases prevailing until the 1750s and 60s.

Although the high proportion of Lowland estates which continued to receive rent payments in kind after 1650 deserves greater prominence as a conclusion, nevertheless the vast majority of such payments were gradually converted into money over the period up to 1760. Some estates had already made this critical conversion by 1700. This was so with the Roxburgh estate, though the careful recording of multure equivalents alongside the cash paid in Books of Charge and Discharge implies a recent process of conversion.[66] A 1706 rental for the Harden estate shows that it too had converted its rents largely to cash,

---

[58] Since this section was written, Whyte, *Agriculture and Society in Seventeenth-Century Scotland*, pp. 154–5, has provided strong empirical support for the spread of leases over the 17th century, but esp. after 1660.

[50] SRO, Bargany MS, GD109/3622. See esp. the entries for Auchneght Wester, half of Muregate, and one half of Knockintibert.

[60] Floors Castle, Roxburgh MSS, Rentals for 1700 and 1701.

[61] See, for instance, those issued by Coupar Abbey estate in Rogers (ed.), op. cit., vol. ii, pp. 181 ff.

[62] SRO, Scott of Harden MSS, GD157, Rentals for crop 1725/6, 'Rental of lands and Barony of Mertoun, Oakwood and Smailholme'.

[63] SRO, Bargany MSS, GD126/Box 1, Tacks.

[64] NLS, Minto MSS, Box 17/117, Tacks of Minto Estate 1713–53.

[65] Hamilton (ed.), *Monymusk Papers (1713–1755)*, pp. 61 ff.

[66] Typical is Floors Castle, Roxburgh MSS, Book of Charge and Discharge by the Compter Gilbert Ker chamberlain . . . crop. 1714 and Money Rents . . . 1715. Entry for

with a total rent yield of £7,672 00 04 Scots.[67] Further north, the 1692 rental for the barony of Corlochie (Angus) likewise shows the conversion to money rents to be almost complete.[68] In the western Lowlands, early eighteenth-century rentals for estates like the Bargany[69] and Shairp of Houston[70] estates show them to have reached a similarly advanced stage of commutation. In other cases, the shift from one rent form to another can be seen as ongoing over the first half of the eighteenth century. The progressive conversion of rent on the Monymusk estate, 1733 to 1761, has been calculated by H. Hamilton (see Table 3).

Table 3: Monymusk Estate Rentals 1733–1761

Year	Scots Money	Meal Bolls	Bear Bolls
1733	3586	830	150
1741	4891	709	83
1753	5151	503	47
1755	5772	423	38
1757	6919	399	38
1759	7160	317	19
1761	7606	298	23[71]

Its late flurry of conversions must have been matched on many other estates, for there were few left by the late eighteenth century on which food rents were still paid. The importance of such conversion cannot be overstated. For the first time, it brought the tenants of many estates into a *direct* relationship with the market, allowing its slumps and demands to shape their decision-making.

Without question, it was the market that formed the most powerful inducement to agrarian change at this stage. As more and more touns became exposed directly to its influence, and as tenant reduction invested more with a greater capacity to respond, it began to exert an increasingly persuasive control over the type of farming system adopted. Stated simply, it induced in farming a greater concern for commercial livestock production.

Carchesters talks of rent 'also converted into money rent price', or Ancrum maines set to 'severall tennants for 128 bolls of Bear being sold at 8 lib. per Boll is 1024.00.00'.

[67] SRO, Scott of Harden MSS, GD157, 'Rental of Willm. Scott of Harden's Lands his lands in Mertoun and Smailholm Parishes for 1703'.

[68] SRO, Airlie MSS, GD16/30/11.

[69] SRO, Bargany MSS, GD109/3622.

[70] SRO. Shairp of Houston, GD30/411/5 and 22 and 611/4 and 5.

[71] Hamilton (ed.), *Monymusk Papers (1713–1755)*, p. lxxiv.

Although we are not yet in a position to decipher its exact chronology, the demand for stock appears to have increased over the period from 1650 to 1760. Although the expanding burghs of central and eastern Scotland played a part, the main source of this demand was the expanding urban markets of England. The gathering response of lowland farming can be assessed in a number of ways.

First, there is the pattern and over-all volume of stock movements across the Border. Using customs lists and contemporary estimates, Smout[72] and latterly D. Woodward[73] have tied to fit a trend to this movement. Their figures suggest that whilst the trade was considerable by the late seventeenth century, there is little obvious sign of a progressive increase before 1700, even after the banning of Irish stock to first the English and then the Scottish markets had given Scottish producers more command over the trade. What stands out from the figures available, particularly those produced by Woodward, is the sharp fluctuations from year to year. Without a more searching study of particular producers, it is impossible to say whether these fluctuations reflected peaks in demand or problems of supply.

The source of the stock involved in this trade raises a further problem. By analysing the number of stock passing through the various customs posts situated near the Border, together with the names of drovers responsible for them, Woodward thought that initially, or before 1700, the main supply area for cattle was probably the south-west, with lesser amounts coming from the eastern Borders and the Highlands.[74] Certainly, descriptions of the south-west *c.*1700 drew particular attention to its cattle trade. 'It affoords also store of Cattle', said one writer on Carrick, 'so that great droves of cowes and bullocks are carried yearly hence south into England and other places of our own kingdom.'[75] After 1700, the relative supply of these three areas may have become more evenly balanced.[76] The importance of the south-

[72] Smout, *Scottish Trade on the Eve of the Union 1660–1707*, pp. 215–15.

[73] D. Woodward, 'A Comparative Study of the Irish and Scottish Livestock Trades in the Seventeenth Century', pp. 147–64, in L. M. Cullen and T. C. Smout (eds.), *Comparative Aspects of Irish Economic and Social History 1600–1900* (Edinburgh, 1977), pp. 152–3.

[74] Ibid., p. 156.

[75] *Geographical Collections*, vol. ii, p. 2.

[76] Sources for the south-east suggest cattle production increased over the middle

west as a producer of cattle has long been recognized. However, in so far as the region's pioneering status in relation to the cattle trade has been built up around personalities like Sir David Dunbar and the Earl of Stair, and the large herds they established on their estates, it is worth noting that the figures published by Woodward suggest that the region may have been producing cattle in quantity as early as 1664.[77] It was the view of some early writers that the shift into cattle production by the south-west reflected the scarcity of tenants and labour following the displacement of Covenanters.[78] A more likely causal factor was the geographical opportunism of the area. Informed of the possibilities by the Irish trade and lying close to the Border with England, it was well placed to capitalize on the growing demand for leanstock from the south. It is quite possible, though, that the introduction of new landowners in place of those Covenanters who forfeited their estates may have created a more mercenary approach to the problem of tenant reduction and enclosure. The spread of cattle enclosures over the late seventeenth and early eighteenth century ultimately provoked a reply in the form of the Levellers, one of Scotland's few documented outbreaks of peasant unrest. The Levellers were so tagged because they sought to dismantle the dykes with which the cattle trade had become associated. Their grievance probably lay as much with the disintegration of opportunities for would-be tenants and cottars as with the new pressures on grazing land and commonties. They were most active in the Stewartry, when gangs of small tenants and labourers sporadically roamed through parishes like Crossmichael, Kelton, Tongland, and Twynholm during 1723 to 1725.[79] The outbreaks were brought to an end by the military and the prosecution of its leader, though the mixed loyalties of the local gentry seems to

decades of the 18th century. See, e.g., the excellent record of stock maintained by Scott of Harden, SRO, Scott of Harden MSS, GD157, Box 130,, Harden's Cattle Books 1760–1783.

[77] Woodward, op. cit., p. 150. His figures are 30,961 cattle at Carlisle and 16,932 cattle at Berwick, *c.*1664.

[78] *OSA* ii (1794), p. 164.

[79] The Levellers have still to receive the detailed analysis they deserve, but discussion can be found in I. Donnachie and I. Macleod. *Old Galloway* (Newton Abbot, 1974), pp. 48–60; J. F. Robertson, *The Story of Galloway* (Castle Douglas, 1963), pp. 195–9.

have moderated their sentences. There are still many un-answered questions about the Levellers.

We need to know more about the level of cattle production by the 1720–5, its economics, the sorts of farmers who were engaged in it, and the impact which it had on the landholding structure of the region. To what extent did it advance the rate of tenant reduction and lead to outright evictions? We also need to know more about those who made common cause with the Levellers. How were they organized and what finally triggered off the outbreaks of dyke levelling?

Whatever answers are eventually given to these sorts of question, the over-all impact of the cattle trade is already clear. It can be summed up by two stories or comments. One, by a writer from the parish of Urr (Kirkcudbrightshire) relates how it 'is not yet quite 100 years, since farms in this neighbourhood, that now pay a rent of 200l per annum, were offered at the church doors, to any tenant, who would pay the land tax, minister's stipend and other public burdens'.[80] The other refers to an auction that was held at the start of the nineteenth century for the tack of a farm on the Baldoon estate in Galloway. Demand and bidding was so fierce that the auctioneer had to restrain those present by reminding them that they were only leasing the farm not buying it![81] Whether embroidered or not, the quite contrasting con-ditions depicted by these two statements owes much to the impact of the livestock trade. Even before the Improvers' Movement, it had attached new values to land and the way it was used.

The shift into stock farming in the middle and eastern Borders was almost as pronounced, but with these differences: first, there was already a strong tradition of stock farming in the region, and secondly, the main enterprise was sheep rather than cattle production. The tradition of stock farming had largely been centred on the upland gerss farms of the Southern Uplands, the Cheviots, and Lammermuir. Over the period 1650 to 1760, such farms seem to have concentrated more and more exclusively on stock. The inducement for this shift was the rising demand for wool and for both mutton and lamb from the markets south of the

---

[80] *OSA*, ii (1974), p. 164.
[81] T. MacLelland, 'On the Agriculture of the Stewartry of Kirkcudbright and Wigtownshire', *Trans. Highland and Agric. Soc. Scotland*, 4th ser., vii (1875), p. 16.

Border. It would enlarge our understanding to know whether this rising demand had an inflationary effect on prices or whether the expansion of supply was sufficient to keep them stable. Unfortunately, both stock and wool prices are difficult to locate before 1760. Those actually found relate to different farms and only cover the post-1700 period. Altogether, they hint at a modest, if uncertain increase between 1700 and 1760, but there are really too many problems of interpretation to allow any firm conclusions to be drawn (see Table 4). An exceptionally fine account-book for the upland farm of Broadlie in Roxburghshire throws light on where the increased demand came from. During the few years on either side of 1750, the tenant of Broadlie sold wool to dealers from Newcastle, Leeds, and Hobberholm Chappel near Halifax, in addition to the wool he sold locally at Hawick and Langholm.[82] His sheep and lambs were despatched along similar routes with sales to fatteners in both Yorkshire and Northumberland, as well as to local farmers.

An equally fine day-book maintained by Walter Grieve,[83] who farmed the upland farms of Branxholm Park, Linhope, Southfield, and Riccarton in Roxburghshire, provides detailed stocking figures from which the economy of such farms can be reconstructed in some detail. Those for Riccarton (1735), Southfield (1740), and Branxholm Park (1741) are presented in Table 5. All appear as commercial sheep farms, committed to the production of wool, skins, sheep, and lambs. Those of Riccarton and Linhope were primarily rearing and store farms with little or no arable land. Those of Southfield and Branxholm Park were better provided for, with fairly substantial amounts of arable but no attempt was made to sell grain. It was devoted solely to the subsistence of those on the farm, though stock were no doubt grazed on the harvest stubble. The economy of such farms, with its strong market orientation, must have been typical of many throughout the Southern Uplands at this point.

A comparable shift towards stock production also occurred in low-ground areas like the Merse, but unlike the situation in the surrounding uplands, enterprises were more evenly balanced between cattle and sheep production. Accounts for both the Scott

[82] Wilton Lodge Museum, Hawick, The Broadlie Day Book, 1748–55.
[83] Ibid., Book of Grieve.

Table 4: Stock and Wool Prices in South-East Scotland 1700–1760

1704/5	Wedders: £3 12s–£4 10s. Scots) Dinmonts: £2 14s–£2 18s. Wool pr. stone: £ 10s1–£5 10s. Oxen: £40 10s–£45
1729	Ewes and lambs: 9/- (Sterling) Ewes: 6/6d Gimmers: 5/8d Hogs: 5/-
1735	Ewes and lambs: 5/-–7/8d Ewes: 3/8d Gimmers: 3/7d Dinmonts: 8/-
1737–9	Ewes: 5/- Lambs: 1/6d Wedders: 6/8d–7/1½d Wool pr. stone: 3/4d
1749	Lambs: 2/4d–2/6d Wedders: 7/3d–9/4d Wool pr. stone: 6/- Oxen: £4 5s.
1750	Ewes: 5/5d Lambs: 2/7d Wool pr. stone: 6/2d
1752/3	Ewes: 5/8d–6/3d Lambs: 2/2d–2/4d Wedders: 8/4d Wool pro. stone: 3/6d–4/3d
1760 (a)	Ewes: 6/8d Lambs: 3/2d Wool pr. stone: 8/4d
1760 (b)	Ewes and lambs: 8/6d Wedders: 10/- Black Cattle £3

Based on Roxburgh MSS, Floors Castle, Accounts of Charge and Discharge, 1704/5, for Stocking Friars Park, Account of Black Cattle and Sheep at Floors and Hallydean, 1737–39; SRO, Scott of Harden MS, GD157, Box 134, Accounts of Charge and Discharge 1949–50, Cattle Books, no. i, 1760; Wilton Park Museum, Hawick, Book of Grieve; J. Hogg, *The Shepherd's Guide* (Edinburgh, 1807), pp. 326–8.

Table 5: Livestock Carried by Select Touns in the Southern Uplands

---

(a)   Stock of Riccarton (Roxburghshire), 1735
19 score 14 ewes and lambs
2 score 08 ewes
3 score 02 dinmonts
3 score 15 hogs
3 score 09 yield gimmers
17 riding tups

32 score 08

(b)   Southfield (Roxburghshire), 1740
4 score 12 ewes and lambs
13 yield ewes
19 yield sheep
2 score 00 yield gimmers
05 hogs
03 tups

8 score 12 sheep plus 5 milk cows

(c)   Branxholm Park (Roxburghshire), 1742
2 score 04 ewes and lambs
1 score 10 gimmers
22 score 08 lambs
10 fat sheep
1 score 13 draught ewes

28 score 05 sheep

(d)   Gross Figures, c.1763, for various farms in upland Roxburghshire

Linhope	110 score sheep		Southfield	8 score sheep
Riccarton	46	do.	Branxholm Park	30	do.
Broadlie	86	do.	Smale	29	do.
Milnholm	10	do. plus 30 cattle		

---

of Harden[84] and the Roxburgh ducal estates[85] show that as well as breeding their own cattle, they were also buying in Highland stots from Falkirk tryst for fattening before the period under review had ended. Whether this interest in cattle can be pushed back into the seventeenth century is uncertain. Figures for the amount of stock crossing on the eastern side of the Border with England c.1700 suggest that whilst the numbers of sheep droved

[84] SRO, Scott of Harden, GD157, Box 130, Harden's Cattle Books 1760–1783.
[85] Floors Castle, Roxburgh MSS, 'Acct. of Black cattel and Sheep at floors & hallyden whit 1737 to Janr. 1 1739'.

were substantial, those of cattle were negligible.[86] This suggests that an interest in cattle as opposed to sheep by Merse farmers was an eighteenth-century development. There was an interesting case raised in 1736 by the tenant of Hyndhope in the Cheviots against various drovers from Northumberland in which the former tried to stop the latter passing through his land with their cattle drove. He argued that 'the Common and ordinary way that the drovers have to goe to Morpeth is by Redeswater and not through Arks or Swinlawhope belonging to Sir John Rutherford of that ilk nor through the Hyndhope Ground belonging to his Grace the Duke of Roxburgh.'[87] Sadly, the case makes no reference to where such droves had come from. If, as in the south-west, the spread of enclosure signals the developing interest in cattle, then the 1720s and 30s may have been an equally significant turning-point in the Merse also, for this is when estates like the Eccles estate cast all its property into enclosures.[88] Its heavy clay soils would have been ideally suited for cattle fattening.

Looking back to the growth of the cattle trade in Galloway, J. Smith talked about how the 'palpable superiority of the herbage about gentlemen's houses, kept constantly in grass, for the accommodation of their families, could not fail to strike' local farmers as a lesson in husbandry.[89] By the end of the seventeenth century grass parks were being laid out around the policies of many Lowland estates. The laird of Urie, for instance, was said to have been at 'considerable charge and expenses in building of dikes and inclosures for the preservation of grass and trees' planted therein 'around his policy in Kincardineshire' in 1701.[90] Whether such parks served as examples to the local farming community or not, they constituted in themselves a major new source of good-quality grazings. Like those which graced the policies of feuars in the parishes around Glasgow,[91] they were a double blessing since they offered a prospect both of an agreeable view as well as an agreeable profit.

---

[86] Woodward, op. cit. pp. 150–1, 155, and Appendix A.
[87] Floors Castle Castle, Roxburgh MSS, 'Advocation Thomson Agt Shortreid 1736'.
[88] SRO, RHP3366.
[89] Smith. *General View of the Agriculture of Galloway (London, 1810), p. 44.*
[90] Barron (ed.), 'Court Book of the Barony of Urie', p. 111.
[91] *Description of the Sheriffdome of Lanark and Renfrew*, Maitland Club (Glasgow, 1831), pp. 28–30, 56, and 66.

Turning to the problem of how this expansion of stock production was accommodated into the farm economy of the south and east, two types of response can be recognized. The first was simply to lay out land to permanent grass. The imparking of land naturally falls into this category. So too does the contraction of arable on upland sheep farms. A 1743 tack for the Cheviot farm of Grubbit on the Biel estate bound the tenant to make the lands 'more convenient for the Breading of Stock than it formerly has been or now is And for that purpose Shall as soon as may be Reduced the Tillage into pasture ground'.[92] There are good reasons for believing that Grubbit was here passing through a transition that many farms in the Southern Uplands underwent in their adjustment to a more complete livestock economy. Quite a number of late eighteenth-century correspondents in the *Old Statistical Account* looked back over their shoulders to a time when arable in the hills had been more extensive.[93] Surveys, like that carried out in 1718 for the Buccleuch estate, confirm that arable acreages were often surprisingly high.[94] Facilitating the contraction of this arable must have been the reduction in tenant numbers which obviously affected the amount that needed to be grown for subsistence. However, there were compelling reasons for converting arable to grass on these upland farms. Arable invariably occupied the best and most sheltered land, the very land needed for the wintering of stock. Since the amount carried in winter determined the summer capacity of the hills, this formed a serious constraint on the number of stock carried.

The second means by which farm economies responded to the enhanced opportunities for livestock marketing was by making adjustments to their cropping rotations. The method most commonly adopted was the restricted cropping of outfield, the latter now being valued as much for its grass as for its arable. Smith appreciated this when writing about Galloway, declaring that with the growth of the cattle trade, grass, 'which had before been an object of no value, and was considered in no other light than as a fallow to enable the land afterwards to produce some oatcrops, now became valuable on its own account'.[95] One way

[92] SRO, Biel MSS, GD6/1601/3.

[93] *OSA*, xvi (1793), p. 66; ibid., 17 (1796), p. 115; *NSA: Roxburghshire* (1844), pp. 26, 28, 78, 94, 202, 276, and 373.

[94] SRO, RHP9628.

[95] Smith, *General View of the Agriculture of Galloway*, p. 43.

in which this revaluation expressed itself was through the restricted cropping of outfield, with some farmers cultivating only a third or less by the early eighteenth century. In fact, Lord Belhaven publicized the improved quantity and quality of grass obtained by restricting the cultivation of outfield when discussing the problem of grass provision in the context of East Lothian.[96] How important outfield grass became for some touns can be illustrated with evidence culled from estate paper collections for the extreme south-east. For instance, when the toun of Nether Ancrum (Roxburghshire) was reorganized in 1738, the six tenants were required immediately to lay out part of the toun under an outfield system so as to provide grass for the farm.[97] Similarly, when a tenant in the nearby toun of Windywalls over-ploughed his outfield *c.*1730, it was said by his fellow tenant that it left him no grass even for his labouring beasts.[98] More explicit evidence was presented during the division of Coldingham Commonty in Berwickshire, the proceedings of which commenced in 1755. Quite a number of touns had allowed their regular use of the commonty to lapse, but with the prospect of a division, they sought to reassert their interest. Speaking generally, a lawyer acting on behalf of one heritor argued that the decline in use of the commonty had been caused by farmers being more inclined to have improved grassland actually on their farms.[99] What this improved grassland might have comprised is hinted at by the herd of Ayton, who told the court that only when too much outfield had been ploughed was use made of the commonty.[1]

Recent papers by Whittington[2] and Whyte[3] have suggested that the changes wrought over roughly the period 1650 to 1760 may have anticipated the Improvers' Movement of the late eighteenth century to such an extent that it questions the neat chronology of the latter. Whilst accepting the importance of

[96] Hamilton, *The Countrey-Man's Rudiments*, p. 16.
[97] Floors Castle, Roxburgh MSS, Tack to James Bell for Nether Ancrum, 1744.
[98] Floors Castle, Roxburgh MSS, Act and Commission John Hood . . . Agt. . . . Robert Davidson, 1758.
[99] SRO, Home-Robertson MSS, GD267, ex Billie no. 621, Decreet of Division of the Commonty of Coldingham, 1772.
[1] Ibid.
[2] Whittington, 'Was there a Scottish Agricultural Revolution?', pp. 204–6.
[3] Whyte, 'The Agricultural Revolution in Scotland: contributions to the debate', pp. 203–5.

these changes, the present writer hesitates to see them as in any way invalidating the concept of a discrete post-1760 Improvers' Movement. As argued at the outset of this section, the changes which occurred before then are best seen as achieving gains by adjustment rather than improvement. The fact that more tenants were drawn into market transactions can be put down to the conversion of multures or grain rents. The fact that more grain was being marketed can be put down to tenant reduction, a concentration of resources in the hands of a few. The expansion of cattle production can be seen as a redirection of these resources. From out of such changes, there emerged farmers and estates tied firmly to the market and in a position to start the long process of accumulating the capital necessary for improvement. The connection was not lost on the rural community. A description of the Barony of Forest or Buchan on the south side of Loch Troul in Galloway declared it to be 'so inclosed and divided for orderly improvement of the sheep and black cattle, that the whole farmers of these grounds have considerable advantage therby to the inriching of the families'.[4] The laying out of new policies and the building of stone farmsteads over this period may represent the first signs of this capital being conspicuously invested. However, this commercial sector of farming must be kept in perspective. With less than half of all touns in the hands of single tenants, and therefore a high proportion of holdings per tenant on the small side, it would be optimistic to see the number of farmers with commercially viable units as constituting more than a third of the total. If we add those factors outlined earlier which constrained and inhibited the strategy of farmers, then the number actually engaged wholeheartedly in production for the market may have been as little as a quarter. Not until the spurt in tenant reduction and holding amalgamation during the closing decades of this period, or during the 1730s, 40s, and 50s, is the balance likely to have been finally tipped towards a market-orientated system.

Rural Domestic Industry

Historians now see the century or so before the take-off of large-scale industrial development in late eighteenth-century Britain

---

[4] *Geographical Collections*, vol. i, p. 401.

as forming a critical preparatory phase during which systems of rural domestic industry spread rapidly in many areas. Their growth was strongest in areas which J. Thirsk has categorized as of a livestock–woodland type.[5] Quite apart from having the suitable raw materials like wool, hides, and timber, these sorts of area possessed other vital preconditions. In particular, their rapid population growth over the seventeenth and early eighteenth centuries, combined with the practice of partible inheritance, meant that the size of family holdings became progressively smaller. Furthermore, the abundant wastelands of these areas, coupled with weak manorial control, encouraged squatting. In consequence of these processes, there slowly emerged systems of smallholdings that were incapable of providing their occupiers with an adequate subsistence. In such circumstances, many turned to domestic industry as a means of supplementing their income. In so far as the essential precondition was the inadequate size of holdings, then such an argument can be applied to parts of south and east Scotland. Here too, the growth of domestic systems of industry can be linked in the first place to the growth of smallholdings in areas like the north-east or with cottars in areas where tenant numbers were being restricted, such as the Southern Uplands. With time, these initially independent producers may have become organized on a putting-out basis, relying on an agent or middleman to supply the materials and market the finished product. Once this stage had been reached, then the pace at which such industry grew was set by the agent in his search for cheap labour, for prior to mechanization, the only way to expand the output of many trades was to find extra hands.

By its very nature, the growth of domestic industry is not easily researched. Inventories of the goods of deceased persons have been used for parts of England, and may offer possibilities for Scotland, but they are likely to be more forthcoming in respect of agents and merchants rather than the actual producers. Scope for examining the latter is provided by chance sources like the 1696 *List of Pollable Persons in the Shire of Aberdeen*. Not only does it indicate which tradesmen were full-time, but also records those cottars who had no supplementary trade as opposed to those who

---

[5] J. Thirsk, 'The Farming Regions of England', pp. 1–112 in J. Thirsk (ed.), *The Agrarian History of England and Wales IV 1500–1640* (Cambridge, 1966), pp. 1–16.

had. The extent of rural industry in the county can be shown by sampling specimen parishes. Thus, the parish of Clatt contained 51 full-time tradesmen, the occupations of whom included weaver, chapman, tailor, merchant, cordoner, carpenter, and smith.[6] That of Monymusk contained 52 full-time tradesmen, plus a number of cottars and tenants who also practised a craft. As in Clatt, the main occupation amongst full-time tradesmen was that of weaving.[7] What the *List of Pollable Persons* does not disclose is the involvement of women and children in trade processes like carding and spinning. Clues as to how such processes were fitted into the rural economy is provided by tacks for the Monymusk estate, for amongst the conditions set for a number of touns was one that their tenants should provide so many hesps or hanks of linen yarn. The 1733 rental for the estate shows that it collected in this way $134\frac{2}{3}$ hesps.[8] In all probability, carding and spinning these hesps must have been the work of the tenant's family, or that of his cottars. Nor is the amount paid in as rent likely to represent the sum total of yarn spun, but merely the estate's share of a much larger product. Farm accounts and day-books sometimes yield similar information. The tenant of Broadlie in Roxburghshire, for instance, hired an Adam Beaty in 1752. Amongst the conditions of his employment was one that his wife had to do some spinning for his master.[9] Nearby, at Southfield, $2\frac{3}{4}$ stones of wool were paid as part of the 'Women's wages' in 1740, though this was insignificant compared with the amounts sold by Grieve to chapmen and dealers.[10]

Until the potential of such sources has been realized, we must rely on general topographic accounts to piece together how widespread rural domestic industry became over this period. The main growth sector was textiles. Branches of it were to be found in many areas. Selkirkshire, for example was reported in the 1720s to produce 'great plenty of well spun Worset, which is sold and carried for the most part unto foreign Nations'.[11] The Selkirk-shire woollen industry demonstrates how purely domestic in-dustries were penetrated by entrepreneurial capital in search of

---

[6] Stuart (ed.), op. cit., vol. i, pp. 463–75.

[7] Ibid., pp. 373–88.

[8] Hamilton (ed.), *Monymusk Papers (1713–1755)*. p. 54.

[9] Broadlie Day Book, 27 April 1752.

[10] Book of Grieve, Accounts for Southfield, 1740.

[11] *Geographical Collections*, vol. iii, p. 168.

cheap labour, for when Andrew Wight visited the area in 1777, he found the women there 'excellent spinners, and are fully employed by the English manufacturers of woollen cloth, who find account in it, by having their wool spun cheaper than at home'.[12] Across in Galloway, an annual fair held at Wigton was 'frequented by merchants from Edinburgh, Glasgow, Air and other places, who here buy great quantities of raw broad cloth and transport part of it over seas and part of it they dy at home and sell for many uses'.[13] In Buchan, one early account informs us of the sort of trade about which the 1696 *List* is silent, or that the 'women of this Countrey are mostly employed in spinning and working of stockings and making of Plaiden-Webs, which the Aberdeen Merchant carry over seas. And it is this which bringeth money to the Comons, other ways of getting it they have not.'[14] The bargain between producers and merchants may have been struck at stocking markets like Old Meldrum. Their face-to-face contact at such markets, though, was not the only linkage between them. References to chapmen in the 1696 *List of Pollable Persons* suggest these also acted as a go-between, as did local shopkeepers in some parishes.[15] Further south, the knitting of stockings gave way to the production of linen cloth. According to Pocock, the cross-over occurred around Inverbervie in Kincardineshire, 'here the linnen Manufacture begins and the knitting of Stockings ends. The Linnen Manufacture to the North being mostly of linnen yarn brought from Banff and sent ... to Nottingham.'[16] Along with Fife and Perthshire, Kincardineshire was the centre of early linen production in Scotland,[17] possessing all stages of the industry from the growing of flax through to the weaving of the cloth itself. When the industry began to grow rapidly from the 1740s onwards, control over it passed more and more to merchants in burghs like Dundee, Forfar, and Dunfermline. The countryside not only in their hinterland, but also, in the Highlands became simply a pool of cheap labour for hand-

[12] Wight, op. cit., vol. iii, pp. 20–1.

[13] *Geographical Collections*, vol. ii, p. 73.

[14] Ibid., vol. iii, p. 225.

[15] *OSA*, v (1793), pp. 61–2.

[16] D. W. Kemp (ed.), *Tours in Scotland, 1747, 1750, 1760 by Richard Pococke*, Scottish History Society, i (1887), p. 212.

[17] See esp. the discussion in H. Hamilton, *The Industrial Revolution in Scotland* (Oxford, 1932), pp. 88 and 91.

intensive processes like heckling and spinning. This urban–rural complementarity was not confined to linen production, but was typical of other textile industries. One need only look at lists such as D. Loch compiled in the 1770s to realize that many burghs in central or eastern Scotland concentrated on the weaving or finishing processes of textile production, relying on cheap rural labour for preparatory processes.[18]

The growth of rural industry was not always a spontaneous affair, a case of smallholders and cottars trying to counter the inadequacy of their domestic economy, but was frequently induced by landowners and merchants. The role of the merchants is a fairly obvious one, but that of landowners needs definition. Their motives were more mixed, being concerned not only with the commercial benefits of encouraging industry but with its capacity for absorbing displaced landholders and enabling smallholders to fulfil servicing roles within the economy of the estate. The simplest way of assisting its growth was through Acts in the local Baron Court. For instance, the court book for the Baronies of Newtyle, Keillours, Cowty, and Bendochy in Angus passed an Act encouraging the spinning of flax yarn.[19] Another form of encouragement adopted by landowners was to establish an annual fair or weekly market at which their tenants or cottars might more easily purchase materials or sell their goods.[20] More ambitious were planned villages. The majority of planned villages date from the period of the Improvers' Movement, but enough were built before then to warrant a mention here. In a comprehensive review of the problem, Smout has uncovered examples dating back to the sixteenth and seventeenth centuries. The Earl of Glencairn, for instance, laid out a new settlement at Kilmaurs (Ayrshire) in 1527, establishing in it not only craftsmen and merchants, but also, forty freemen in tofts or smallholdings that extended to five acres (2 ha) apiece.[21] Those planned after 1650 were similarly designed as a focus for rural trades and crafts.

---

[18] Sir Arthur Mitchell, 'David Loch's Tour in Scotland 1778', pp. 19–28.

[19] HMC, *5th Report*, p. 623.

[20] Examples include the Earl of Aberdeen's weekly market and bi-annual fairs at Kirktoun of Methlick 1681 (*ASP* viii, p. 439) and John Abercromby of Glassock's bi-annual fairs on the Muir of Glassock (Banff), 1681 (*APS* viii, p. 441).

[21] T. C. Smout, 'The Landowners and the Planned Village in Scotland 1730–1830', pp. 73–106 in N. T. Phillipson and R. Mitchison (eds.), *Scotland in the Age of Improvement* (Edinburgh, 1970), pp. 73–4.

A well-documented example is that of Ormiston (Midlothian). Built in 1738, it soon boasted a variety of trades, from spinning and shoemakers to candlemakers and maltsters.[22] In trying to explain why the planned village became established in Scotland, we possibly need to look more at changing conditions within rural society than at external factors like the growth of trade. Given the general reduction in tenant numbers in the south and east of the country, the planned village may represent an attempt to create a suitable focus for vital trades and crafts that were threatened by the eventual decline of the small tenant.

The foregoing discussion of rural industry has been confined to those branches which were integrated into the rural economy, either as a supplement to farming or as a means of using up female and child labour within the domestic economy. Excluded by such a definition are those branches of industry whose changing organization and scale of working increasingly divorced them from the rural, domestic context which had originally nurtured them. Coal-working is one example. With its increasing expansion after 1650, there emerged concentrations of pits and workings in coastal areas on either side of the Forth, whilst those around Glasgow grew more extensive still.[23] At the same time, its organization became more capital-intensive as workings became deeper and posed more technical problems. The industry became dominated by capitalist entrepreneurs like Sir Charles Dundas or Sir William Dick, men who combined coal-working with related activities such as salt-working and shipping. Within this system, the role of the ordinary tenant, working a surface pit on his farm in his spare time, receded rapidly. In his place, the labour force of the industry became more organized, with whole communities of full-time coal-workers developing, such as those of Falkirk, Airth, Kinnaird, and Quarrel.[24] The new organization and scale of the industry comes over from the application by William Baillie of Ladrington for two yearly fairs and a weekly market at Painstone (East Lothian) in 1690. Baillie submitted that he had a coal heugh there which served the eastern half of the county. Its output was sufficient for him 'to

[22] Ibid., P. 85
[23] *Geographical Collections*, vol. i, pp. 316 and 330; *Sheriffdome of Lanark and Renfrew*, p. 138.
[24] Ibid., p. 330.

keep a considerable number of Coalizers and other workmen constantle at work, upwards of fourscore of persones'.[25]

Even agricultural servicing and primary processing industries acquired substantial non-agrarian sectors, whose linkage with farming was measured solely in terms of material supply. In a sense, the growing concentration of weaving and textile-finishing processes in the burghs is one aspect of this deepening dichotomy between agriculture and the industries based upon it. However, there was a whole range of servicing and processing industries that began to gravitate to central places. Naturally, it was the burghs that attracted most activity. The experience of Montrose probably matched that of many others. 'They are constantly building', said an early eighteenth-century account, 'both in the toune and suburbs which is at a considerable distance from the toune in the links and is ther malthouses and kilns and granaries for cornes, of thrie storie high and some more and are increased to such a number that in a short tyme its thought they will equall if not exceed the toune in greatness'.[26] Nor was Scotland's premier burgh, Edinburgh, aloof from such activity, with paper, linen, ale-making, grain, and saw mills all jostling each other for position along the Water of Leith.[27] How much the burghs shared in an expanding trade and how much they gained at the expense of the countryside is impossible to say. Certainly, landowners must have recognized the dangers. Indeed, this may have been the reason why estates persisted for so long in trying to control where tenants had their grain milled or their barley malted. It could also be the reason why so many sought to establish non-burghal markets and fairs on their own estates.

Inventory and Prospect

Having acceded to an incorporating Union with her more prosperous southern neighbour in 1707, Scotland had cause to face the eighteenth century with some degree of expectancy. There were, of course, some who voiced their misgivings over such a close and binding alliance with the 'auld enemy'. A 'Union on base unjust conditions' and much more, said one

[25] *APS* viii, p. 527.
[26] *Geographical Collections*, ii, p. 42.
[27] Ibid., p. 67.

anonymous pasquil of the times.[28] Others took a different line. The flaughter spade had done more damage to Scotland than the Union promised, proclaimed one Aberdeenshire laird.[29] In fact, at risk of mouthing Hugh MacDiarmid's 'parrot cry' and telling how:

> ... the Union brocht
> Puir Scotland into being
> As a country worth a thocht[30]

she could not have chosen a more appropriate partner for the times. After the trials of King William's lean years and being reminded that much of her agriculture was still largely concerned with scarcity and survival rather than surplus and profit, she suddenly found herself with the prospect of quite different economic horizons. She was now firmly set within an enlarged and much more vigorously growing market system. It not only opened 'a road west-awa' yonder' for Glasgow merchants, as Baille Nicol Jarvie put it,[31] but brought Scottish agriculture under the shadow of a powerful new market stimulus. The greater social and economic interaction with England which followed the Union also brought her into contact with new ideas on husbandry and farming techniques generally which provided her with the know-how and means by which she could respond more fully to these new market opportunities. This agrarian improvement required capital. The growing volume of trade in livestock products with England provided some capital early on, whilst the inflation of agricultural prices generally after the Union may have provided much more,[32] albeit at the expense of the ordinary Scottish consumer. Of course, once agricultural improvement was under way, then increased output would itself

---

[28] Scott (ed.), *Penguin Book of Scottish Verse*, p. 277.
[29] A. C. Cameron, 'On Ancient Farming Customs in Scotland', *Trans. Highland & Agricultural Soc. Scotland*, 4th ser., v (1873), p. 298.
[30] Scott (ed.), *Penguin Book of Scottish Verse*, p. 443.
[31] Sir Walter Scott, *Rob Roy*, Centenary edn. pub. A. & C. Black (Edinburgh, 1886), p. 305.
[32] The author fully endorses the view expressed by Smout and Fenton, op. cit., p. 89 that the Scottish 'agricultural revolution could come about in the eighteenth century only after new markets had been discovered and developed', and, in particular, the English market.

have generated capital. However, before such gains had been reaped, it must be conceded that Scotland at the point of the Union was not a wealthy country. Not long before, she had gone through the trauma of the Darien scheme failure, when as much as half of the country's circulating captial and even more of her morale evaporated in the unyielding jungle of Central America. With the Union, however, she became a principal beneficiary in the world's largest and most rapidly growing commerical empire. Quite apart from providing her with cheap raw materials for industrial development, it conferred upon her a share in the extremely remunerative trade which bound the colonies to Europe. We need only look at the way the Glasgow merchant community (the Spiers, Dennistouns, Houstons, Cunninghames, Glassfords, and Dunlops) re-invested its accumulating wealth into land to appreciate that here was a source of capital for agriculture, a 'contribution of the first order' as T. M. Devine phrased it,[33] and a factor which greatly affected the Scottish land market over the eighteenth and nineteenth centuries.

It is possibly because of these problems of capital supply that—for all the early promise that Scotland would reap major economic benefits from the Union—it was not until the middle of the eighteenth century that anything like a general movement for change and improvement began to transform her rural sector. This gap between stimulus and response was interpreted by some contemporaries as signifying that Scotland's loss of independence was not so readily compensated for by forces making for her economic transformation. One can only answer their scepticism by stressing that it would be unrealistic to suppose that a traditional rural society still bedevilled by chronically low productivity and an excess of farm propulation could respond any more quickly, at least within the framework of a *laissez-faire* economic system. Besides, the over-all configuration of rural change in Scotland, with a 'pioneer' phase lasting two or three decades (1730s, 1740s, and 1750s), followed by a more general Improving Movement, is consistent with a normal diffusion curve, however else one might try to explain it.

Whatever doubts may be entered against the precise con-

[33] T. M. Devine, 'Glasgow Colonial Merchants and Land 1770–1815', pp. 205–44 in J. T. Ward and R. G. Wilson (eds.), *Land and Industry* (Newton Abbot, 1971), p. 206.

ditions which engendered rural change and improvement, there
can be none regarding the character of such change. Every aspect
of traditional farming began to give way before a belief in new
and better husbandry that swept like a religion through the
countryside. The familiar toun, for so long the basic social unit of
Scottish society, disappeared. In its place, there emerged large
well-appointed farmsteads, supplemented on the really large
holdings by a small row of cottages set at a measured distance for
the use of farm labourers. The open, irregular landscape which
surrounded the old fermtouns took on a more disciplined form, as
shots were regularized in shape, as patches of muir and moss were
reclaimed to produce a more continuous arable area, and as the
whole was subdivided into regular, geometrical enclosures that
characterize so much of the Lowlands today. These represented
changes in the framework of farming. Equally vital were changes
in the character of farming systems and husbandry. The
uniformity which pervaded so much of early farming, with its
infield–outfield systems and emphasis on grain cropping, was
dissolved and more flexible and varied farming systems were
adopted which integrated stock and crop in new and more
productive ways. Essential to these new systems were crops like
turnips and sown grasses, and the development of new livestock
breeds like the improved Cheviot, the Leicester, the Shorthorn,
and the Aberdeen-Angus. The tools of husbandry were also
subject to radical change: improved ploughs, drilling machines,
harvesting tools, reaping machines, and threshing machines were
all developed. Perhaps most of all, farming became much more
commercially-orientated, and as regions evolved links to particular markets, there emerged broad regional differences in
farming type.

These changes in farm structure and husbandry were accompanied by dramatic social changes. The disappearance of the
fermtoun had a particularly profound effect. Fewer people could
now hope to be tenants. Those who realized this hope found
themselves managing much larger and more profitable units.
Those who failed were confronted with the alternatives of
becoming farm labourers or moving out of the countryside
altogether to join a rapidly swelling urban proletariat. Social
contrasts, therefore, were accentuated as a few were elevated in
status and many more were depressed. Superimposed on these

changes at the tenurial level were important changes in land-ownership. Traditional ties between landowners and tenants were broken as new social groups—merchants, industrialists, and lawyers—bought landed estates. Radically new social values were also forged. Perhaps the most significant was an all-pervading belief in the virtues of improvement and a search for betterment. Change became not just a single event through which farming passed but a continuous, ongoing affair, in which successive generations claimed theirs as the ultimate and finest contribution. Viewing the problem in retrospect, we might highlight the idea of change in the late eighteenth century because it then seemed to have more novelty, but, in doing so, we must not overlook the fact that the search for new and better husbandry was itself to prove one of the more enduring innovations. Naturally, as the profits of improvement began to flow back to the rural community, life-styles began to alter. As one writer exclaimed in 1799, 'an astonishing change has taken place even in the memory of man! About half a century ago . . . the farmer went on foot to market; now he rides well dressed and mounted: formerly he ate his food off his knee, and it consisted of meal, vegetables and milk; now his table is covered, his knife and fork are laid down before him to dine on meat.'[34] A number of parish reports in the *Old Statistical Account* drew similar comparisons which confirm these changes of habit and diet, with wheaten bread, butcher's meat, tea-drinking, being especially noted.[35]

Speaking of the Earl of Hopetoun's West Lothian estate and the enclosing and farm reorganization that was in progress during the 1750s, A. Geddes once said that he 'would be safe in saying that had some countryman of the later Middle Ages come back when the surveyor was still at his work, he would have noted but little external difference from his own time; but that had we ourselves visited the estate a dozen years later, we should have found the present layout already begun.'[36] Geddes's comment here is really a gloss on what was happening to the entire fabric of

[34] J. Robertson, *General View of the Agriculture of the County of Perth (Perth, 1799)*, p. 100.
[35] *OSA*, v (1793), p. 247.
[36] A. Geddes, 'The Changing Landscape of the Lothians', *SGM* lxxi (1938), p. 129.

rural society, and not just farm layout. Patterns and institutions of great age and maturity were swept aside by the Improvers' Movement and replaced by forms we would ourselves recognize as familiar and modern.

Chapter 8

Rural Society and Economy in the Highlands and Islands 1650–1780

Looking back across the recent history of the Highlands and Islands in 1800, the Duke of Argyll described what he saw as 'a picture of Celtic feudalism dying hard'.[1] Even if events like Culloden, the coming of sheep, the clearances, the collapse of the kelp trade, or the potato famines had not happened, though, it is unlikely that we would be in a position to reverse his verdict. The problems of the region were deeper and more structural in nature, and cannot be put down to the relentless assertion of new political forces or land uses. Put in simple terms, the Highlands and Islands had too many people dependent on too little arable land. This was a predicament it faced before its Jacobite aspirations had been dashed at Culloden and certainly before sheep began to displace men. Indeed, as soon as the documentary material becomes fuller after 1650, it depicts a society sinking more and more into a condition of overpopulation, manifesting all the disfunctions one would expect under these circumstances. The central theme of this chapter therefore must be how the region compounded rather than eased its problems over the period 1650 to 1780, thereby making ultimately dramatic solutions of some sort necessary rather than a matter of choice.

The Farming Township: Its Structure

As with farming communities in the south and south-east of the country, the structure of those in the Highlands and Islands can be considered in terms of both landholding and the physical scale and disposition of touns.

Landholding The availability of a number of rentals or lists of occupiers for touns in the Highlands and Islands makes the study of landholding from 1650 to 1780 a relatively easy task.

[1] George Douglas, Duke of Argyll, *Scotland as it is and as it was* (Edinburgh, 1887), p. 387.

Altogether, nine have been examined: they consist of a 1660 to 1670 rental of the Gairloch estate (Wester Ross),[2] a 1678 rental for the Reay estate (Sutherland),[3] a 1683 rental for the MacLeod of MacLeod estate on Skye,[4] 1695 to 1743 lists of occupiers and tenants on the Menzies estate in Rannoch,[5] a 1727 rental of the Seaforth estate lands on Lewis and in Lochaber, Kintail, and Lochcarron on the mainland,[6] a 1723 list of occupiers on the Ardnamurchan and Sunart property of Sir Alexander Murray of Stanhope,[7] a 1739 rental of the Bishop of Orkney's lands in Orkney,[8] a 1755 list of occupiers and tenants on the Annexed estate lands of Strathyre (Perthshire), Barrasdale (Skye), Beulie, Lovat, and Corgach (Cromarty),[9] and lastly, a 1769 rental of the Breadalbane estate lands in Perthshire.[10]

Taking rentals at their face value leads to the impression that a great deal of variety existed between estates in respect of landholding. Thus, estates like those of Corgach or MacLeod of MacLeod had barely a third of their touns in the hands of multiple tenants, whilst the Reay, Lochtayside, and Menzies estates had over two-thirds in the hands of multiple tenants. A similar degree of variation can be found within the bounds of individual estates. On the large, sprawling Seaforth estate, for example, multiple tenancy varied from as low as around a fifth of all touns in Kintail (49 touns) to around three-fifths of all touns in Lochalsh Barony (29 touns). In all probability, these proportions do not faithfully reflect on-the-ground differences in the amount of multiple tenancy, but are likely to be distorted by differences in the way each rental or tenant list was compiled and by the presence or absence of the tacksman system.

---

[2] W. Macgill, *Old Ross-shire and Scotland* (Inverness, 1909), vol. ii, pp. 162–3.

[3] A. Mackay, *Book of the Mackay* (Edinburgh, 1896), pp. 471–5.

[4] MacLeod, *Book of Dunvegan*, vol. i, pp. 148–53.

[5] SRO, Macgregor Collection, GD150/156, lists for 1695, 1698, 1735, 1739, and 1745.

[6] This rental is reproduced in two sources. The most detailed is *Report to the Secretary for Scotland by the Crofters Commission on the Social Conditions of the People of Lewis in 1901, as Compared with Twenty Years Ago* (Glasgow, 1902), Appendix O. The alternative is J. R. N. Macphail (ed.), *Highland Papers*, Scottish History Society, xii (1916), vol. ii, pp. 313–39.

[7] Stanhope, *True Interest of Great Britain, Ireland and Our Plantations*, Table vi.

[8] Peterkin, *Rentals*, nos. V and VI, 'True and Just Rentall of All Farms Dewties and Gersumers of Bishopric of Orkney'.

[9] Wills (ed.), *Statistics of the Annexed Estates 1755–56*, pp. 1 ff.

[10] McArthur (ed.), *Survey of Lochtayside 1769*, pp. 1 ff. Use was also made of SRO, Macgregor Collection, GD50/16, Breadalbane rentals 1731 and 1761.

According to M. Gray, cottars and sub-tenants—individuals who held land of the tenant(s) of a toun—were as numerous in the Highlands and Islands as tenants, or individuals who held land directly of the landowner.[11] Since rentals dealt primarily, if not exclusively with the latter, we must expect them to conceal as many landholders or occupiers as they reveal. Various lists of occupiers, as well as the more explicit rentals, enable us to quantify the extent to which the less detailed rentals understate the number of occupiers in a toun. Some lists, like that for the Ardnamurchan and Sunart property of Sir John Murray are themselves rather basic, itemizing merely the number of families in each toun with little clue as to whether some were tenants and others, sub-tenants or cottars.[12] However, what they tell us about the group nature of fermtouns is still very revealing. Out of 32 touns in Ardnamurchan, 31 were occupied by more than one family, the odd one out being a vacant toun. Equally pertinent, out of the 31 touns so occupied, 27 were inhabited by four families or more. In Sunart, 15 out of the 20 touns had more than one family, two of the remaining five being vacant. Altogether, ten had four families or more.[13] A particularly informative rental is that for Gairloch 1660 to 1670. In addition to giving the number of tenants in each toun, it details the number of cottars or mailers. Eleven of the twenty touns mentioned were held by multiple tenants, whilst 16 had at least one cottar. All the nine touns which were held by one tenant had at least one cottar, five having as many as three. Altogether, there were 48 tenants listed in the rental compared with 52 cottars or mailers.[14]

A more analytical approach can be made using 'Lists of Inhabitants' for the Rannoch portion of the Menzies estate. They cover the period 1695 to 1747. The early lists distinguish between tacksmen, tenants, servants, hirds, and cottars. For instance, in 1695, eight tacksmen are recorded, one in each of the main touns. Beneath them were others of varying status. For example, at Leragean, there was also the tacksman's hird, eight tenants, their

[11] M. Gray, *The Highland Economy 1750–1850* (Edinburgh, 1957), pp. 202–3.
[12] Stanhope, *True Interest of Great Britain, Ireland and Our Plantations*, Table vi. In addition to the number of families, Stanhope's list also details the number of male adults, female adults, and children.
[13] Ibid., Table vi. Broadly speaking, touns in Sunart appear to have been smaller, tenurially and socially, than those of Ardnamurchan.
[14] Mackay, *Book of Mackay*, pp. 471–5.

four sons, and a shoemaker. At Camerachmore, apart from the two joint tacksmen, there were four tenants, the son of one of them, a servant, two hirds, and a weaver. By the 1735 list, references to tacksmen disappear instead, there are simply listed the 68 different tenants who held the 16 touns, plus 18 servants and 15 cottars. All but four touns were held by multiple tenants. As one might expect in such a lawless area, conditions were fluid. By 1743, the number of tenants had risen slightly to 70, but the number of cottars sharply to 35. The number of servants, meanwhile, fell back slightly to one. More revealingly, on seven of the larger touns, only eighteen tenants remained in 1743 out of the 43 who had possessed them in 1735. Apart from the increase in cottars and general turnover of tenants, one further feature of the 1743 list is that every toun had passed into the hands of multiple tenants.[15].

An equally detailed picture is afforded by the survey carried out on the Annexed estates in 1755. The survey states the number of possessers, families, and total number of people in each toun. On the Barrasdale and Strathyre estates, we find that the number of possessors and the number of families tally exactly with each other. However, elsewhere, the relationship was not so straightforward. On the Corgach portion of the Cromarty estate the majority of touns carried more families than possessors. Taking the more extreme examples first, touns like Achnahard and Reiff, Achroscaildruisk and Achillibuy each had one possessor but were inhabited by 20, 12, and 11 families respectively. Almost half the remainder had likewise only one possessor, with up to eight families in occupation. Unfortunately, it cannot be determined from the context of these figures whether they signify the presence of a tacksman system, or a system of single-tenant touns plus cottars.[16]

Such a distinction, of course, had far-reaching significance for landholding. It could mean the difference between a toun held nominally by a tacksman but in actuality sub-let by him to, a number of tenants, either wholly or in part, or a toun farmed by a single tenant as a consolidated holding but with the help of cottars. How different these two types of system were can be pieced together using material for a number of estates.

[15] SRO, Macgregor Collection, GD150/156, lists of inhabitants 1695–1747.
[16] Wills (ed.), *Statistics of the Annexed Estates 1755–56*, pp. 1 ff.

As regards tacksmen, there still persisted the old system whereby large portions of an estate spanning a number of settlements were leased to a near relation of the clan chief, the head of a sub-branch of the clan, or a close ally. Such tacksmen had a political role to play by helping to secure the support of an area or at least stabilize it. As Cregeen has said, 'they were the middlemen in a military organization.'[17] The same author has documented examples of this old style of tacksmen using the Argyll estate rental of 1715. Thus, the 24 pennylands of Torosay were set to Colin Campbell of Braglen, who, in turn, sub-let 20 pennylands to a total of 41 tenants. Similarly, the 115 pennylands of Morvern were leased to Cameron of Glendessary who, in turn, sub-let all but 20 pennylands to a whole battery of large and small tenants.[18] As well as this military role, whose prime purpose was to fill the rent-roll with loyal tenants, tacksmen had a more organizational role to play within the estate economy. As the examples just quoted demonstrate, each tacksman acted 'as farmer of the rents of his district'.[19] It was a means whereby the large clan chiefs could gather rent from their vast and sometimes inaccessible estates. By leasing large segments to intermediaries or tacksmen, landowners delegated the responsibility for collecting rent from the many small landholders which Highland estates usually carried. Of course, as Dr Johnson was quick to observe, tacksmen made a handsome profit from their position as farmers of rent, often leasing land at 6*d* per acre and sub-letting it at 10*d*.[20] According to Cregeen, when the Argyll estate raised its rents in the 1730s, it did so without cost to the ordinary tenant, a manoeuvre it accomplished simply by cutting out the middleman or the tacksman.[21]

By contrast with these large territorial tacksmen, there were also to be found tacksmen whose interests lay within the confines of a single toun. The role of this sort appears more bound up with the organizational needs of the estate than of a military character, though this is not to say that they did not have a

---

[17] E. Cregeen (ed.), *Argyll Estate Instructions*, p. xvi.
[18] Idem, 'The Tacksmen and their Successors. A Study of Tenurial Reorganisation in Mull, Morvern and Tiree in the Early 18th Century', *SS* xiii (1969), pp. 101–1.
[19] Ibid., p. 101.
[20] S. Johnson, *A Journey to the Western Islands of Scotland*, ed. M. Lascelles (New Haven and London, 1971), p. 87.
[21] Cregeen, 'Tacksmen and their Successors', p. 116.

military role to play when the occasion arose. It was a question of emphasis. Their function appears as representatives or spokesmen for a toun, charged with the task of mediating between landowners and tenants of a toun in matters of rent and services. For example, when the early lists of inhabitants were drawn up for the Rannoch portion of the Menzies estate, it was the local tacksman in each toun who signed the list as a true statement of the tenants and cottars in that toun.[22] A similar representative role can be gleaned from references to tacksmen in the early eighteenth-century rentals for Strathavon on the Marquis of Huntly's estate. The rentals were concerned not just with the rent of each tacksmen, but also, with the liabilities of the sub-tenants under him. The manner in which the rentals were compiled is also of interest. It took the form of a roll-call before the Marquis's Baillie. The proceedings had the status of a court, with the rental declaring the 'Court fenced' before commencing its business. Significantly, sub-tenants as well as tacksmen were presented before the court. When, as in the case of Webster Culfoich, sub-tenants were unable to attend, the Baillie took the oath of John Grant 'an principall tacksman' on what they paid him.[23] The court took an equal interest in what all other sub-tenants paid their various tacksman. The implication is that the tacksmen were acting almost as agents of the estate, rather than on their own behalf. The limited scale of their interest property-wise can be illustrated by two examples. Thus, in 1736, Patrick Grant was noted as tacksman of the seven oxgates of Achlichay. Beneath him were three sub-tenants holding an oxgate each, and three holding half an oxgate.[24] On the 12-oxgate toun of Inverlochy, the main tack holder was Donald Grant, who declared that he had 'seall. subtennents that possesses oxgates and half oxgates amounting in all to seven oxgates and thrie quarters. And that each oxgate pays fourteen merks & a half for duty & customes & sixteen or eighteen poultry among them, he does not know which And that he & each of his subtennents pay a reek hen & that only for each reeking house'.[25]

Whatever their precise role, there can be little doubt that the

---

[22] See esp. SRO, Macgregor Collection, GD150/156, list for 1695.
[23] Gaffney (ed.), *Lordship of Strathavon*, Appendix I, p. 213.
[24] Ibid., p. 216.
[25] Ibid., p. 218.

traditional standing of tacksmen was being threatened by the middle decades of the eighteenth century. When he surveyed the Argyll estate in 1737 preparatory to its being re-leased, Duncan Forbes of Culloden concluded that they had outlived their usefulness. In particular, he accused them of causing peasant hardship by rack-renting.[26] At the subsequent re-leasing of the estate, they were excluded largely on his recommendation. Although Cregeen has pleaded their defence on the grounds that adverse market conditions were a more likely cause of peasant hardship,[27] it has to be admitted that criticism of tacksmen was fairly general at this point. When the Assynt estate in Sutherland fell due for re-leasing in the 1770s, it was 'taken under consideration the former practice of giving Leases of Extensive farms and Grasings to one Tenant with a Power of Subsetting the same whereby The principal Tacksman commonly Exacts an additional Rent from his Subtenants imposing heavy Services and other Conditions oppressive to the Subtenents and detrimental to the improvement of the Country.'[28] In fact, from the 1760s onwards, the Tutors responsible for the running of the estate had sought to curb the power and influence of tacksmen. They were prevented from having more than one toun in their possession and other touns were set directly to joint-tenants.[29] Visitors to the Highlands also castigated them. The views of Dr Johnson regarding tacksmen are well known.[30] Less well known but equally pertinent are the views of T. Garnett. In a sentence, he believed that tacksmen 'begger those beneath them, as well as intercept the advantages due to those above them'.[31]

In a sense, the criticism which tacksmen were increasingly subjected to over the eighteenth century reflected their predicament. This predicament is encapsulated in the comment by Cregeen that they formed their 'Chief's mainstay, serving to unify the clan proper of blood relations, and by their wider authority

[26] Forbes's report is reprinted in *Report of the Commissioners of Inquiry into the Conditions of the Crofters and Cottars in the Highlands and Islands* (Edinburgh, 1884), p. 389.
[27] Cregeen, 'Tacksmen and their Successors', pp. 110–11.
[28] R. J. Adam (ed.), *John Home's Survey of Assynt*, Scottish History Society, 3rd ser., lii (1960), p. xxxi, n. 106.
[29] Ibid., pp. xxxiii–xxxv.
[30] Johnson, op. cit., p. 87.
[31] T. Garnett, *Observations on a Tour through the Highlands and Part of the Western Isles of Scotland* (London, 1810 edn.), vol. i, p. 173.

over their locality binding together all the diverse groups dwelling in the clan's territory into a political entity'.[32] In trying to accomplish the former, they were naturally inclined to display patronage towards their own kin. A report on Tiree in 1771, for example, observed that there was not a tacksman in the island 'whose portion of land is not sub-let in whole or in part to his children or other near relation for their support'.[33] This was a widespread tendency. On the Assynt estate, 59 per cent of all tacksmen and tenants in the 1770s were either MacLeods or Mackenzies, the two clans who had held the estate successively. The former tended to concentrate on the coast from Clashmore to around Unapool, and the latter, inland or around Lochinver Bay.[34] In these instances, the very real affinity between tacksman and sub-tenant must have engendered a fairly close and warm relationship. How else do we explain situations like that which arose on the MacLeod of MacLeod estate in northern Skye? When MacLeod tried to force up rents sharply at the end of the eighteenth century, not only did some of his tacksmen emigrate but their sub-tenants went with them.[35] The real problems and conflict arose when political control over an area passed out of the hands of the clan who formed its main occupiers. The group which bore the brunt of the subsequent changes and adjustments were the tacksmen. As Cregeen said, they had the task of 'binding together all the diverse groups dwelling in the clan's territory'. Thus, when the Argyll estate gained control over the Maclean lands on Mull in 1679, it was Campbell tacksmen that spearheaded the estate's assertion of authority over the area. Their action was twofold. Either they showed little favour to Maclean tenants when fixing rents or they established Campbells in their

[32] Cregreen, 'Tacksmen and their Successors', p. 94. E. Burt made a similar observation when discussing the clan system generally. 'If, by Increase of the Tribe,' he wrote, 'any small Farms are wanting for the Support of such Addition, he splits others into lesser Portions, because all must somehow be provided for.' See *Burt's Letters*, vol. ii, p. 109.

[33] Cregeen (ed.), *Argyll Estate Instructions*, p. xxii.

[34] Adam (ed.), *Survey of Assynt*, p. xlii.

[35] MacLeod (ed.), *Book of Dunvegan*, vol. ii, p. 113. Adam has some valuable comments to make on the link between tacksmen and emigration during the 18th century. The agents acting for the estate, he argued, 'deplored emigration—and above all they deplored the part played in it by the tacksmen, whom they singled out as the villains of the situation. The importance of the tacksmen as the natural leader of emigration, and as its possible financier, repeatedly appears in agent's letters.' See Adam (ed.), *Survey of Assynt*, p. xxx.

place. Both were guaranteed to produce social conflict and to invest the tacksman with an odious reputation.[36] The process can be seen at work in Morvern. The house of Argyll acquired two-thirds of Morvern when they took over the Maclean of Duart estates in 1679. At first, the area was set to local clansmen who could be trusted, such as Cameron of Glendessary, who acted as tacksmen for the area, rather than to local Macleans. When Forbes appeared on the scene with his recommendation of letting as much directly to sub-tenants as possible, the landholders of Morvern resisted the change, with tacksmen and sub-tenants combining in their opposition. Perhaps they sensed it would weaken the Camerons' control, for they formed the bulk of the sub-tenants. Forbes eventually compromised by introducing changes only in the northern part of Morvern, and even there, he retained the old tacksman system. The tacksmen which 'he chose were still local people, not yet Campbells from the south, but they were smaller men than their predecessors had been, and their power in the district was proportionately less'.[37] In fact, it was not until 1754 that half the leases in the area were granted to Campbells.

No matter what form it took so long as it lasted then the tacksman system poses problems for the interpretation of rentals. Unless supplementary information is available, as it is for the aforementioned estates, there is no way of determining the extent to which sub-tenants formed groups of multiple tenants. We can only infer from the better-documented examples that it was generally the case. Such touns must have contrasted sharply with those on which there existed a single tenant plus cottars. Cottars were of course, also commonplace on multiple-tenant touns. However, their presence on touns farmed by a single tenant is noteworthy because of the possible confusion with the system of tacksmen and sub-tenants. Whereas sub-tenants could hold substantial holdings and frequently shared the entire toun between themselves, cottars usually had only an acre or so plus their cottage. Moreover, whilst sub-tenants often had services to

[36] See discussion in Cregeen, 'Tacksmen and their Successors', pp. 97–101, and E. Cregeen, 'The Changing Role of the House of Argyll in the Scottish Highlands', pp. 153–92 in I. M. Lewis (ed.), *History and Social Anthropology*, ASA monograph no. 7 (London, 1968), pp. 155–7.

[37] Gaskell, *Morvern Transformed*, p. 3.

perform, it was not the essence of their contract as it was with cottars. In short, cottars were farm labourers. They carried out the husbandry tasks necessary on a large holding. Naturally, the larger the toun, the more necessary the cottars. The nature of their status is enlarged upon by the Rannoch lists. Throughout the later lists, which tend to be more systematically organized, cottars are linked closely with particular tenants. For instance, in the 1743 list, four of the ten tenants holding Aulich are shown as having cottars. In Camserachmore, three of the four tenants had one cottar, and the remaining tenant, three.[38] This tied relationship between particular tenants and cottars is best highlighted by the exception. In the 1735 list, a John McOnell is described as having 'a house as a Cottar but is own'd by none of the town for Cottar'.[39] The Menzies lists show a marked increase in the number of cottars over the early eighteenth century. More information is needed for other estates before this can be turned into a general trend, but it is what might be expected given the known increase of population over the eighteenth century. What we can be certain about is that cottars were widespread by the middle decades. This is supported not only by the rentals and lists cited above, but also, by evidence for areas like Glen Urquhart, Netherlorn, and Tiree.[40]

Cottars were not the only smallholders. There were also crofters and pendiclers. These differed from cottars by holding their land directly from the landowners rather than via a tacksman or sub-tenant.[41] It has also been suggested that their land was fixed in its layout rather than shifted around as cottars' land tended to be.[42] Nor were cottars the only hired labour. Many lists of inhabitants, such as those for Rannoch and Assynt, refer to servants.[43] To judge from their sheer number on certain estates, some were simply cottars by another name. Others were possibly landless, living in with a tenant as part of his household,

---

[38] SRO, Macgregor Collection, GD150/156, list for 1743.

[39] Ibid., list for 1735.

[40] Gray, *The Highland Economy 1750–1850*, p. 23; Cregeen (ed.), *Argyll Estate Instructions*, list on plan at rear of book.

[41] Most were holders of specifically designated crofts that were tied to specific duties, like brewhouses, ferries, and the like.

[42] Gray, *The Highland Economy 1750–1850*, p. 22.

[43] SRO, Macgregor Collection, GD150/156, list for 1739; Adam (ed.), *Survey of Assynt*, pp. 68–88.

the equivalent of the Lewis *scallog*.[44] What is missing from the Highlands is any substantial reference to independent tradesmen. There were many cottars or crofters who practised a trade, such as weaving or shoemaking, but few who derived their living in this way. Subsistence in the Highlands meant land, and few were entirely removed from it, either directly or indirectly.[45]

Toun and Holding Size Like their Lowland counterpart, Highland touns varied greatly in acreage. However, mere acreage is misleading, for most combined vast acreages of hill or mountain pasture with small amounts of arable. The extent of this imbalance is evident from a series of fine estate surveys dating from the 1760s and 1770s (see Table 6). Especially informative is a survey drawn up for the Lochtayside portion of the Breadalbane estate in 1769. Altogether, it covers 115 touns on both sides of the Loch. Of the 56 units on the north side of the Loch, only nine exceeded 250 acres (101 ha), whereas on the south side (57 touns), the number in excess was 43. If the comparison is narrowed to one of arable acreages, though, their differences are lessened. Apart from a small handful of touns on the north side with over 75 acres (30 ha) of croft and outfield arable, most touns on the estate had barely 20 to 30 acres (8 to 12 ha) of cultivated land. On the Assynt estate in Sutherland the imbalance was more extreme. Of 44 touns detailed in a survey of the estate carried out in the 1770s, as many as 33 touns had over 1,000 acres (405 ha) credited to them. A few, such as Ledbeg, Stroncuby, and Unapool had over 3,000 acres (1,215 ha). Yet only three touns could boast infields of more than 100 acres (40 ha). In fact, out of a total of 33,335 acres (13,496 ha) on land making up the coastal touns, only 2,038 acres (825 ha) was classed as infield or cultivated shieling. Out of the 56,698 acres (22,955) comprising the touns of the interior, only 1,672 (677 ha) acres was so classified.

[44] See *Report of the Commissioners of Inquiry into the Condition of the Crofters and Cottars*, pp. 3–5.
[45] The Rannoch lists record one or two cottars as shoemakers or weavers. Adam Smith had thoughts on the matter. 'In the lone houses and very small villages of which are scattered about in so desert a country as the Highlands and Islands', he wrote, 'every farmer must be butcher, baker, and brewer for his own family.' See A. Smith, *An Inquiry into the Nature and Causes of the Wealth of Nations*, ed. E. Cannan (London, 1930, 5th edn.), vol. i, p. 19.

Table 6: *The Relationship Between Arable and Pasture in Highland Touns*

	Date	Nos. of Touns	Total Acreage (Arable + Pasture)	Arable Acreage	Total Acreage Per Toun (Arable + Pasture)	Arable Per Toun
Ardnamurchan	1723	32	53859	608	1683	19
Sunart	1723	20	47344	240	2367	12
Strathyre Barony	1755	14		511		37
Barrasdale	1755	17		53		3
Tiree	1768/9	32	13833	772	432	24
Breadalbane Estate:						
Lochtay–Northside	1769	56	7713	2595	138	46
Lochtay–Southside	1769	57	22432	1649	393	29
Assynt	1775	43	88174	3738	2051	87

Based on Stanhope, *True Interest of Great Britain, Ireland and Our Plantations*, Table vi; Wills (ed.), *Statistics of the Annexed Estates 1755–56*, pp. 1–5; Cregeen (ed.), *Argyll Estate Instructions*, plan of Tiree; McArthur (ed.), *Survey of Lochtayside*, pp. i ff.; Home (ed.), *Survey of Assynt*, pp. 1–88. It should be noted that the arable figures for Ardnamurchan, Sunart, and Tiree are estimates, based on the assumption that a pennyland equalled four acres in the case of the first two districts and that a maleland (or meilland) equalled two acres in the case of Tiree. The arable figures for Assynt include the 'sheelings' recorded as cultivated, whilst those for the Breadalbane estate include the land recorded as outfield as well as infield.

Not all surveys are so specific. But even so, they can still demonstrate the gross imbalance between arable and pasture. For instance, Sir Alexander Murray's model survey of 'Anatomie of Ardnamoruchan and Swinard' in 1723 sets the pennyland assessment of each town against its total acreage. Except for two touns with eight and nine pennylands, most of the touns in Ardnamurchan were only six pennylands, and therefore could not have commanded much more than 50 acres (20 ha) of arable infield. Despite this, 24 had a total acreage of over 1,000 (405 ha). A 1760 survey of touns in Glenlivet belonging to the Gordon estate notes the arable acreage of both infield and outfield but not the acreage of the surrounding pasture. It shows that most touns had access to 50 to 100 acres (20 to 40 ha). A glance at the various plans drawn up, though, soon confirms that their available grazings were much more extensive. On Tiree, a 1768/9 survey records the 'mail land' assessment of each toun plus their total acreage. If a mail land is assumed to have been equal to two acres at the most, then all but three touns had less than 100 acres of infield. Again, their pasture formed the more extensive sector, generally being four or five times more extensive. Over-all, mail lands accounted for around 700 to 800 acres (282–324 ha) out of a total of 13,833 acres (5,600 ha).

Of cardinal importance to the trend of Highland history after 1650 is the reduction in the amount of land per tenant, family, or per capita, a reduction which reached critical levels by the mid-eighteenth century. The availability of detailed surveys, coupled with lists of tenants or inhabitants, enables this problem to be framed in fairly precise terms. Calculations based on a number of estates are presented in Table 7. Four types of indices have been derived: the amounts of arable per tenant, family, and person together with the total acreage (arable plus pasture) per person. In the case of those relating to families, the figures employed are those provided by the original surveys under this heading. The over-all conclusion to be drawn from Table 7, is that, given the nature of the environment and the vagaries of climate, the subsistence of many communities must have been narrowly and precariously based. Somewhat surprisingly, the rugged Assynt estate was one of only two estates (the other was Strathyre) with anything like a reasonable amount of arable per family. The average for other estates works out at around three to four acres

Table 7: The Amount of Arable and Arable plus Pasture per Tenant, Family, and Person on Highland Estates.

	Date	Arable	Arable plus Pasture
Ardnamurchan	1727		
	Family	3.0	267
	Person	0.6	58
Sunart	1723		
	Family	3.0	707
	Person	0.6	120
Strathyre	1755		
	Tenant	7	
	Family	7	
	Person	1.7	
Barrasdale	1755		
	Tenant	1.39	
	Family	1.39	
	Person	0.2	
Tiree	1768/9		57
	Tenant	13	57
	Tenant/Cottar	7.5	34
	Person	1.8	8.2
Breadalbane	1769		
Lochtay–Northside	Tenant	11.8	35
Lochtay–Southside	Tenant	9.2	125
Assynt	1775		
	Tenant	9.4	222
	Household	11	260
	Person	2.1	52

Based on Stanhope, *True interest of Great Britain, Ireland and our Plantations*, Table vi; Wills (ed.), *Statistics of the Annexed Estates 1755–56*, pp. 1–5; Cregeen (ed.), *Argyll Estate Instructions*, plan of Tiree; McArthur (ed.), *Survey of Lochtayside*, pp. 1 ff.; Home (ed.), *Survey of Assynt*, pp. 1–88.

per family, but falls to as little as two acres on the Barrasdale and Slisgarrow estates. Recalculated in terms of arable acreage per person, the general average on all estates falls to two acres or less. Because of its large household size, even the Assynt estate fared badly with only two acres per person. Other estates, such as Barrasdale, Slisgarrow, or Kinloch and Merlagan, averaged under one acre. Of course, in terms of the total acreage available (or arable plus pasture), these figures need uprating, with estates like Assynt and Ardnamurchan having between them as much as 20 to 30 acres (8 to 12 ha) per person. Nor did each person or family command equal access to these resources. Those who were actually tenants or tacksmen must have managed much better than those who were only cottars or even landless. Even amongst tenants, there could be significant differences. Those on the Assynt estate, for instance, can be grouped into tenants who possessed the large pastoral holdings of the interior as individual tenures, and those of lesser status who shared a multiple-tenant toun on the coast with a group of other farmers.[46] The same contrast between large and small tenants prevailed on Mull, at least by the time of a 1742 to 1743 rental.[47] Islay too, was an island where tenants were of unequal status. 'Islay is occupy'd by two class of tenants' declared a letter of 1770, 'viz., the great, or gentlemen tenants, and the small tenants,—the gentlemen tenants possessing several quarterlands extending to three or four thousand acres and upwards . . . The small tenants, four, five, six or eight of them, enjoy a quarterland promiscuously among them.'[48]

The figures in Table 7 must be seen in the context of a steady downward trend. The lists of inhabitants for Rannoch suggest this downward trend was certainly in progress by the late seventeenth century, and was ongoing over the first half of the eighteenth century.[49] A view of trends during the middle decades is available for Ardnamurchan and Sunart. Between 1723 and 1792, their population rose by almost 90 per cent, two-thirds of this increase occurring after Dr Webster's census in 1755.[50] The acreages per family and per person given in Table 7 and based on 1723 data, therefore, were probably diminished still further in 1792. The rapid increase which had set in by the second half of the eighteenth century is clearly delineated by evidence for Tiree. In 1755, its population was 1509. By 1768, it had risen to

---

[46] Adam (ed.), *Survey of Assynt*, pp. xlv–xlviii. See also the analysis and discussion in A. Simms, *Assynt. Die Kulturlandschaft eines keltischen Reliktgevietes im nordwestschottischen Hochland*, Giessener Geographiche Schriften no. 16 (Giessen, 1969), pp. 16–25 and maps in rear folder.

[47] Cregeen (ed.), *Argyll Estate Instructions*, p. xiv.

[48] Smith, *Book of Islay*, p. 470.

[49] Altogether, the numbers of tenants, cottars, and servants increased from 104 to 165 between 1695 and 1743, the main increase occurring after 1735.

[50] Early figures based on Stanhope, *True Interest of Great Britain, Ireland and Our Plantations*, Table vi. For Dr Webster's figures, see J. G. Kyd (ed.), *Scottish Population Statistics*, SHS, 3rd ser., xliv (1949–50), p. 33. For 1792 figures, see *OSA* xx (1793), pp. 290–1.

1676 and, by 1792, to 2443.[51] Already, by 1768, all but three of its
31 touns carried more than one tenant, whilst all but two had at
least one cottar. The combined figures for the island at this point
were 241 tenants and 170 cottars.[52] Planned changes by the estate
disguise the fortunes of particular categories, but it is clear that
the number of small tenants increased dramatically over the next
two or three decades. Its average population per toun rose from
56 in 1768 to 82 in 1792, and by 1800 had reached 90.[53] Even by
1771, the island was being described by the Duke of Argyll
himself as 'over-peopled, and my farms oppress'd with a
numerous set of indigent tenants & cottars'.[54] This vigorous
growth of population after 1755 was part of a wider pattern of
growth that affected all parts of the Highlands and Islands.
Acting on the averages presented in Table 7, it would make M.
Gray's general estimate of barely 2½ acres (1 ha) per family by the
late eighteenth century plausible.[55] By then, many touns in the
western Highlands and Islands must have joined those described
in a mid-seventeenth-century survey of Shetland. In answer to an
inquiry about the parish of Erie and whether it was over-
populated, it was said that 'famelys ar here susteyned upon verie
small peeces of ground unworthie of appelation of rowmes' and, in
a glance at conditions around, 'touching the demand whether
there be any townmes in the paroche so burdened with
indwalleres for commoditite to the masters that the land may not
susteyne them, we answer, that not onlie here in this paroche, but
everie where in the whole country it is so.'[56] For comparison the
surveyor of the Forfeited Estates in 1755 was of the same opinion
about touns which he came across on estates like those of Lovat
and Cromarty, arguing that the holdings they provided for
tenants were 'too small'.[57] It hardly surprises that a later observer
classed the tenants there as 'the most beggardly wretches he ever
saw'.[58]

[51] Kyd (ed.), *Scottish Population Statistics*, p. 35; Cregeen (ed.), *Argyll Estate Instructions*, pp. xxviii–xxix; *OSA* x (1794), p. 403.
[52] Cregeen (ed.), *Argyll Estate Instructions*, list on map in rear folder.
[53] George Douglas, Duke of Argyll, *Crofts aand Farms in the Hebrides—an Account of the Management of an Island Estate for 130 Years* (Edinburgh, 1883), pp. 4–19.
[54] Cregeen (ed.), *Argyll Estate Instructions*, p. 1.
[55] Gray, *The Highland Economy 1750–1850*, pp. 240–1.
[56] Peterkin, *Rentals*, no. III, Documents Relating to the Bishopric of Orkney, p. 72.
[57] Wills (ed.), *Reports on the Annexed Estates 1755–1769*, p. 47.
[58] Millar (ed.), *Scottish Forfeited Estate Papers 1715–45*, p. 72.

(a)   The Farming Township: Its Layout

The disposition of Highland touns was marked not only by an excess of hill pasture over arable, but also, by the sprawling, fragmented nature of the latter. Surveyors' reports for estates like those of Assynt and Breadalbane constantly stress its broken nature, drawing out its responsiveness to the discontinuous and begrudging opportunities of the Highland environment with its mosaic of moss and machair, peat and pasture.[59] Moreover, the further north and west, the more were such opportunities confined to coastal sites. In 1700, it was said of Lewis that 'the arable land of the countrie lyes be the sea-syde round about.'[60] A. Brand passed a similar observation on Sutherland, dismissing its arable as 'a few ridges nigh to the Coasts'.[61] The interior of both areas contained vast expanses of hill grazings. This juxtapositioning and proportioning of arable and pasture was commonplace throughout the northern and western Highlands. However, although the amount of arable was limited, most commentators were impressed by its extent under the circumstances. In one of his valuable letters written from the Highlands in the 1720s, E. Burt, an English army officer, reflected that he had not 'seen the least spot that would bear corn uncultivated, not even upon the sides of the hills, where it could be no otherwise broke up than with a spade'.[62] In a phrase, he was expressing the very crux of the Highland problem. Here was Britain's least favourably endowed region as regards the potential for arable farming, with its rugged, mountainous terrain, high rainfall, strong winds, short growing season, and thin, acid soils—conditions designed to inhibit all but the hardiest of crops and cultivators—and yet, it was one in which tillage was fundamental to the rural economy.

The lengths to which the Highlander went in order to secure his arable are manifest in the marginal lands he was prepared to

---

[59] Adam (ed.), *Survey of Assynt*, p. 42. provides a not untypical example with the corn lands of Oldernay being described as 'much broke and interjected with Rocks, and Stony Baulks'. McArthur (ed.), *Survey of Lochtayside*, p. 46 provides the example of Drummaglass, which had its 'high outfds.', together with those of adjacent touns, described as 'divided into so many small spotts that it was thought unnecessary to distinguish the divisions'.

[60] *Geographical Collections*, vol. ii, p. 213.

[61] Brand, *A Brief Description of Orkney, Zetland, Pightland-Firth and Caithness*, p. 112.

[62] *Burt's Letters*, p. 51.

crop, land so difficult that it demanded of him almost a garden-like approach to its preparation and cultivation. On the Assynt estate, for example, many touns were described in the 1700 survey as having recently cultivated 'mossland'.[63] Others, like Clachtoll, had their arable described as 'extremely rocky and so much interjected with that ploughing with Horses or Cattle would be quite impracticable'.[64] The arable of Inver, mean-while, was of 'the poorest Soil, and most interjected with Rocks and Baulks, the last . . . full of Oak Roots'.[65] That of Culack likewise, was 'very much broke and interjected with patches of Wet Moss, and craigy Banks, so that one half it can only be reckon'd tillable'.[66] Tenants on the Breadalbane estate nego-tiated their ploughs and spades around similar obstacles. On Blarliargen, part of the infield was classed 'rocky; uneavenly and not all so good. There are others above the road very steep and craggy . . .'[67] On Little Comry, the outfields were noted as 'high, scattered and bare',[68] whilst those of Marrag-ness rated as 'steep and rising'.[69]

Epitomizing the way in which the evolving layout of the Highland toun was adjusted to the sparse opportunities present is the cultivation of shieling sites, a practice which became common by the end of the seventeenth century as the pressure on land increased. The salient factor here was not the extreme barrenness or ruggedness of such sites, for as R. Miller reasoned, centuries of grazing by stock must have fertilized the spots around the shieling huts themselves.[70] Rather was their problem one of sheer physical isolation and inaccessibility from the main arable core of the toun. This is demonstrated by Henry Home's plan of the Assynt estate, 1774. The cultivated shieling sites marked on the plan mostly comprised plots of a few acres located in the very heart of Assynt, up to five or six miles from the toun to which they were

---

[63] See, e.g., Adam (ed.), *Survey of Assynt*, p. 44.
[64] Ibid., p. 12.
[65] Ibid., p. 28.
[66] Ibid., p. 17.
[67] McArthur (ed.), *Survey of Lochtayside*, p. 18.
[68] Ibid., p. 65.
[69] Ibid., p. 11.
[70] R. Miller, 'Land Use by Summer Shielings', *SS* ii (1967), p. 198. His point was anticipated by the surveyor of the Assynt estate, John Home. Writing of the farm of Store, he reported that the 'Sheelings ly scatter'd among the Hills and are very rich and fertile by toathing.' See Adam (ed.), *Survey of Assynt*, p. 44.

linked.[71] In fact, where shielings were cultivated, their isolation from the main body of the toun often led to their separation and incorporation as independent touns. V. Gaffney's work on Strathavon uncovered a number of examples. For instance, the tenant of Achriachan and Findron was required in an agreement of 1721 to renounce all rights in the shielings of Lettermore and Blairnamorrow, whilst the tenants of West Camdell were compelled by a tack of 1735 to improve their shielings only to see them to be set as a separate toun at a later date.[72] This hiving-off of shieling sites must be seen in the context of an ongoing process of new settlement formation involving marginal or peripheral sites. A set of plans for touns in Inveravon (Banffshire) that was drawn up in 1761 reveals this wider process graphically with ample signs of outfields and pasture grounds succumbing to new encroachments and settlement. One actually bore the note that it 'Exhibits the New Land that is lately taken Inn to Corn Land off the pasture And is not Incorporate with the Old plows But are in Separate Tacks and Crofts'.[73]

Another manifestation of the pressures acting on the layout of Highland touns was the cultivation of haugh land. In the Highlands, this constituted attractive land for the farmer, being both level and fertile. However, it carried a high risk with it for many rivers in the Highlands, but especially those which are highly braided, were prone to extensive flooding and changes of channel. But many farmers, it seems, were prepared to take this risk during the late seventeenth and eighteenth centuries. Early eighteenth-century rentals for the Seaforth properties in Easter Ross, for instance, refer to a number of touns in which arable land had been swept away when the highly-braided streams of the area flooded or changed course.[74] In Argyllshire, a description of the River Shira around the turn of the century talks of both homesteads and arable being swept away: where they once ploughed, it was said, they now catch salmon, and vice versa.[75]

[71] Ibid., see map at frontispiece.
[72] Gaffney (ed.), *Lordship of Strathavon*, p. 31.
[73] SRO, RHP2487.
[74] MacPhail (ed.), *Highland Papers*, vol. ii, p. 343.
[75] *Geographical Collections*, vol. ii, p. 146. Other examples can be found in *Black Book of Taymouth*, pp. 359–60 and MacLeod (ed.), *Book of Dunvegan*, vol. ii, p. 79. The latter cites the conditions that were to be inserted in tacks *c.*1769. One was that when 'rivers overflow

Although the physical disposition of Highland touns is relatively well documented, that of landholding within them is not.
A number of runrig plans, most dating from the mid- or late
nineteenth century, exist for the Northern Isles (see Plate 3).
However, for the main body of the Highlands and Islands runrig
plans are scarce. Early surveys were content to record the
disposition of arable, pasture, and settlement and no more (see
Figs. 8.1 and 2 and Plates 4, 5, and 6). Presumably, this was a

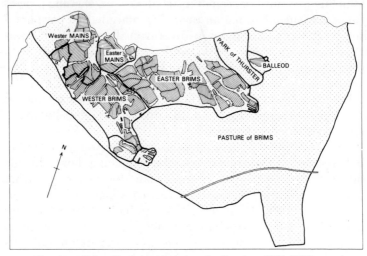

FIG. 8.1.   Brims Estate (Caithness), 1769. Based on SRO, RHP 1219

function of the transient nature of landholding for there was
hardly much point in mapping, at a greatly increased cost, a
layout of individual strips or rigs if it was liable to change from
year to year. Some surveyors, however, pleaded the sheer
intricacy of landholding as the main reason for not depicting
runrig in their surveys. Thus, a 1761 plan of the Daugh of
Fodderletter (Banffshire) carried the note that its four ploughs
'are subset to Different Tenants and so Runridged they cannot be
easily cast in plows'.[76] Likewise, when surveying the touns of

and do damage, all the neighbouring tenants are bound to give their services to manage
the waters'.
   [76] SRO, RHP2487, Daugh of Fodderletter.

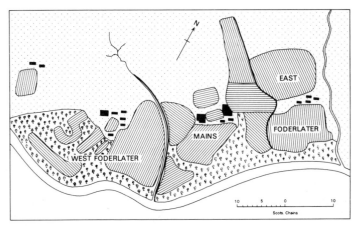

Fig. 8.2.   West, Mains, and East Fod(d)erlater (Banffshire), 1761. Based on SRO, RHP 2488/3

Nether and Upper Dalachy in the Barony of Fochaber, the surveyor excused himself with the words that the 'two Dalachy are all Runridged and could not be well nor exactly shown here as the Scale is small'.[77]

(b)   The Farming System

Farming in the Highlands and Islands continued to be structured around infield–outfield systems throughout this period. Indeed, it is only from this period that we get the first really explicit descriptions of its nature in the region. A 1769 survey of the Breadalbane property in the Netherlorn distict of Argyll provides one of the best for detail. According to the survey, the farms were

divided into Two great Divisions, The one Infield or wintertown as they Called it and the other outfield or Teath ground. This outfield may be about Two thirds of the farm and divided into Three divisions, one of these Divisions teathed all Summer with the Cattle and brock up the insuing spring for oats then take Two or three Crops of oats of this in a succession without any more manure and afterwards let it lye out in ley till they go over the rest in the same rotation. The infield which may be

[77] SRO, RHP2313/7.

about one third of the farm Divided into Three Divisions one in Barley, one in Oats, one in rye and potatoes. This they follow in rotation, by giving all the dung the farm produces to this portion of land, Of course the other Two thirds must be in an impoverished State.[78]

A similar cropping system existed on the Perthshire section of the Breadalbane estate.[79] However, it must not be taken as typical of all parts of the Highlands nor representative of all periods. Descriptions of other areas suggest that more elemental cropping systems prevailed on infield with only bear and oats being grown.[80] Outfield too, varied, with many touns reportedly cropping up to half.[81] There were also variations of a more fundamental character. On the Assynt estate, infield was supplemented not by an outfield as such, but by cultivated 'sheelings'.[82] A nineteenth-century account of farming on Heisgier in the Hebrides varied in the opposite way, consisting solely of an outfield-type cropping system, with arable being moved to a new plot every three years, the entire arable being cultivated on a nine-year long rotation.[83]

It needs little familiarity with the evidence for Highland farming from 1650 to 1780, to realize it contains many symptoms of a population rapidly outstripping its resources. In his report about Oldernay on the Assynt estate, Home exclaimed that nothing 'can exceed the richness and luxuriance of both Corn and Bear which this and all the Coasting Farms upon the Estate produce, both growing to the height of an ordinary Man, particularly Bear which is the principal Crop, yielding no less for common than sixty peaks from sowing one ...'[84] There are reports of similar high yields for parts of the Hebrides. However, generally speaking, they were much lower, even where turf and seaweed were available in quantity.[85] As more and more difficult

[78] SRO, RHP972/5.

[79] McArthur (ed.), *Survey of Lochtayside*, p. 11.

[80] See, e.g., *OSA* ii (1794), p. 264; ibid., ix (1793), p. 494; D. W. Kempe (ed.), *Tours in Scotland 1747, 1750 and 1760 by Richard Pococke*, Scottish History Society, i (1887), p. 149; Brand, *A Brief Description of Zetland, Pightland-Firth and Caithness*, p. 27; Marwick, *Place Names of Birsay*, p. 115.

[81] Individual cases of cropping are given in McArthur (ed.), *Survey of Lochtayside*, pp. 8–9; Wills (ed.), *Reports on the Annexed Estates 1755–1769*, p. 66; *OSA* viii (1793), p. 99.

[82] Adam (ed.), *Survey of Assynt*, pp. 3 ff.

[83] Skene, *Celtic Scotland*, vol. iii, p. 378.

[84] Adam (ed.), *Survey of Assynt*, p. 42.

[85] *Geographical Collections*, vol. iii, p. 22; Martin, op. cit., pp. 42 and 53.

ground was cropped, returns of only three or four became the norm. This decline in yields is embodied in the experience of Tiree. Known by the Iona monks as *terra ethica* or land of corn, and described by Dr Johnson (admittedly not an authority on the matter) as 'eminent for its fertility',[86] its productivity was already in decline before the latter visited it. Martin toured the island in 1699 and reported that although it had 'always been valued for its extraordinary fruitfulness in corn, yet being in tillage every year, it has become less fruitful than formerly'.[87] An official survey of the Argyll ducal estate in 1737 put it more bluntly: continuous cropping and inadequate manuring, it concluded, had reduced yields sharply, and whilst the fields appeared thick with herbage, 'hardly one tenth of them is corn, the rest is all wild carrot, mustard, etc'.[88]

Critical to the subsistence of many Highland touns was the broad strategy of using the resources of their vast non-agricultural sector to sustain their vital but small arable sector. This meant the continuation and probable expansion of techniques like the heavy application of seaweed, soils, peat, and turf to cultivated land. As cultivation spread on to more and more difficult ground, the use of hand-intensive tools like the spade of caschrom spread apace. Delving with a spade or caschrom was reported on islands like Toronsay or St Kilda back in the sixteenth century.[89] Although 'a severe and tedious manner' of cultivation,[90] it had the advantage of being practical where the plough was not and of preparing the ground more thoroughly. Martin, for instance, wrote that ground prepared in this way on Skye and Lewis actually yielded more than when prepared with the conventional plough.[91] However, there was more to the use of the spade or caschrom than practical necessity. It made full use of a plentiful resource, namely, labour. Home saw this connection when commenting on its practice on the Assynt estate in 1774. Talking specifically about the use of the caschrom, he wrote that it 'is carryed on throughout all the coasting Farms, and it would surprise a Stranger who knew nothing of the strength and

---

[86] Johnson, op. cit., p. 133.
[87] Martin, op. cit., p. 267.
[88] *Report of the Commissioners of Inquiry into the Conditions of the Crofters and Cottars*, p. 392.
[89] Skene, *Celtic Scotland*, vol. iii, p. 431.
[90] Adam (ed.), *Survey of Assynt*, p. 42.
[91] Martin, op. cit., pp. 3 and 140.

number of the people so that they would not readily believe so great an extent of Ground as they have in tillage could be done in this way'.[92] Bound up with its use was the technique of lazy beds to achieve a greater soil depth. Again, there was a virtue in necessity, for writing of lazy beds or *Timiy* on Lewis, Martin believed they produced 'a greater Increase then dyging or plowing otherwise'.[93] Considered altogether, these various husbandry techniques suggest a labour-intensive system, a system in which the high labour input was vital in maintaining the equilibrium between land and people, especially in marginal areas. This role of human effort in sustaining such large numbers of people on the land is summed up in a phrase about Shetland, an area where land pressure had been reached early on. 'The industrie of the poor labourers', it was said, 'doeth exceed the fertilitie of the ground.'[94] It is perhaps to this period that we should look for the origin of the Lewis saying that 'work without a threesome is hard, and sore it is without a foursome.'[95]

(c)   The Farm Economy

The farm economy of the Highlands was geared to subsistence, not exclusively but certainly as a matter of priority. Everything else was subordinate, at least in the mind of the peasant. However, if the commercial side of the farm economy was given a low priority by the peasant, it must not be neglected by the historian. However unwilling he may have been, the Highlander was drawn into a regular trade in farm produce, notably livestock and livestock produce. This trade was bound up with his rent obligations. But, unlike the south and east of the country, it was not solely a case of landowners trading produce paid as rent. Contrary to usual assumptions on the backward nature of upland areas, but consistent with the constraints imposed by its isolation, many touns in the western and northern Highlands paid a money rent by the late seventeenth century. The Highland tenant, therefore, often had a more direct involvement in marketing than his Lowland counterpart over

[92] Adam (ed.), *Survey of Assynt*, p. 42.
[93] Martin, op. cit., p. 3.
[94] Peterkin, *Rentals*, no. III, Documents Relating to Bishopric of Orkney, p. 70.
[95] A. Geddes, *The Isles of Lewis and Harris* (Edinburgh, 1955), p. 21; idem, 'Conjoint-Tenants and Tacksmen in the Isle of Lewis, 1715–26', *ECHR*, 2nd ser., i (1948–49), p. 57.

this period. This was not a spontaneous involvement in the marketing process, simply something into which tenants were drawn by their rent obligations. Only during the opening decades of the eighteenth century did Highland farmers begin to shift more wholeheartedly into stock production because they perceived market opportunities for it.

Basically, the subsistence economy of Highland touns revolved largely around grain-cropping. There were some areas, like Durness, which relied on livestock produce (though not meat) all year round[96] and others, particularly in the northern Isles, where fish was important,[97] but the staple diet of most Highlanders was oatmeal and barley, with fish or dairy produce being only supplementary.[98] This dependence on grain was only relaxed with the introduction and spread of the potato from the 1730s onwards. First cultivated in the Uists, it diffused slowly at first.[99] Only during the closing two or three decades of the eighteenth century did its adoption become widespread, establishing itself as the staple food of many of the more marginal touns for over half the year.[1] For most of the period 1650–1780, it was still the nature of the grain harvest that determined whether communities faced a crisis of subsistence or not. Broadly speaking, the various parts of the Highlands and Islands can be grouped into those which were self-sufficient in meal or grain in all but the poorest of years, and those which faced the risks of scarcity year in, year out. Into the former category fell areas like Caithness, Orkney, and surprisingly Lewis. Into the latter fell areas like Rannoch, Strathnaver, and Shetland. The experience of these two types of area diverged, but not radically so. Those with inadequate provision constantly faced the need to import meal. Shetland, for instance, was

[96] Kempe (ed.), op. cit., p. 127.

[97] See the comments of Brand, *A Brief Description of Orkney, Zetland, Pightland-Firth and Caithness*, p. 110.

[98] See, e.g., the stress on oats and barley in *Geographical Collections*, vol. ii, p. 212 and vol. iii, pp. 61 and 83.

[99] The most informative account of the spread of potatoes through the Highlands and Islands is J. E. Handley, *Scottish Farming in the Eighteenth Century* (London, 1953), pp. 176–89 but esp. pp. 181–4. Since writing this section, a 1729 reference to potatoes in Rannoch has been found in SRO, GD50, Menzies Book of Tacks 1684–1738.

[1] The *OSA* reporter for Dornoch parish in Sutherland, viii (1793), p. 4 conveyed a widespread situation when he declared that potatoes 'serve as the chief subsistence of the people during a third part of the year, with many for *one half*, and with some even for *two thirds* of the year'.

estimated to grow only one-third of its needs, the rest being made up by shipments from Orkney and Caithness.[2] The constant threat of starvation that was endemic to some of these areas was met with rent rebates, enabling tenants to buy extra meal on the open market, or largesse, in the form of meal. Its recurrent nature is well conveyed by Burt's comment that in parts of the northern Highlands, the 'Poverty of the Tenants has rendered it Customary for the Chief, or Laird, to free some of them, every Year, from all Arrears of Rent; this is supposed, upon an Average to be about one Year in five of the whole Estate.'[3] Similarly, in Struan and Lochgarry (Perthshire), it was reported that tenants could not grow enough grain even in 'the best years' and 200 bolls of meal were imported annually,[4] whilst the inhabitants of Lochaber were said to need 6,000 bolls annually.[5] On a visit to the higher parts of Perthsire, Andrew Wight confirmed the difficulty which the area had in feeding itself. He wrote in his report for the Forfeited Estate Commissioners that the 'state of the Country, with respect to provisions, is truly deplorable. Meal is the chief article used by the farmers, and all of the lower class, for food; and at the time I was among them, a few of the tenants excepted, no family had oatmeal in their houses, nor could get any; and they were living on bear-meal only, and not even mixed with pease.'[6]

On the face of it, areas like Caithness and Orkney fared much better, producing regular surpluses of grain and meal for export to other parts of Scotland and abroad.[7] However, it was precisely in these areas that grain rents persisted longest, and much of the trade generated consisted of grain abstracted from the local market economy by landowners. In Orkney it was collected in the form of either skat or rent victuals. Although it formed only part of the tenant's liabilities, alongside geese, poultry, *screa*, or dried fish, and oil, the cumulative amount so collected seems to have been considerable.[8] A hint at the highly organized nature of

[2] Brand, *A Brief Description of Orkney, Zetland, Pightland-Firth and Caithness*, p. 110.

[3] *Burt's Letters*, vol. i, p. 158.

[4] Millar (ed.), *Scottish Forfeited Estate Papers 1715–45*, p. 263.

[5] Pennant, *A Tour in Scotland 1769*, p. 228.

[6] Wight, *Present State of Husbandry in Scotland*, vol. i, pp. 87–8.

[7] Kemp (ed.), op. cit., p. 139; Brand, *A Brief Description of Orkney, Zetland, Pightland-Firth and Caithness*, p. 225; Donaldson, *Caithness in the Eighteenth Century*, p. 186. According to the figures assembled by Donaldson, the amount of grain dispatched from Caithness effectively doubled over the first half of the 18th century.

[8] Instances of rent being paid in these commodities can be found in 'Rentall of the

the grain trade in Caithness is provided by the agreement by which Sir James Sinclair of Mey, David Sinclair of Southdun, and Patrick Dunbar contracted to provide from their respective estates 900 bolls of grain (half bear, half meal) and to deliver it on board a ship at Staxigo. The buyers were merchants from Leven and Winthank. Later the same year, a further contract was drawn up for 238 bolls of bear and 195 bolls of meal.[9] Staxigo was obviously a major transhipment port for the trade, for in the late seventeenth century, the Earl of Caithness constructed warehouses there capable of holding 4,000 bolls of bear and 4,000 bolls of oats.[10] Had he been able to fill them, he would have been responsible for almost half the grain exported out of Caithness, for Brand put the amount exported at 16,000 bolls per annum.[11] The involuntary participation of tenants in such trade, however, had its problems. Brand saw this when he complained that the 'Rents when Collected, whether payed in Money, Meal, Oats, Barly or Butter are ordinarily sent south, when causeth a great grudge among the People, some of them there being redacted to great straits not getting Meal, Barley or the like sometimes to buy as in the late dearth.'[12] Others too, felt this was a real grievance on Orkney. According to one inhabitant, the Orkney tenant was trapped by his circumstances. Remote in physical and organizational terms from the main grain markets, he was unable himself to capitalize on his good harvests. Only his landlord had the means and will to overcome these problems. When his crop failed, and he was forced to pay the current market price for his grain rents, these same problems of isolation ensured that this price would be high, a misfortune that 'reduced many to beggary'. There was no prospect, therefore, of balancing the good with the bad, for 'the good years is nothing more tollerable to us nor the deir yeare.'[13] That such areas could suffer along with their less productive neighbours in really poor years is readily documented. Orkney, for instance, was said to have lost

---

Neithertown of Stroma 1719', p. 125 in A. W. Johnston (ed.), *Old Lore Miscellany of Orkney, Shetland, Caithness and Sutherland* ix, *Old Lore Series*, xi (1933); Peterkin, *Rentals*, book VI.

[9] Donaldson, *Caithness in the Eighteenth Century*, p. 157.

[10] Ibid., p. 186.

[11] Brand, *A Brief Description of Orkney, Zetland, Pightland-Firth and Caithness*, p. 225.

[12] Ibid., pp. 39–40.

[13] Peterkin, *Rentals*, Appendix, section III, pp. 74–5.

one-third of its inhabitants during the succession of poor harvests from 1695 to 1702.[14] Further sporadic crop failures litter the eighteenth century, bringing with them financial crisis, starvation, or both. Thus, on the Earl of Moray's lands in Caithness, crop failures in both 1716 and 1722 led to many tenants becoming bankrupt, despite rents being waived.[15] Further south, in Easter Ross, a comparable dilemma arose during the poor harvests of the early 1770s. On the Lovat estate lands in Kilmorack parish, meal was ordered to be bought from Aberdeenshire or Banffshire and 'sold to the tenants in small quantities, and some given to the poor to prevent them from starving, most of the gentlemen of estate in that neighbourhood in the Higlands finding themselves under the necessity of nursing their tenants on this melancholy occasion'.[16]

For most Highland tenants, trade to them meant livestock or livestock products. Surveys of stock carried by touns (see Table 8)

Table 8: Number of Livestock Per Toun on Highland Estates

	Date	Number of Sheep Per Toun	Number of Cattle Per Toun
Ardnamurchan	1727	63	63
Sunart	1727	159	159
Strathyre	1755	86	44
Barrasdale	1755	29	33
Breadalbane:			
Lochtay–Southside	1769	90	24

Based on Stanhope, *True Interest of Great Britain, Ireland and Our Plantations*, Table vi; Wills (ed.), *Statistics of the Annexed Estates 1755–56*, pp. 1–5; McArthur (ed.), *Survey of Lochtayside*, pp. 1 ff.

suggest that most touns and most tenants possessed both sheep and cattle. Compared with the stocking balance of more recent times, with its vastly greater emphasis on sheep, the outstanding feature of these pre-1780 stocking figures is the more equal balance between the two. In Ardnamurchan and Sunart, for

[14] Storer Clouston (ed.), *The Orkney Parishes*, p. 153, note. For a considered appraisal of such claims, see Flinn (ed.), *Scottish Population History*, pp. 164–85.

[15] Donaldson, *Caithness in the Eighteenth Century*, pp. 22–4.

[16] Millar (ed.), *Scottish Forfeited Estate Papers 1715–45*, p. 85.

example, a rigid system of stents or soums meant that their numbers were exactly equal, with 2,016 of each in Ardnamurchan and 1,160 of each in Sunart. On the various Forfeited Estates, there were some, like Barrasdale or the Baronies of Corgach (Cromarty estate), Beauly (Lovat estate), and Stratherrick (Lovat estate) on which cattle predominated, but others, like Lix, Strathyre, Balquidder, and Comrie, on which sheep did. In terms of value, though, cattle must have been the more important everywhere, possibly more so in the north and west than in the southern Highlands.[17] Certainly, it was the sale of cattle that provided tenants with their prime source of money for rent. Each year, tenants would subscribe a few cattle to the large organized droves that made their way to the great cattle fairs at Dunbeath in the far north or Crieff and Falkirk to the south, where up to 30,000 cattle might be assembled.[18] Needless to say, information tends to be more readily forthcoming for the larger cattle dealers and farmers than for the great mass of tenants who contributed one or two stock per year to a drove. However, typical of the latter must have been the group of 24 tenants from 10 different touns on the Forfeited Estates whose dealings were analysed by M. Gray. Between them they sold 68 cattle in a year, raising £150 13s. Of this, £79.3s.8d. was spent on their rent, and the rest on meal.[19] Altogether, he estimated that tenants on the estates of Stratherrick, Clunie, Strathgartney, and Strathyre derived one-half of their rent from the sale of their cattle.[20] Cattle were a logical item of farm produce to trade. There was a demand for them, their sale did not jeopardize subsistence of the toun, they made use of an abundant resource, and they walked themselves to market.

However, beyond the sale of a few cattle, the average Highland toun had little to spare. Their inability to generate a broader- or larger-scale trade in farm produce is emphatically captured in a description of Inverness market by Burt. 'Here are four or five Fairs in the Year', he wrote in one letter,

[17] M. Gray, 'Economic Welfare and Money Income in the Highlands, 1750–1850', *Scottish Jnl. of Political Economy*, ii (196), p. 52.
[18] Descriptions of the trysts at both Crieff and Falkirk during the early 18th century can be found in A. R. B. Haldane, *The Drove Roads of Scotland* (London, 1952), pp. 24 and 138–44.
[19] Gray, 'Economic Welfare and Money Income in the Highlands, 1750–1850', p. 53.
[20] Ibid., p. 53. See also *OSA* viii (1793), p. 375.

When the Highlanders bring their Commodities to the Market: but, good God! you could not conceive there was such misery in this island. One has under his arm a small Roll of linen, another a Piece of coarse Plaiding: these are considerable Dealers. But the Merchandise of the greatest Part of them is of a most contemptible Value, such as these; viz.—two or three cheeses, of about three or four Pounds weight a piece; a kid sold for sixpence or Eight pence at most; a small Quantity of Butter, in something that looks like a Bladder, and is sometimes set down upon the dirt in the street; three or four Goat skins; a Piece of Wood for an Axeltree to one of the little Carts, &c.[21]

Nor was Inverness alone in having little to show for its hinterland. J. Knox was equally damming of boroughs like Wick, Dornoch, Tain, Dingwall, and Fortrose, touns which carried the 'high-sounding appelation of royal boroughs, but which, in reality, are nothing more than ruinous villages, exhibiting all the symptons of decay, poverty and distress'.[22]

But even as Burt wrote back in the 1720s, vital changes were afoot which affected the orientation of the Highland farm economy and its responsiveness to market opportunities. The change developed from an enhanced awareness of the commercial value of cattle. Initially, cattle held a somewhat ambivalent place in the farm economy of the region. They provided part of the manure that was essential to cultivation in an area of high rainfall and leaching. But in many touns, they did so only through the tathing of outfield. Infield received little stock manure largely because it was not everywhere customary for stock to be grazed on the harvest stubble. This was because the cereal crop was harvested by pulling it up, roots and all, rather than by cutting it with a sickle or scythe. The grain itself was extracted by *graddaning*, or burning away the husk and straw. Not only was there no stubble for grazing by this method but, after burning, there was little straw either.[23] In some areas, cattle were not even housed during winter, so that there was not even a supply of manure from the byre. Broadly speaking, cattle in such areas were maintained by pasture and pasture alone, either

[21] *Burt's Letters*, vol. ii, p. 83.

[22] J. Knox, *A View of the British Empire More Especially Scotland* (London, 1784), p. 17.

[23] Early references to graddaning include Martin, op. cit., pp. 204–5; *The Highlands of Scotland in 1750*, pp. 93–4; Mitchell, 'James Robertson's Tour Through Some of the Western Islands, ETC, of Scotland', p. 15.

machair or hill grazings. Furthermore, where pressure on land was acute, such pasture was confined to the poorest land or the uncultivated parts of outfield.[24] Quite a number of surveys stress the disinterest of Highland touns in making adequate provision for the grassing of their stock, especially during winter. Since the summer carrying capacity of the hills was set by the number that could be over-wintered in a toun, this lack of any provision during winter was especially serious. And yet, in spite of this marginal or scavenger-like existence on some touns, cattle represented the one item which tenants could sell in order to raise their cash rents.

Over the opening decades of the eighteenth century, some tenants and landowners began to perceive the growing commercial possibilities of cattle-rearing. In so far as cattle had long been marketed, this was not outwardly a radical change. But it did represent an important change in attitude, a positive response to the rising level of demand for lean stock from English graziers or fatteners. Alongside the small tenant selling one or two animals a year, there now appeared tacksmen holding large pastoral holdings whose interest and dealings in cattle were on an entirely new scale. Cregeen has traced the emergence of this new outlook on the Argyll estate. Its pioneers were men like Archibald Campbell of Lochbuy, who devoted much of his Lochfyneside estate to cattle from 1728 onwards.[25] Following a reorganization of landholding in 1737, touns in the northern part of the estate were set to single tenants at a greatly increased rent. This increase was designed to realize their full commercial value, a value related to the opportunities offered by large-scale cattle production.[26] The large pastoral holdings held by single tacksmen in the interior parts of the Assynt have also been linked with the growth of cattle production on a new scale.[27] Some insight into the cause of this expanded production is provided by a document amongst the Breadalbane papers. It was drawn up in

[24] Quite the best illustration of this neglect of pasture is the story of an Englishman's reaction to conditions in early 18th-century Sutherland. At home, he said, they build their houses of stone and pasture their cattle on grass, but here, they build their houses of turf and pasture their cattle on stone. See *OSA* viii (1793), pp. 6–7.

[25] Cregeen, 'Tacksmen and their Successors', p. 114.

[26] Cregeen (ed.), *Argyll Estate Instructions*, p. xvi.

[27] Adam (ed.), *Survey of Assynt*, p. xlviii. Inland farms 'specialised in the raising of cattle for southern markets'.

1758 as a reasoned complaint against proposed legislation
allowing the import of Irish cattle into England. The author
argued that it would undermine the Highland cattle trade which
had grown up since the Union in 1707, and would threaten the
high rents that were based on it.[28] This stated relationship
between high rents and the growth of the cattle trade helps to
explain why many Highland estates did experience an increased
rent yield over the eighteenth century, *before the coming of sheep*. In
his *Wealth of Nations* (1776), Adam Smith put it down as a three-
or four-fold increase since the beginning of the century.[29] Actual
rent figures for estates like that of the MacLeods on Skye show he
was not far wrong (see Table 9). The rents of Harris and Glenelg
displayed similar increases. Much of the increase can no doubt be
put down to the higher profits on cattle, though part of it was
probably due to the general inflation of food prices after the
Union.[30] Of course, cattle prices shared in this inflation.
However, not all Highlanders gained as a result. For those
reduced to begging, it had a quite opposite effect. '. . . before the
Union they never presumed to ask for more than a *Bodle* (or the
sixth Part of a Penny), but now they beg for a *Baubee* (or
Halfpenny).'[31]

Table 9: Rent Increases on the MacLeod of MacLeod Estate

	1708	1724	1744	1754	1769	1777	
Duirinish	£269	285	352	521	896	829	
Bracadale	£277	278	335	450	818	690	*All figs. in*
Minginish	£215	231	249	318	538	451	*pounds sterling*
Waternish	£228	214	252	355	579	503	

Based on MacLeod (ed.), *Book of Dunvegan*, vol. ii, pp. 79 ff.

[28] M. McArthur, 'Some Eighteenth-Century Scottish Opinions on the Importation of
Irish Cattle Into Great Britain', *Scottish Jnl. of Agriculture*, xviii (1935), pp. 237–9.

[29] Smith, *Wealth of Nations*, vol. i, p. 222. Comment on this early 18th-century increase
in cattle prices and its impact on rents is fairly easy to come by. The anonymous *Highlands
of Scotland in 1750*, pp. 39–40, e.g., touched a common theme when he wrote that the
McKenzie tacksmen in Lewis 'are Remarkably disposed to grow Rich. They screwed
their rents to extravagant Height (which they vitiously term improving their Estates).'

[30] The general inflationary trend of prices after the Union deserves greater attention
from scholars, given its role in turning the ordinary Scotsman against it.

[31] *Burt's Letters*, vol. i, p. 144.

Late eighteenth-century commentators on the problems of the Highlands were quick to point out the need for economic diversification to drain off from agriculture what they saw as its supernumeraries.[32] Yet long before planned solutions with this intent were applied, many Highland communities had begun 'naturally' to exploit the potential of existing non-agricultural activities, like fishing and domestic industry, to a much greater degree. This growing diversification was instrumental in bringing Highland population to the critical levels reached by the late eighteenth century, stretching it finally beyond the capacity of agriculture as the sole means of livelihood and support.

With so many settlements fringing the coast, it was inevitable that pressure on land should engender a deeper commitment to fishing as a dietary and income supplement. However, whilst the opportunities for fishing were evenly spread around the coast, there were strong regional variations in the response to them. The area of greatest activity, where fishing formed 'the Foundation both of their Trade and wealth', was Shetland.[33] Perhaps because of its adverse ratio of people to land, as much as the richness of its fishing grounds, this had long been the case. Its importance was manifest in the way some households derived their entire means of support from it. As Brand remarked, there 'are many who follow no trade but their fishing'.[34] Its commercial organization, though, was something that developed late. In this aspect, they were, said J. Knox, 'animated and instructed by the Dutch',[35] who, along with Bremers and Hamburgers, had long fished the seas around Shetland, using its ports as a base for supplies. But over the seventeenth century, the Dutch found themselves inceasingly in conflict with the growing interests of the Shetlanders themselves. The outcome was that the number of Dutch *busses* fell and the number of local boats increased. According to O'Dell, a significant turning-point

---

[32] This is well exemplified by the writings of J. Knox. See *A Discourse on the Expediency of Establishing Fishing Stations or Small Towns in the Highlands of Scotland and Hebride Islands* (London, 1786). Pennant too, saw the need for diversification. Talking of Lochaber on his 1769 tour, he referred to the 'rage for raising rents' and then said that 'the great men begin at the wrong end, with sqeezing the bag, before they have helped the poor tenant to fill it, by the introduction of manufactures.' See Pennant, *A Tour in Scotland 1769*, p. 208.

[33] Martin, op. cit., p. 384.

[34] Brand, *A Brief Description of Orkney, Zetland, Pightland-Firth and Caithness*, p. 110.

[35] Knox, *View of the British Empire*, p. 21.

occurred in 1712 when a heavy duty was imposed on the import of foreign salt. Although this did not mean salt imports ceased, it did encourage Shetlanders to take over from the Dutch the role of fish curers and dealers.[36] The initiative was seized largely by landlords and merchants rather than ordinary peasants or fishermen. The role of the former was as suppliers as well as merchants, for some began to demand green or unsalted fish from coastal touns as part of their rent. A glimpse at the role of merchants is provided by the letter-book of Gifford of Busta, a merchant-landmaster who traded during the second quarter of the eighteenth century. We cannot say whether he was representative of his type, but his letter-book is certainly informative. Altogether, he declared his 'Commodities yearly exported are, salt well dried, cod, ling, tusk, and saith fish, some stock fish and salted herrings' as well as butter, oil, and stockings.[37] The scale of his dealings is conveyed by the three vessels he sent to Hamburg in 1744, and whose combined cargoes comprised 54,430 dried ling, 1,320 cod, 12 barrels of herring, 3 barrels of fish oil, 81 barrels of butter, and 100 pairs of stocking.[38] A hint at the gross trade in fish from Lerwick is afforded by customs lists detailing the export of fish cured with imported salt. During the 1740s and 1750s the main export was dried cod and ling, of which over 12,000 cwts was exported in 1750 alone. As with Gifford of Busta's trade, the main destination was Hamburg, with lesser amounts to Cadiz, Barcelona, and Lisbon. Imported by return cargo from the latter were considerable quantities of salt.[39]

Although contemporary accounts also credit Orkney with a sizeable trade in fish, the amounts involved were less. But it did share some of the characteristics of the Shetland industry. For instance, the economy of some communities was reported to be almost entirely devoted to fishing.[40] Furthermore, there are signs that landlords may have been responsible for broadening its value from an item of subsistence to being one of trade by collecting fish as part of a tenant's rent The 1719 rental for the Neithertoune of Stromay, with its payments of screa, was

---

[36] O'Dell, *Historical Geography of the Shetland Islands*, p. 114. See also, pp. 300–13.
[37] Extended extracts reprinted ibid., p. 303.
[38] Ibid., p. 305.
[39] Ibid.
[40] Brand, *A Brief Description of Orkney, Zetland, Pightland-Firth and Caithness*, p. 110.

probably no different to that of many coastal touns.[41] Most important of all, there was, as in Shetland, an instinctive attachment to fishing which made its expansion in step with population growth a natural progression. 'Most of the people of the Barony and Marwick', reflected one Orcadian of Birsay and Harray, 'are bred fishermen.'[42]

The west Highlander appears as a more unwilling partner to fishing. His unwillingness had deep roots. Back in the sixteenth century, the report drawn up on the Hebrides stated that large quantities of cod, ling, and herring were caught in the lochs that fretted the western seaboard, especially Gairloch and Lochs Broom, Hourne, and Fyne. However, most of the fish caught was by fleets of fishing boats that moved into the region in spring with the herring shoals, rather than by locals.[43] The west Highlander generally was in this respect like the men of Harris, 'unskilful in slaying of the fishes and salmond that cummis as thair neighbours are'.[44] His disinclination towards fishing puzzled many authorities who felt that it 'is, and certainly ought to be esteemed their proper harvest'.[45] Part of the reason for it, though, may have been the unpredictable nature of this harvest especially with regard to a fish like the herring. T. Pennant put this in a phrase when he said that 'their visits to the western isles and coasts, [was] certain; but their attachment to one particular loch, extremely precarious'.[46] Another may have been the lack of facility and organization for marketing fish through local outlets. An attempt to generate greater local involvement was made by establishing fishing stations, with curing houses, at Lochmaddy and Rodel in the early seventeenth century, but both ventures failed.[47] Attempts by the Earl of Seaforth to use Dutch fishermen to 'animate interest' also failed through the opposition of Scottish herring fleets, the latter being accused by the Dutch of breaking up their equipment and 'the schooles of their hering'.[48] By the

[41] 'Rentall of the Neithertown of Stroma 1719', *Old Lore Miscellany*, p. 155.
[42] *OSA* xiv (1795), p. 320.
[43] See, for instance, *Highlands of Scotland in 1750*, p. 33.
[44] Skene, *Celtic Scotland*, vol. iii, p. 430.
[45] *An Essay Upon the British Fisheries by a Caledonian Fisher* (Edinburgh, 1785).
[46] Pennant, *A Tour in Scotland 1769*, p. 239.
[47] *Report to the Secretary for Scotland by the Crofters Commission on the Social Conditions of the People of Lewis*, pp. xi and lv–lvi.
[48] *Collectanea de Rebus Albanicis*, p. 111

eighteenth century, the growth of population and pressure on land appears to have persuaded the west Highlander to think otherwise. Some, like the inhabitants of Durness, were still accused of neglecting the opportunities present,[49] but generally speaking, fishing assumed much more importance by the middle of the century. Estates responded differently. Some, like Gairloch, placed a levy on each fish caught by tenants.[50] Others, like that of Barrasdale, placed fishing on the list of services extracted from them.[51] On still others, tacksmen if not the estate took a share of the tenant's catch. There were even communities for whom it had become a primary source of income. Thus, when Home visited Baddindarroch on the Assynt estate in the 1770s, he found that in addition to the tenants, there were 'sundry others residing upon the Farm, whose chief Employment is at the Fishings'.[52] Its growing value is underlined by his further comment that 'as the Fishings are become an object worth attention any part of the Coast having a convenient landing place has the fairest chance for Establishing new settlements.'[53]

The eighteenth century also witnessed an expansion of textile production in the Highlands. The product mix was a varied one, ranging from both woollen and flax yarn to finished goods like linen cloth, stockings, hats, and gloves. Although the expansion of domestic industry was welcomed by some contemporaries as an antidote to the 'idleness' of the Highlanders[54] and a panacea for the economic problems of the region, its growth over this period had more complex mechanisms and motivations behind it. In the first place, it had no novelty about it. Cloth had long been demanded as part of a tenant's rent in many parts of the Highlands and Islands. In the north-east, it was called lining

---

[49] Brand, *A Brief Description of Orkney, Zetland, Pightland-Firth and Caithness*, p. 127.
[50] Gray, *Highland Economy, 1750–1850*, p. 116.
[51] Ibid.
[52] Adam (ed.), *Survey of Assynt*, p. 10. See also, pp. 17–19.
[53] Ibid., p. 14.
[54] See comments of A. J. Durie, 'Linen Spinning in the North of Scotland, 1746–1773', *Northern Scotland*, ii (1974–5), p. 13. The myth of the Highlander's idleness is a recurring theme in early accounts. *Burt's Letters*, vol. i, p. 148 tells of seeing a man basking 'in full dress' whilst his wife and mother-in-law worked at reaping the oats. On complaining, he was told by the mother-in-law that 'her Son-in-Law was a *Gentleman*, and it would be a Disparagement to him to do any such Work'.

cloth.[55] In Orkney and Shetland, it was wodmel or landmel.[56] In the case of the Hebridean islands like Harris, Tiree, and Islay, it was simply white cloth.[57] Such cloths continued to be manufactured, but over the first half of the eighteenth century, the emphasis was shifted more on to yarn, especially flax yarn. From the peasant's point of view, producing flax yarn was a valuable addition to the domestic economy, not least because it employed mainly women and children, leaving the men free for farm work and fishing. In so far as women had previously done more than a fair share of the latter, this was quite a significant adjustment in the labour regime of Highland touns. The point was not lost on contemporary observers. A survey of Balquidder (Perthshire) in 1755, for instance, found that the men were now more inclined to do the farm work themselves 'rather than take the women from the spinning'.[58] A petition submitted to the Forfeited Estates Commissioners in 1763, talks of the tenantry 'and their little ones' in Struan and Lochgarry being 'all winter employed in spinning, which draws considerable money into them yearly and former indolence and sloth banished the country'.[59] From the agent or manufacturer's point of view, the Highlands were an abundant source of cheap labour. This fact was often proclaimed in support of their claim for grants and loans from agencies like the Board of Trustees for Manufacturers and the British Linen Bank.[60] The former started its operations in 1727 and the latter in 1746. Both were extremely active in the Highlands, providing forward loans for dealers and investing directly in heckling stations, spinning schools, and equipment like spinning wheels.[61] The Forfeited Estates Commissioners discharged a similar function in respect of the estates under their care.[62] Such investment was concentrated in areas where labour was plentiful but cheap, like Glenmoriston and by Lochs Broom and Carron. Encouraged in this way, the

[55] See, for instance, *Miscellany of the Spalding Club*, iv, pp. 261–319.
[56] O'Dell, *Historical Geography of the Shetland Islands*, p. 251 provides detailed rental transcripts with lists of cloth collected.
[57] MacLeod (ed.), *Book of Dunvegan*, vol. i, p. 155; *Collectanea de Rebus Albanicis*, p. 171.
[58] Wills (ed.), *Reports on the Annexed Estates 1755–1769*, p. 3.
[59] Millar (ed.), *Scottish Forfeited Estate Papers 1715–45*, pp. 252–3.
[60] Durie, op. cit., p. 16.
[61] Ibid., pp. 13–36; H. Hamilton, *The Industrial Revolution in Scotland* (Oxford, 1932), pp. 87–9; Gaffney, *Lordship of Strathavon*, pp. 44–8.
[62] Hamilton, *Industrial Revolution in Scotland*, pp. 82–90; Kemp (ed.), op. cit., p. 101.

industry spread from its initial centres in Argyllshire, Perthshire, and Inverness-shire northwards and westwards into Ross and Cromarty, Sutherland, Caithness, and across into the Northern Isles.[63] At the same time, output rose. There are no figures for the amount of yarn spun, but we can monitor the growth in output of linen cloth. From only 21,972 yards in 1727/8, its production in the Highland counties rose steadily to 313,006 yards by 1778.[64] Such growth, however, is deceptive. Many agents found great difficulty in maintaining a regular supply of cheap yarn from all but the most accessible areas, whilst the bulk of linen cloth produced came from one county, Inverness-shire. So discouraged were agencies like the Board of Trustees and the British Linen Bank by their failure to establish a really viable industry that each, in turn, pulled out of the region, the latter in the 1770s and the former in 1789.

A great deal of flax-spinning was organized on a putting-out basis. The key figures in such a system were the agents or dealers like Munro of Inverness or Sandeman of Perth. Acting for themselves or for commercial institutions like the British Linen Bank, the agent had the task of feeding the materials through the system, giving out lint and gathering in the spun yarn. The scattered and isolated nature of many touns meant this was far from being an easy task. One agent, Duncan Grant, complained that 'he could never expect to have his lint returned as yarn in less than six months'.[65] As in other putting-out systems, spinners sometimes became dependent on the merchants or dealers not just for lint but also for credit. In Perthshire, one of the main areas, it was 'very common that when a tenant comes to pay his rent and wants a small part of it, that he goes out and borrows it from one or other of the Crieff merchants to be repaid by him to the lender in linen yarn'.[66] As with so many other items, yarn was also collected as part of a tenant's rent. Both the Breadalbane and Mey estates followed this practice, the estate feeding it through to the manufacturer.[67] Alternatively, there are also signs of a pure

---

[63] Durie, op. cit., pp. 16–19.
[64] Hamilton, *Industrial Revolution in Scotland*, p. 88.
[65] Gaffney, *Lordship of Strathavon*, p. 48.
[66] Wills (ed.), *Reports on the Annexed Estates 1755–1769*, p. 25.
[67] McArthur (ed.), *Survey of Lochtayside 1769*, p. lxiii; Donaldson, *Caithness in the Eighteenth Century*, p. 108.

domestic system, with tenants growing their own flax, spinning it, and then marketing the yarn themselves at centres like Inverness, Crieff, or Perth.[68] Although weaving was carried out in the main market centres around the periphery of the Highlands, possibly the greatest proportion of yarn was dispatched south, either to touns like Glasgow and Paisley, or else to English textile centres like Nottingham.[69]

With fewer problems over raw-material supply, the various trades based on wool, like knitted stockings or woollen cloths, tended to lack the entrepreneurial dominance of the flax trades. Instead, production was commonly in the hands of the peasant. Only at the marketing stage did it involve merchants. This pure domestic system of production can be seen in Shetland, where a variety of woollen goods were manufactured: stockings, gloves, hats, garters, and cloths. The part-time nature of the industry is not only conveyed by the way tenants paid cloth as rent, but also, by the more explicit descriptions. Knitting, for instance, was 'the work of servants and labourers, who derive the principal part of their subsistence from some other employment'.[70] The marketing procedure varied. Where woollen goods were paid as rent, then the estate factor must have acted as agent. If made nearby, some were probably sold direct to merchants or fishermen at ports like Lerwick. However, it is clear from Gifford of Busta's letter-book that the more remote touns were served by pedlars who bought items on behalf of merchants like Gifford himself.[71] Market control was channelled back to the knitters and weavers by way of commissions, with merchants ordering so many hats or pairs of stockings from them in response to market demand. In many ways, the domestic industries of Shetland lived off its fishing trade, for boats involved in the latter gave them access to a wide range of markets.

Yet another aspect of the domestic economy that was turned increasingly to commercial advantage was the making of ale and *aqua vitae*. Despite being widespread in the Highlands and Islands

---

[68] Wills (ed.), *Reports on the Annexed Estates 1755–1769*, p. 22 refers to the 'great quantities of linen yarn brought to market here (Crief) weekly, and which is brought up and sent in packs to Glasgow, Paisley &c from this place'.

[69] Ibid., p. 22; Kemp (ed.), op. cit., p. 212.

[70] Smith, *Wealth of Nations*, vol. i, p. 119.

[71] O'Dell, *Historical Geography of the Shetland Islands*, p. 306. See also p. 156.

by 1650, the role of brewing and distilling has not been given the attention it deserves. On some estates, they were fastidiously regulated. Only official brewers and *aqua vitae* men were permitted to make ale or whisky for sale. The extent of such a system may be measurable by the provision which estates made for 'brewseats' or 'ailhouses'. If so, then estates differed widely. Thus, the Huntly estate had quite a number,[72] the Breadalbane a few,[73] and the Assynt estate none at all.[74] These differences do not measure the amount of brewing or distilling only the extent of its control by these estates. In some cases, we glimpse these controls directly through their enactment by estates. For instance, in 1703, the Regality Court of Grant bound

all the tenants to carry their bear for malt to the malt kiln at Castle Grant, and to get 8 merks for it each boll, to be sold at 16d. the pynt. None to import malt out of any place but the four parishes. No aquavitie to be imported to the four parishes, and the brewers to brew acquavitie of the country malt, and to serve the four parishes ate reasonable rates.[75]

A less patently feudal system prevailed in Rannoch. There a 1677 court act empowered the birleymen to 'take tryall of all sorts of liquor, brandie or acqua vitae that sall happen to be provin, tapit and sold in the countri; and ordainit to sell the same at such prices as they think the same to be worth'.[76] Invariably, these courts also provide instances of these sorts of regulations being infringed. In an action that leaves much to the imagination, the Glenurchay court book recorded that the 'Laird perseis the men of Corrygyll and Sockoch for drinking of aquavitae. Donald M'Ille Phadrisk V'Nicoll confessis the aquavitae man to have beine ane nicht with him in his howss.'[77]

A number of areas achieved notoriety for the amount of grain distilled. Tenants on the Lovat and Cromarty estates, for example, were reported in 1755 to be 'a lazy, idle set of people,

---

[72] Based on *Miscellany of the Spalding Club*, iv, pp. 261–319 and rental lists in Gaffney, *Lordship of Strathavon*, Appendix I.

[73] McArthur (ed.), *Survey of Lochtayside 1769*, pp. 1 ff. and SRO, Macgregor Collection, GD150/16, rentals for 1731 and 1761.

[74] Adam (ed.), *Survey of Assynt*, pp. 1 ff.

[75] Cramond (ed.), *Court Book of the Regality of Grant*, p. 17.

[76] Gillies, 'Extracts from the Baron Court Book of Menzies', p. 113.

[77] *Black Book of Taymouth*, p. 384.

who instead of cultivating and improving their farms, employ lots of their time distilling spirits, for which they imported an incredible quantity from other counties . . . the whisky is mostly consumed among themselves.'[78] The Barony of Beauly alone, had fourteen to fifteen stills and as many ale houses.[79] Likewise, the Campeltown area was said by Pennant to import large amounts of barley for distilling.[80] According to J. E. Handley, most of the barley grown in the northern and north-eastern counties was used for brewing or distilling.[81] If so, then a county like Caithness must have been closely linked with the trade. Rentals suggest that this was the case, for those relating to estates like that of Mey[82] or to Dungasby in Brabster[83] show their tenants were all required to pay malt as rent or skat.

The benefits of the industry were not accepted by all who wrote about it. For some, it was a source of cash which utilized labour during the slack periods in the farming calendar. The amount of cash generated may have increased following the imposition of malt duty in 1714, for the latter triggered off a great deal of smuggling.[84] However, most outside observers were concerned more about its excesses of consumption rather than profit, seeing it as consuming valuable grain during times of food scarcity and contributing to the disorder of Highland society. Stories of these excesses are legion, but there can be few richer in pathos than the tragi-comedy played out at Castle Grant in 1701. Four women were

accused for contriving to bring such quantity of acqwavite to the said Donalich, old and young John Broackie that were sentenced to be hanged for crimes wherby the said condemned persons might dy by the said acqwavite, being in prison at Castle Grant. Three pints and a mutchkin were conveyed to the prison by them and given to the said persons, and they drank till Donalich dyed thereby immediatly, and young Broackie dyed throw the stress therof going to the gallows.

---

[78] Millar (ed.), *Scottish Forfeited Estate Papers 1715–45*, p. 78.

[79] Ibid., p. 61.

[80] Pennant, *A Tour in Scotland and Voyage to the Hebrides*, part i, p. 194.

[81] Handley, *Scottish Farming in the Eighteenth Century*, p. 54.

[82] Donaldson, *Caithness in the Eighteenth Century*, p. 107.

[83] 'Rental of Brabster, Caithness, 1697', *Old Lore Miscellany of Orkney, Shetland, Caithness and Sutherland* ix, Old Lore Series, xi (1933), pp 46–50.

[84] M. C. Storrie, 'The Scotch Whisky Industry', *TIBG* xxxi (1962), pp. 98–9.

The four women were found guilty of supplying whisky to excess and ordered to be scourged with thirty stripes of a cord before all but one were banished from the Regality for life.[85]

Yet another example of the Highlander's resourcefulness in the face of growing land pressure was the adoption of kelp-making in the 1730s. Kelp was the calcined ashes of seaweed from which carbonate of soda and iodine could be obtained. Its production began on the Uists, spreading to other parts of the Hebrides and the adjacent mainland and ultimately northwards into Orkney.[86] Output remained modest until 1790, when the outbreak of the Napoleonic Wars restricted the imports of barilla, an alternative source of soda, from Spain. Thereafter, or at least for the remainder of the Wars, prices and output rose sharply.[87] Even before 1790, though, it established itself as a valued addition to the money-making opportunities of coastal touns. But like other opportunities, its full benefits were moderated by the demands of landlords. In fact, as Gray's work demonstrated, estates like the Seaforth estate in Lewis, reserved the rights of kelp to themselves, employing tenants as paid labour to exploit it.[88] Others reaped the same profit by imposing a duty on the kelp produced by tenants or by raising rents.[89]

Conclusion

The transition from the Old to New Orders in the Highlands and Islands has not the sharpness of chronology which characterizes the Lowlands. Whatever single date we choose to break off the narrative on the Old Order will be makeshift, but that of 1780 has much to recommend it. A visitor to the region then would still have found himself amidst a society whose traditions and

[85] Cramond, *Court Book of the Regality of Grant*, p. 16.
[86] *Report to the Secretary for Scotland by the Crofters Commission on the Social Condition of the People of Lewis*, p. lxxxi recites the story of kelp-burning being introduced into the Hebrides in 1735 by an Irishman, Roderick MacDonald, but goes on to say it was practised in Orkney as early as 1722.
[87] Garnett, op. cit., vol. i, p. 188 quotes prices as 1740–60, £2. 5*s*; 1760–70, £4. 4*s*; 1770–80, £5. 0*s*; 1780–90, £6. 0*s*. After 1790, the price rose sharply to £20. per ton. See J. MacCulloch, *The Highlands and Western Isles of Scotland* (London, 1824), vol. iii, p. 152. The growth of output can be exemplified by Tiree, where it doubled over the 1790s alone. See *New Statistical Account of Scotland: Argyll* (1845), p. 348.
[88] Gray, *The Highland Economy 1750–1850*, pp. 131–2.
[89] Ibid., pp. 130–1.

institutions had matured over centuries. Yet for all its archaism and timelessness, it was one that could not disguise the acute problems that now beset it. A few estates only excepted, wrote Knox in 1784, the Highlands and Islands were 'seats of oppression, poverty, famine, anguish, and wild despair'.[90] Here, in a sentence, were all the manifest disfunctions of the region. With a rapidly growing excess of people over land, its agricultural base was stretched to the limit. Nor was it solely a resource problem. As on Lewis, the ordinary peasant was often 'enslav'd by those amongst them'.[91] Few could have argued—indeed, few did argue—that at this point, Highland society had progressed as far as it could without radical reform. Whilst those who planned and executed the reforms that were eventually adopted have often been condemned for their disregard of humane values, this prior need for radical solutions of some sort cannot be overlooked.

A really perceptive observer *c.*1780, though, would not only have grasped the urgency of change, but could well have foreseen how events were to unfold over the following half-century or so. This is because the various development options open to the region were already being tried and tested by then. Fishing, kelp production, and domestic industry had all demonstrated the potential of diversification as a panacea for the region's problems. Each had their supporters as growth sectors for the Highland economy. However, each had a susceptibility to fluctuations, which made any excessive dependence on them ultimately precarious. Also heralding future trends were adjustments and changes in the farm economy of touns. Despite the inadequate supply of land for the overwhelming majority of Highland peasants, there were still some who enjoyed large holdings. The response of the latter to market opportunities over the early eighteenth century demonstrated a lesson that was not missed, and that is, the Highlands were more profitable to landowners when farming stock rather than men. Although initially, the stock enterprises adopted on these farms were based on cattle, the sharp increases in rent which they sustained bred an entirely new attitude towards land amongst those who owned it. When the market demand for sheep rose, it was inevitable that attention should be switched to them. But the whole principle of a stock-

---

[90] Knox, *View of the British Empire*, p. 8.
[91] *Highlands of Scotland in 1750*, p. 46.

based farming enterprise, with its higher and more reliable rent yield, had already been made by early cattle farms. Indeed, the debate on the relative merits or otherwise of having farms stocked with men or beasts was in full swing by the end of the 1770s, when sheep were only just beginning to spread into the southern Highlands on a large scale, though the pioneers had been engaged in sheep production for almost a decade.[92] By 1780, too, the first planned attempts to reorganize landholding were being made, a process that did much to shake out the supernumeraries from the Highlands. Of course, there were other factors which ensured that emigration out of the region had deeper roots. As early as the 1730s, the levying of higher rents on a number of estates had induced emigration. The regular trickle of migrants that probably seeped out of the region at the best of times over the eighteenth century was further swelled to a spate during times of famine or poor harvests, such as in the 1770s. To sum up, then, the strands out of which Highland history was to be woven over the critical years of the late eighteenth and the nineteenth century were perceptible by 1780. Their fuller working out over these years erased or transformed patterns and institutions that can be traced back through most of the chapters in this book.

---

[92] The chronology of sheep farming is well reviewed by J. A. S. Watson, 'The Rise and Development of the Sheep Industry in the Highlands and North of Scotland', *Trans. Highland & Agricultural Soc.*, 5th ser., xlvi (1932), pp. 1–25.

Bibliography

1. *Manuscript Sources*
At the Scottish Record Office, Edinburgh:
GD6, Biel Papers
GD16, Airlie Muniments
GD24, Abercairny Papers
GD30, Shairp of Houston Papers
GD36, Rose of Montcoffer Papers
GD45, Dalhousie Muniments
GD50, John Macgregor Collection
GD52, Forbes Collection
GD72, Hay of Park Papers
GD109, Bargany Papers
GD124, Mar and Kellie Papers
GD126, Balfour and Melville Papers
GD150, Morton Collection
GD224, Buccleuch Muniments
GD225, Leith Hall Muniments
GD237, Lothian Papers
GD267, Home-Robertson Papers

At the National Library of Scotland, Edinburgh:
Minto Estate Papers

At Floors Castle, Kelso:
Roxburgh MSS

At Jedburgh:
Roxburghshire Sheriff Court Records

At Duns:
Berwickshire Sheriff Court Records

2. *Printed Sources*
Aberbrothoc, Liber S. Thome de, Bannatyne Club (Edinburgh, 1848–56), 2 vols.
Adam, R. J. (ed.), *John Home's Survey of Assynt*, Scottish History Soc., 3rd ser., lii (1960).
Anderson, J., *General View of the Agriculture of the County of Aberdeen* (Edinburgh, 1794).
—— (ed.), *Calendar of the Laing Charters A.D.854–1837* (Edinburgh, 1899).
Anderson, A. O. (ed.), *Early Sources of Scottish History A.D.500 to 1286* (Edinburgh, 1922), 2 vols.
Anderson, M. O., *Kings and Kingship in Early Scotland* (Edinburgh, 1973).
Argyll, George Douglas, Duke of, *Crofts and Farms in the Hebrides—An Account of the Management of an Island Estate for 130 Years* Edinburgh, 1883).
Balfour, D. (ed.) *Oppressions of the Sixteenth Century in the Islands of Orkney and Zetland*, Maitland Club (Edinburgh, 1859).

Bannerman, J., 'Senchus Fer nAlban' *Celtica*, vii (1966), pp. 142–62; viii (1968), pp. 90–111; ix (1971), pp. 217–65.
— *Studies in the History of Dalriada* (Edinburgh, 1974).
Barclay, R. S. (ed.), *The Court Book of the Orkney and Shetland 1612–1613* (Kirkwall, 1962).
Barron, D. G. (ed.), *The Court Book of the Barony of Urie*, Scottish History Soc., 1st ser., xii (1892).
Barrow, G. W. S. (ed.), *The Acts of Malcolm IV, King of Scots 1153–1165, Regesta Regum Scottorum* (Edinburgh, 1960).
— — (ed. with collaboration of W. W. Scott), *The Acts of William I, King of the Scots 1165–1214, Regesta Regum Scottorum*, vol. ii (Edinburgh, 1971).
— — *The Kingdom of the Scots* (London, 1973).
— — 'The Pattern of Lordship and Feudal Settlement in Cumbria', *Jnl. of Medieval History*, i (1975), pp. 117–38.
— — *The Anglo-Norman Era in Scottish History* (Oxford, 1980).
Beaufoy, H., *The Substance of a Speech by Henry Beaufoy Esq. to the British Society for Extending the Fisheries* (London, 1788).
Beresford, M. W. and Hurst, J. G. (eds.), *Deserted Medieval Villages* (London, 1969).
Beveridge, J. and Donaldson, J. (eds.) *Register of the Privy Seal of Scotland 1556–1567* (Edinburgh, 1957).
Birks, H. H., 'Studies in the Vegetational History of Scotland II. Two Pollen Diagrams from the Galloway Hills, Kirkcudbrightshire', *Jnl. of Ecology*, lx (1972), pp. 183–217.
— — 'Studies in the Vegetational History of Scotland III. A Radiocarbon-Dated Diagram from Loch Maree, Ross and Cromarty', *New Phytologist*, lxxi (1972), pp. 731–54.
Boyle, A., 'Matrilineal Succession in the Pictish Monarchy', *SHR* lvi (1977), pp. 1–10.
Brand, J., *A Brief Description of Orkney, Zetland, Pightland-Firth and Caithness*, 1701 edition edited by W. Brown (Edinburgh, 1883).
Breeze, D. J., 'The Abandonment of the Antonine Wall. Its Date and Implications', *SAF* (1975), pp. 67–80.
Brown, P. Hume, *Early Travellers in Scotland* (Edinburgh, 1891).
— — *Scotland Before 1700 from Contemporary Documents* (Edinburgh, 1893).
Browne, G. F., *Echt- Forbes Family Charters 1345–1727* (Edinburgh, 1923).
Burnett, J. G., *Powis Papers 1507–1594* (Aberdeen, 1951).
Calder, C. S. T., 'Report on the Discovery of Numerous Stone Age House-Sites in Shetland', *PSAS* lxxxix (1955–6), pp. 340–97.
Campbell, A., *A Journey from Edinburgh through parts of North Britain* (London, 1802), 2 vols.
Carter, I., 'Marriage Patterns and Social Sectors in Scotland before the Eighteenth Century', *SS* xvii (1973), pp. 51–60.
Chadwick, H. M., *Early Scotland* (Cambridge, 1949).
Childe, V. G., *The Prehistory of Scotland* (London, 1935).
— — *Scotland Before the Scots* (London, 1946).
— — *Ancient Dwellings at Skara Brae* (Edinburgh, 1950).
Clouston, J. Storer (ed.), *Records of the Earldom of Orkney 1299–1614*, Scottish History Soc., 2nd ser., vii (1914).
— — 'The Orkney Townships', *SHR* xxvii (1920), pp. 16–45.
— — *The Orkney Parishes—Containing the Statistical Account of 1795–1798* (Kirkwall, 1927).
Clyde, J. A. (ed.), *The Jus Feudale by Sir Thomas Craig of Riccarton* (Edinburgh, 1934), 2 vols.
— — (ed.), *Hope's Major Practicks 1608–1633*, The Stair Soc. (Edinburgh, 1938), 2 vols.
Coles, J. M., 'The Early Settlement of Scotland: Excavations at Morton, Fife', *Proc. Prehistoric Soc.*, xxxvii (1971), pp. 284–366.
Collectanea de Rebus Albanicis, Consisting of Original Papers and Documents Relating to the History of the Highlands and Islands of Scotland, edited by the Iona Club (Edinburgh, 1847).

Cooper, Lord, 'The Numbers and Distribution of the Population of Scotland', *SHR* xxvi (1947), pp. 2–6.

Cormack, W. F. and Coles, J. M., 'A Mesolithic Site at Low Clone, Wigtonshire', *Trans. Dumfr. & Galloway Nat. Hist. & Antiq. Soc.*, xlv (1968).

'Corshill Baron Court Book', pp. 65–249 in *Archaeological and Historical Collections Relating to the Counties of Ayr and Wigton*, iv (Edinburgh, 1844).

Cottam, M. B. and Small, A., 'The Distribution of Settlements in Southern Pictland', *Medieval Archaeology*, xviii (1974), pp. 43–65.

Coull, J. R., 'Fisheries in Scotland in the 16th, 17th and 18th Centuries'. *SGM* xciii (1977), pp. 5–14.

Report to the Secretary for Scotland by the Crofters Commission on the Social Condition of the People of Lewis in 1901, as Compared with Twenty Years Ago (Glasgow, 1902).

Craw, J. Hewart, 'Chirnside Common', *Proc. of the Berwickshire Naturalist Club*, xxiv (1922), pp. 423–50.

Crawford, I. A., 'Contributions to a History of Domestic Settlement in North Uist', *SS* ix (1965), pp. 34–65.

—— 'Scot (?), Norsemen and Gael', *SAF* vi (1974), pp. 1–16.

—— and Switsur, R., 'Sandscaping and C14: the Udal, N. Uist', *Antiquity*, li (1977), pp. 124–36.

Cregeen, E. R. (ed.), *Argyll Estate Instructions* [Mull, Morvern, Tiree] *1771–1805*, Scottish History Soc., 4th ser., (1964).

—— 'The Tacksman and their Successors. A Study of Tenurial Reorganization in Mull, Morvern and Tiree in the Early 18th Century', *SS* xiii (1969), pp. 93–144.

Cruickshank, F., *Navar and Lethnot* (Brechin, 1899).

Cruickshank, J., 'The Court Book of the Barony of Fintray 1711–1726', pp. 1–66 in *The Miscellany of the Third Spalding Club*, vol. i. Third Spalding Club (Aberdeen, 1935).

Cullen, L. M. and Smout, T. C. (eds.), *Comparative Aspects of Scottish and Irish Economic and Social History 1600–1900* (Edinburgh, 1977).

Dalyell, Sir James, and Beveridge, J. (eds.), *The Binns Papers 1320–1864*, SRS (Edinburgh, 1938).

Davidson, D. A., Jones R. L., and Renfrew, C., 'Paleoenvironmental Reconstruction and Evaluation. A Case Study from Orkney', *TIBG*, n.s., i (1976), pp. 46–61.

Devine, T. M., 'Glasgow Colonial Merchants and Land 1770–1815', pp. 205–44 in Ward, J. T. and Wilson, R. G. (eds.), *Land and Industry* (Newton Abbot, 1971).

—— and Lythe, S. G. E., 'The Economy of Scotland under James VI', *SHR* l (1971), pp. 91–106.

Dickinson, W. C. (ed.), *The Sheriff Court Book of Fife 1515–1522*, Scottish History Soc., 3rd ser., xii (1928).

—— (ed.), *The Court Book of the Barony of Carnwath 1523–1542*, Scottish History Soc., 3rd ser., xxix (1937).

—— *A New History of Scotland vol. I. Scotland From the Earliest Times to 1603* (Edinburgh, 1961).

Dodgshon, R. A. 'The Nature and Development of Infield–Outfield in Scotland', *TIBG* lix (1973), pp. 1–23.

—— 'The Landholding Foundations of the Open Field System', *Past and Present*, lxvii (1975), pp. 3–29.

—— 'Farming in Roxburghshire and Berwickshire on the Eve of Improvement', *SHR* liv (1975), pp. 140–54

—— 'Towards an Understanding and Definition of Runrig: the Evidence for Roxburghshire and Berwickshire', *TIBG* lxiv (1975), pp. 15–33.

—— 'Runrig and the Communal Origins of Property in Land', *Juridical Rev.* (1975), pp. 189–208.

— — 'Scandinavian Solskifte and the Sunwise Division of Land in Eastern Scotland', *SS* xix (1975), pp. 1–14.

— — 'Changes in Scottish Township Organisation During the Medieval and Early Modern Periods', *Geografiska Annaler*, 58B (1977), pp. 51–65.

— — 'Law and Landscape in Early Scotland: A Study of the Relationship Between Tenure and Landholding', pp. 127–45 in Harding, A. (ed.), *Lawmakers and Lawmaking in British History*, Royal Historical Society's Studies in History series (London, 1980).

Donaldson, J. E., *Caithness in the Eighteenth Century* (Edinburgh, 1938).

Donaldson, G. (ed.), *Accounts of the Collectors of Thirds of Benefices 1561–1572*, Scottish History Soc., 3rd ser., xlii (1949).

— — (ed.), *The Court Book of Shetland 1602–1604*, SRC (Edinburgh, 1958).

— — *Shetland Life Under Earl Patrick* (Edinburgh, 1958).

Dunbar, J. G. and Hay, G. D., 'Excavations at Lour, Stobo, 1959–60', *PSAS*, xcvi (1959–60), pp. 196–210.

Duncan, A. A. M., *Scotland: The Making of the Kingdom. Vol. I: The Edinburgh History of Scotland* (Edinburgh, 1975).

— — and Brown, A. L., 'Argyll and the Isles in the Earlier Middle Ages', *PSAS* xc (1956–7), pp. 192–219.

Dunlop, J. (ed.), *Court Minutes of Balgair 1706–1736*, SRS (Edinburgh, 1957).

Durie, A. J., 'Linen-Spinning in the North of Scotland 1746–1773', *Northern Scotland*, ii (1974–5), pp. 13–36.

Easson, D. E. (ed.), *Charters of the Abbey of Couper Angus*, Scottish History Soc., 3rd ser., xl–xli (1947), 2 vols.

— — and Macdonald, A. (eds.), *Charters of the Abbey of Incholm*, Scottish History Soc., 3rd ser., xxxii (1938).

Edmonston, A., *A View of the Ancient and Present State of the Zetland Islands* (Lerwick, 1809).

Evans, J. G., Limbrey, S., and Cleere, H. (eds.), *The Effect of Man on the Landscape: The Highland Zone*, Council for British Archaeology, Research Report no. 11 (London, 1975).

Fairhurst, H., 'Kilphedir and the Hut Circle Sites in Northern Scotland', *SAF* iii (1971), pp. 1–10.

— — and Taylor, D. B., 'A Hut Circle Settlement at Kilphedir, Sutherland', *PSAS* ciii (1970–1), pp. 65–99.

Farran, C. D'Olivier, 'Runrig and the English Open Field System', *Juridical Rev.*, lxv (1953), pp. 134–59.

Feachem, R., *The North Britons* (London, 1965).

— — 'Ancient Agriculture in the Highland of Britain', *PPS* xxxviii (1972), pp. 339–47.

Fenton, A., 'Skene of Hallyard's Manuscript of Husbandrie', *AHR* xi (1963), pp. 65–81.

— — *Scottish Country Life* (Edinburgh, 1976).

— — Franklin, T. Bedford, *A History of Scottish Farming* (London, 1952).

Flinn, M. W. (ed.), *Scottish Population History* (Cambridge, 1977).

Frere, S., *Britannia. A History of Roman Britain* (London, 1978).

Gaffney, V. (ed.) *The Lordship of Strathavon*, Third Spalding Club (Aberdeen, 1960).

— — 'Shielings of the Drumochter', *SS* xi (1967), pp. 91–9.

Gailey, R. A., 'The Evolution of Highland Rural Settlement With Particular Reference to Argyllshire', *SS* vi (1960), pp. 155–77.

— — 'The Peasant Houses of the South-West Highlands of Scotland: Distribution, Parallels and Evolution', *Gwerin*, v (1962), pp. 1–16.

Garnett, T., *Observations on a Tour Through the Highlands and Part of the Western Isles of Scotland* (London, 1810), 2 vols.

Gaskell, P., *Morvern Transformed* (Cambridge, 1968).

Geddes, A., 'The Changing Landscape of the Lothians, 1600–1800, As Revealed by Old Estate Plans', *SGM* liv (1938), pp. 129–43.

—— 'Conjoint-Tenants and Tacksmen on the Isle of Lewis 1715–26', *EcHR*, 2nd ser., i (1948–9), pp. 54–60.

Grant, Sir Alexander, *A Dissertation on the Chief Obstacles to the Improvement of Land* (Aberdeen, 1760).

Grant, I. F., *Everyday Life on an Old Highland Farm 1769–1782* (London, 1924).

—— *The Social and Economic Development of Scotland Before 1603* (Edinburgh, 1930).

Gray, M., 'The Abolition of Runrig in the Highlands of Scotland', *EcHR*, 2nd ser., v (1952–3), pp. 46–57.

—— *The Highland Economy 1750–1850* (Edinburgh, 1957).

—— 'Economic Welfare and Money Income in the Highlands 1750–1850', *Scottish Jnl. of Political Economy*, ii (1955), pp. 47–63.

Guido, M., 'A Scottish Crannog Re-Dated, *Antiquity*, xlviii (1974), pp. 54–6.

Gunn, G. B. (ed.), *Records of the Baron Court of Stithcill 1655–1807*, Scottish History Soc., 1st ser., I (1905).

Hamilton, H. (ed.), *Monymusk Papers (1713–1755)*, Scottish History Soc., 3rd ser., xxxix (1945).

—— *An Economic History of Scotland in the Eighteenth Century* (Oxford, 1963).

Hamilton, J. (2nd Lord Belhaven), *The Countrey-Man's Rudiments or Advice to the Farmers in East Lothian, How to Labour and Improve their Ground* (Edinburgh, 1899).

Hamilton, J. R. C., *Excavations at Jarlshof, Shetland* (Edinburgh, 1956).

[Hamilton, W.] *Description of the Sheriffdoms of Lanark and Renfrew.* Compiled about 1710 by William Hamilton of Glasgow, Maitland Club (Glasgow, 1831).

Hamilton-Grierson, Sir Philip J. (ed.), *Habakkuk Bisset's Rolment of Courtis*, STS (Edinburgh, 1920).

Handley, J. E., *Scottish Farming in the Eighteenth Century* (London, 1953).

Hannay, R. K. (ed.), *Rentale Dunkeldense 1505–1517*, Scottish History Soc., 2nd ser., x (1915).

Harding, D. W. (ed.), *Hillforts* (London, 1977).

Harvey, C. C. H. and Macleod, J. (eds.), *Calendar of Writs at Yester House 1166–1625* SRS (Edinburgh, 1930).

Henderson, I, *The Picts* (London, 1967).

Henshall, A., *Chambered Tombs in Scotland* (Edinburgh, 1963–72), 2 vols.

Higgs, E. S. (ed.), *Papers in Economic Prehistory* (Cambridge, 1973).

The Highlands of Scotland in 1750. With an Introduction by A. Lang (Edinburgh and London, 1898).

HMC, *Third Report of the Royal Commission on Historical Manuscripts* (London, 1872).

—— *Fourth Report of the Royal Commission on Historical Manuscripts, Part I, Report and Appendix* (London, 1874).

—— *Fifth Report of the Royal Commission on Historical Manuscripts, Part I, Report and Appendix* (London 1876).

—— *Report on Manuscripts in Various Collections*, vol. v (London, 1909).

Hodd, A. N. L., 'Runrig on the Eve of the Agricultural Revolution', *SGM* xc (1974), pp. 130–3.

Hogg, J., *The Shepherd's Guide* (Edinburgh, 1807).

Huntly, Charles, XI Marquis of (ed.), *The Records of Aboyne 1230–1681*, New Spalding Club (Aberdeen, 1894).

Imrie, J., Rae, T. I., and Ritchie, W. D. (eds.), *The Burgh Court Book of Selkirk 1503–45, part I, 1505–31*, SRS (Edinburgh, 1960).

Innes, C. (ed.), *The Black Book of Taymouth*, Bannatyne Club (Edinburgh, 1855).

—— *Scotch Legal Antiquities* (Edinburgh, 1872).

—— and Brichan, J. E. (eds.), *Origines Parochiales Scotiae*, Bannatyne Club (Edinburgh, 1851–55), 2 vols.

Jackson, A., 'Pictish Social Structure and Symbol Stones', *SS* xv (1971), pp. 121–40.

Jackson, K. H., *Language and History in Early Britain* (Edinburgh, 1953).

—— 'Britons and Angles in Southern Scotland', *Antiquity*, xxix (1955), pp. 77–88.

—— *The Gaelic Notes in the Book of Deer* (Cambridge, 1972).

Jervise, A., *Memorials of Angus and Mearns* (Edinburgh, 1761).

Jobey, G., 'Excavations at Boonies, Westerkirk, and the Nature of Romano-British Settlement in Eastern Dumfries-shire', *PSAS* cv (1972), pp. 118–40.

Johnston, A. W., 'The Alleged Prevalence of Gavelkind in Orkney and Shetland', *Saga-Book of the Viking Club*, vi (1908–9), pp. 305–7.

—— 'Rental of Brabster, Caithness, 1697', *Old Lore Miscellany of Orkney, Shetland, Caithness and Sutherland, vol. IX, Old Lore Series, vol. XI* (London, 1933), pp. 46–52.

—— 'Notes on the Fiscal Antiquities of Orkney and Shetland', ibid., pp. 53–64.

Johnson, S., *A Journey to the Western Islands of Scotland*, ed. by M. Lascelles (New Haven and London, 1971).

Keith, G. S., *General View of the Agriculture of Aberdeenshire* (Aberdeen, 1811).

Kemp, D. W. (ed.), *Tours in Scotland, 1747, 1750, 1760 by Richard Pococke*, Scottish History Soc., 1st ser., i. (1887).

Kerr, R., *General View of the Agriculture of the County of Berwick* (London, 1809).

Kirby, D. P., 'Strathclyde and Cumbria. A Survey of Historical Development to 1902', *Trans. Cumberland & Westmorland Antiq. & Arch. Soc.*, n.s., lxii (1962), pp. 77–94.

Kirk, W., 'The Primary Agricultural Colonisation of Scotland', *SGM* lxxiii (1957), pp. 65–90.

Knox, J., *A View of the British Empire More Especially Scotland* (London, 1784).

—— *A Discourse on the Expediency of Establishing Fishing Stations or Small Towns in the Highlands of Scotland and the Hebride Islands* (London, 1786).

Lacaille, A. D., *The Stone Age in Scotland* (Oxford, 1954).

Laing, D. (ed.), *The Orygynale Cronykil of Scotland by Andrew of Wyntoun* (Edinburgh, 1872), 3 vols.

Laing, L. R., 'Medieval Settlement Archaeology in Scotland', *SAF* (1969), pp. 69–79.

—— *Orkney and Shetland: An Archaeological Guide* (Newton Abbot, 1974).

—— *Settlement Types in Post-Roman Scotland*, British Archaeological Reports, no. 13 (Oxford, 1975).

Lamont, W. D., 'Old Land Denominations and Old Extent in Islay', *SS* i (1957), pp. 183–203 and ii (1958), pp. 86–107.

—— 'The Islay Charter of 1408', *Proc. Royal Irish Academy*, 60C (1959–60), pp. 163–87.

Lebon, J. G. H., 'The Face of the Countryside in Central Ayrshire during the 18th and 19th Centuries', *SGM* lxii (1946), pp. 7–15.

—— 'The Process of Enclosure in the Western Lowlands', *SGM*, lxii (1946), pp. 100–115.

Levie, W. Elder, 'Celtic Tribal Law and Custom in Scotland', *Juridical Rev.*, xxxix (1927), pp. 191–208.

—— 'The Scottish Davach or Dauch', *Scottish Gaelic Studies*, iii (1931), pp. 99–110.

Liber Sancte Marie De Calchou 1113–1567, Bannatyne Club (Edinburgh, 1846), 2 vols.

Liber Sancte Marie De Melros, Bannatyne Club (Edinburgh, 1837), 2 vols.

McArthur, M., 'Some Eighteenth Century Scottish Opinions on the Importation of Irish Cattle into Great Britain', *Scottish Jnl. of Agriculture*, xviii (1935), pp. 236–43.

—— (ed.), *Survey of Lochtayside*, Scottish History Soc., 3rd ser., xxvii (1936).

MacDonald, A., 'Old Highland Records: A Miscellany of', *Trans. of the Gaelic Soc. of Inverness*, xliii (1960–3), pp. 1–10.

Macfarlane, W. *Geographical Collections Relating to Scotland Made by W. Macfarlane*, Scottish History Soc., 1st ser., li–liii (1906–8), 3 vols.

Macgill, W., *Old Ross-shire and Scotland* (Inverness, 1909), 2 vols.

Mackay, A., *Book of the Mackay* (Inverness, 1909).

Mackay, A. J. G., 'Notes and Queries on the Custom of Gavelkind in Kent, Ireland, Wales and Scotland', *PSAS* xxxii (1897–8), pp. 133–58.

Mackay, W. (ed.), *Chronicles of the Frasers—The Wardlaw Manuscript*, Scottish History Soc., 1st ser., xlvii (1905).

McKerral, A., 'Ancient Denominations of Agricultural Land in Scotland. A Summary of Recorded Opinions, with some Notes, Observations and References', *PSAS* lxxviii (1943–4), pp. 39–80.

—— 'The Tacksman and His Holding in the South-West Highlands', *SHR* xxvi (1947), pp. 10–25.

MacKie, E. W. 'The Origin and Development of the Broch and Wheelhouse Building Cultures of the Scottish Iron Age', *Proc. Prehistoric Soc.*, xxxi (1965), pp. 93–146.

—— 'Radio-Carbon Dates and the Scottish Iron Age', *Antiquity*, xliii (1969), pp. 15–26.

—— 'The Scottish Iron Age', *SHR* xlix (1970), pp. 1–32.

—— *Scotland: An Archaeological Guide* (London, 1975).

Mackie, J. D. (ed.), *Thomas Thomson's Memorial on Old Extent*, The Stair Soc. (Edinburgh, 1946).

MacLeod, R. C. (ed.), *The Book of Dunvegan 1340–1920*, Third Spalding Club (Aberdeen, 1938), 2 vols.

McNeill, G. P. (ed.), *The Exchequer Rolls of Scotland, vol. XVII, A.D. 1537–1542* (Edinburgh, 1897).

McNeill, P. and Nicholson, R. (eds.), *An Historical Atlas of Scotland c.400–c.1600* (St Andrews, 1975).

Macphail, J. R. N. (ed.), *Highland Papers*, vol. ii, Scottish History Soc., 2nd ser., xii (1916).

Macpherson, A., *Glimpses of Church and Social Life in the Highlands in Olden Times* (Edinburgh and London, 1893).

—— 'An Old Highland Genealogy and the Evolution of a Scottish Clan', *SS* x (1966), pp. 1–43,

—— 'An Old Highland Parish Register, Survivals of Clanship and Social Change in Laggan, Inverness-shire, 1775–1854', *SS* ii (1967), pp. 149–92.

Macqueen, J., 'The Gaelic Speakers of Galloway and Carrick', *SS* xvii (1972), pp. 17–33.

Martin, M., *A Description of the Western Islands of Scotland* (London, 1716 edn.).

Marwick, H., 'Naval Defence in Norse Scotland', *SHR* cv (1949), pp. 1–11.

—— *Orkney Field Names* (Kirkwall, 1952).

Mason, J., 'Conditions in the Highlands after the Forty-Five', *SHR* xxvi (1947), pp. 134–46.

Mather, A. S., 'Pre-1745 Land Use and Conservation in a Highland Glen: an Example from Glen Strathfarrar, North Inverness-shire', *SGM* 86 (1970), pp. 160–9.

Maxwell, G., 'Duns and Forts. A Note on Some Iron Age Monuments of the Atlantic Province', *SAF* (1969), pp. 41–52.

Maxwell, R., *Select Transactions of the Honourable The Society of Improvers in the Knowledge of Agriculture in Scotland* (Edinburgh, 1743).

Menzies, G. (ed.), *Who Are the Scots?* (London, 1971).

Mercer, J., 'Flint Tools from the Present Tidal Zone, Lussa Bay, Isle of Jura, Argyll', *PSAS* cii (1969–70), pp. 1–30.

—— 'New C14 Dates from the Isle of Jura, Argyll', *Antiquity*, xlviii (1974), pp. 65–6.

Millar, A. (ed.), *The Glamis Book of Record*, Scottish History Soc., 1st ser., ix (1890).

—— (ed.), *A Selection of Scottish Forfeited Estates Papers 1715:1745*, Scottish History Soc., 1st ser., lvii (1909).

Miller, R., 'Land Use by Summer Shielings', *SS* xi (1967), pp. 193–221.

Mitchell, G. F., 'The Larnian Culture: A Review', *Jnl. Royal Soc. Antiq. Ireland*, lxxix (1949), pp. 170–81.

— — 'The Larnian Culture. A Minimal View', *Proc. Prehistoric Soc.*, xxxviii (1971), pp. 274–83.

Mitchie, J. S. (ed.), *The Records of Invercauld 1547–1828*, Spalding Club (Aberdeen, 1901).

Mitchison, R., 'The Movements of Scottish Corn Prices in the Seventeenth and Eighteenth Centuries', *Econ. Hist. Rev.*, 2nd ser., xviii (1965), pp. 78–91.

Munro, R. W. (ed.), *Monro's Western Isles of Scotland* (Edinburgh, 1961).

Murray, Sir Alexander, *The True Interest of Great Britain Ireland and Our Plantations* (London, 1740).

Murray, J. A. H. (ed.), *The Complaynt of Scotlande 1554*, Early Text Soc., extra series, xvii (1872).

Neilson, G. and Paton, H. (eds.) *Acts of the Lords of Council in Civil Causes, vol. II, A.D. 1496–1501* (Edinburgh, 1918).

New Statistical Account of Scotland (Edinburgh, 1845), 15 vols.

Nicholson, R., *Scotland: The Later Middle Ages, vol. II, The Edinburgh History of Scotland* (Edinburgh, 1974).

Nicolaisen, W. F. H., 'Celts and Anglo-Saxons in the Scottish Border Counties: The Place Name Evidence', *SS* viii (1964), pp. 141–71.

— — 'Norse Settlement in the Northern and Western Isles', *SHR* xlviii (1969), pp. 6–17.

— — 'Gaelic Place-Names in Southern Scotland', *Studia Celtica*, v (1970), pp. 15–35.

— — *Scottish Place-Names* (London, 1976).

O'Dell, A. C., *The Historical Geography of Shetland* (Lerwick, 1939).

The Old Statistical Account of Scotland (Edinburgh, 1791–99), 20 vols.

Parish Lists for Wigtonshire and Minnigaff 1684, SRS (Edinburgh, 1916).

Parry, M. L. and Slater, T. R. (eds.), *The Making of the Scottish Countryside* (London, 1980).

Paton, H. (ed.), *The Mackintosh Muniments 1442–1820* (Edinburgh, 1903).

Paul, J. B. and Thompson, J. M. (eds.), *The Register of the Great Seal of Scotland 1513–1546* (Edinburgh, 1883).

Pennant, T., *A Tour in Scotland 1769* (London, 1776 edn.).

— — *A Tour in Scotland and a Voyage to the Hebrides* (Chester, 1772) 2 vols.

Peterkin, A., *Rentals of the Ancient Earldom and Bishoprick of Orkney* (Edinburgh, 1820).

— — *Notes on Orkney and Zetland* (Edinburgh, 1822).

Piggot, S. (ed.), *The Prehistoric Peoples of Scotland* (London, 1952).

— — 'The Dalladies Long Barrow, N.E. Scotland', *Antiquity*, xlvii (1973), pp. 32–6.

[Pont, T.] *Topographical Account of the District of Cunningham and Ayrshire*, compiled about the year 1600 by Timothy Pont, Maitland Club (Glasgow, 1848).

Rae, T. I., *The Union of 1707* (Edinburgh, 1974).

Raine, J. (ed.), *The Priory of Coldingham, The Correspondence, Inventories, Account Rolls and Law Proceedings of the Priory of Coldingham*, Surtees Soc. (London, 1841).

— — (ed.), *The History and Antiquities of North Durham* (London, 1852).

Ramsay, J. H. (ed.), *Bamff Charters A.D. 1232–1703* (Oxford, 1915).

RCAM, *An Inventory of the Ancient Monuments . . . of Argyll* (Edinburgh, 1971–), vols. on *Kintyre* (1971) and *Lorn* (1974).

— — *An Inventory of the Ancient Monuments . . . of Lanark* (Edinburgh, 1978).

— — *An Inventory of the Ancient Monuments . . . of Peebles-shire* (Edinburgh, 1967), 2 vols.

— — *An Inventory of the Ancient Monuments . . . of Roxburghshire* (Edinburgh, 1956), 2 vols.

— — *An Inventory of the Ancient Monuments . . . of Selkirkshire* (Edinburgh, 1957).

Registrum de Dunfermelyn, Bannatynne Club (Edinburgh, 1842).

Registrum Episcopatus Moraviensis, Bannatyne Club (Edinburgh, 1837).

Registrum Honoris de Morton, Bannatyne Club (Edinburgh, 1853).

Reid, R. C. (ed.), *Wigtownshire Charters*, Scottish History Soc., 3rd ser., li (1960).

Renfrew, C. (ed.), *British Prehistory* (London, 1974).

— — Harkness D., and Switsur, R., 'Quanterness, Radiocarbon and the Orkney Cairns', *Antiquity*, i (1976), pp. 194–204.

Reports on the State of Certain Parishes in Scotland 1627, Maitland Club (Edinburgh, 1835).

Richmond, I. A. (ed.), *Roman and Native in North Britain* (London, 1958).

Ritchie, A., 'Palisaded Sites in North Britain: Their Context and Affinities', *SAF* ii (1974), pp. 48–67.

—— 'Pict and Norseman in Northern Scotland', *SAF* vi (1974), pp. 23–36.

Ritchie, R. L. G., *The Normans in Scotland* (Edinburgh, 1954).

Ritchie, W. Tod (ed.), *The Bannatyne Manuscript by George Bannatyne*, STS (London, 1934).

Rivet, A. L. F. (ed.), *The Iron Age in Northern Britain* (Edinburgh, 1966).

Robertson, A. S., *The Antonine Wall*, (Glasgow, 1970).

Robertson, E. W., *Historical Essays in Connexion with the Land, the Church &c* (Edinburgh, 1872),

Robertson, J., *General View of the Agriculture of the County of Perth* (Perth, 1799).

—— (ed.), *Illustrations of the Topography and Antiquities of the Shires of Aberdeen and Banff*, Spalding Club (Aberdeen, 1862), 4 vols.

Robertson, J. F. *The Story of Galloway* (Castle Douglas, 1963).

Rogers, A. (ed.) *Rental Book of the Cistercian Abbey of Cupar Angus* (London, 1880), 2 vols.

Romanes, C. S. (ed.), *Selections from the Records of the Regality of Melrose*, Scottish History Soc., 2nd ser., *1605–1661*, vi (1914); *1662–1676*, viii (1915); *1547–1706*, xiii (1917).

—— 'The Land System of the Scottish Burgh', *Juridical Rev.*, xlvii (1935), pp. 103–19.

Romanes, J. H., 'The Kindly Tenants of the Abbey of Melrose', *Juridical Rev.*, li (1939), pp. 201–16.

Sanderson, M. H. B., 'The Feuars of Kirklands', *SHR* lii (1973), pp. 117–36. *Session Cases*, 4th ser., iii (1875–6).

Sinclair, Sir John, *General Report of the Agricultural State and Political Circumstances of Scotland* (Edinburgh, 1814), 3 vols.

[Skene, Leys, and Whitehaugh] 'Court Books of the Baronies of Skene, Leys Whitehaugh, 1613–1687', pp. 215–38 in *The Miscellany of the Spalding Club*, vol. v (Aberdeen, 1852).

Skene, W. F. (ed.), *John of Fordun's Chronicle of the Scottish Nation* (Edinburgh, 1872), 2 vols.

—— *Celtic Scotland* (Edinburgh, 1890 edn.), 3 vols.

Small, A., 'The Historical Geography of the Norse Viking Colonization of the Scottish Highlands', *Norsk Geografisk Tidsskrift*, xxii (1968), pp. 1–16.

—— 'Burghead', *SAF* i (1969), pp. 61–8.

—— and Cottam, B., *Craig Phadraig*, Dundee University, Department of Geography occasional paper, no. 1 (1972).

Smith, A., *General View of the Agriculture of Galloway* (London, 1810).

—— *An Inquiry into the Nature and Causes of the Wealth of Nations*, ed. E. Cannan (London, 1930 edn.).

Smith, G. G., *The Book of Islay* (Edinburgh, 1895).

Smith, J., *General View of the Agriculture of the Hebrides or Western Isles of Scotland* (Edinburgh, 1811).

Smith, J., *The Gordon's Mill Farming Club 1758–1764* (Aberdeen, 1962).

Smout, T. C., *Scottish Trade on the Eve of the Union 1660–1707* (Edinburgh, 1963).

—— 'Scottish Landowners and Economic Growth 1650–1850', *Scottish Jnl. of Political Economy*, ii (1964), pp. 218–34.

—— *A History of the Scottish People 1560–1830* (London and Glasgow, 1969).

—— and Fenton, A., 'Scottish Agriculture before the Improvers—An Exploration', *Agric. Hist. Rev.*, xiii (1965), pp. 73–93.

Stevenson, J. H. (ed.), *The Register of the Great Seal of Scotland 1660–1668* (Edinburgh, 1914).

Stevenson, R. B. K., 'Medieval Dwelling Sites and a Primitive Village in the Parish of Manor, Peebles-shire', *PSAS* lxxv (1942–3), pp. 72–115.

Steinnes, A., 'The Huseby System in Orkney', *SHR* xxxviii (1959), pp. 36–46.

Stuart, J. (ed.), *Lists of Pollable Persons Within the Shire of Aberdeen 1696* (Aberdeen, 1844), 2 vols.

Symon, J. A. *Scottish Farming: Past and Present* (Edinburgh, 1963).

Thomson, J. M. (ed.), *The Register of the Great Seal of Scotland 1620–1633* (Edinburgh, 1884).

—— *The Register of the Great Seal of Scotland 1546–1580* (Edinburgh, 1886).

—— *The Register of the Great Seal of Scotland 1580–1593* (Edinburgh, 1888).

—— (ed.), *The Register of the Great Seal of Scotland 1593–1608* (Edinburgh, 1890).

Thomson, W. P. L., 'Funzie, Fetlar: A Shetland Run-rig Township in the Nineteenth Century', *SGM* lxxxvi (1970), pp. 170–185.

Ure, D., *General View of the Agriculture of the County of Roxburgh* (London, 1794).

Wainwright, F. T. (ed.), *The Problem of the Picts* (Edinburgh, 1955).

—— (ed.), *The Northern Isles* (Edinburgh, 1964).

Walker, D. and West, R. G. (eds.), *Studies in the Vegetational History of the British Isles* (Cambridge, 1970).

Walton, K., 'The Distribution of Population in Aberdeenshire, 1686', *SGM* lxvi (1950), pp. 17–26.

Watson, J. A. S., 'The Rise and Development of the Sheep Industry in the Highlands and North of Scotland', *Trans. Highland & Agric. Soc. Scotland*, 5th ser., xliv (1932), pp. 1–25.

Watson, W. J., *The History of Celtic Place-Names in Scotland* (Edinburgh, 1926).

Webster, J., *General View of the Agriculture of Galloway* (Edinburgh, 1794).

Whittington, G., 'Field Systems of Scotland', pp. 530–79 in Baker, A. R. H. and Butlin, R. A. (eds.), *Studies on Field Systems in the British Isles* (Cambridge, 1973).

—— 'Was there a Scottish Agricultural Revolution?', *Area*, vii (1975) pp. 204–6.

—— 'Placenames and the Settlement Pattern of Dark-Age Scotland', *PSAS* cvi (1974–5), pp. 99–110.

—— and Soulsby, J. A., 'A Preliminary Report on an Investigation into *Pit* Placenames', *SGM* lxxxiv (1968), pp. 117–25.

—— and Brett, D. U., 'Locational Decision-Making on a Scottish Estate Prior to Enclosure', *Jnl. of Historical Geography*, v (1979), pp. 33–43.

Wight, A., *Present State of Husbandry in Scotland* (Edinburgh, 1778–84), 3 vols.

Wills, V. (ed.), *Reports on the Annexed Estates 1755–1769*, Scottish Record Office (Edinburgh, 1973).

—— (ed.), *Statistics of the Annexed Estates 1755–1756*, Scottish Record Office (Edinburgh, 1973).

Whyte, I. D. (ed.), 'Rural Housing in Lowland Scotland in the Seventeenth Century—the Evidence of Estate Papers', *SS* xix (1975), pp. 55–68.

—— 'Infield–Outfield Farming on a Seventeenth-Century Scottish Estate', *Jnl. of Historical Geography*, v (1979), pp. 391–401.

—— 'Written Leases and Their Impact on Scottish Agriculture in the Seventeenth Century', *Agric. Hist. Rev.*, xxvii (1979), pp. 1–9.

—— *Agriculture and Society in Seventeenth-Century Scotland* (Edinburgh, 1979).

Yeaman, W., 'Kavels', *Juridical Rev.*, xxxix (1927), pp. 38–49.

Index

Abercairny estate (Perthshire), 251
Abercorn (Peeblesshire), 195
Aberdeen, 188, 268
Aberdeen, bishop of, 181
Aberdeenshire, 14, 95, 158, 182, 200, 203, 208–13, 215, 222, 224, 229, 239–40, 243, 252, 254, 266, 304
Aberlady, 162
Abernethy vitrified fort, 13
Abirbrothy (Angus), 191
Achedor (Aberdeenshire), 169, 238
Achillibuy (Corgach), 280
Achinbothy–Langmure estate, 200
Achlichay (Huntly), 282
Achnagathill (Aberdeenshire), 200
Achnahand and Reiff (Corgach), 280
Achroscaildruisk (Corgach), 280
Acts of Parliament, 70, 101, 170, 191–3, 235, 239
Agricola, Julius, 21
Aird, The, 180
Airth (Stirlingshire), 270
Alba, 32, 37, 42
Albanie, De Situ, 27–8, 30
Alcluith (Dumbarton Rock), 38
Ale, 143, 271, 315–16
Ale-brewing, 143, 271, 315–16
Alehouses (brew-seats), 143, 315–16
Alexander I (1107–24), 93, 96
Alishes -beg and -moir (Strathnaver), 200
Altrie, lordship of, 124
Alyth (Angus), 83
Ancrum, Nether (Roxburghshire), 264
Ancrum Mill, 250
Anderson, J., 229–30
Angles and Anglian settlement, 48–51, 64, 76
Anglo-Normans, 90–6
Angus, 12, 14, 93, 158, 185, 211, 215, 224, 244–6
Angus, earl of, 120
Annandale, 20, 22, 65, 94, 178–9
Annexed estates, 278, 280
Antonine Wall, 22–3, 39
Applecross, 30
Aqua vitae, 143, 167, 316–17
Arable, 9–11, 16, 20, 24–5, 35–6, 51, 56, 75–7, 85, 121, 123–6, 130–1, 146, 157–62, 229–35, 297–300; contraction, 263
Arbroath, 119–20, 122, 126
Arbuthnott, Bailie, 247
Arbuthnott par., 185
Arbuthnott thanage, 61, 83
Ard, 20, 24–5
Ardchattan, 119
Ardclach barony, 143
Ardle valley, 121
Ardmannoch, 146
Ard -more and -beg (Strathnaver), 200
Ardnamurchan, 44, 65, 181, 278–9, 289–90, 304–5
Argyll, 1, 6, 12, 19, 26, 41, 96, 295, 297, 314; bishop of, 68; duke of, 277, 292; estate, 281, 283–4, 299, 307; Sir Ewen of, 68
Arinskachar (Kintyre), 146
Arran, 7–8, 53
Assynt, 83, 283–4, 286–7, 289–90, 293–4, 298–9, 307, 312, 316
Atholl, 95; earl of, 120; earldom of, 95; forest of, 165
Auch- (=achadh), 42
Auchencraw (Berwickshire), 50, 143, 153, 163, 215, 218, 231
Auchihove (Strathisla), 103
Auchindory (Angus), 104
Auchinhabrick (Banff), 192
Auchinory (Moray), 177
Augustinian canons, 119
Aurochs, 2
Ayrshire, 1–2, 19–20, 120, 212, 234, 244
Ayton, Great and Little, 125, 142, 163, 264

Badenoch, 108, 136
Baglillie barony (Fife), 211
baile, 140, 171
Baillie of Ladrington, William, 270
Bal-, 32–3, 42, 46
Balbrogy, grange of (Angus), 98, 104, 121, 126, 153, 198
Baldoon estate (Wigtonshire), 258
Balfour–Melville estate, 254
Balgair (Stirlingshire), 238, 249

Butt, J., 208
Butter, 303, 310
-*byr*, 54

Cadiz, 310
Cain, 68–9
Cair, 39
Cairns, clearance, 9–10, 15
Caisteal nan Gillean (Oronsay), 3
Caithness, 6, 27, 31, 53, 73, 187, 301–4,
  314, 317; earl of, 303
Caledonii, 22, 27
Callanish (Lewis), 13
Calpe, 107–8
Cambuskenneth, 119
Camerachmore (Rannoch), 280, 286
Cameron of Glendessary, 281, 285
Cameston par. (Roxburghshire), 120
Campbell of Braglen, Colin, 281
Campbell of Glenorchy, Sir Duncan, 97
Campbell of Lochbuy, Archibald, 307
Campbells, 106, 284–5
Campeltown, 317
Candlemakers, 270
Canoby par. (Dumfriesshire), 216
Canterbury abbey, 119
Cantred, 82
Capital, 265, 273
Caputh (Perthshire), 103
Caraldie (Inverness-shire), 108
Cardon (Fife), 211
Carham, battle of, 48
Carlisle, 39
Carriages, 68, 97, 249
Carrict, 66, 254, 256
Carrowran, 150
Carse of Gowrie, 60, 93, 218
Carsebank, East and West, 203
Carter, I., 107
Carucate, 73, 75, 143, 149, 182–4
Caschrom, 299–300
Cash rents, 98–9, 136, 254–5, 300–1, 305;
  conversion to, 98–9, 254–5
Castle Grant, 317
Castlebay (Shetland), 150
Cattle, 20, 68–9, 165, 230, 237, 256–8,
  306–8; disease, 131; highland, 256, 261,
  306–8; prices, 135, 308
Caverton (Roxburghshire), 198, 207; mill,
  250
Celtic earls, 105
Cenel Comgaill, 44; Loairn, 43; nGabrain,
  44; nOengusa, 44

Chadwick, H. M., 37, 42
Chambered tombs, 6–8, 10; clyde cairns,
  6–7; passage graves, 6–7
Cheese, 306
Cheviots, 121–2, 126–7, 163–4, 175, 207,
  215, 258, 262–3
Childe, G., 7, 13
Chirnside (Berwickshire), 164, 231, 235
Christianity, 35–7, 40
Chronicle of the Picts, 27
Church lands, 98, 100–4, 118–21, 157;
  farming out of, 123; feuing of, 101–4
Cistercians, 119, 121
Clachans, 46, 170
Clackmannanshire, 178
Clactonian glaciation, 1
Clan system, 104–14, 281–5; chiefdoms,
  72–3; chiefs, 69, 96, 281, 302; *clann*, 105;
  sliochd, 105, 108; territories, 106–9,
  281–5
Clanchattan, 108
Clarilaw (Roxburghshire), 120
Clatt par. (Aberdeenshire), 169, 203, 215,
  224, 238, 267
Clerk of Penicuick, 208
Clerkington (Midlothian), 186
Clickhimmin (Shetland), 18
Clientship, 107–8
Climatic deterioration, 25
Cloth, 97, 312
Clouston, J. Storer, 77, 115–17, 199
Cluniacs, 119
Clunie estate, 305
Clyde valley, 22, 38, 160, 178; -dale, 25,
  93, 95
Cnoc Sligeach (Oronsay), 3–4
Coal-working, 270
Cobach, 69
Coldingham, 49–50, 125, 142–3, 208, 215;
  Commonty, 131, 163, 264; priory, 63,
  103, 125, 127, 131, 149, 181; shire, 62–3,
  181
Coldstane par. (Aberdeenshire), 246, 252
Coll, 44, 52, 57, 74, 79
Colonization, 174–89
Colonsay, 52
Columba, 30
Commonty, 125–6, 163–4, 187–8, 190–5;
  division of, 191–5; encroachments on,
  188–95; grazing on, 157, 189–95
Comrie, 305
Coneway par. (Moray), 185
Conveth (=waiting), 68–9

Premonstratensians, 119
Preston (Lothian), 120
Prestwick (Ayrshire), 49
Price, L., 33–4
Prices, 134–6, 258–61, 303, 308; Price Revolution, 134–6
Primside barony (Roxburghshire), 147, 216
Privy Council, 123
Putting-out system of industrial production, 266, 314–15

Quarrel, 270
Quarterland, 46–8, 79, 150, 291
Quarterness (Orkney), 7
Quowart, 79
Quoy, 55
Quoyness (Orkney), 55

Raedykes (Kincardineshire), 22
Raith barony (Fife), 211
Rannoch, 278–9, 282, 286, 291, 301, 316
Reay estate (Sutherland), 278
Redpath par. (Berwickshire), 120
Reeking hens, 78, 282
Reformation, 123
Regality Courts, 166–8, 316–18
Regiam Majestam, 75
Reginald, son of Somerled, 78
Register of the Great Seal of Scotland, 151, 196
Renders, 68–73, 76–7, 80, 85–6
Renfrew, 1, 19
Rent augmentation, 136–40, 186–7, 248, 281–4, 308, 319; conversion to cash, 254–5; in kind, 69–71, 97–9, 246–9, 303, 318; rack-renting, 136–40, 186, 283
Rentale Dunkeldense, 162
Reston, West (Berwickshire), 125, 236
Rheged, 39, 48
Riccarton (Roxburghshire), 259
Rievaulx abbey, 119
Ring of Brodgar (Orkney), 13
Ringwood (Roxburghshire), 121
Rinyo (Orkney), 5, 8–9
Risga Island (L. Sunart), 3
Ritchie, A., 14
Robert II (1371–90), 68
Roberton (Lanarkshire), 95
Robertson, W., 59, 61, 65, 67, 73, 82
Rodel (Harris), 311
Romano-British settlement, 23–5, 67
Romans, 16, 21–5, 40
Ronaldsway, South (Orkney), 117

Roonies, 9
Ross, 146; earldom of, 106; Easter, 53, 95, 106, 295, 304; Wester, 278
Rothiemurchus, 61
Rousay (Orkney), 78, 117
Roxburgh, barony, 207, 224, 235; duke of, 124, 235, 262; estate, 207, 215–16, 232, 250, 254, 261; mill, 250
Roxburghshire, 21, 24, 51, 69, 142, 194, 198, 207–8, 216, 224, 226, 232, 236, 238, 244–5, 250, 254, 259, 264
Runrig, 141–57, 168, 186, 200–1, 208, 217–23, 296–7; proprietary, 145, 208

St. Andrews, 4; abbey, 122; bishopric of, 119
St. Boswells par. (Roxburghshire), 120
St. Cuthbert monks, 119
St. Fergus par. (Aberdeenshire), 126
St. Kilda, 299
St. Ninian, 40
St. Ola (Orkney), 117
Sahlins, M., 71
Salmon, 295
Sandeman of Perth, 314
Sanderson, M. H. B., 103
Sandwatt (Strathnaver), 200
Sandwick par. (Orkney), 199
Sandy (Orkney), 117
Sandyhill (Perthshire), 104, 155–6
Scallog, 287
Scandinavian settlements, 19, 51–7
Scat and scatland, 54–6, 65, 77, 79
Scatnes (Shetland), 195
Scattald, 194
Scone abbey, 102, 104, 119, 155–6
Scord of Brouster (Shetland), 9
Scotia, 32
Scotland, central, 10, 12–13, 17, 22, 175, 215, 242, 245; eastern, 6, 12, 33, 64, 88, 205–76; north-east, 12, 16, 22, 60, 64, 75–6, 149, 187, 214, 217, 222, 317; northern, 60, 82; south-east, 16, 26, 48, 51, 62, 64, 75, 82, 84–5, 88, 154, 205–76; south-west, 12–14, 16, 94, 159, 242; southern, 11, 16, 40, 49, 142; western, 60, 82
Scott of Harden estate, 232, 254, 261
Scotti, 32–3, 40–8
Scrabster (Caithness), 52
Seafield, earl of, 248
Seaforth estate, 278, 295, 318; earl of, 311
Seaweed, 159, 231, 235, 299; *see also* Kelp

Whales, 4
Wheat, 157–9, 231–3, 244
Whisky, 143, 167, 315–18
White Meldon Hill (Peeblesshire), 14, 24–5
Whithorn (=Candida Casa), 40; abbey, 119
Whitrig (Berwickshire), 153
Whittingham (East Lothian), 49
Whittington, G., 33–4, 177, 265
Whyte, I. D., 226, 265
Wick, 306
Wight, A., 222, 240, 268, 302
Wigton, 268
Wigtonshire, 6, 158

Wildfowling, 2, 4
William's 'dear years', King, 251, 272
Windywalls (Roxburghshire), 264
Winthank, 303
Wiston (Lanarkshire), 95
Woodward, D., 256–7
Wool, 127, 258–60, 266–7
Woollens, 312, 315
Wyntoun's *Orygynall Cronykill*, 132–3

Yarramanna, 153
Yetholm shire, 63, 67
Yields, 243–4, 298–9
Yorkshire, 94, 259
Ythan valley, 243, 253